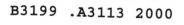

W9-BCV-044

0 1341 0944066 6

Adorno Reader

BLACKWELL READERS

In a number of disciplines, across a number of decades, and in a number of languages, writers and texts have emerged which require the attention of students and scholars around the world. United only by a concern with radical ideas, Blackwell Readers collect and introduce the works of pre-eminent theorists. Often translating works for the first time (Levinas, Irigaray, Lyotard, Blanchot, Kristeva), or presenting material previously inaccessible (C. L. R. James, Fanon, Elias), each volume in the series introduces and represents work which is now fundamental to study in the humanities and social sciences.

The Adorno Reader

Edited by
Brian O'Connor

Blackwell
Publishing

BLACKWELL PUBLISHING
350 Main Street, Malden, MA 02148-5020, USA
9600 Garsington Road, Oxford OX4 2DQ, UK
550 Swanston Street, Carlton, Victoria 3053, Australia

First published 2000

4   2006

Library of Congress Cataloging-in-Publication Data

Adorno, Theodor W., 1903–1969.
  [Selections. English. 2000]
  The Adorno reader / edited by Brian O'Connor.
     p.   cm. – (Blackwell readers)
  Includes bibliographical references and index.
  ISBN 0-631-21076-8 (alk. paper); ISBN 0-631-21077-6 (pbk. : alk. paper)
  1. Philosophy. 2. Sociology. 3. Criticism. I. O'Connor, Brian. II. Title. III. Series.

B3199.A31 2000
193 – dc21

99-046075

ISBN-13: 978-0-631-21076-4 (alk. paper); ISBN-13: 978-0-631-21077-1 (pbk. : alk. paper)

A catalogue record for this title is available from the British Library.

Set in 10½ on 12½ pt Bembo
by Best-set Typesetter Ltd, Hong Kong
Printed and bound in India
by Gopsons Papers Ltd, Noida

The publisher's policy is to use permanent paper from mills that operate a sustainable forestry policy, and which has been manufactured from pulp processed using acid-free and elementary chlorine-free practices. Furthermore, the publisher ensures that the text paper and cover board used have met acceptable environmental accreditation standards.

For further information on
Blackwell Publishing, visit our website:
www.blackwellpublishing.com

Contents

Acknowledgements

For their helpful suggestions on various aspects of this book I am very grateful to Martin Jay, Richard Kearney, Beth Remmes of Blackwells, and Michael Rosen. My greatest debt, however, is to my wife, Eileen Brennan. Her detailed comments and criticisms proved as ever to be a precious philosophical resource.

The editor and publishers gratefully acknowledge the following for permission to reproduce copyright material:

1. The Actuality of Philosophy
Telos, no. 31 (Spring 1977), pp. 120–33 (trans. Benjamin Snow).

2. Why Philosophy?
from *Man and Philosophy*, pp. 11–24 (ed. Walter Leifer, trans. Margaret D. Senft-Howie and Reginald Freeston) (Max Heuber Verlag, Munich/Germany, 1964 [Hueber-No. 1075]).

3. Negative Dialectics and The Possibility of Philosophy
Introduction, *Negative Dialectics*, pp. 3–31 (trans. E. B. Ashton) (Routledge and Kegan Paul, London, 1973; Suhrkamp Verlag, Frankfurt).

4. The Melancholy Science
Minima Moralia: Reflections from Damaged Life, pp. 15–18 (trans. E. F. N. Jephcott) (Verso, London, 1978).

5. Meditations on Metaphysics: After Auschwitz
Meditations on Metaphysics. *Negative Dialectics*, pp. 361–5 (trans. E. B. Ashton) (Routledge and Kegan Paul, London, 1973; Suhrkamp Verlag, Frankfurt).

6. The Essay as Form
New German Critique, no. 32 (Spring–Summer, 1984), pp. 151–71 (trans. Bob Hullot-Kentor and Frederic Will).

7. The Metacritique of Epistemology
Introduction. *Against Epistemology: A Metacritique*, pp. 3–29 (trans. Willis Domingo) (Blackwell, Oxford, 1982).

8. Subject and Object
from *The Essential Frankfurt School Reader*, pp. 497–511 (trans. Andrew Arato and Eike Gebhardt) (Blackwell, Oxford, 1978).

9. The Concept of Enlightenment
Introduction, *Dialectic of Enlightenment*, pp. 3–32 (abridged) (trans. John Cumming) (Verso, London, 1979).

10. Sociology and Empirical Research
from *The Positivist Dispute in German Sociology*, pp. 66–86 (trans. Glyn Adey and David Frisby) (Heinemann, London, 1976).

11. Cultural Criticism and Society
from *Prisms*, pp. 17–34 (trans. Samuel and Shierry Weber) (Copyright © The MIT Press, Cambridge, Mass., 1981).

12. Lyric Poetry and Society
Telos, no. 20, pp. 56–70 (Summer, 1974) (trans. Bruce Mayo).

13. Culture Industry Reconsidered
New German Critique, No. 6, pp. 12–19 (Fall, 1975) (trans. Anson G. Rabinbach).

14. The Autonomy of Art
Aesthetic Theory, pp. 320–52 (abridged) (trans. C. Lenhardt) (Routledge and Kegan Paul, London, 1984; and Suhrkamp Verlag, Frankfurt).

15. Perennial Fashion – Jazz
from *Prisms*, pp. 119–32 (trans. Samuel and Shierry Weber) (Copyright © The MIT Press, Cambridge, Mass., 1981).

16. Arnold Schoenberg, 1874–1951
from *Prisms*, pp. 147–72 (trans. Samuel and Shierry Weber) (Copyright © The MIT Press, Cambridge, Mass., 1981).

17. Alienated Masterpiece: The Missa Solemnis
Telos, no. 28, pp. 113–24 (Summer, 1976) (trans. Duncan Smith).

18. Trying to Understand *Endgame*
New German Critique, no. 26, pp. 119–50 (Spring–Summer, 1982) (trans. Michael J. Jones).

The publishers apologize for any errors or omissions in the above list and would be grateful to be notified of any corrections that should be incorporated in the next edition or reprint of this book.

A Note on Selections

If the criterion of selection for an anthology of Adorno's writings were that all of the material should be capable of helping us to think more, then that anthology would be almost co-extensive with Adorno's collected works. The criterion of the *Adorno Reader* is to choose texts which are simply indispensable to the effort of understanding Adorno's various theoretical positions, and it is clear enough that some of Adorno's writings are more useful than others in precisely that respect. In these writings we find his philosophical programme meticulously argued, or sometimes reference made, in the course of critique, to what Adorno takes to be his basic concepts.

In order to allow a ready appreciation of a specific area of Adorno's thought, this *Reader* organizes the material into five sections. Although Adorno's writings do not fall very neatly within disciplinary boundaries many of them tend to emphasize particular lines of thought, and the first four sections follow those lines. The fifth comprises critical essays on specific cultural topics.

Finally, the individual introductions are intended in no way to pre-empt the experience of Adorno's texts. Their purpose is to facilitate an appreciation of some of the more difficult ideas and also to elucidate the theoretical presuppositions which Adorno very often takes as read.

Introduction

It is difficult not to be intimidated by the work of Theodor Wiesengrund Adorno. With few exceptions his writings demand of the reader an unusual level of concentration in order to be able to stay with the vastness of detail, complexity of argument, nuances of style. For some this tells against Adorno as compelling evidence that he is a pretentious obscurantist. In an environment where the rules of thought are prescribed in advance of the matter of thought such a rejection of Adorno is inevitable. But it is against that very environment that Adorno rails by presenting ideas in a unique way. The brilliant 'Essay as Form' sets out Adorno's reflections on the form of presentation most conducive to philosophical thought. Philosophical motivations alone, however, do not explain the remarkable structure of Adorno's writings. His extraordinary intellect, his ability for unrelentingly sophisticated thought, shapes his texts. Jürgen Habermas, once Adorno's assistant at the University of Frankfurt, relates: 'Adorno was a genius . . . [He] had a presence of mind, a spontaneity of thought, a power of formulation that I have never seen before or since. One was unable to grasp the emerging process of Adorno's thoughts; they emerged, as it were, finished. That was his virtuosity. He also did not have the freedom to go below his level; he could not let up on the effort of his thought even for a moment. When you were with Adorno you were in the movement of his thought. Adorno was not trivial; it was denied him, in a clearly painful way, ever to be trivial.'[1] Adorno's genius accounts not only for the complexity of his thought, but also for the unequalled facility with which, in contributing powerfully to the diverse fields of sociology, musicology, aesthetics, and the traditional problems of philosophy, his intellect ranges across disciplinary boundaries.

I   Adorno's Life in Writings

Adorno's intellectual formation was no less extraordinary than we might expect of a person of these achievements. The son of a Catholic mother and assimilated Jewish father he was born in 1903 in Frankfurt am Main, a city that has no special significance in his writings, but one nevertheless with which he is always to be associated. Whilst in his early teens he spent his Saturdays reading the *Critique of Pure Reason* under the tutelage of Siegfried Kracauer. According to Rolf Wiggershaus, Kant's book was not read straightforwardly as an epistemological treatise. Rather, 'Adorno experienced the book . . . as a kind of coded writing from which the historical condition of the spirit could be deciphered, and in which objectivism and subjectivism, ontology and idealism were joined in battle.'[2] If this is so then Kracauer's influence on what was to become Adorno's philosophy was enormous. Adorno's mature philosophical writings attempt to discover the historical and social forces at work behind philosophical ideas, the ideologies which drive philosophers to certain conclusions. Furthermore this analysis is without that kind of reductionism which treats philosophical ideas superficially by explaining them merely as social forces in disguise. Adorno's sensitivity to detail ensures that his philosophical criticism has scholarly credibility.

   Given Kracauer's part in this early intellectual training it is hardly surprising that Adorno should have chosen among his subjects philosophy, sociology, and psychology when he enrolled as an undergraduate at the University of Frankfurt. His academic progress was rapid. Before reaching his twenty-first birthday, in 1924, he presented a doctoral dissertation, still at Frankfurt, entitled *The Transcendence of the Real and the Noematic in Husserl's Phenomenology*. The dissertation, a critique of Edmund Husserl's *Ideas*, owed its central contentions to Adorno's supervisor, Hans Cornelius, the author of several neo-Kantian tracts, now forgotten by the history of philosophy. Though remarkably precocious, the dissertation was largely an academic exercise. Nevertheless it does contain in simple form an argumentative strategy which is worth noting because it is a constant feature, albeit with greater sophistication, of Adorno's later critiques of philosophy. The strategy in question is that of identifying contradictions or antinomies which, in Adorno's distinctly Kantian view, emerge inevitably from any philosophical position with an erroneous account of the relationship of consciousness to reality. The contradiction in Husserl, according to the twenty year-old Adorno, is that

'Husserl, on the one hand, demands the grounding of all real things only by way of a return to unmediated givennesses. On the other hand, he holds that things are "absolute transcendences" which in fact identify themselves epistemologically only in their relatedness to consciousness . . .'[3] Although this is a curious anticipation of an element of Adorno's fully developed strategies of philosophical criticism it is the only one to be found in the doctoral dissertation. More interesting than that, however, is the complete absence of Kracauer's influence at this stage.

To a large extent the same might be said of *The Concept of the Unconscious in the Transcendental Theory of the Soul*, a *Habilitationsschrift*, which Adorno completed in 1927. Once again Cornelius is a significant presence. Indeed in the Preface Adorno states that 'The theoretical position which we presuppose here is that of Hans Cornelius, as represented in his book, *Transcendental Systematic*. We presuppose this standpoint everywhere and thus refrain from expressly citing it everywhere.'[4] Rolf Tiedemann, Adorno's editor, ever loyal to Adorno's expressed intentions, notes that this *Habilitationsschrift* and the doctoral dissertation, are 'school philosophy, works of a student of Cornelius'.[5] However, the criticism of phenomenology, that it cannot accommodate the unconscious, shows a concern which falls outside orthodox neo-Kantianism. As, obviously enough, does the argument that the unconscious has a social (or material) basis. In this contention, Adorno, anticipating some of the psychoanalytic elements of later critical theory, enlists Freud in the critique of ideology. Freud's theory of the unconscious apparently exposes the social at work behind what is taken to be natural. In this light, Freud's theory not only has its intended consequences for what we might think of personality, it also confirms the Marxist thesis that society determines consciousness, that is, for Adorno, that the individual is never self-constituted. He concluded the *Habilitationsschrift* with the observation, 'It is not for nothing that against psychoanalysis is directed the scandalized outrage of all of those who see psychoanalytic enlightenment endangering the unconscious as their ideological refuge and private possession'.[6] But for all the work's understated innovations Adorno withdrew from the examination as he came to realize that it did not possess sufficient originality to meet the strict requirements of the *Habilitation*.

The most surprising thing about the *Habilitationsschrift* is that Adorno made no systematic use of ideas which, as his correspondence shows, excited him far more than anything that Cornelius or Husserl had to say. Prior to attending university he had been introduced by Kracauer to Georg Lukács' *Theory of the Novel* (1920). Although Lukács became well known as one of the most important neo-Marxists, *Theory of the Novel*, his first book, showed no commitment to Marxism, though it was certainly compatible with that position.

Lukács argued that the novel is the inevitable product of a society whose individuals no longer communicate directly. Instead, their communication is mediated through the institutions of modern society, a fact reflected in the indirectness to experience of the novel. The very possibility of the novel, then, is inseparable from the configuration of its particular social basis. Adorno maintained a version of this Lukácsian insight right up to the unfinished *Aesthetic Theory* (cf. 'The Autonomy of Art'). For Adorno the relationship between culture and society is always a critical one. Art does not exist in a spiritual realm, nor is it simply entertainment. Its 'autonomy' from society defines it as authentic art. That autonomy sets up a relation of criticism between society and art, the latter which, by virtue of its autonomy, cannot be reduced to the purposes of bourgeois society. Particular art works, if correctly interpreted, in some way intimate the material conditions of society. But what, in this context, is involved in interpretation?

Not very long after withdrawing his *Habilitationsschrift* Adorno discovered, in the arcane writings of Walter Benjamin, the promising possibility for a theory of interpretation which might illuminate the presence of the material in the aesthetic and other cultural products. So impressed was Adorno with what he found in Benjamin's *The Origin of German Tragic Drama* (1928) that he arranged a personal meeting, one which began a profound friendship. The 'Epistemo-Critical Prologue' of *The Origin of German Tragic Drama* outlines a theory of philosophical truth which Adorno regarded as having immediate implications for the question of interpretation. Benjamin's theory posits the idea of constellations, a metaphor which expresses the practice of philosophical truth. In this practice the subject mediates phenomena, striving to arrange them in such a way, in 'constellations', that they might reveal their idea. Importantly, ideas are neither generalizations nor subjective reconstructions in that they are the very intelligibility and truth of the phenomena: 'Ideas are, rather, [the phenomenas'] objective virtual arrangement, their objective interpretation.'[7] Undoubtedly this is a strange procedure but Benjamin saw it as a necessary alternative to the conventional model of understanding in which concepts (which he always understands as universals) absorb the particularity of phenomena. In a constellation particular phenomena are not subsumed under universals. Rather the meaning of any phenomenon can emerge only when the phenomenon is understood as configured with certain other phenomena. The relationship between the idea and the phenomena can, in a sense, be regarded as metaphysical in that ideas are not reducible to individual phenomena: 'Ideas are not among the given elements of the world of phenomena.'[8] However, ideas are not, at the same time, to be taken as extra-materialist, in the sense that Plato might be said to claim. Quite challengingly Benjamin suggests that ideas exist in language, and he attempts to underpin this claim with arguments which are at least quasi-mystical (referring to the 'primordial form of perception' as the basis of his claim for 'the symbolic character of the word').[9] Adorno – as we shall see in 'The Actuality of Philosophy', 'The Essay as Form', and 'Sociology and Empirical Research' – attempts to exploit this theory, though he sunders it from its mystical commitments. It represents for him a possible method for understanding how the general (society and its ideology) lies hidden in the particular.

We might, in a way, be grateful for the problems that Adorno had with the Husserl *Habilitationsschrift*, for they had the effect of pushing him towards the production of new work, much of which was foundational for thoughts and concepts that preoccupied him for the remainder of his career. He decided to write a second *Habilitationsschrift*, and this time it was his own voice, albeit one which had been nurtured by Lukács, Benjamin, and Kracauer, the latter to whom, in fact, the book was dedicated. In 1931 he presented his work which was accepted and, in 1933, published under the title *Kierkegaard: Construction of the Aesthetic*. In 1966, in the Preface to *Negative Dialectics*, Adorno wrote, 'To use the strength of the subject to break through the fallacy of constitutive subjectivity – that is what the author felt to be his task ever since he came to trust his own intellectual impulses.'[10] The Kierkegaard book marks the first instance of that philosophical programme. Adorno's choice of subject was fashionable, though his argument was highly controversial. Kierkegaard's works had assumed a central place in German existential philosophy. The critique of Kierkegaard was by implication, therefore, a critique of contemporary existentialism. Here, as in later works, Adorno finds the idea of a subject with no constitutive attachments to an environment to be antinomical. The antinomy manifests itself in a particular way in Kierkegaard: on the one hand Kierkegaard sets up a model of the individual characterized by inwardness and detachment from history. On the other hand, as Adorno puts it, 'the inner history of the person is bound anthropologically to external history through the unity of the "race."'[11] The aporias in Kierkegaard's writings on the nature of the individual can all be traced back to this antinomy. With regard to the idea of abstract subjectivity Adorno ingeniously interprets Kierkegaard's various references to the interior of a bourgeois house. These references, intended rather innocently by Kierkegaard, convey a hidden truth: the historical state of the subject in which its relation to nature has been problematized. Instead its engagements are with semblance, false nature: 'the *intérieur* is the incarnate imago of Kierkegaard's philosophical "point": everything truly external has shrunken to the point. The same spacelessness can be recognized in the structure of his philosophy.'[12] It is clear that Adorno thought that the critique of Kierkegaard raised serious difficulties for existential philosophy in general. We can find similar accusations levelled in other works at Heidegger's fundamental ontology. Adorno's final conclusions about Heidegger appear in embryonic form in 'The Actuality of Philosophy', a lecture completed in the same year as the Kierkegaard study. Heidegger, in Adorno's view, is irrationalist in that he is committed to the idea of unmediated truth and idealist in that his theory of being locates meaning exclusively within subjectivity.[13]

Between 1924 and 1931, then, Adorno, quite astonishingly, presented three dissertations. What makes this productivity all the more remarkable is that he spent a large part of 1925 in Vienna undertaking intensive musical instruction. In some respects Adorno's musical life is inseparable from his development as a thinker. He came from a musical family. His mother, Maria Calvelli-Adorno, had been a professional singer, whilst her sister, Agathe, who lived in Adorno's family home, had been Maria's accompanist and also a successful pianist in her own right. As a teenager Adorno attended the local music conservatory. Music was also one of his undergraduate subjects. Soon after completing his doctorate he set out to explore the full potential of his compositional talent. He moved to Vienna to study composition under Alban Berg (and piano with Eduard Steuermann). Berg was not randomly chosen by Adorno. He was profoundly impressed by Berg's music after hearing a performance of the opera *Wozzeck*. But Adorno in any case was already an ardent admirer of the new music of the Second Viennese School, particularly of its patriarch, Arnold Schoenberg. He felt that instruction from Berg would reveal the techniques of what he took to be the most progressive contemporary music. But Berg, like others whom Adorno admired, was often impatient with Adorno's philosophical pronouncements on what he, Berg, was attempting to achieve. It is possible that the intellectual gulf between the two men prejudiced Berg in his assessment of Adorno as a composer as he did not pretend to deem Adorno suitably equipped with all the prerequisite skills and natural abilities. At that point Adorno decided to abandon the idea of making a career as a composer. On listening to some of Adorno's music one cannot help thinking that he had more talent than this decision might suggest.[14] Undoubtedly, the inner circle of the Second Viennese School, with its austerity and uncompromising musicological convictions, would have felt duty bound to deliver the truth, regardless of personal consequences (they had all themselves had to endure sacrifice and, at times, public opprobrium). And these after all were the people whom Adorno had chosen not only as his teachers but also as his judges. But perhaps Adorno's intellectual gifts were an obstacle to the freedom required for musical creativity.[15] He did not, however, leave Vienna empty-handed. He gained access to the compositional techniques of Schoenberg and Berg, knowledge that he would use in numerous seminal works on twentieth-century music, most notably in *Philosophy of Modern Music* (1949) and *Alban Berg* (1968). These books are not simply musicological in that they also explore the experience of the composer, that is, his attitude to the available musical conventions and his attempts to transform the idioms of music. 'Arnold Schoenberg, 1874–1951' provides an excellent overview of this form of music criticism, arguing that the task of composition is 'dialectical' (see below), in that valuable compositional possibilities are generated by a response to the tensions in the matter, music itself. In many ways the activity of philosophical thought, as we see in 'The Essay as Form', parallels the authentic compositional one.

By 1931 Adorno had secured an academic position at the University of Frankfurt. In the same year Max Horkheimer, who had been Adorno's *Habilitationsschrift* examiner, was appointed as Professor of Social Philosophy and, simultaneously, Director of the Institute of Social Research which was affiliated with the University. The Institute was founded by Felix Weil, the son of a millionaire, who wanted its work to contribute to an understanding of society which would lead ultimately to the realization of a Marxist state. This practical purpose was reflected in the work of its first director, Carl Grünberg, editor of the journal *Archive for the History of Socialism and the Workers' Movement* (*Archiv für die Geschichte des Sozialismus und der Arbeiterbewegung*). The appointment of somebody with Horkheimer's impeccable philosophical credentials as Grünberg's successor meant, inevitably, a change of emphasis in the work of the Institute. This was perhaps at its most obvious in the replacement of Grünberg's journal with a new title, *Journal of Social Research* (*Zeitschrift für Sozialforschung*). Under Horkheimer's direction the Institute attracted an exceptional range of talents, including among its members Friedrich Pollock, Leo Lowenthal, Erich Fromm, and Herbert Marcuse. Walter Benjamin was a Research Associate. An admiration for Marx was shared by all at the Institute, though some saw Marx as primarily a philosopher whilst others insisted on the continuing and immediate political relevance of his writings. Although the political character of the Institute's members was not universally radical they all held the belief, as Benjamin put it, 'that the teaching about society can only be developed in the most tightly integrated connection of disciplines; above all, economics, psychology, history and philosophy'.[16] This methodology defines the critical theory of what was informally to become known as the Frankfurt School. Adorno was intellectually and personally close to several of the Institute's members, but because he was financially comfortable – his father was a successful merchant – it seems that Horkheimer at first did not think it necessary to offer him a position, given the attendant stipend. Adorno, however, did contribute several articles to the *Journal of Social Research*. *De facto* Adorno was part of the Frankfurt School from the moment Horkheimer assumed directorship of the Institute.

With the National Socialists' accession to power in 1933 Adorno was removed from the University on account of his Jewish background. That same year the Institute of Social Research was relocated to Geneva, giving continuity to its work and, importantly, financial support for its members. Adorno, at that stage not yet a member, was obliged to make his own arrangements for emigration, a situation which was a source of some difficulty in his personal relationship with Horkheimer. Poorly advised, Adorno believed that he might find an academic position at one of the constituent colleges of the University of London. He corresponded with Ernst Cassirer, the most prominent German philosopher to have moved to England, in the expectation that Cassirer might be able to use his influence to secure the appointment. But Cassirer had neither the authority nor, it appears, the enthusiasm. However a solution was found by John Maynard Keynes, who just so happened to be a friend of Adorno's father. He suggested that Adorno enrol as a DPhil student at the University of Oxford. This would serve the twin purposes of giving Adorno a legitimate reason to be in Britain as well as integrating him into the educational structure. This integration might then lead to an appointment. In 1934 Adorno matriculated at Oxford as a member of Merton College. For a certain period he was able to make trips back to Germany. Whilst in Oxford (1934–7) Adorno, supervised by Gilbert Ryle, returned to Husserl studies. The labours of this period eventually appeared in 1956 as *Against Epistemology: A Metacritique*. The differences between the Oxford work and the two Husserl dissertations mark the significant transformation of Adorno as a philosopher. *Against Epistemology*, whilst highly proficient on issues in epistemology, is no simple epistemological treatise. In fact it continues with the approach of *Kierkegaard* in that it attempts to locate the social and material sources of the multiple antinomies which Adorno identifies in the various phases of Husserl's philosophy (cf. 'Metacritique of Epistemology').

Adorno never completed his DPhil degree. For him it was always a means to an end, but that end presented itself more quickly than he expected. Horkheimer, with the Institute of Social Research now attached to Columbia University in New York since 1935, had organized a position for Adorno on a project which would turn out to be a formative one. Adorno, if he was interested, could work under Paul Lazarsfeld at the Princeton Radio Project. This would involve research into the listening habits of Americans in order to discern the effects of radio on the listenership's relation to society. Adorno accepted. The project encouraged him to develop an empirical specificity which was lacking in his sociology. (Sociology for Adorno and many other

Europeans of the time was really a branch of political philosophy.) That is not to say that Adorno would ever be able to endorse entirely empirical methodologies, which he regarded as largely superficial and highly misleading (cf. 'Sociology and Empirical Research'). However, he felt that empirical methods could probably supply him with the sort of concrete data to which intepretation, in the form of critical theory, could then be applied. Through analysis of radio listening Adorno believed that he could uncover some of the hidden forces of society, particularly its mechanisms of conformism. Another opportunity for this more empirical sociology came in *The Authoritarian Personality* (1950), a volume in the series *Studies in Prejudice* which was supported by the Institute of Social Research. Together with three psychologists from the University of California at Berkeley Adorno was involved in an empirical analysis, through rigorous interview, of different personality types in order to discover which ones were amenable to the authoritarianism which had facilitated Fascism. Adorno regarded his contribution to the project as the central one as he had, in his view, developed the F-scale (F = fascism) in personality analysis.[17]

It was only during its American phase that Adorno became a member of the Institute (1938). During this period Horkheimer was moving towards a theoretical work – conceiving a never to be realized project on dialectical logic – and saw Adorno as his natural collaborator. He wanted Adorno close to him. So when in 1941 Horkheimer moved to California for reasons of health, Adorno – unlike some other members of the Institute – soon followed. There they worked on what was to become the classic text of critical theory, *Dialectic of Enlightenment*. The book, at first published privately in 1944, brought together many of the issues which had concerned both philosophers. In addition to the critique of instrumental reason – which can be seen in 'The Concept of Enlightenment' – there was also an examination of the rise of bourgeois subjectivity, with the philosophical implications as a proto-history of idealism. Particular emphasis was placed on the constriction of experience as the means by which modern subjectivity had been produced. Adorno and Horkheimer also offered an analysis of the culture industry, a thoroughly uncompromising critique of what they saw as the complicity of would-be entertainment in social conformism. Finally, *Dialectic of Enlightenment* examined anti-Semitism in a curiously non-specific way for the times in that it did not particularize the case of European Jews under the Nazis, seeing anti-Semitism instead as an element of society's drive for conformism and cohesion.

Adorno made his return to Germany in 1949, resuming teaching at the University of Frankfurt and soon afterwards his position at the Institute of Social Research, once again restored to Frankfurt. He was prolific, writing

numerous essays on music, society and literature, many of which were to
appear later in collections edited by Adorno himself. The following are,
perhaps, the most notable: on literature, *Notes to Literature*, 3 vols (1956, 1961,
1965) (cf. 'The Essay as Form', 'Lyric Poetry and Society', and 'Trying to
Understand *Endgame*'); on society and critical theory, *Prisms: Cultural Criticism and Society* (1955) (cf. 'Cultural Criticism and Society', 'Perennial Fashion
– Jazz', and 'Arnold Schoenberg 1874–1951'), *Without a Model: Parva Aesthetica* (1967) (cf. 'Culture Industry Reconsidered'), *Interventions* (1963) (cf.
'Why Philosophy?') and *Catchwords* (1969) (cf. 'Subject and Object'); on
music, *Soundfigures* (1959), *Quasi una fantasia* (1963), *Moments musicaux* (1964)
(cf. 'Alienated Masterpiece: The *Missa Solemnis*'), and *Impromtus* (1968). The
important monographs of this post-war period are *Minima Moralia* (1951) (cf.
'The Melancholy Science'), *Against Epistemology* (1956) (cf. 'Metacritique
of Epistemology'), *Hegel: Three Studies* (1963), *Negative Dialectics* (1966) (cf.
'Negative Dialectics and the Possibility of Philosophy' and 'Meditations on
Metaphysics'), and the unfinished *Aesthetic Theory* (1970) (cf. 'The Autonomy
of Art').

This period, though staggeringly productive, was not without its inter-
ruptions. Adorno found himself at odds with a highly volatile, sometimes hys-
terical, student movement. For several years he was probed constantly about
his political intentions. He was held in high regard, not least because of *Dialectic of Enlightenment*, taken by the students as an anti-bourgeois *credo*. But the
students were deluded about Adorno's thoughts on revolution, and when the
reality eventually became clear confrontation ensued. Adorno, committed
so deeply to ideas, could not sympathize with the practice of boycotts and
sit-ins. In 1969 there was an incident when he thought that the Institute's
building was about to be occupied. With his assistant he implored the students to leave. Their efforts were unsuccessful and the police were duly called.
From then on the hostility against Adorno became febrile to the extent that
he was harassed and his lectures were interrupted by demonstrations. Sadly
Adorno's death in September of that year meant that a generation of students had not the opportunity in calmer times to reconcile themselves with
a thinker whose writings had given them part of the critical apparatus with
which they idealistically called for reform and freedom.

II Experience: the Central Concept of Adorno's Thought

The enormity of Adorno's *oeuvre* sometimes threatens to overwhelm the
reader. But although it extends over the twenty volumes of his collected writings (and perhaps thirty more of unpublished manuscripts and lectures) we

are surely tempted to ask whether there is any idea which might allow us to see his works as anything more than the disparate ideas of a single person? One possibility is Adorno's concept of experience, a concept which appears to direct, not always explicitly, the very substance of Adorno's enquiries. Through various media Adorno presses the argument that experience might provide an alternative and potentially liberating model of rationality.

Adorno's concept of experience is largely indebted to the version offered by Hegel in the Introduction to the *Phenomenology of Spirit*. There Hegel argues that experience is the dialectical movement of consciousness.[18] In order to make sense of this idea it is important to understand what Hegel means by consciousness. Hegel understands consciousness as the judging mind through which the world is mediated. This process is never passive in that consciousness brings presuppositions to the world. It is these presuppositions which determine what we know and what we take to be true. Consciousness, then, has two elements: what is known and, more importantly, the criterion, or standard (as Hegel puts it[19]), of what we take to be true. Consciousness represents, Hegel writes elsewhere, 'the attitude of thought towards objectivity'. It is quite evident that consciousness is dynamic in the sense that human beings do change their criterion of truth (this is spectacularly obvious in the case of the succession of cultures that form the history of civilization). Hegel argues that this change is a rational process in that it occurs when consciousness is faced with certain pressures which challenge its criterion of truth. It is this process which Hegel calls experience. Consciousness can be transformed when its criterion of truth is revealed as no longer adequately achieving some particular knowledge. Contradiction is the term Hegel gives to these situations. In a contradiction of this sort, Hegel states, 'consciousness suffers . . . violence at its own hands: it spoils its own limited satisfaction'[20] as it recognizes that it cannot achieve knowledge so long as it maintains its current criterion. Consciousness in effect transforms itself as it evolves a more satisfactory criterion. This movement is dialectical since it is one which is generated by a problem within the matter itself, as opposed to an externally imposed standard of what ought to count as true. This motion is, in a sense, negative, in that something is denied (i.e. the adequacy of the criterion) but Hegel argues that it is a determinate negation in that it is a negation which generates a consciousness of a revised criterion which proves to be more adequate. As he puts it, in 'a *determinate* negation a new form has thereby immediately arisen'.[21] This idea of determinate negation is an innovation which allows Hegel to explain experience as a process of judgment and revision, a process in which experience is conceptual.

Experience, then, is the process of consciousness revising its criterion of truth. Charles Taylor explains it well: 'Now we cannot compare the world-as-I-see-it, or the world-as-I-claim-to-know it with the world-in-itself as yardstick. But what can serve as yardstick is the conception we have formed of what it is for a claim to be successful, i.e., what is veridical knowledge. And this involves no appeal to a standard outside consciousness. We rather appeal to its own conception of truth . . . What we compare with this is its effective knowing. If we can show that this could not meet its own standard, if we can show that in trying to meet this standard, we cannot but produce something incompatible with it, then we have uncovered a contradiction which cannot leave our conception of knowledge unchanged.'[22] This cognitive process, in which we reflect on the presuppositions through which we know and adjust our criterion of knowing, continues until, 'Concept (*Begriff*) corresponds to object and object to concept (*Begriff*)'.[23] For Hegel, the only alternative to this movement is 'unthinking inertia'.[24] Because what he is describing is not a rarefied activity of philosophers but the process or logic of ordinary consciousness, 'unthinking inertia' – the refusal to revise our understanding – would be something like not thinking at all.

This account of experience provides Adorno with an invaluable model in that it allows him to explain what he takes to be the irrational acceptance by individuals in society of a social totality which is fundamentally antagonistic to them. Whereas Hegel sees 'unthinking inertia' as inevitably challenged by the ineluctable demands of thought, Adorno argues, in effect, that contemporary consciousness is sustained by that very inertia. Adorno agrees with Hegel that experience as the very process of rationality should compel us to move beyond contradictory judgements, those judgements in which our criterion of truth is clearly inadequate. As Adorno's terminology puts it, there is a nonidentity between our concepts and the object, and consciousness of that nonidentity produces a revision – a self-reflection – in our use of those concepts. Yet, Adorno argues, this consciousness does not always arise with respect to certain contradictory social beliefs. The contradiction in these beliefs is between the definition of society as a collective of autonomous individuals and the reality that society dominates individuals and moulds them to those purposes which effectively contribute to the preservation of society. (This explains why the exemplary models of experience are to be found in philosophy and art: these are spheres which are not totally encompassed by the needs of society.) Recognition of a contradiction compels us to revise the criterion, and in this instance it could lead to a revision of society itself since the criterion misleads us about the antagonistic nature of society. Once revealed to consciousness this contradiction could no longer be tolerated. But in the case of social beliefs thought remains at the initial stage: it affirms the given situation without recognizing the problematic nature of its criterion.

Adorno takes it that the maintenance of the contradiction is somehow caused by a problematic consciousness, one which, in effect, fails to perceive the contradiction. He shares the Hegelian-Marxist view that consciousness is determined by its society in ways which are specifically required for the stabilization of that society. Adorno's argument is that the essence of this society is the principle of exchange, a mechanism to which individuals are entirely subordinate in even the most basic features of their lives. Society strives to preserve and reproduce itself through the activities of individuals. In these activities, however, as the critique holds, individuals help to maintain a society which is fundamentally antagonistic to their needs. Accordingly Adorno develops a theory of ideology or false consciousness, as he sometimes terms it, in order to explain how individuals willingly contribute to the maintenance of exchange society. In false consciousness one is not simply in error in the way that can be corrected by a more competent judge of the situation. Rather, in false consciousness the subject cannot accept arguments which point to autonomy as semblance. The social constitution of consciousness entails, in this regard, the foundational belief in autonomy as the self-founding essence of the individual: without it we are nothing, nonpersons. The notion that autonomy is compromised, indeed 'contradicted', by the needs of society is unrecognizable from within a false consciousness. Since this contradiction remains unrecognized, Adorno argues that false consciousness generates irrationality in that it disguises a state of affairs which has to be transformed. What is missing is the revolutionary moment of experience in which the criterion of truth is challenged. Instead consciousness in its 'unthinking inertia' is restricted to the given. But, as Adorno puts it, 'such a rigid and invariant basis contradicts that which experience tells us about itself, about the change that occurs constantly in the forms of experience, the more open it is, and the more it is actualized. To be incapable of this change is to be incapable of experience.'[25] The key difference, then, between Adorno and Hegel is that whereas Hegel presents experience as an irrevocable process, Adorno argues that it is absent from those who cannot perceive the contradiction which clearly shapes their lives.

A corollary of false consciousness is reification. By reification Adorno means the perception of what is qualitative as quantitative. That misperception is to be regarded as reductive in that unique qualitative characteristics are missed. Reification, it should be clear, is a state of consciousness in that it is consciousness that perceives the world in a reified way. Adorno, like Lukács before him,[26] argues that the particular structure of exchange society produces reification. For its operation exchange requires a purely quantitative world, and this can only be realized by the translation of qualities into abstract value. Through mechanisms which Adorno never satisfactorily explains, the exchange imperative (that all should be amenable to exchange) has the power to influence consciousness such that consciousness perceives the world in precisely the manner required to preserve the exchange society. Through this process of exchange-oriented reification thought must become limited to socially affirming tasks: labour must become abstract, art must become consumable. Most fundamental of all, however, is the perception of the person not as a unique individual, but as an entity with certain socially useful capacities. To say that society is reified, as Adorno frequently does, is to say that it is composed of individuals who perceive themselves as externally related to others, abstract subjects linked only to other subjects by the principle of exchange. According to Adorno the aim of society is total integration, that is, to have no sphere of life which is independent of the requirements of society (which, as mentioned above, strives to reproduce and preserve itself). Reification contributes to that end by legitimating the exchange principle: it legitimates it by making it appear to be the natural product of human nature.

Reification also affects rationality. The official model of rationality – that is, the model required by society for its self-preservation as an exchange society – takes the form, according to Adorno, of category thinking, which he also terms positivist rationality. Category thinking affirms the priority of categories. Since categorization is simply a matter of finding one of a number of available categories for all objects it can be described as a quantitative process. This sort of rationality is obviously at odds with critical rationality in which thought responds openly to its objects: positivist rationality, by contrast, has its alternatives established, as it were, a priori. It follows from this that the form of experience available to a reified consciousness in no way resembles the form presented by Adorno in that the reified consciousness judges unreflectively through categories (since they are finite and the only alternatives), and can never, therefore, recognize the nonidentity between concept and object which would motivate a new judgement. In precisely this respect positivist rationality facilitates the modern belief that subjectivity has the power of mastery over its environment: environment must be subject to categories. The reality, however – one which Adorno describes as a contradiction – is that subjectivity is neither sovereign nor autonomous but is constituted, in so far as individuals define themselves, by the roles which are required for the preservation of the society. (It should be noted that Adorno sometimes makes excessive claims about the operations of reification by positing total reification. That idea leaves no scope for experience understood as a qualitative process and consequently ensures that non-positivist rationality is irretrievably lost. More plausible is his view that reification is a dominant perspective, but not the only one.)

Adorno's work, in its numerous different ways, attempts to restore experience to contemporary thought in order that a transformation of consciousness might be effectuated. In his critique of the philosophical tradition Adorno posits his particular model of experience against which, through various complex arguments, the success or failure of that tradition's efforts to explain the role of subjectivity may be judged. To this end he employs the concept of mediation, a concept borrowed from Hegel but modified to operate in a non-metaphysical context.[27] The idea of mediation, as we can see in 'Metacritique of Epistemology', is that nothing is independently constituted. In effect, every positive thing – what might appear to be immediately given – is effectively dependent on conditions which are sometimes wrongly construed as merely external conditions. Certain forms of subjective idealism – for example, those of Descartes or Fichte – appear to hold that some pure part of subjectivity is immediate in that it is independent of the reality in which it actually operates. It is immediate (or unmediated) in the sense that it is not known through inference, deduction, or abstraction. Adorno argues, however, that subjectivity is coherent only in its relation to what idealism takes to be the other of the subject, an otherness which he designates under the general term 'object'. Society, for instance, is no external relation but is largely constitutive of the practices and values of the subject. The subject is also determined, to an extent, by the linguistic possibilities of its context. In purely epistemological terms, a transcendental subject dualistically situated towards an object is abstract and devoid of any qualities which allow us to describe it coherently. (Kant's 'I think' and the subsequent theories of subjectivity proposed by Fichte and Schopenhauer all evince that difficulty.) As something which is not an object it begins to lose the conditions which normally allow us to individuate things. Needless to say, the countless difficulties of mind–body dualism spring from this subtraction from subjectivity of anything which is supposedly non-I. For these reasons the claim that subjectivity is immediate must be false since it disincludes the essentially mediating conditions of subjectivity. For Adorno experience properly understood constantly undermines the model of a subject detached from its environment: 'experience lives by consuming the [detached] stand-point; not until the stand-point is submerged in it would there be philosophy'.[28] The detached model absolutizes a relation which cannot be sustained since experience is the process of interaction. Against these extremes Adorno attempts to articulate a model of experience in which the subject might be seen to engage with the object without either being reduced to the object or choosing in Sartrean manner its own mode of experience. By allowing the process of experience to enter philosophy – the discipline which attempts to explain experience – Adorno thinks that he can undermine the abstractions of philosophy. These abstractions set up a static relation of subject and object, whereas experience shows the process to be dynamic. An important implication of this is the retrieval of particularity. Positivist epistemology which holds that subjects categorize objects leaves itself with the difficulty of explaining how particularity is to be specified, since categories – general concepts – precede the object. In experience subjectivity responds to what Adorno calls the priority of the object. This priority explains the process in which our concepts adjust to objects. As such it captures the experience of particularity, whereas the mechanisms of positivist thinking (which are manifest in philosophy too) grasp only 'the essential' or universal.

The problem with empirical sociology is that it makes no distinction between appearance and reality. It takes society as a totality of given facts and understands its task as the orderly arrangement of those facts. Adorno, as we saw from his American experiences, allowed the methodology, but never without qualification: it is incomplete unless it can provide some way – interpretation – of understanding the reality which gives rise to the appearances. Adorno, as 'Sociology and Empirical Research' clearly argues, is especially critical of the unreflective sociological practice of gathering information about a society by means of opinion surveys. These surveys operate with the assumption that individuals can be explained by reference to their opinions, or to put it in more Adornian language, that consciousness is the unmediated property of the individual. In this procedure sociology is ideological. In attempting to offer a theory of society it simply takes individualism at face value and will affirm society as it is, failing to reveal or represent its real processes. The contradiction below the surface is beyond the reach of empirical sociology. In this way empirical sociology contributes nothing to the transformation of consciousness: in fact it preserves contemporary consciousness by never questioning its ability to be a reliable interpreter of its own circumstances. A further problem with empirical sociology is that in setting up a finite set of possible answers – classifications – it reneges on its own claims to be guided by particularity. Now of course Adorno claims that individuals are limited by modern society and, as such, are amenable to classification. However the difference in his view is that these limitations are not to be analyzed neutrally as though they were natural.

The idea of the potentially revolutionary qualities of experience is a central part of Adorno's aesthetic theory. Important aesthetic productions are those which emerge from an artist's authentic response to experience. Following the idealist aesthetics of Schelling and Hegel, Adorno, to put it broadly at first, believes that art, albeit individualist in expression, is the product of the culture within which the artist lives. That idea obviously accords with the intuitive notion that artworks have their place in history and that this place somehow explains their artistic value. (For instance, no new painting in a style technically identical with Rembrandt has, it might be argued, the aesthetic quality of Rembrandt's paintings. Yet, it may be allowed that artists 'in the school of . . .' who were almost contemporaneous with the painter have produced works with aesthetic value.) Hegel set out to show how different periods in art are the unique product of the consciousness of that time (for example, the Egyptians' materialist imagination compelled them to monumental art).

Adorno is clearly situated within Hegel's general aesthetic theory, however his views of modern society necessarily give rise to significant adjustments in the theory. For Adorno the whole notion of culture has become problematical. The once complementary relationship between culture and society is no longer sustainable because society itself has become the realm of appearance. That is, it is a false harmony which can only problematically be manifested in art. Culture and society are now at odds with each other. If society is, as Adorno claims, ideological then culture, art specifically, cannot exist harmoniously with society without merely repeating the ideology. The appearance of a natural social order cannot be reproduced in art without art becoming a vehicle for the ideology of the 'second nature' of society. To merely repeat society is not, Adorno contends, to create an authentic art which responds to the experience of modern society. The experience of modern society – its real truth – is that of contradiction, and art must somehow express this. The ways in which it does so are quite oblique in that it provokes the experience of contradiction without naming society directly. Adorno insists that it should never attempt to be didactic. Didactic art is not, Adorno argues, genuinely aesthetic and as such does not generate those experiences which are needed to push false consciousness into dialectic. (Cf. 'The Autonomy of Art'.) In line with Hegel's view of the isomorphism of context and form, Adorno finds something uniquely apt about the dissonant, atonal qualities of the music of Arnold Schoenberg in a society which, contrary to appearance, is dissonant. As Richard Wolin puts it: 'the fragmentariness of the de-aestheticized works of art originates in opposition to the concept of totality and the false reconciliation that concept implies.'[29] The aesthetic reception of modernist, dissonant works can never be achieved without serious effort, and that effort challenges the passive consumption of popular culture which merely sustains unthinking inertia. Aesthetic appreciation is a heightened form of experience, one which contrasts therefore in a critical way with the reduced experience of a reified consciousness.

Again and again Adorno endeavours to illuminate experience as a process, to contrast it with the reified forms endorsed by conventional philosophy and social theory. All of this sits unhappily with the general assessment that

Adorno's allegedly pessimistic views of society render intellectual reflection literally hopeless. In so much of Adorno's theoretical work the effort is to transform, to appeal to a readership not yet beyond the reach of reasons. Whether, in the end, we agree with Adorno's portrait of modern society, his works still leave us with a deepened sense of the idea of experience, one which opens up to us the awareness that our interaction with the world is never separate from its social mediation. Adorno never pretends that this mediation is easily discerned. However, his legacy is not only his exemplary effort to render the world intelligible, but the considerable contents of that effort.

Notes

1   Jürgen Habermas, trans. James Swindal, 'A generation apart from Adorno (an interview)', *Philosophy and Social Criticism*, 18 (1992): 122–3.
2   Rolf Wiggershaus, trans. Michael Robertson, *The Frankfurt School: Its History, Theories and Political Significance* (Cambridge: Polity Press, 1994), p. 67.
3   Theodor W. Adorno, *Philosophische Frühschriften, Gesammelte Schriften*, Band 1 (Frankfurt: Suhrkamp Verlag, 1973), p. 375.
4   Ibid., p. 81.
5   Ibid., p. 382. Editor's Postscript.
6   Ibid., pp. 320–1.
7   Walter Benjamin, trans. John Osborne, *The Origin of German Tragic Drama* (London: NLB, 1977), p. 34.
8   Ibid., p. 35.
9   Ibid., p. 36.
10 Theodor W. Adorno, trans. E. B. Ashton, *Negative Dialectics* (London: Routledge, 1973), p. xx.
11 Theodor W. Adorno, trans. Robert Hullot-Kentor, *Kierkegaard: Construction of the Aesthetic* (Minneapolis: University of Minnesota Press, 1989), p. 32.
12 Ibid., p. 44.
13 Cf. Brian O'Connor, 'Adorno, Heidegger and the Critique of Epistemology', *Philosophy and Social Criticism*, vol. 24 (1998) for further discussion of Adorno's view of Heidegger.
14 Some of Adorno's music can be heard on a recent recording, Theodor W. Adorno, Hans Eisler, *Works for String Quartet* (CPO 999 341-2) (1996).
15 This is Susan Buck-Morss's suggestion. Cf. *The Origin of Negative Dialectics: Theodor W. Adorno, Walter Benjamin, and the Frankfurt Institute* (Sussex: The Harvester Press, 1977), p. 16.
16 Walter Benjamin, 'Ein deutsches Institut freier Forschung', *Gesammelte Schriften*, vol. 3 (Frankfurt: Suhrkamp, 1972). Quoted in David Held, *Introduction to Critical Theory: Horkheimer to Habermas* (Berkeley: University of California Press, 1980), p. 32.

17   Cf. Wiggershaus, *The Frankfurt School*, p. 411, for details on the question of who, exactly, suggested the F-scale.

18   G. W. F. Hegel, trans. A. V. Miller, *Hegel's Phenomenology of Spirit* (Oxford: Oxford University Press, 1977), p. 55.

19   Ibid., p. 53.

20   Ibid., p. 51.

21   Ibid., p. 51.

22   Charles Taylor, *Hegel* (Cambridge: Cambridge University Press, 1975), p. 135. Robert Pippin also takes up the idea of a separation in consciousness which can allow this comparison to be made: 'This is Hegel's way of making what is now a familiar point: that in, say, assertoric judgements, we self-consciously assert; the act of asserting is complex, since it involves not only the representation of what we assert but our fulfilling a criterion for asserting, a component of experience that cannot be isolated from what it is we are asserting. Both what we take to be "the truth" . . . and our taking it to be "the truth" are involved'. *Hegel's Idealism: The Satisfaction of Self-Consciousness* (Cambridge: Cambridge University Press, 1989), p. 104.

23   Hegel, *Hegel's Phenomenology of Spirit*, p. 51, emended.

24   Ibid., p. 51.

25   Adorno, *Negative Dialectics*, p. 388.

26   Cf. Georg Lukács, trans. Rodney Livingstone, *History and Class Consciousness: Studies in Marxist Dialectics* (London: Merlin Press, 1971), 'The Phenomenon of Reification'.

27   Although the concept of mediation is not unproblematic in either context. Cf. Brian O'Connor, 'The Concept of Mediation in Hegel and Adorno', *Bulletin of the Hegel Society of Great Britain*, vol. 39/40 (1999).

28   *Adorno Reader*, p. 77.

29   Richard Wolin, 'The De-Aestheticization of Art: on Adorno's *Ästhetische Theorie*', *Telos*, 41 (Fall, 1979) p. 112.

Part I

The Task of Philosophy

1

The Actuality of Philosophy

'The Actuality of Philosophy' is the earliest and undoubtedly the clearest of Adorno's efforts to define the task of philosophy. In this 1931 inaugural lecture at the University of Frankfurt Adorno assesses the possibility of philosophy by examining the context of the philosophical enterprise, that is, the alternative models offered by contemporary philosophy and also the condition of society. He contends that there can be no totalizing philosophy. This is a conclusion drawn from the apparent failure of the Hegelian enterprise. The ambition of revealing the rational structure of the world, as traditionally pursued, is undermined by the complexity and inherent irrationality of the object, the world itself. Adorno also holds that any philosophy which presents merely the appearances of reality will be ideological, in that it will affirm and preserve those appearances rather than critically search for 'true and just reality'.

Armed with these two ideas Adorno finds that the main positions of contemporary philosophy lapse into either totalitarianism or ideology. As an alternative he proposes a model of philosophy as interpretation. At this point in his career Adorno sees interpretation as analogous to riddle-solving. Following Benjamin he contends that interpretation (as riddle-solving) in achieved by realizing a particular configuration of the elements of the riddle. Adorno is suggesting that placing elements in this configuration actually produces some kind of compelling illumination. This, in fact, is Adorno's first statement of the idea of constellations. We can see that Adorno is proposing a form of interpretation which commits itself to the possibility of truth. For him interpretation is therefore no matter of approximation, nor is it one of open-endedness. It cannot be since it aims to expose the falseness of social appearances, to reveal the illusions of second nature which sustain contemporary society.

A further important principle introduced in 'The Actuality of Philosophy' is the compatibility of interpretation with a materialist conception of the world. Adorno's use of the concept of materialism is borrowed from Marx. It pertains to Marx's rejection of Hegel's idea that society and history are guided by the extra-material forces of *Geist*. Famously, the Young Hegelians re-read theology as the concealed history of humanity. Marx applied this to Hegel to reveal that the world of *Geist* is nothing more than the world of society. Furthermore, society does not move forward by means of the self-developments of *Geist*. It moves because of the activities – the class-antagonisms according to Marx – of human beings. This is a materialist conception in that it sees the world as explicable entirely in terms of human action. There is a further characteristic: materialism rejects the concept of an inherently meaningful reality as this could only be justified by appeal to some metaphysical conception of the nature of reality. It should be noted that Adorno was never to share the orthodox Marxist view about the revolutionary potential of the proletariat. He held the less sanguine belief that regardless of class structures no individual is free from the ideology which underpins society. In that respect, at least, all are equally dominated.

'The Actuality of Philosophy' [1931], *Telos*, no. 31 (Spring, 1977), pp. 120–33.
Translated by Benjamin Snow.

Whoever chooses philosophy as a profession today must first reject the illusion that earlier philosophical enterprises began with: that the power of thought is sufficient to grasp the totality of the real. No justifying reason could rediscover itself in a reality whose order and form suppresses every claim to reason; only polemically does reason present itself to the knower as total reality, while only in traces and ruins is it prepared to hope that it will ever come across correct and just reality. Philosophy which presents reality as such today only veils reality and eternalizes its present condition. Prior to every answer, such a function is already implicit in the question – that question which today is called radical and which is really the least radical of all: the question of being (*Sein*) itself, as expressly formulated by the new ontological blueprints,[1] and as, despite all contradictions, fundamental to the idealist systems, now allegedly overcome. This question assumes as the possibility of its answer that being itself is appropriate to thought and available to it, that the idea of existing being (*des Seienden*) can be examined. The adequacy of thinking about being as a totality, however, has degenerated and consequently the idea of existing being has itself become impervious to questioning, for the idea could stand only over a round and closed reality as a star in clear transparence, and has now perhaps faded from view for all time, ever since the images of our life are guaranteed through history alone. The idea of being has become powerless in philosophy; it is nothing more than an empty form-principle whose archaic dignity helps to cover any content whatsoever. The fullness of the real, as totality, does not let itself be subsumed under the idea of being which might allocate meaning to it; nor can the idea of existing being be built up out of elements of reality. It [the idea of being] is lost for philosophy, and thereby its claim to the totality of the real is struck at its source.

The history of philosophy itself bears witness to this. The crisis of idealism comes at the same time as a crisis in philosophy's pretensions to totality. The *autonome ratio* [autonomous reason] – this was the thesis of every idealistic system – was supposed to be capable of developing the concept of reality, and in fact all reality, from out of itself. This thesis has disintegrated. The Neo-Kantianism of the Marburg School, which labored most strenuously to gain the content of reality from logical categories, has indeed preserved its self-contained form as a system, but has thereby renounced every right over reality and has withdrawn into a formal region in which every determination of content is condemned to virtually the farthest point of an unending process. Within idealism, the position opposed to the Marburg School, Simmel's *Lebensphilosophie* with its psychologistic and irrationalist orientations, has admittedly maintained contact with the reality with which it deals, but in so doing has lost all claim to make sense out of the empirical world which presses in upon it, and becomes resigned to "the living" as a blind and unenlightened concept of nature which it vainly attempts to raise the unclear, illusory transcendence of the "more-than-life." The southwest-German School of Rickert, finally, which mediates between the extremes, purports that its "values" represent more concrete and applicable philosophical criteria than the ideas of the Marburg School, and has developed a method which sets empirical reality in relation, however questionable, to those values. But the locus and source of the values remains undetermined; they lie between logical necessity and psychological multiplicity somewhere, not binding within reality, not transparent within the mind, an ontology of appearances which is as little able to bear the question of value-from-whence as that of value-for-what. Working apart from the attempts at grand resolutions of idealist philosophy are the scientistic philosophies, which give up from the beginning the basic idealist question regarding the constitution of reality and, still within the frame of a propadeutics of the separate, developed disciplines, grant validity only to the natural sciences, and thereby mean to possess secure ground in the given, be it the unity of consciousness (*Bewusstseinszusammenhang*), or be it the research of the separate disciplines. Losing contact with the historical problems of philosophy, they forgot that in every assumption their own statements are inextricably bound to historical prob-

lems and the history of those problems, and are not to be resolved independent of them.

Inserted into this situation is the effort of the philosophic spirit which is
known to us in present day under the name of phenomenology: the effort,
following the disintegration of the idealist systems and with the instrument
of idealism, the *autonome ratio*, to gain a trans-subjective, binding order of
being. It is the deepest paradox of all phenomenological intentions that, by
means of the same categories produced by subjective, post-Cartesian thought,
they strive to gain just that objectivity which these intentions originally
opposed. It is thus no accident that phenomenology in Husserl took precisely
its starting point from transcendental idealism, and the late products of phenomenology are all the less able to disavow this origin, the more they try to
conceal it. It was the authentically productive and fruitful discovery of Husserl
– more important than the externally more effective method of *Wesenschau*
[essential intuition] – that he recognized in the meaning of the concept of
the non-deducible given (*unableitbaren Gegebenheit*), as developed by the positivist schools, the fundamental problem of the relationship between reason
and reality. He rescued from psychology the concept of the originally given
intuition, and in the development of the descriptive method of philosophy,
he won back a certainty of limited analysis which had long been lost in the
separate disciplines. But it cannot be denied – and the fact that Husserl
expressed it so openly is proof of his great and clear honesty – that every
one of the Husserlian analyses of the given rests in an implicit system of transcendental idealism, which Husserl ultimately formulated: that the "jurisdiction of reason" (*Rechtsrechnung der Vernunft*) remains the court of final appeal
for the relation between reason and reality and that therefore all Husserlian
descriptions belong to the domain of this reason. Husserl purified idealism
from every excess of speculation and brought it up to the standard of the
highest reality within its reach. But he didn't burst it [idealism] open. As with
Cohen and Natorp, his domain is ruled by the autonomous mind, with the
important difference, however, that he has renounced the claim of the productive power of mind, the Kantian and Fichtean spontaneity, and resigns
himself, as only Kant himself had done, to take possession of the sphere of
that which is adequately within his reach. The traditional interpretation of
philosophical history of the last thirty years would like to understand this
self-resignation of Husserlian phenomenology as its limitation, and views it
as the beginning of a development which leads ultimately to the plan of
working out just that order of being which in Husserl's description of the
noetic–noematic relationship could be only formally laid out. I must explicitly contradict this interpretation. The transition to "material phenomenology" has only apparently succeeded, and at the price of that certainty of the

findings which alone provided the legitimacy of the phenomenological method. If in Max Scheler's development the eternal, basic truths alternate in sudden changes, to be exiled finally into the powerlessness of transcendence, then one can certainly recognize the tirelessly questioning impulse of a thinking which takes part in truth only in moving from error to error. But Scheler's puzzling and disquieting development needs to be understood more rigorously than as the fate of an individual mind. On the contrary, it indicates that the transition of phenomenology from the formal-idealist to the material and objective region cannot succeed with continuity or total assurance, that instead the images of transhistorical truth, which at one time [Scheler's] philosophy projected so seductively onto the background of closed, Catholic theory, became confused and disintegrated as soon as they were sought for in just that reality, the comprehension of which was in fact precisely what constituted the program of "material phenomenology." Scheler's last change of direction appears to me to possess its authentic, exemplary validity in his recognition of the gap between the eternal ideas and reality, the overcoming of which led phenomenology to enter the material sphere, as itself material-metaphysical, and thus he abandoned reality to a blind impulse (*Drang*) with a relationship to the heaven of ideas that is dark and problematic, and leaves room for only the weakest trace of hope. With Scheler, material phenomenology has dialectically revoked itself. Only the metaphysics of the impulse is left over from the ontological design; the only remaining eternity over which his philosophy has disposal is that of a boundless and uncontrolled dynamic. Viewed under the aspect of this self-revocation of phenomenology, Heidegger's theory also presents itself differently than is apparent from the pathos of the beginning which is responsible for its external effect.

With Heidegger, at least in his published writings, the question of objective ideas and objective being has been replaced by the subjective. The challenge of material ontology is reduced to the realm of subjectivity, within the depths of which it searches for what it was not able to locate in the open fullness of reality. It is thus no accident, in the philosophical-historical sense as well, that Heidegger falls back on precisely the latest plan for a subjective ontology produced by Western thinking: the existentialist philosophy of Sören Kierkegaard. But Kierkegaard's plan is irreparably shattered. No firmly grounded being has been able to reach Kierkegaard's restless, inner-subjective dialectic; the last depth which opened up to it was that of the despair into which subjectivity disintegrated, an objective despair which transformed the design of being within subjectivity into a design of hell. It knows of no other way to escape this hellish space than by a "leap" into transcendence which remains an inauthentic and empty act of thought, itself subjective, and which finds its highest determination in the paradox that here the subjective mind must sacrifice itself and retain belief instead, the contents of which, accidental for subjectivity, derive solely from the Biblical word. Only through the assumption of an essentially undialectical and historically pre-dialectical "ready at hand" (*zurhanden*) reality is Heidegger able to evade such a consequence. However, a leap and an undialectical negation (*Negat*) of subjective being is also Heidegger's ultimate justification, with the sole difference that the analysis of the "existing there" (*Vorfindlichen*), whereby Heidegger remains bound to phenomenology and breaks in principle with Kierkegaard's idealist speculation, avoids the transcendence of belief which is grasped spontaneously with the sacrifice of subjective mind, and instead recognizes solely the transcendence to a vitalist "thus being" (*Sosein*): in death. With Heidegger's metaphysics of death, phenomenology seals a development which Scheler already inaugurated with the theory of impulse. It cannot be concealed that phenomenology is on the verge of ending in precisely that vitalism against which it originally declared battle: the transcendence of death with Simmel is distinguished from Heidegger's solely in that it remains within psychological categories whereas Heidegger speaks in ontological ones. However, in the material itself, for example in the analysis of the anxiety phenomenon, it would be hard to find a sure way to distinguish them.

In accordance with this interpretation of the transition of phenomenology into vitalism, Heidegger could evade the second great threat to phenomenological ontology, that posed by historicism, only by ontologizing time itself, i.e., putting it forth as that which constituted the essence of man whereby the effort of material phenomenology to discover the eternal in man paradoxically dissolved: as eternal, only temporality remained. The claims of phenomenology are satisfied only by those categories, from the absolute rule of which phenomenology wanted thought to be exempt: mere subjectivity and mere temporality. With the concept of "thrownness" (*Geworfenheit*), which is set forth as the ultimate condition of man's being, life by itself becomes as blind and meaningless as only it was in *Lebensphilosophie*, and death is as incapable of alotting a positive meaning here as there. The claim to totality made by thought is thrown back upon thought itself, and it is finally shattered there too. All that is needed is an understanding of the narrowness of the Heideggerian existential categories of thrownness, anxiety, and death, which are in fact not able to banish the fullness of what is living, and the pure concept of "life" completely seizes the Heideggerian ontological blueprint. If appearances are not deceiving, then with this further development, phenomenological philosophy is preparing for its own final disintegration. For the second time, philosophy stands powerless before the question of being. It can no more describe being as free-standing and fundamental than it was able earlier to develop it from out of itself.

I have discussed the most recent history of philosophy, not for a general intellectual history orientation, but because only out of the historical entanglement of questions and answers does the question of philosophy's actuality emerge precisely. And that simply means, after the failure of efforts for a grand and total philosophy: whether philosophy is itself at all actual. By "actuality" is understood not its vague "maturity" or immaturity on the basis of non-binding conceptions regarding the general intellectual situation, but much more: whether, after the failure of the last great efforts, there exists an adequacy between the philosophic questions and the possibility of their being answered at all; whether the authentic results of the recent history of these problems is the essential unanswerability of the cardinal philosophic questions. The question is in no way rhetorical, but should be taken very literally. Every philosophy which today does not depend on the security of current intellectual and social conditions, but instead upon truth, sees itself facing the problem of a liquidation of philosophy. The sciences, particularly the logical and mathematical sciences, have set about the liquidation of philosophy with an earnestness which hardly ever existed before. This earnestness is so significant because the separate sciences, including the mathematical natural sciences, have long since rid themselves of the naturalistic conceptual apparatus that, in the 19th century, made them inferior to idealist theories of knowledge, and they have totally annexed the contents of cognitive criticism. With the help of sharpened, critical, cognitive methods, the most advanced logic – I am thinking of the new Vienna School as it proceeded from Schlick, and is now carried on by Carnap and Dubislav in close connection with Russell and the logical analysts – is attempting to keep all authentic, wider-reaching knowledge of experience in exclusive reserve, and tries to search for all propositions which in any way reach out beyond the circle of experience and its relativity, solely in tautologies, in analytical propositions. According to this, the Kantian question as to the constitution of *a priori* synthetic judgments would be utterly meaningless, because there is absolutely no such thing as this kind of judgment; every move beyond that which is verifiable by the power of experience is prevented; philosophy becomes solely an occasion for ordering and controlling the separate sciences, without being allowed to append anything essential from itself to their findings. Associated as complement and supplement to the ideal of such absolutely scientific philosophy – not, to be sure, for the Vienna School, but for every view which wants to defend philosophy from the claims of an exclusively scientific method – while in fact itself recognizing that this claim is a concept of philosophy as an art form, whose lack of binding force before truth is excelled only by its unfamiliarity with art and its own aesthetic inferiority. It would be better just to liquidate philosophy once and for all and dissolve it into the particular disciplines than to come to its aid with a poetic ideal which means nothing more than a poor ornamental cover for faulty thinking.

It must be said here that the thesis that all philosophic questioning in principle can be dissolved into that of the separate sciences is even today in no way so philosophically presuppositionless as it makes itself out to be. I would simply like to recall two problems which could not be mastered on the basis of this thesis. First, the problem of the meaning of the "given" itself, the fundamental category of all empiricism, which maintains the question of the accompanying subject, which in turn can only be answered historico-philosophically, because the subject of the given is not ahistorically identical and transcendental, but rather assumes changing and historically comprehensible forms. This problem is not even posed in the frame of empirio-criticism, including the most modern, but instead it naively accepts the Kantian point of departure. The other problem is familiar to it, but solved only arbitrarily and without any stringency. The problem of the unknown consciousness, the alien ego, can be made accessible for empirio-criticism only through analogy, composed subsequently on the basis of one's own experience, whereas in fact the empirio-critical method already necessarily assumes unknown consciousness in the language it has at its disposal. Solely by posing these problems, the theory of the Vienna School is drawn into precisely that philosophic continuity from which it wanted to distance itself. Yet that says nothing against the extraordinary importance of this School. I view its significance less in that it might have successfully converted philosophy into science than in that its rigorous formulation of the scientific in philosophy sharpens the contours of the contents of philosophy not subject to logic and the separate sciences. Philosophy will not be transformed into science, but under the pressure of the empiricist attack it will banish from itself all questioning which, as specifically scientific, belongs of right to the separate sciences and clouds philosophic questioning. I do not mean to suggest that philosophy should give up or even slacken that contact with separate sciences which it has finally regained, and the attainment of which counts among the most fortunate results of the most recent intellectual history. Quite the contrary. Philosophy will be able to understand the material content and concretion of problems only within the present standing of the separate sciences. It will also not be allowed to raise itself above such sciences by accepting their "results" as finished and meditating upon them from a safe distance. Rather, philosophic problems will lie always, and in a certain sense irredeemably, locked within the most specific questions of the separate sciences. Philosophy distinguishes itself from science not by a higher level of generality, as the banal view still today assumes, nor through the abstraction of its categories nor through the nature of its materials. The central difference lies far more in that the separate sciences accept their findings, at least their final and deepest findings, as indestructible and static, whereas philosophy perceives the first findings which it lights upon as a sign that needs unriddling. Plainly put: the idea of science (*Wissenschaft*) is research; that of philosophy is interpretation. In this remains the great, perhaps the everlasting paradox: philosophy persistently and with the claim of truth, must proceed interpretively without ever possessing a sure key to interpretation; nothing more is given to it than fleeting, disappearing traces within the riddle figures of that which exists and their astonishing entwinings. The history of philosophy is nothing other than the history of such entwinings. Thus it reaches so few "results." It must always begin anew and therefore cannot do without the least thread which earlier times have spun, and through which the lineature is perhaps completed which could transform the ciphers into a text.

It follows, then, that the idea of interpretation in no way coincides with the problem of "meaning," with which it is mostly confused. It just is not the task of philosophy to present such a meaning positively, to portray reality as "meaningful" and thereby justify it. Every such justification of that which exists is prohibited by the fragmentation in being itself. While our images of perceived reality may very well be *Gestalten*, the world in which we live is not; it is constituted differently than out of mere images of perception. The text which philosophy has to read is incomplete, contradictory and fragmentary, and much in it may be delivered up to blind demons; in fact perhaps the reading of it is our task precisely so that we, by reading, can better learn to recognize the demonic forces and to banish them. At the same time the idea of interpretation does not mean to suggest a second, a secret world which is to be opened up through an analysis of appearances. The dualism of the intelligible and the empirical, as was formulated by Kant and only from the post-Kantian perspective was attributed to Plato, whose heaven of ideas still lies undisguised and open to the mind – this dualism is better ascribed to the idea of research than that of interpretation – the idea of research, which assumes the reduction of the question to given and known elements where nothing would seem necessary except the answer. He who interprets by searching behind the phenomenal world for a world-in-itself (*Welt an sich*) which forms its foundation and support, acts mistakenly like someone who wants to find in the riddle the reflection of a being which lies behind it, a being mirrored in the riddle, in which it is contained. Instead, the function of riddle-solving is to light up the riddle-*Gestalt* like lightning and to negate it (*aufzuheben*), not to persist behind the riddle and imitate it. Authentic philosophic interpretation does not meet up with a fixed meaning which already lies behind the question, but lights it up suddenly and momentarily, and consumes it at the same time. Just as riddle-solving is constituted, in that the singular and dispersed elements of the question are brought into various groupings long enough for them to close together in a figure out of which the solution springs forth, while the question disappears – so philosophy has to bring its elements, which it receives from the sciences, into changing constellations, or, to say it with less astrological and scientifically more current expression, into changing trial combinations, until they fall into a figure which can be read as an answer, while at the same time the question disappears. The task of philosophy is not to search for concealed and manifest intentions of reality, but to interpret unintentional reality, in that, by the power of constructing figures, or images (*Bilder*), out of the isolated elements of reality it negates (*aufhebt*) questions, the exact articulation of which is the task of science,[2] a task to which philosophy always remains bound, because its power of illumination is not able to catch fire otherwise than on these solid questions. Here one can discover what appears as such an astounding and strange affinity existing between interpretive philosophy and that type of thinking which most strongly rejects the concept of the intentional, the meaningful: the thinking of materialism. Interpretation of the unintentional through a juxtaposition of the analytically isolated elements and illumination of the real by the power of such interpretation is the program of every authentically materialist knowledge, a program to which the materialist procedure does all the more justice, the more it distances itself from every "meaning" of its objects and the less it relates itself to an implicit, quasi-religious meaning. For long ago, interpretation divorced itself from all questions of meaning or, in other words, the symbols of philosophy are decayed. If philosophy must learn to renounce the question of totality, then it implies that it must learn to do without the symbolic function, in which for a long time, at least in idealism, the particular appeared to represent the general. It must give up the great problems, the size of which once hoped to guarantee the totality, whereas today between the wide meshes of big questions, interpretation slips away. If true interpretation succeeds only through a juxtaposition of the smallest elements, then it no longer has a role in the great problems in the traditional sense, or only in the sense that it deposits within a concrete finding the total question which that finding previously seemed to represent symbolically. Construction out of small and unintentional elements thus counts among the basic assumptions of philosophic interpretation; turning to the "refuse of the physical world" (*Abhub der Erscheinungswelt*) which Freud proclaimed, has validity beyond the realm of psychoanalysis, just as the turning of progressive social philosophy to economics has validity not merely due to the empirical superiority of economics, but just as much because of the immanent requirements of philosophic interpretation itself. Should philosophy today ask about the absolute relationship between the thing-in-itself and appearance, or, to grasp a more current formulation, about simply the meaning of being, it would either remain formal and unbinding, or it would split itself into a multitude of possible and arbitrary world-view positions (*weltanschaulicher Standpunkte*).

Suppose, however – I give an example as a thought experiment, without suggesting its actual feasibility – suppose it were possible to group the elements of a social analysis in such a manner that the way they came together made a figure which certainly does not lie before us organically, but which must first be posited: the commodity structure. This would hardly solve the thing-in-itself problem, not even in the sense that somehow the social conditions might be revealed under which the thing-in-itself problem came into existence, as Lukács even thought the solution to be;[3] for the truth content of a problem is in principle different from the historical and psychological conditions out of which it grows. But it might be possible that, from a sufficient construction of the commodity structure, the thing-in-itself problem absolutely disappeared. Like a source of light, the historical figure of commodity and of exchange value may free the form of a reality, the hidden meaning of which remained closed to investigation of the thing-in-itself problem, because there is no hidden meaning which could be redeemable from its one-time and first-time historical appearance. I don't want to give any material statements here, but only point out the direction for what I perceive as the tasks of philosophic interpretation. But even simply the correct formulation of these tasks would establish several things concerning those questions of philosophic principle, the explicit expression of which I would like to avoid. Namely this: that the function which the traditional philosophic inquiry expected from meta-historical, symbolically meaningful ideas is accomplished by inner-historically constituted, non-symbolic ones. With this, however, the relationship between ontology and history would also be differently posited, in principle, without thereby allowing the device of ontologizing history as totality in the form of mere "historicity," whereby every specific tension between interpretation and the object would be lost, and merely a masked historicism would remain. Instead of this, according to my conception, history would no more be the place from which ideas arise, stand out independently and disappear again. On the contrary, the historical images (*geschichtliche Bilder*) would at the same time be themselves ideas, the configuration of which constituted unintentional truth (*intentionslose Wahrheit*), rather than that truth appeared in history as intention.

But I break off the thought here: for nowhere are general statements more questionable than in a philosophy which wants to exclude abstract and general statements and requires them only in the necessity of transition. Instead, I would like to point out a second essential connection between interpretive philosophy and materialism. I said that the riddle's answer was not the "meaning" of the riddle in the sense that both could exist at the same time. The answer was contained within the riddle, and the riddle portrayed only its own appearance and contained the answer within itself as intention. Far more, the answer stands in strict antithesis to the riddle, needs to be constructed out of the riddle's elements, and destroys the riddle, which is not meaningful, but meaningless, as soon as the answer is decisively given to it. The movement which occurs in this process is executed in earnestness by materialism. Earnestness means here that the answer does not remain mistakenly in the closed area of knowledge, but that praxis is granted to it. The interpretation of given reality and its abolition are connected to each other, not, of course, in the sense that reality is negated in the concept, but that out of the construction of a configuration of reality the demand for its [reality's] real change always follows promptly. The change-causing gesture of the riddle process – not its mere resolution as such – provides the image of resolutions to which materialist praxis alone has access. Materialism has named this relationship with a name that is philosophically certified: dialectic. Only dialectically, it seems to me, is philosophic interpretation possible. When Marx reproached the philosophers, saying that they had only variously interpreted the world, and contraposed to them that the point was to change it, then the sentence receives its legitimacy not only out of political praxis, but also out of philosophic theory. Only in the annihilation of the question is the authenticity of philosophic interpretation first successfully proven, and mere thought by itself cannot accomplish this [authenticity]: therefore the annihilation of the question compels praxis. It is superfluous to separate out explicitly a conception of pragmatism, in which theory and praxis entwine with each other as they do in the dialectic.

I am clearly conscious of the impossibility of developing the program which I presented you – an impossibility which stems not only from the limits of time, but exists generally, because precisely as a program it does not allow itself to be worked out in completeness and generality. Nevertheless, I clearly see it as my duty to give you several suggestions. First: the idea of philosophic interpretation does not shrink back from that liquidation of philosophy which to me seems signalled by the collapse of the last philosophic claims to totality. For the strict exclusion of all ontological questions in the traditional sense, the avoidance of invariant general concepts, also perhaps the concept of man, the exclusion of every conception of a self-sufficient totality of mind (Geist), or of a self-contained "history of mind"; the concentration of philosophic questions on concrete inner-historical complexes from which they are not to be detached – these postulates indeed become extremely similar to a dissolution of that which has long been called philosophy. Whereas (at least the official) contemporary philosophic thinking has long kept its distance from these demands, or in any case has attempted to assimilate them singly in a watered-down form, one of the first and most actual tasks would appear to be the radical criticism of the ruling philosophic thinking. I am not afraid of the reproach of unfruitful negativity – an expression which Gottfried Keller once characterized as a "gingerbread expression" (*Pfefferkuchenausdruck*). If philosophic interpretation can in fact only prosper dialectically, then the first dialectical point of attack is given by a philosophy which cultivates precisely those problems whose removal appears more pressingly necessary than the addition of a new answer to so many old ones. Only an essentially undialectical philosophy, one which aims at ahistorical truth, could maintain that the old problems could simply be removed by forgetting them and starting fresh from the beginning. In fact, the deception of beginning is precisely that which in Heidegger's philosophy comes under criticism first of all. Only in the strictest dialectical communication with the most recent solution-attempts of philosophy and of philosophic terminology can a real change in philosophic consciousness prevail. This communication will have to take its specific scientific material preponderantly from sociology and, as the interpretive grouping process demands, crystalize out the small, unintentional elements which are nonetheless still bound to philosophic material.

One of the most powerful academic philosophers of the present [Heidegger] is said to have answered the question of the relationship between philosophy and sociology somewhat like this: while the philosopher is like an architect who presents and develops the blueprint of a house, the sociologist is like the cat burglar who climbs the walls from outside and takes out what he can reach. I would be inclined to acknowledge the comparison and to interpret positively the function he gave sociology for philosophy. For the house, this big house, has long since decayed in its foundations and threatens not only to destroy all those inside it, but to cause all the things to vanish which are stored within it, much of which is irreplaceable. If the cat burglar steals these things, these singular, indeed often half-forgotten things, he does a good deed, provided that they are only rescued; he will scarcely hold onto them for long, since they are for him only of scant worth. Of course, the appreciation of sociology by philosophic interpretation requires some limitations. The point of interpretive philosophy is to construct keys, before which reality springs open. As to the size of the key categories, they are specially made to order. The old idealism chose categories too large; so they did not even come close to fitting the keyhole. Pure philosophic sociologism chooses them too small; the key indeed goes in, but the door doesn't open. A great number of sociologists carry nominalism so far that the concepts become too small to align the others with themselves, to enter with them into a constellation. What remains is a vast, inconsistent connection of simple this-here determinations, which scoffs at every cognitive ordering and in no way provides a critical criterion. Thus, for example, the concept of class is nullified and replaced by countless descriptions of separate groups so that they can no longer be arranged into overlapping unities, although they in fact appear as such in empirical reality. Similarly, one of the most important concepts, that of ideology,[4] is robbed of its cutting edge by defining it formally as the arrangement of contents of consciousness in regard to particular groups, without allowing the question to arise any longer as to the truth or falsity of the contents themselves. This sociology classifies itself as a kind of general relativism, the generality of which can be no more recognized by philosophic interpretation than can any other generality, and for the correction of which philosophy possesses a sufficient means in the dialectical method.

In regard to the manipulation of conceptual material by philosophy, I speak purposely of grouping and trial arrangement, of constellation and construction. The historical images, which do not constitute the meaning of being (*Dasein*) but dissolve and resolve its questions are not simply self-given. They do not lie organically ready in history; not showing (*Schau* [Husserl]) or intuition is required to become aware of them. They are not magically sent by the gods to be taken in and venerated. Rather, they must be produced by human beings and are legitimated in the last analysis alone by the fact that reality crystalizes about them in striking conclusiveness (*Evidenz* [Husserl]). Here they divorce themselves centrally from the archaic, the mythic archetypes (*Urbilder*) which psychoanalysis lights upon, and which [Ludwig] Klages hopes to preserve as categories of our knowledge. Should they be equivalent to them in a hundred characteristics, they separate themselves at the point where those [archetypes] describe their fatalistic orbit in the heads of human beings. The historical images are manageable and comprehensible, instruments of human reason, even there where they seem to align themselves objectively, as magnetic centers of objective being. They are models, by means of which the *ratio*, examining and testing, approaches a reality which refuses to submit to laws, yet can imitate the pattern of the model every time, provided that pattern is imprinted correctly. One may see here an attempt to re-establish that old concept of philosophy which was formulated by Bacon and passionately contended around the time of Leibniz, a conception which idealism derided as a fad: that of the *ars inveniendi* [art of invention]. Every other conception of models would be gnostic and indefensible. But the *organon* of this *ars inveniendi* is fantasy. An exact fantasy; fantasy which abides strictly within the material which the sciences present to it, and reaches beyond them only in the smallest aspects of their arrangement: aspects, granted, which fantasy itself must originally generate. If the idea of philosophic interpretation which I tried to develop for you is valid, then it can be expressed as the demand to answer the questions of a pre-given reality each time, through a fantasy which rearranges the elements of the question without going beyond the circumference of the elements, the exactitude of which has its control in the disappearance of the question.

I know full well that many, perhaps most of you are not in agreement with what I am presenting here. Not only scientific thinking but, still more, fundamental ontology contradicts my conviction as to the current tasks of philosophy. But thinking which aims at relations with the object, and not at validity isolated in itself, is accustomed to prove its right to exist not by refuting the objections which are voiced against it and which consider themselves irrefutable, but by its fruitfulness, in the sense in which Goethe used the term. Nonetheless, may I still perhaps address a word to the most current objections, not as I have construed them, but as the representatives of fundamental ontology formulate them, and as they first led me to formulate the theory according to which, up until then, I had proceeded solely in the praxis of philosophic interpretation.

The central objection is that my conception, too, is based on a concept of man, a blueprint of Being (*Entwurf des Daseins*); only, out of blind anxiety before the power of history, I allegedly shrank from putting these invariants forth clearly and left them clouded; instead I bestowed upon historical facticity, or its arrangement, the power which actually belongs to the invariant, ontological first principles, practiced idolatry with historically produced being, destroyed in philosophy every permanent standard, sublimated it into an aesthetic picture game (*Bilderspiel*), and transformed the *prima philosophia* [philosophy of first principles] into essayism.

In response, I can relate to these objections only by admitting of their content, but I defend it as philosophically legitimate. I will not decide whether a particular conception of man and being lies at the base of my theory, but I do deny the necessity of resorting to this conception. It is an idealist demand, that of an absolute beginning, as only pure thought by itself can accomplish. It is a Cartesian demand, which believes it necessary to raise thinking to the form of its thought presuppositions and axioms. However, philosophy which no longer makes the assumption of autonomy, which no longer believes reality to be grounded in the *ratio*, but instead assumes always and forever that the law-giving of autonomous reason pierces through a being which is not adequate to it and cannot be laid out rationally as a totality – such a philosophy will not go the entire path to the rational presuppositions, but instead will stop there where irreducible reality breaks in upon it. If it proceeds further into the region of presuppositions, then it will be able to reach them only formally, and at the price of that reality in which its actual tasks are laid. The break-in of what is irreducible, however, occurs concrete-historically and thus it is history which retards the movement of thought to its presuppositions. The productivity of thinking is able to prove itself only dialectically, in historical concreteness. Both thought and history come into communication within the models. Regarding efforts to achieve a form for such communication, I gladly put up with the reproach of essayism. The English empiricists called their philosophic writings essays, as did Leibniz, because the power of freshly disclosed reality, upon which their thinking struck, continuously forced upon them the risk of experimentation. Not until the post-Kantian century was the risk of experimentation lost, along with the power of reality. Thus from a form of great philosophy the essay became an insignificant form of aesthetics, in which a concretion of inter-pretation nonetheless takes refuge as appearance (*Schein*), over which authen-tic philosophy, in the grand dimensions of its problems, has long since lost disposal.

If, with the disintegration of all security within great philosophy, experi-ment makes its entry; if it thereby ties onto the limited, contoured and unsymbolic interpretations of aesthetic essays, then that does not appear to be condemnable, provided that the objects are chosen correctly, that they are real. For the mind (*Geist*) is indeed not capable of producing or grasping the totality of the real, but it may be possible to penetrate the detail, to explode in miniature the mass of merely existing reality.

Translator's Notes

This speech was delivered by Adorno 7 May 1931, as his inaugural lecture to the philosophy faculty of the University of Frankfurt where he taught until 1933. The topic of Adorno's first seminar was Walter Benjamin's book, *Ursprung des deutschen Trauerspiels* (completed in 1925 and published in 1928), a study which Benjamin intended as his *Habilitationsschrift* but which was rejected by the academic establish-ment. Adorno's speech reflects strongly the influence of Benjamin's *Trauerspiel* study. It was to have been dedicated to Benjamin in published form, but the planned pub-lication did not take place. The speech was found in Adorno's estate after his death and appears for the first time in vol. 1 of his *Gesammelte Schriften*.

1   Adorno is referring to Martin Heidegger's *Being and Time* (1927) trans. John Mac-
     quarrie and Edward Robinson (Oxford: Blackwell, 1962), which by 1931 had
     made a significant impact within academic circles.
2   Cf. Walter Benjamin, *The Origin of German Tragic Drama*, trans. John Osborne
     (London: NLB, 1977), pp. 27–56, especially pp. 34–6.
3   Cf. Georg Lukács, *History and Class Consciousness*, trans. Rodney Livingstone
     (London: Merlin Press, 1971).
4   Adorno is referring to Karl Mannheim, *Ideology and Utopia*, trans. Louis Wirth and
     Edward Shils (London: Routledge, 1960).

2

Why Philosophy?

The essay 'Why Philosophy?' was originally written by Adorno for a radio broadcast in 1962. Here Adorno returns to the question of what philosophy must achieve in order to recover its critical vocation. The essay reflects on the idea that for many, philosophy has come to be seen, as Adorno puts it, as 'good for nothing'. He agrees that philosophy has indeed lost its former pre-eminent position, however, that loss can be attributed to certain predominant intellectual preferences. According to Adorno, philosophy has fallen into two nonviable alternatives: positivism or scientific method and fundamental ontology. Critical philosophy has given way to positivism with the result that there are areas of experience that have been withdrawn from philosophical reflection altogether. Reading positivism in a manner characteristic of critical theory, Adorno sees it as the product of a particular historical consciousness. Since contemporary consciousness is affected by ideology it follows, for Adorno, that positivism, as the preferred method of contemporary thought, must be ideological. In a general way Adorno claims that the division of labour in society is reflected in positivism itself in that positivism accepts a division between the tasks of knowledge. Furthermore, positivist method, according to Adorno, is conformist in that its approach is merely classificatory. In opposition to this state of affairs philosophy must be reconstituted in order to restore (as Adorno sees it) its essentially critical character. For Adorno criticism is resistance to immediacy and for that reason he denies that Heidegger's philosophy can provide an alternative to positivism. Fundamental ontology like positivism, the argument goes, merely affirms being rather than investigating the social structures which give rise to it. In contrast to positivism and fundamental ontology, Adorno proposes dialectics which he makes equivalent to criticism for the reason that it overturns immediacy, immediacy in this case being the given meanings of society. A further point of interest is Adorno's evocation of idealism. He attempts to revise idealism since he values one aspect of its description of the human condition, namely, that human beings are not brute facts but have a positive 'spontaneous' capacity. As such idealism, the epistemology of which Adorno neither here nor elsewhere defends, provides a structure in which an emancipatory model of the subject – a critical individual – might be constructed. Adorno's conclusions in 'Why Philosophy?' are not tentative. They offer a broad programme for a new philosophy.

'Why Philosophy?' [1962], in *Man and Philosophy* (Munich: Max Hueber Verlag), pp. 11–24, ed. by Walter Leifer. Translated by Margaret D. Senft-Howie and Reginald Freeston.

To a question like "Why Philosophy?", for the formulation of which I am myself responsible – although not unaware of its amateurish sound – most people would expect an answer along lines which assembled every imaginable difficulty and reservation, and eventually gave birth to an affirmative conclusion, hedged around with due limitations, confirming what had been rhetorically doubted. This all-too-familiar course discloses the conformist, apologetic approach, expressed in positive terms and counting on agreement in advance. That, indeed, is all one might expect from a professional lecturer in philosophy whose living depends on a continuance of such studies and whose own, tangible interests are damaged by any suggestion to the contrary. I have, nevertheless, some sort of right to pose the question, if only because I am not at all sure of the answer.

Anyone who is defending something that the spirit of an age rejects as out of date and obsolete, is in an awkward position. The arguments put forward sound lame and overdone. He addresses his audience as though he is trying to talk them into buying something they don't want. This drawback has to be reckoned with by those who are not prepared to be dissuaded from philosophy. He knows that it is no longer suited to the modern techniques that control our lives – "technical" in the figurative, as well as in the literal, sense – and with which it was once so inextricably entwined. Nor is philosophy any longer a cultural medium transcending technical affairs, as it was in Hegel's time, for instance, when, for a few short decades, the tight little circle of German intellectuals exchanged ideas in the common language of philosophy. From about the time Kant died, philosophy came under a cloud because it had got out of step with the more exact sciences – and the physical sciences in particular – and forfeited its public position as the leading discipline. That trend is relevant to the crisis over the value of humanistic studies in education, and on this subject I need say little. The Kantian and Hegelian revivals, characterised by the appearance of the less imposing aspects of their namesakes' teachings, have left the situation substantially unchanged. Finally, caught up in the general urge to specialize, philosophy too settled into the grooves of a specialist study, that of the pure theory from which all incidental content has been purged. This involved denying the original philosophical concept – intellectual freedom, or refusal to acknowledge the supremacy of technical science. At the same time, by abstaining from a fixed content, be it a formal doctrine of logic or science, or the myth of pure being divorced from all that exists, "pure" philosophy declared itself bankrupt when confronted with the social objectives of the world around us. In this, of course, it was merely setting the seal to a process that broadly matched the course of its own historical development. Whole areas were continually being withdrawn from its sphere of influence and subjected to scientific method, so that it almost lost the power to choose between becoming a science itself or persisting in the form of a tiny, tolerated enclave, opposed thereby to what it set out to be – a universal system of truth. Even Newtonian physics had been known as "philosophy". The modern scientific intelligence would regard it as an archaic relic, a rudiment from that age of early Greek speculation in which bold explanations of natural phenomena and sublime metaphysical insight into the nature of things were still inextricably interwoven. For this reason, some resolute souls have announced that such archaic anachronisms constitute the only true philosophy and have sought to restore their one-time pre-eminence. But the schizophrenic mentality which casts about and seeks its own reunion in the harmonious unities of the past, falsifies the substance of its own quest. It is like working, by choice, in the medium of a primitive language. In philosophy, as much as elsewhere, restorations are doomed to failure. For philosophy needs to protect itself from cultural rantings, as well as from the magical incantations of ideologies. Neither should it be imagined that specialist work along the lines suggested by scientific method, or whatever else prides itself on being research, is philosophy. And, in the end, philosophical method that is free from all those things is diametrically opposed to current thinking. But nothing less frees it from the taint of apologetics. Philosophical speculation that satisfies the aims of genuine metaphysical enquiry, instead of sheepishly hiding behind the facts of its own history, draws its strength from its resistance to modern methodology and serves to counter the present-day nonchalant acceptance of the material world around us.

Even the greatest triumphs so far achieved in philosophical speculation, as exemplified in the work done by Hegel, no longer hold us. In accordance with the categories of public opinion – which apply to everyone – it is precisely those whose actions are public property, and who are thereby numbered among the dialecticians, that quote Hegelian differential dicta. No opinion rests upon personal conviction. Views are implicit from the direction taken by the subject–matter itself, its entire freedom to move, and freedom for our thought to follow it, being postulated by no less an authority than Hegel himself. The comprehensiveness claimed by traditional philosophical method, culminating in the thesis that reality is reasonable, is indistinguishable from apologetics, which has, however, been taken to absurd limits. By claiming to be an all–embracing system, philosophy runs the risk of ending in a series of crazy delusions. Immediately it abandons the claim to omniscence, however, and gives up the idea of crystallizing all truth within itself, it denies the whole weight of its own traditions. This is the price it must pay in exchanging its delusions for reality, in purging itself of crazy notions and linking reality with reason. It then loses its character of a self–sufficing and cogent body of justificatory proofs. Its place in society – which it would do well to promote and not to deny – corresponds to its own desperate need to define what, today, is defined by the hackneyed term of the absurd. Philosophy guided by a sense of responsibility for everything should no longer lay claim to a mastery of the absolute, should in fact renounce all such notions, in order not to betray them in the event, without, however, sacrificing the concept of truth itself. The province of philosophy lies in such contradictions as these. They confer on it a negative character. Kant's famous dictum that the path of criticism is the only one still open to us, belongs among those propositions by which the philosophy in which they originate, passes its test, inasmuch as the saying or axiom outlives the system which conceived it. The critical idea itself may indeed be included amongst the philosophical traditions that have been disrupted in the modern age. And while, in the meantime, the arena of every kind of knowledge has been invaded to so great an extent by scientific specialisations – so that speculation along philosophic lines is attended by a kind of persecution complex and the ever–present fear that it must yield to rejection as a dilettante occupation, wherever it does light upon some substantial aspect of reality, the concept of original truth raises its reactionary head – and gobbles down undeserved credit for it. The more reified our world becomes, and the thicker the veil under which we hide the face of nature, the more the ideas around which that veil is spun are accepted as the only true experience of this world, and of natural phenomena. From the vaunted pre–Socratic era onwards, however, traditional philosophers have played a critical role. Xenophanes, to whose school of thought the concept of being is due which is, today, contrasted to any fixed philosophical notion, wanted to liberate natural forces from a mythological content. And then Aristotle saw through the Platonic trend towards elevating a proposition to the status of a being in itself. More recently, the scholastic dogmas were criticized by Descartes as being essentially opinions. Leibniz became the critic of the empirical method; then Kant refuted Leibniz and Hume at one and the same time; Hegel criticized Kant, and Marx came out against Hegel. In all these cases criticism was not merely a seasoning to what, thirty years ago would have been called, in the jargon of ontology, their "design." It did not seek to document attitudes that could be taken up according to taste or inclination. It had its being, rather, in the sphere of cogent argument. In criticism, these philosophers expressed their own truth. Criticism, rather than the passive acceptance of received theory, the unifying factor between the various problems, and an ingredient in each argument, has laid the foundations of what may be termed the constructive unity of the history of philosophy. In the progressive continuity of such lines of criticism, even those philosophies that base their teachings upon the supposedly eternal, a-temporal, verities, contain within themselves the crystallized metaphysical thought of their age.

Modern philosophical criticism should be conducted in the presence of two schools of thought which, in the spirit of our age, operate, willy-nilly, beyond the academic frontiers. They both diverge and, at the same time, run complementary to each other. In the Anglo-Saxon world especially, logical positivism, first inaugurated in the Viennese school, has gained ground to the point of virtual monopoly. In the sense that it is modern by reason of its remarkably consistent faculty of enlightenment, it strikes many as the doctrine most suited to the needs of a technological and scientifically-minded era. What it is unable to absorb – the indigestible residues – are the offshoots from metaphysics, the remains of a mythology it no longer heeds – or, in the terminology of those who know little of it, art. Against this – above all in the Germanic countries – there are the ontological approaches. The word ontology itself is somewhat out of favour, to judge at least from what Heidegger has published since *Sein und Zeit*. His approach is an "archaic" one; while his French variant, existentialism, has remoulded the ontological framework in a spirit of enlightenment and with political commitment. The positivist and the ontological schools are anathema to each other. Heidegger's doctrine was – unjustly, by the way – attacked by Rudolf Carnap, one of the foremost exponents of the positivist school, as being devoid of sense. Positivist thinking, on the other hand, is looked on by ontologists of the Heidegger brand, as oblivious of being itself ("*Seins-vergessen*"), and tending to vulgarize and cheapen the essential question. It is feared that too much preoccupation with the mere fact of existence – the tool of positivist views – will besmirch the hands of those who make use of it. All the more striking, then, is the coincident tendency of each of these standpoints. Metaphysics is their common enemy. The fact that it proceeds considerably beyond the limitations of known circumstance and is hence intolerable to the positivist, whose very name indicates an adherence to positive, existing and received evidence, requires no emphasis. But Heidegger too, schooled as he is in traditional metaphysics, has expressly tried to detach his work from its influence. He calls metaphysics, somewhat derogatorily, philosophy from the time of Aristotle at least – if not from that of Plato as well – inasmuch as it distinguishes between being and existing, idea and meaning – one might also say, using language of which Heidegger would, however, not approve – subject from object. Thinking that seeks to analyse and separate and break up the ideas suggested by the words that describe them, in short, all that Hegel called the operation and working efforts of "the concept", and equated with philosophy, is regarded as the betrayal of the latter, not even capable of being amended, but as being dictated by the nature of being itself. On these two counts, in both positivist theory and that of Heidegger – in his later work, at all events – the current is set against speculation. The idea which arises independently from, and indicatively of, the facts, and cannot be separated from them without leaving a residue behind – a remainder, as it were – is stigmatized as vain and profitless cerebration: according to Heidegger, however, ways of thinking that follow the typical pattern prescribed by the historical evolution of thought in the West at bottom fall short of the real truth. The latter comes to light of itself, and stands revealed: correct thinking is no more than the ability to perceive it. In the last resort, the final court of appeal for philosophy is philology. On this view of the common aversion to metaphysical method it appears less of a paradox than at first when we learn that Walter Bröcker, a disciple of Heidegger's working in Kiel, attempted to combine positivism and the philosophy of being by leaving the whole field of existence clear to positivist theory and superimposing over it, on a higher plane, the principles of the philosophy of being, in the form of a deliberately contrived mythology. Being, under which heading Heidegger's philosophy seems to range itself more and more closely is, for him, simply an impression made on the passive consciousness, in similarly direct independence from the mediation of the subject as the sensory data are for the positivists. The processes of thought are, for both, a necessary evil and held in less esteem, as involving tendentious risks. Thought loses the power of being something independent. The autonomy of reason is disappearing, inasmuch as it does not satisfy itself by measuring and comparing present and past data, and adjusting itself to them. By the same token, the concept of liberty of thought also disappears and, in effect, the idea of self-determination in human society. Most positivists, were they not deeply imbued with humanistic tendencies, would be obliged in practice to devise some form of adaption to the facts of existence which would render thought of no avail, and make it a mere anticipation or classification. With Heideg-ger, however, thought, in its character of a reverent, meaningless and passive listener to a continual reiteration of the formula of being, would lose its right to criticize and would be forced to capitulate indiscriminately to everything that might be referred to the equivocal superiority implied in the notion of being. Heideggers's absorption into Hitler's "*Führerstaat*" was not an oppor-tunist manoeuvre: it followed from a philosophic attitude of mind in which the "Führer" and the dominant power of being were virtually identified.

Is philosophy still necessary, as it has been from time immemorial, as a critical method, as a check to the expanding influence of heteronomy? Is philosophical thought involved in a vain attempt to remain its own master and to convert a falsely imposed mythology and a resigned adaptation in accordance with its own standards of what is true and what is not true? Unless it were forbidden to do so, as it was in the Christian Athens of late antiquity, philosophy should provide a refuge for intellectual freedom and liberty, without having any hope, however, of being able to break the politi-cal trends that are stifling physical and mental freedoms throughout the world and continually sending powerful roots down into the substrata of phi-losophical discussion and argument. Changes in the substance of ideas always reflect something of external realities, however. But if those two heteronomous schools of thought exclude the truth, and can be shown to do so in a compelling manner, this not only adds a new link to the chain of hopeless philosophies but also gives some grounds for hoping that slavery and repression – evils in as little need of philosophical proof that they are evil, as that they exist – may not, after all, have the last word. Criticism would have the task of establishing that the two dominant trends in philosophy were separate, insufficient, and yet irreconcilable aspects of truth, which had diverged in the course of historical evolution. Little as they lend themselves to fusion in what is known as a "synthesis", they would nevertheless call for critical reflection, each within itself. What is wrong with positivist theory is that it accepts the division of labour between the sciences, as it is socially enforced, as a standard of truth itself, admitting no theory in which the divi-sion of labour itself emerges clearly as being derived, an epiphenomenon the authority of which is falsely assumed. If philosophy wished to found a science in the present age of emancipation, and if she had seen her image as inter-preted by Fichte and Hegel, as the only real science, the very general frame-work positivism borrowed from the sciences, and its refined and socially polished methods, would become a philosophy in an urge for self-justification – an example of thinking in a circle that appears to disturb the fanatical adherents of logical tidiness to a remarkably small extent. Philosophy resigned when she elevated to her own status the science which she alone was intended to illumine. The existence of science, telle quelle, as it appears in the weft and warp of social life, with all its inadequacies and irrationalities, has become the criterion of its own truth. Positivism, with its fanatical reverence for the reified veneer of facts, tends to become reified itself. With all its animosity towards mythology, it betrays the anti-mythological impulses of philosophy, throwing down what is merely man-made achievement and reducing its significance to the standards of its human origin.

Such a fundamental ontology, however, blinds itself to the mediatory role, not only of what is factual, but of concept. It suppresses recognition of the fact that the real entities, or whatever a progressive process of sublimation may call them, with which it confronts the facts of positivism, are still thought, subjective thinking, and mind. It is precisely the existence of subjectivity and subjective determination that takes us back to forms of existence that originate otherwise than entirely from the fact of being, in human social groupings, for example. In the sanctuary of the edifice in which the philosophy of repristination lies entrenched from the profanity of mere fact, as well as from the rationality of concepts, we come again upon the philosophical schism from which the heralds of unity, of indivisible wholes, imagined themselves immune. The words they use are necessarily concepts, inasmuch as they are intended to be meaningful at all; the philosophy of being wishes to be thought even after it has definitely turned towards archaism. Since, however, ideas, by their very nature, require some kind of complementarity; and since Hegel's unsurpassed speculative perception informs us that the mere thought of identity evokes, nay demands, the corresponding concept of non-identity against which alone we may demonstrate the idea of identity: the purest concepts still postulate their reverse aspect. Thought itself, of which all ideas are a function, cannot be represented in the absence of thinking activity, which the word thought implies. This retrospect already includes for its motive force what was, on an idealistic view, first formulated in the concept and what, from the viewpoint of mythological being, in addition to the concept, is an epiphenomenon, a third factor. Without the determination afforded by these two impulses, the third factor would be quite indeterminate; the mere mention of it goes beyond the fact of determination occasioned by such forces, the existence of which has been so assiduously denied. Even Kant's transcendental subject, from which transcendent, unsubjective being would gladly inherit the legacy, requires a complementary diversity to become a whole, just as, on the other hand, diversity requires the unifying complement of reason. Apart from the contents, which are those of the whole entity, the idea of the latter cannot be grasped, and the factual traces remaining in the contents are as little susceptible of exorcism as their differentiation from the concept of which they are a necessary ingredient. No unified concept, however formal or approximating to the abstractions of pure logic, can be detached – even in theory – from the subject-matter with which it is concerned: even the content of formal logic includes a material essence which pure logic prided itself on having eliminated. The basis of what Günther Anders has called the "pseudo-concretion" of Heidegger's philosophy of being, however – and of all the fallacious imposture to which it has given rise – resides in the fact that it claims to be pure of what it is ultimately in itself, and from the concreteness of which it profits. It celebrates victory in the course of a strategic withdrawal. Its mythical ambiguity merely camouflages the fixed interaction of impulse from which it is no more able to detach itself than the conditioned consciousness ever could. Because, in the mythology of being, the factual and the conceptual remain artificially confused, being is represented as on a higher plane than either existence or concept, and hence, in Kant's words, surreptitiously acquires absoluteness. It too is a product of reified consciousness, since it suppresses the human element in the most elevated concepts and idolizes them. Dialectics, however, insists upon the "mediation" of what is seemingly immediate, and upon the reciprocity at all levels of what is immediate and what requires intermediary processes. Dialectics is not a third approach but it represents an attempt, by means of an immanent criticism, to elevate philosophical viewpoints above themselves and above the despotism of such viewpoints. In contrast to the ingenuousness of a controlled, free consciousness which regards its own limitations and data as unlimited, philosophy would then have a binding obligation to be disingenuous. In a world which, permeated through and through with the structures of social order, is so heavily weighted against all individualistic tendencies that the individual has little other choice but to accept them for what they are, such naivety continually grows apace and takes on sinister connotations. What is forced upon the individual by an all-pervasive apparatus of his own construction, and in the toils of which he is held enmeshed, to the virtual exclusion of all spontaneous impulse, becomes natural to him. The reified consciousness is entirely naive, and yet it has also lost its naivety completely. The task before philosophy is to break up the seemingly obvious and the apparently incomprehensible.

The integration of philosophy and science, which showed itself in the earliest writings on metaphysics in the West, sought to liberate ideas from the tutelage of dogma, towards which they tended by reason of the despotic will, the negation of all freedom. At this, however, was aimed the postulate of the direct "association" of a lively intellectual activity in all branches of knowledge, the ineradicable criterion of "evidence" since the time of Spinoza. In purely logical terms, this was the anticipatory image of an actual situation in which man was free, at last, of any form of unseeing authority. The wheel has now come full circle, however. The appeal to science, the rules by which it functions, the absolute validity of the methods to which it owes its development, together constitute an authority which penalises free, untrammelled, "untrained" thinking and will not allow the minds of men to dwell on matters that do not bear the stamp of its approval. Science, the means to autonomy, has degenerated into an instrument of heteronomy. Its original raison d'être has become detached, a plaything of the slanderous comment, demeaned to an isolated existence in the limbo of speculative small-talk. The critical method of scientivism, which roundly refutes such ways of thinking is not, therefore, what its well-intentioned opponents reproach it for being, but is, rather, a destruction of what is already destructive. Criticism of the existing philosophies is not a plea for the disappearance of philosophy as such, or even for its replacement by a single discipline, social science, for instance. It may, in a formal and material way, even assist those forms of intellectual liberty that fail to find a foothold in the tide of present-day philosophic fashion. Speculation on a broad basis that proceeds consistently and works from the firm ground of progress towards an objective, is, on the other hand, also free in the sense that it refuses to be governed by the rules of organised knowledge. It directs the essence of its own accumulated experience towards the objects, strips away the social fabric that veils them, and gives them a new look. If philosophy could liberate itself from the aura of fearfulness spread about by the tyranny of current trends − from the ontological pressures to imagine only what is conceptually "pure"; and from the scientific compulsion to think solely along paths "in line with" the dictates of approved scientifically tested principle − it would be capable, in an atmosphere cleared of anxiety, of seeing what its inhibited perceptions had failed to descry. The dream of philosophic phenomenology, like the dream in which we imagine we are awake, of "getting at the facts", could only come true for a philosophy that hopes to acquire knowledge without waving the magic wand of intuition, but by reflecting upon subjective as well as objective intermediary phases, not however, in accordance with the dogmatic primacy of a superimposed method which, instead of the objects desired, merely offers the phenomenological processes a series of fetishes, or "home-made" imaginings. Were not all positive phraseology so profoundly suspect, one might asseverate that, finally, what traditional philosophy has failed to achieve by confusing its own identity with what it wished to clarify, was revealed to a consciousness that was free and, at the same time, capable of "internal refraction". The attenuous weariness of a traditional philosophy that stems from the interplay of its own mutations, is still potentially philosophy, since it possesses the latent dynamism of one which has broken the spell of its own evolution.

Problematic it may yet be, whether philosophy, as a form of occupation for the searching intellect, is still suited to the times; or whether it remains behind its present task i.e. that of diagnosing the malady which is driving the world to disaster. The time for speculation seems to have gone. The obvious absurdity of the situation makes one boggle at the idea of understanding it. The abolition of philosophy was forecast more than a century ago. The fact that, in the East, Marxist philosophy has congealed to "diamat", as though such a philosophy were compatible with Marxist theory, is evidence of Marxism's divergence into a truncated, static dogma, refuting its own content; its retrogression, as they themselves call it, towards an ideology. Philosophers can continue their endeavours only if they deny the Marxist proposition of the obsolescence of reflection. Marx considered that opportunities to change society from top to bottom existed here and now. But it would be sheer obstinacy to stick to this expectation of Marx. The proletariat to which he addressed himself was not yet integrated into society; it was manifestly sunk in misery while the community still lacked the means of asserting its dominance, should the need arise. Philosophy, as a free and coherent body of thought, is in an entirely different position. Marx would have been the last to separate thought from the realities of historical evolution. Hegel was aware of the impermanence of art, and foretold its demise, associating its continued existence with a "consciousness of want". But what is right for art is applicable to philosophy, which contains an essence of truth in line with that expressed in art, although its methods are dissimilar. The undiminished continuance of suffering, anxiety and threats obliges thought which is unable to develop profitably, to preserve itself. After missing its cue philosophy would then have to ask, without any illusions, why the world which could be a paradise on earth today, could become very hell tomorrow. Such knowledge would certainly be philosophical. To replace it in favour of practical politics which perpetuated necessarily the present situation, the condition it was the function of philosophy to criticize, would be anachronistic. Politics aimed at the formation of a reasonable and mature mankind remain under an evil spell, as long as they lack a theory that takes account of the totality that is false. That this does not mean that one should warm up idealism, but rather that one should accept the facts of social and political realities and their relative strengths, goes without saying.

During the last forty or fifty years, philosophy has, generally quite spuriously, declared its opposition to idealism. What was genuine in this contention, was its objection to decorative phraseology, intellectual conceit which ascribes absolute authority to the mind, and the glorification of this world, in the name of freedom. The anthropocentricity inherent in all idealistic theory is beyond aid; we need only call to mind the bare outlines of the changes taking place in cosmology during the last century and a half. Among the tasks awaiting the attention of philosophy, by no means the last is the adaptation, without amatenurish analogies and syntheses, of the results of experience gained in the natural sciences, to the province of the mind. A deep and sterile gulf has grown up between such experience and what we call the world of the mind, to the point, in fact, that intellectual preoccupation with the mind itself and social phenomena appears, at times, like a vain conceit. If the sole purpose of philosophy consisted in bringing the human intellect to the stage where it could identify itself with what it has learned about natural phenomena, instead of leaving mankind to live out its life like a troglodyte sheltering behind its own knowledge of the cosmos in which the imprudent species, "homo", goes his graceless way, at least something would have been achieved. In view of this task, and of an unimpaired insight into the kinetic laws of society, it would hardly be tempted to claim to be able to set forth something like positive "meaning" to the world. To that extent it makes common cause with the positivist view, but still more with modern art, the manifestations of which remain beyond the ken of the greater part of what passes today for philosophic thinking. But the much overstated trend of neo-ontology against idealism ends, not in a dynamic restatement of its aims and purpose, but in resignation. Thought has allowed itself to become, as it were, intimidated, and no longer possesses the self-confidence to go beyond the mere reproduction of what is anyway. In contrast to such resigned attitudes, idealism at least retained an element of spontaneity. On the other hand, materialism, if carried to its logical conclusions, would mean the end of materialism, of man's blind, humiliating dependence on material circumstance. Far as the mind of man is from being absolute, it is not a mere duplication of brute fact either. It will only come to a proper awareness of things if it avoids its own limitations. The human mind's powers of resistance are the only criteria in philosophy today. It is as irreconcilable with reified consciousness as once Platonic enthusiasm was; its transcendence beyond the factual allows it to call the universally conditioned phenomena by their own names. It hopes for reconciliation with the non–identical that is being degraded continuously by affirmative philosophies. The latter regard everything in its functional aspect; even seeing in the adaptation to natural phenomena a pretext for subjugating the phenomenon of the mind. But what exists does not want to be manipulated. Anything that has function is bewitched in a functional world. Thought alone, unfettered by mental reservations, and freely admitting, without any illusions as to its inner sovereignty, its own absence of function and material impotence, may be vouchsafed a glimpse of a non-existent yet feasible order of things where men and things each occupy their appointed place. Philosophy is not outmoded simply

because it is good-for-nothing; it should not even make that claim to attention if it wishes to avoid the heedless repetition of its cardinal sin, that of
self-assertiveness.

That fault was a traditional one, inherited from the concept of a
"philosophia perennis" in which the eternal verities were vested. Hegel sprang
that trap with his remarkable adage that philosophy was the essence of a
period, distilled by thought. He considered it such an evident requirement
that he did not hesitate to define philosophy by it. He was the first to gain
an insight into the temporal nucleus of time itself. He linked it to the belief
that, by expressing its own stage of consciousness as a necessary, and dynamic,
part of a whole, every significant philosophy also expressed itself as a whole.
That this confidence, and the efficacy of the philosophy, was invalidated,
diminishes not merely the emphatic claim of subsequent systems, but also
their intrinsic quality. What was self-evident to Hegel, however, cannot by
any means be said of the philosophies currently fashionable. They are no
longer the essential substance of their times, expressed in ideas. In their
"provincial" sphere, the ontologists are indeed doing themselves some good.
This is duly parallelled by the impotent poverty of ideas evinced by the positivists. They have so modified the rules of the game that the reified consciousness of mindless "bright boys" may consider itself the cream of the
"Zeitgeist". They are, however, but a symptom of the current mentality, and
falsify what they want in the incorruptible virtue of those whom nobody
will deceive. Both tendencies represent, at most, the spirit of regression, and
Nietzsche's "Hinterweltler" (those remote from the main currents of life in
the world) have literally reverted to being backwoodsmen. From such, philosophy, as the most advanced kind of awareness, should preserve itself, per-
vaded as it is with the possibility of becoming something different – and
equal to the resistance of the forces of regression – should what it has
absorbed and understood as so much ballast be raised to new, unforseen
heights. If, in the face of such a claim – of which it is well aware – the
philosophical archaism of today is evasive concerning the older kind of verity;
if it treats casually the idea of progress, which it is engaged in obstructing,
much as though it had got the better of it, we can put it down to humbug.
No dialectic of progress could legitimize an intellectual attitude that considers itself sound and "healthy" merely because it has not so far felt the pressures of that objectivity in which it is itself involved – and which ensures
that the appeal to soundness directly strengthens the evil. That self-righteous
meditation that treats the progressive type of consciousness with contempt,
is hackneyed. Reflections that go beyond the neo-ontological incantations,
as well as beyond the "verities of fact" of the positivists, are not fashionable
extremes, but are cogently motivated. As long as philosophy retains the slight-

est trace of the particular atmosphere diffused by the title of a book published more than thirty years ago by an early Kantian: *Aus der Philosophenecke* (*Out of the Philosopher's Corner*), it will continue to be the plaything of its detractors. Avuncular advice will not suffice to raise it above the hum and whirr of scientific activity. All wisdom has degenerated to the pontifical. Neither is philosophy turning to advantage the approach of that professor who, in the pre-Fascist era, experienced an urge to rectify the ills of the times, and examined Marlene Dietrich's film, *The Blue Angel*, in order to obtain, at first hand, an idea of how bad things really were. Excursions of that kind into tangible realities turn philosophy into the refuse of history, with the subject-matter of which it is confused, in the manner of a fetishistic belief in culture per se. A fair measure of the worth of a philosophy in these days would be its ability to counteract all such tendencies. It should not merely aim at the supercilious assembly of facts of various kinds and then take more or less arbitrary decisions, but it should seek, without mental reservations, to learn what those who cling to certain tenets wish to avoid, guided by the superstition that philosophy should, when all is said and done, have something constructive to offer. Rimbaud's phrase: "il faut être absolument moderne" is not a programme of an aesthetic nature, nor one likely to appeal to lovers of neat and tidy schemes. It is a categorical imperative of philosophy. Those lines of enquiry that expressly seek to avoid it, are the first to fall victims to historical bias. It does not hold the key to salvation, but allows some hope only to the movement of concept followed by the intellect wherever the path may lead.

3

Negative Dialectics and the Possibility of Philosophy

When *Negative Dialectics* first appeared in 1966 it caused dismay among those who wanted to believe that Adorno's philosophy was fundamentally compatible with a Marxist politics. The reasons for this reaction can be appreciated from the Introduction to *Negative Dialectics*. In that Introduction Adorno undermines the idea of political praxis for the reason that praxis must be a response to a correct and indeed contemporary interpretation of experience. That interpretation, he claims, is still awaited. This claim gives rise to the criticism that *Negative Dialectics* is a retreat into theory. A more favourable intepretation of the book, however, is to see it as the beginning of a new theory which generates a different praxis, namely, a transformation of consciousness. In essence that transformation would see a different understanding of the relationship of subject to object, one in which the object is not reified and thereby distanced from the subject.

The Introduction to *Negative Dialectics* outlines the problems of how we are to understand the function of concepts. For Adorno this understanding involves a critique of common philosophical assumptions about concepts. Traditional philosophy, Adorno with some hyperbole suggests, assumes that concepts can be hypostatized, that is, that they can be divorced from the particularity which they attempt to capture. Following this thought he sets up the schema of (a) concept as universal and (b) nonconceptual (or nonidentical) as particular, arguing that it is a misunderstanding of the function of concepts to see them as having priority in cognition. This is because concepts can only be realized by particulars, and that entails, in effect, that concepts are functionally related to nonconceptuality. In Adorno's terminology dialectics as the cognition of that tension between concept and nonconceptuality is consciousness of the limits of the concept. This cognition is critical, one which Adorno sees as negative in that it denies that hypostatization of concepts can be the basis of a coherent theory. But, following Hegel's Introduction to the *Phenomenology of Spirit*, that negativity is not abstract: it is induced by the nature of the concept and, as such, suggests a more complex understanding of the function and possibility of concepts. This, Adorno holds, contributes to a process of reconciliation (*Versöhnung*) between universal and particular as opposed to the oppressive relationship expressed both in philosophy and, more widely, by the reified consciousness which reduces qualities to categories. Adorno dramatically identifies this consciousness with guilt. Undoubtedly the possible ambiguities of the word in German, *Schuld*, as guilt and as that which is owed, explain that consciousness must, as it were, give to the object the concepts that are appropriate if cognition is to happen at all. A further point of interest in this section is Adorno's use of the term *mimesis*. It names a reconciled experience in which there is reciprocity between universal and particular. Arguably, in this context, the idea of *mimesis* multiplies terms which effectively denote the same thing in that *mimesis* and reconciliation (and affinity elsewhere) appear to express a similar relationship.

Introduction, *Negative Dialectics* [1966] (London: Routledge, 1973), pp. 3–31.
Translated by E. B. Ashton.

Philosophy, which once seemed obsolete, lives on because the moment to realize it was missed. The summary judgment that it had merely interpreted the world, that resignation in the face of reality had crippled it in itself, becomes a defeatism of reason after the attempt to change the world miscarried. Philosophy offers no place from which theory as such might be concretely convicted of the anachronisms it is suspected of, now as before. Perhaps it was an inadequate interpretation which promised that it would be put into practice. Theory cannot prolong the moment its critique depended on. A practice indefinitely delayed is no longer the forum for appeals against self-satisfied speculation; it is mostly the pretext used by executive authorities to choke, as vain, whatever critical thoughts the practical change would require.

Having broken its pledge to be as one with reality or at the point of realization, philosophy is obliged ruthlessly to criticize itself. Once upon a time, compared with sense perception and every kind of external experience, it was felt to be the very opposite of naïveté; now it has objectively grown as naïve in its turn as the seedy scholars feasting on subjective speculation seemed to Goethe, one hundred and fifty years ago. The introverted thought architect dwells behind the moon that is taken over by extroverted technicians. The conceptual shells that were to house the whole, according to philosophical custom, have in view of the immense expansion of society and of the strides made by positive natural science come to seem like relics of a simple barter economy amidst the late stage of industrial capitalism. The discrepancy (since decayed into a commonplace) between power and any sort of spirit has grown so vast as to foil whatever attempts to understand the preponderance might be inspired by the spirit's own concept. The will to this understanding bespeaks a power claim denied by that which is to be understood.

The most patent expression of philosophy's historical fate is the way the special sciences compelled it to turn back into a special science. If Kant had, as he put it, "freed himself from the school concept of philosophy for its world concept,"[1] it has now, perforce, regressed to its school concept. Whenever philosophers mistake that for the world concept, their pretensions grow ridiculous. Hegel, despite his doctrine of the absolute spirit in which he included philosophy, knew philosophy as a mere element of reality, an activity in the division of labor, and thus restricted it. This has since led to the narrowness of philosophy, to a disproportionateness to reality that became the more marked the more thoroughly philosophers forgot about the restriction – the more they disdained, as alien, any thought of their position in a whole which they monopolized as their object, instead of recognizing how much they depended on it all the way to the internal composition of their philosophy, to its immanent truth.

To be worth another thought, philosophy must rid itself of such naïveté. But its critical self-reflection must not halt before the highest peaks of its history. Its task would be to inquire whether and how there can still be a philosophy at all, now that Hegel's has fallen, just as Kant inquired into the possibility of metaphysics after the critique of rationalism. If Hegel's dialectics constituted the unsuccessful attempt to use philosophical concepts for coping with all that is heterogeneous to those concepts, the relationship to dialectics is due for an accounting insofar as his attempt failed.

Dialectics not a Standpoint

No theory today escapes the marketplace. Each one is offered as a possibility among competing opinions; all are put up for choice; all are swallowed. There are no blinders for thought to don against this, and the self-righteous conviction that my own theory is spared that fate will surely deteriorate into self-advertising. But neither need dialectics be muted by such rebuke, or by the concomitant charge of its superfluity, of being a method slapped on outwardly, at random. The name of dialectics says no more, to begin with, than that objects do not go into their concepts without leaving a remainder, that they come to contradict the traditional norm of adequacy. Contradiction is not what Hegel's absolute idealism was bound to transfigure it into: it is not of the essence in a Heraclitean sense. It indicates the untruth of identity, the fact that the concept does not exhaust the thing conceived.

Yet the appearance of identity is inherent in thought itself, in its pure form. To think is to identify. Conceptual order is content to screen what thinking seeks to comprehend. The semblance and the truth of thought entwine. The semblance cannot be decreed away, as by avowal of a being-in-itself outside the totality of cogitative definitions. It is a thesis secretly implied by Kant – and mobilized against him by Hegel – that the transconceptual "in itself" is void, being wholly indefinite. Aware that the conceptual totality is mere appearance, I have no way but to break immanently, in its own measure, through the appearance of total identity. Since that totality is structured to accord with logic, however, whose core is the principle of the excluded middle, whatever will not fit this principle, whatever differs in quality, comes to be designated as a contradiction. Contradiction is nonidentity under the aspect of identity; the dialectical primacy of the principle of contradiction makes the thought of unity the measure of heterogeneity. As the heterogeneous collides with its limit it exceeds itself.

Dialectics is the consistent sense of nonidentity. It does not begin by taking a standpoint. My thought is driven to it by its own inevitable insufficiency, by my guilt of what I am thinking. We are blaming the method for the fault of the matter when we object to dialectics on the ground (repeated from Hegel's Aristotelian critics on[2]) that whatever happens to come into the dialectical mill will be reduced to the merely logical form of contradiction, and that (an argument still advanced by Croce[3]) the full diversity of the noncontradictory, of that which is simply differentiated, will be ignored. What we differentiate will appear divergent, dissonant, negative for just as long as the structure of our consciousness obliges it to strive for unity: as long as its demand for totality will be its measure for whatever is not identical with it. This is what dialectics holds up to our consciousness as a contradiction. Because of the immanent nature of consciousness, contradictoriness itself has an inescapably and fatefully legal character. Identity and contradiction of thought are welded together. Total contradiction is nothing but the manifested untruth of total identification. Contradiction is nonidentity under the rule of a law that affects the nonidentical as well.

Reality and Dialectics

This law is not a cogitative law, however. It is real. Unquestionably, one who submits to the dialectical discipline has to pay dearly in the qualitative variety of experience. Still, in the administered world the impoverishment of experience by dialectics, which outrages healthy opinion, proves appropriate to the abstract monotony of that world. Its agony is the world's agony raised to a concept. Cognition must bow to it, unless concretion is once more to be debased into the ideology it starts becoming in fact.

Another version of dialectics contented itself with a debilitated renascence: with its intellectual-historical derivation from Kant's *aporias* and from that which the systems of his successors projected but failed to achieve. It can be achieved only negatively. Dialectics unfolds the difference between the particular and the universal, dictated by the universal. As the subject–object dichotomy is brought to mind it becomes inescapable for the subject, furrowing whatever the subject thinks, even objectively – but it would come to an end in reconcilement. Reconcilement would release the nonidentical, would rid it of coercion, including spiritualized coercion; it would open the road to the multiplicity of different things and strip dialectics of its power over them. Reconcilement would be the thought of the many as no longer inimical, a thought that is anathema to subjective reason.

Dialectics serves the end of reconcilement. It dismantles the coercive logical character of its own course; that is why it is denounced as "panlogism." As idealistic dialectics, it was bracketed with the absolute subject's predominance as the negative impulse of each single move of the concept and of its course as a whole. Historically, such primacy of the subject has been condemned even in the Hegelian conception that eclipsed the individual human consciousness as well as the transcendental one of Kant and Fichte. Subjective primacy was not only supplanted by the impotence of the weakening thought, which the world's overpowering course deters from construing it; but none of the reconcilements claimed by absolute idealism – and no other kind remained consistent – has stood up, whether in logic or in politics and history. The inability of consistent idealism to constitute itself as anything but the epitome of contradiction is as much the logical consequence of its truth as it is the punishment incurred by its logicity *qua* logicity; it is appearance as much as necessity.

Yet reopening the case of dialectics, whose non-idealistic form has since degenerated into a dogma as its idealistic one did into a cultural asset, will not decide solely about the actuality of a traditional mode of philosophizing, nor about the actuality of the philosophical structure of cognitive objects.

Through Hegel, philosophy had regained the right and the capacity to think substantively instead of being put off with the analysis of cognitive forms that were empty and, in an emphatic sense, null and void. Where present philosophy deals with anything substantive at all, it lapses either into the randomness of a weltanschauung or into that formalism, that "matter of indifference," against which Hegel had risen. There is historical evidence of this in the evolution of phenomenology, which once was animated by the need for contents and became an invocation of being, a repudiation of any content as unclean.

The fundament and result of Hegel's substantive philosophizing was the primacy of the subject, or – in the famous phrase from the Introduction to his *Logic* – the "identity of identity and nonidentity."[4] He held the definite particular to be definable by the mind because its immanent definition was to be nothing but the mind. Without this supposition, according to Hegel, philosophy would be incapable of knowing anything substantive or essential. Unless the idealistically acquired concept of dialectics harbors experiences contrary to the Hegelian emphasis, experiences independent of the idealistic machinery, philosophy must inevitably do without substantive insight, confine itself to the methodology of science, call that philosophy, and virtually cross itself out.

The Concern of Philosophy

The matters of true philosophical interest at this point in history are those in which Hegel, agreeing with tradition, expressed his disinterest. They are nonconceptuality, individuality, and particularity – things which ever since Plato used to be dismissed as transitory and insignificant, and which Hegel labeled "lazy Existenz." Philosophy's theme would consist of the qualities it downgrades as contingent, as a *quantité négligeable*. A matter of urgency to the concept would be what it fails to cover, what its abstractionist mechanism eliminates, what is not already a case of the concept.

Bergson and Husserl, carriers of philosophical modernism, both have innervated this idea but withdrawn from it to traditional metaphysics. Bergson, in a tour de force, created another type of cognition for nonconceptuality's sake. The dialectical salt was washed away in an undifferentiated tide of life; solidified reality was disposed of as subaltern, not comprehended along with its subalternity. The hater of the rigid general concept established a cult of irrational immediacy, of sovereign freedom in the midst of unfreedom. He drafted his two cognitive modes in as dualistic an opposition as that of the Cartesian and Kantian doctrines he fought had ever been; the causal-mechanical mode, as pragmatistic knowledge, was no more affected by the intuitive one than the bourgeois establishment was by the relaxed unself-consciousness of those who owe their privileges to that establishment.

The celebrated intuitions themselves seem rather abstract in Bergson's philosophy; they scarcely go beyond the phenomenal time consciousness which even Kant had underlying chronological-physical time – spatial time, according to Bergson's insight. Although it takes an effort to develop, the intuitive mode of mental conduct does continue to exist in fact as an archaic rudiment of mimetic reactions. What preceded its past holds a promise beyond the ossified present. Intuitions succeed only desultorily, however. Every cognition including Bergson's own needs the rationality he scorns, and needs it precisely at the moment of concretion. Absolutized duration, pure becoming, the pure act – these would recoil into the same timelessness which Bergson chides in metaphysics since Plato and Aristotle. He did not mind that the thing he groped for, if it is not to remain a mirage, is visible solely with the equipment of cognition, by reflection upon its own means, and that it grows arbitrary in a procedure unrelated, from the start, to that of cognition.

Husserl the logician, on the other hand, would indeed sharply distinguish the mode of apprehending the essence from generalizing abstraction – what he had in mind was a specific mental experience capable of perceiving the essence in the particular – but the essence to which this experience referred did not differ in any respect from the familiar general concepts. There is a glaring discrepancy between the arrangements of essence perception and its *terminus ad quem*. Neither attempt to break out of idealism was successful: Bergson's bearings, like those of his positivistic arch-enemies, came from the *données immédiates de la conscience*; Husserl's came in similar fashion from phenomena of the stream of consciousness. Both men stay within range of immanent subjectivity.[5] To be insisted upon, against both, would be the goal they pursue in vain: to counter Wittgenstein by uttering the unutterable.

The plain contradictoriness of this challenge is that of philosophy itself, which is thereby qualified as dialectics before getting entangled in its individual contradictions. The work of philosophical self-reflection consists in unraveling that paradox. Everything else is signification, secondhand construction, pre-philosophical activity, today as in Hegel's time. Though doubtful as ever, a confidence that philosophy can make it after all – that the concept can transcend the concept, the preparatory and concluding element, and can thus reach the nonconceptual – is one of philosophy's inalienable features and part of the naïveté that ails it. Otherwise it must capitulate, and the human mind with it. We could not conceive the simplest operation; there would be no truth; emphatically, everything would be just nothing. But whatever truth the concepts cover beyond their abstract range can have no other stage than what the concepts suppress, disparage, and discard. The cognitive utopia would be to use concepts to unseal the nonconceptual with concepts, without making it their equal.

The Antagonistic Entirety

Such a concept of dialectics makes us doubt its possibility. However varied, the anticipation of moving in contradictions throughout seems to teach a mental totality – the very identity thesis we have just rendered inoperative. The mind which ceaselessly reflects on contradiction in the thing itself, we hear, must be the thing itself if it is to be organized in the form of contradiction; the truth which in idealistic dialectics drives beyond every particular, as onesided and wrong, is the truth of the whole, and if that were not preconceived, the dialectical steps would lack motivation and direction. We have to answer that the object of a mental experience is an antagonistic system in itself – antagonistic in reality, not just in its conveyance to the knowing subject that rediscovers itself therein. The coercive state of reality, which idealism had projected into the region of the subject and the mind, must be retranslated from that region. What remains of idealism is that society, the objective determinant of the mind, is as much an epitome of subjects as it is their negation. In society the subjects are unknowable and incapacitated; hence its desperate objectivity and conceptuality, which idealism mistakes for something positive.

The system is not one of the absolute spirit; it is one of the most conditioned spirit of those who have it and cannot even know how much it is their own. The subjective preconception of the material production process in society – basically different from its theoretical constitution – is the unresolved part, the part unreconciled with the subjects. Their own reason, unconscious like the transcendental subject and establishing identity by barter (*Tausch*), remains incommensurable with the subjects it reduces to the same denominator: the subject as the subject's foe. The preceding generality is both true and untrue: true, because it forms that "ether" which Hegel calls spirit; untrue, because its reason is no reason yet, because its universality is the product of particular interests. This is why a philosophical critique of identity transcends philosophy. But the ineffable part of the utopia is that what defies subsumption under identity – the "use value," in Marxist terminology – is necessary anyway if life is to go on at all, even under the prevailing circumstances of production. The utopia extends to the sworn enemies of its realization. Regarding the concrete utopian possibility, dialectics is the ontology of the wrong state of things. The right state of things would be free of it: neither a system nor a contradiction.

Disenchantment of the Concept

Philosophy, Hegel's included, invites the general objection that by inevitably having concepts for its material it anticipates an idealistic decision. In fact no philosophy, not even extreme empiricism, can drag in the *facta bruta* and present them like cases in anatomy or experiments in physics; no philosophy can paste the particulars into the text, as seductive paintings would hoodwink it into believing. But the argument in its formality and generality takes as fetishistic a view of the concept as the concept does in interpreting itself naïvely in its own domain: in either case it is regarded as a self-sufficient totality over which philosophical thought has no power. In truth, all concepts, even the philosophical ones, refer to nonconceptualities, because concepts on their part are moments of the reality that requires their formation, primarily for the control of nature. What conceptualization appears to be from within, to one engaged in it – the predominance of its sphere, without which nothing is known – must not be mistaken for what it is in itself. Such a semblance of being-in-itself is conferred upon it by the motion that exempts it from reality, to which it is harnessed in turn.

Necessity compels philosophy to operate with concepts, but this necessity must not be turned into the virtue of their priority – no more than, conversely, criticism of that virtue can be turned into a summary verdict against philosophy. On the other hand, the insight that philosophy's conceptual knowledge is not the absolute of philosophy – this insight, for all its inescapability, is again due to the nature of the concept. It is not a dogmatic thesis, much less a naïvely realistic one. Initially, such concepts as that of "being" at the start of Hegel's *Logic* emphatically mean nonconceptualities; as Lask put it, they "mean beyond themselves." Dissatisfaction with their own conceptuality is part of their meaning, although the inclusion of nonconceptuality in their meaning makes it tendentially their equal and thus keeps them trapped within themselves. The substance of concepts is to them both immanent, as far as the mind is concerned, and transcendent as far as being is concerned. To be aware of this is to be able to get rid of concept fetishism. Philosophical reflection makes sure of the nonconceptual in the concept. It would be empty otherwise, according to Kant's dictum; in the end, having ceased to be a concept of anything at all, it would be nothing.

A philosophy that lets us know this, that extinguishes the autarky of the concept, strips the blindfold from our eyes. That the concept is a concept even when dealing with things in being does not change the fact that on its part it is entwined with a nonconceptual whole. Its only insulation from that whole is its reification – that which establishes it as a concept. The concept is an element in dialectical logic, like any other. What survives in it is the fact that nonconceptuality has conveyed it by way of its meaning, which in turn establishes its conceptuality. To refer to nonconceptualities – as ultimately, according to traditional epistemology, every definition of concepts requires nonconceptual, deictic elements – is characteristic of the concept, and so is the contrary: that as the abstract unit of the noumena subsumed thereunder it will depart from the noumenal. To change this direction of conceptuality, to give it a turn toward nonidentity, is the hinge of negative dialectics. Insight into the constitutive character of the nonconceptual in the concept would end the compulsive identification which the concept brings unless halted by such reflection. Reflection upon its own meaning is the way out of the concept's seeming being-in-itself as a unit of meaning.

"Infinity"

Disenchantment of the concept is the antidote of philosophy. It keeps it from growing rampant and becoming an absolute to itself. An idea bequeathed to us by idealism – and corrupted by it, more than any other – needs a change in its function: the idea of the infinite. It is not up to philosophy to exhaust things according to scientific usage, to reduce the phenomena to a minimum of propositions; there are hints of that in Hegel's polemic against Fichte, whom he accused of starting out with a "dictum." Instead, in philosophy we literally seek to immerse ourselves in things that are heterogeneous to it, without placing those things in prefabricated categories. We want to adhere as closely to the heterogeneous as the programs of phenomenology and of Simmel tried in vain to do; our aim is total self-relinquishment. Philosophical contents can only be grasped where philosophy does not impose them. The illusion that it might confine the essence in its finite definitions will have to be given up.

The fatal ease with which the word "infinite" rolled off the idealistic philosophers' tongues may have been due only to a wish to allay gnawing doubts about the meager finiteness of their conceptual machinery – including Hegel's, his intentions notwithstanding. Traditional philosophy thinks of itself as possessing an infinite object, and in that belief it becomes a finite, conclusive philosophy. A changed philosophy would have to cancel that claim, to cease persuading others and itself that it has the infinite at its disposal.

Instead, if it were delicately understood, the changed philosophy itself would be infinite in the sense of scorning solidification in a body of enumerable theorems. Its substance would lie in the diversity of objects that impinge upon it and of the objects it seeks, a diversity not wrought by any schema; to those objects, philosophy would truly give itself rather than use them as a mirror in which to reread itself, mistaking its own image for concretion. It would be nothing but full, unreduced experience in the medium of conceptual reflection, whereas even the "science of empirical conscious-ness" reduced the contents of such experience to cases of categories. What makes philosophy risk the strain of its own infinity is the unwarranted expec-tation that each individual and particular puzzle it solves will be like Leibniz's monad, the ever-elusive entirety in itself – although, of course, in line with a pre-established disharmony rather than a pre-established harmony. The metacritical turn against the *prima philosophia* is at the same time a turn against the finiteness of a philosophy that prates about infinity without respecting it.

No object is wholly known; knowledge is not supposed to prepare the phantasm of a whole. Thus the goal of a philosophical interpretation of works of art cannot be their identification with the concept, their absorption in the concept; yet it is through such interpretation that the truth of the work unfolds. What can be envisioned, however – whether as the regularly con-tinued abstraction or as an application of the concepts to whatever comes under their definition – may be useful as technology in the broadest sense of the word; but to philosophy, which refuses to fit in, it is irrelevant. In prin-ciple, philosophy can always go astray, which is the sole reason why it can go forward. This has been recognized in skepticism and in pragmatism, most recently in Dewey's wholly humane version of the latter; but we ought to add it as a ferment to an emphatic philosophy instead of renouncing phi-losophy, from the outset, in favor of the test it has to stand.

As a corrective to the total rule of method, philosophy contains a playful element which the traditional view of it as a science would like to exorcise. For Hegel, too, this was a sensitive point; he rejects "types and distinctions determined by external chance and by play, not by reason."[6] The un-naïve thinker knows how far he remains from the object of his thinking, and yet he must always talk as if he had it entirely. This brings him to the point of clowning. He must not deny his clownish traits, least of all since they alone can give him hope for what is denied him. Philosophy is the most serious of things, but then again it is not all that serious. A thing that aims at what it is not a priori and is not authorized to control – such a thing, according to its own concept, is simultaneously part of a sphere beyond control, a sphere tabooed by conceptuality. To represent the mimesis it supplanted, the concept has no other way than to adopt something mimetic in its own conduct, without abandoning itself.

The esthetic moment is thus not accidental to philosophy, though on grounds quite different from Schelling's; but it is no less incumbent upon philosophy to void its estheticism, to sublimate the esthetic into the real, by cogent insights. Cogency and play are the two poles of philosophy. Its affinity to art does not entitle it to borrow from art, least of all by virtue of the intuitions which barbarians take for the prerogatives of art. Intuitions hardly ever strike in isolation, as lightning from above; they do not strike the artist's work like that either. They hang together with the formal law of the work; if one tried to extract and preserve them, they would dissolve. Finally, thought is no protector of springs whose freshness might deliver us from thinking. We have no type of cognition at our disposal that differs absolutely from the disposing type, the type which intuitionism flees in panic and in vain.

A philosophy that tried to imitate art, that would turn itself into a work of art, would be expunging itself. It would be postulating the demand for identity, claiming to exhaust its object by endowing its procedure with a supremacy to which the heterogeneous bows a priori, as material – whereas to genuine philosophy its relation to the heterogeneous is virtually thematic. Common to art and philosophy is not the form, not the forming process, but a mode of conduct that forbids pseudomorphosis. Both keep faith with their own substance through their opposites: art by making itself resistant to its meanings; philosophy, by refusing to clutch at any immediate thing. What the philosophical concept will not abandon is the yearning that animates the nonconceptual side of art, and whose fulfillment shuns the immediate side of art as mere appearance. The concept – the organon of thinking, and yet the wall between thinking and the thought – negates that yearning. Philosophy can neither circumvent such negation nor submit to it. It must strive, by way of the concept, to transcend the concept.

The Speculative Moment

Even after breaking with idealism, philosophy cannot do without speculation, which was exalted by idealism and tabooed with it – meaning speculation, of course, in a sense broader than the overly positive Hegelian one.[7] For positivists it is not difficult to attribute speculation to Marxian materialism, which starts out from laws of objective being, by no means from immediate data or protocol statements. To cleanse himself of the suspicion of ideology, it is now safer for a man to call Marx a metaphysician than to call him a class enemy.

But the safe ground is a phantasm where the claims of truth demand that one rise above it. Philosophy is not to be put off with theorems that would talk it out of its essential concern instead of satisfying that concern, albeit with a No. In the counter-movements to Kant, from the nineteenth century on, this was sensed but always compromised again by obscurantism. The resistance of philosophy needs to unfold, however. Even in music – as in all art, presumably – the impulse animating the first bar will not be fulfilled at once, but only in further articulation. To this extent, however much it may be phenomenal as a totality, music is a critique of phenomenality, of the appearance that the substance is present here and now. Such a mediate role befits philosophy no less. When it presumes to say things forthwith it invites Hegel's verdict on empty profundity. Mouthing profundities will no more make a man profound than narrating the metaphysical views of its characters will make a novel metaphysical.

To ask philosophy to deal with the question of being, or with other cardinal themes of Western metaphysics, shows a primitive topical faith. The objective worth of those themes is indeed inescapable in philosophy, but neither can we rely on our ability to cope with the great topics. We must be so wary of the beaten tracks of philosophical reflection that our emphatic interest will seek refuge in ephemeral objects not yet overdetermined by intentions. Though chained to the questions of traditional philosophical problematics, we certainly must negate that problematics. A world that is objectively set for totality will not release the human consciousness, will ceaselessly fasten it to points it wants to get away from; but a thinking that blithely begins afresh, heedless of the historic form of its problems, will so much more be their prey.

That philosophy shares in the idea of depth is due to its cogitative breath alone. A prime example from the modern age is the Kantian deduction of pure intellectual concepts, which the author, with abysmally apologetic irony, called "somewhat profoundly arranged."[8] Profundity, as Hegel did not fail to note, is another element of dialectics, not an isolated trait. A dreadful German tradition equates profound thoughts with thoughts ready to swear by the theodicy of death and evil. A theological *terminus ad quem* is tacitly passed over and passed under, as if the worth of a thought were decided by its result, the confirmation of transcendence, or by its immersion in inwardness, its sheer being-for-itself; as if withdrawal from the world were flatly tantamount to consciousness of the world ground. As for the phantasms of profundity – which in the history of the human spirit have always been well-disposed toward an existing state of affairs they find insipid – resistance would be their true measure.

The power of the status quo puts up the façades into which our consciousness crashes. It must seek to crash through them. This alone would free the postulate of depth from ideology. Surviving in such resistance is the speculative moment: what will not have its law prescribed for it by given facts transcends them even in the closest contact with the objects, and in repudiating a sacrosanct transcendence. Where the thought transcends the bonds it tied in resistance – there is its freedom. Freedom follows the subject's urge to express itself. The need to lend a voice to suffering is a condition of all truth. For suffering is objectivity that weighs upon the subject; its most subjective experience, its expression, is objectively conveyed.

Presentation

This may help to explain why the presentation of philosophy is not an external matter of indifference to it but immanent to its idea. Its integral, nonconceptually mimetic moment of expression is objectified only by presentation in language. The freedom of philosophy is nothing but the capacity to lend a voice to its unfreedom. If more is claimed for the expressive moment, it will degenerate into a weltanschauung; where the expressive moment and the duty of presentation are given up, philosophy comes to resemble science.

To philosophy, expression and stringency are not two dichotomous possibilities. They need each other; neither one can be without the other. Expression is relieved of its accidental character by thought, on which it toils as thought toils on expression. Only an expressed thought is succinct, rendered succinct by its presentation in language; what is vaguely put is poorly thought. Expression compels stringency in what it expresses. It is not an end in itself at the latter's expense; rather, expression removes the expressed from the materialized mischief which in its turn is an object of philosophical criticism. Speculative philosophy without an idealistic substructure requires observance of stringency to break the authoritarian power claim of stringency. Benjamin, whose original draft of his passage theory combined incomparable speculative skill with micrological proximity to factual contents, later remarked in a correspondence about the first properly metaphysical stratum of this work that it could be accomplished only as an "impermissible 'poetic' one."[9] This admission of surrender denotes as much the difficulty of a philosophy loath to decline as the point at which its concept can be carried further. It was probably due to Benjamin's acceptance of dialectical materialism as a weltanschauung, so to speak, with closed eyes. But the fact that he could not bring himself to put the definitive version of the passage theory in writing reminds us that philosophy is more than bustle only where it runs the risk of total failure – this in reply to the absolute certainty that has traditionally been obtained by stealth. Benjamin's defeatism about his own thought was conditioned by the undialectical positivity of which he carried a formally unchanged remnant from his theological phase into his material-istic phase. By comparison, Hegel's equating negativity with the thought that keeps philosophy from both the positivity of science and the contingency of dilettantism has empirical substance.

Thought as such, before all particular contents, is an act of negation, of resistance to that which is forced upon it; this is what thought has inherited from its archetype, the relation between labor and material. Today, when ide-ologues tend more than ever to encourage thought to be positive, they clev-erly note that positivity runs precisely counter to thought and that it takes friendly persuasion by social authority to accustom thought to positivity. The effort implied in the concept of thought itself, as the counter-part of passive contemplation, is negative already – a revolt against being importuned to bow to every immediate thing. Critical germs are contained in judgment and inference, the thought forms without which not even the critique of thought can do: they are never definite without simultaneously excluding what they have failed to achieve, and whatever does not bear their stamp will be denied – although with questionable authority – by the truth they seek to organize. The judgment that a thing is such and such is a potential rebuttal to claims of any relation of its subject and predicate other than the one expressed in the judgment. Thought forms tend beyond that which merely exists, is merely "given." The point which thinking aims at its material is not solely a spiri-tualized control of nature. While doing violence to the object of its syntheses, our thinking heeds a potential that waits in the object, and it unconsciously obeys the idea of making amends to the pieces for what it has done. In philosophy, this unconscious tendency becomes conscious. Accom-panying irreconcilable thoughts is the hope for reconcilement, because the resistance of thought to mere things in being, the commanding freedom of the subject, intends in the object even that of which the object was deprived by objectification.

Attitude Toward Systems

Traditional speculation has developed the synthesis of diversity – which it conceived as chaotic, on Kantian grounds – and its ultimate aim was to divest itself of any kind of content. By contrast, the *telos* of philosophy, its open and unshielded part, is as anti-systematic as its freedom to interpret the phe-nomena with which it joins unarmed issue. Philosophy retains respect for systems to the extent to which things heterogeneous to it face it in the form

of a system. The administered world moves in this direction. It is the negative objectivity that is a system, not the positive subject. In a historical phase
in which systems — insofar as they deal seriously with contents — have been
relegated to the ominous realm of conceptual poetry and nothing but the
pale outline of their schematic order has been retained, it is difficult to
imagine vividly what used to attract a philosophical spirit to the system.

When we contemplate philosophical history, the virtue of partisanship
must not keep us from perceiving how superior the system, whether rationalistic or idealistic, has been to its opponents for more than two centuries.
Compared with the systems, the opposition seems trivial. Systems elaborate
things; they interpret the world while the others really keep protesting only
that it can't be done. The others display resignation, denial, failure — if they
had more truth in the end, it would indicate the transience of philosophy.
In any case, it would be up to philosophy to elevate such truth from its subaltern state and to champion it against the philosophies which not only boast
of their "higher" rank: materialism in particular shows to this day that it was
spawned in Abdera. According to Nietzsche's critique, systems no longer
documented anything but the finickiness of scholars compensating themselves
for political impotence by conceptually construing their, so to speak, administrative authority over things in being. But the systematic need, the need not
to put up with the *membra disiecta* of knowledge but to achieve the absolute
knowledge that is already, involuntarily, claimed in each succinct individual
judgment — this need was more, at times, than a pseudomorphosis of the
spirit into the irresistibly successful method of mathematical and natural
science.

In the philosophy of history, the systems of the seventeenth century especially served a compensatory purpose. The *ratio* which in accordance with
bourgeois class interests had smashed the feudal order and scholastic ontology, the form of the intellectual reflection of that order — this same *ratio* no
sooner faced the ruins, its own handiwork, than it would be struck by fear
of chaos. It trembled before the menace that continued underneath its own
domain, waxing stronger in proportion to its own power. This fear shaped
the beginnings of a mode of conduct constitutive for bourgeois existence as
a whole: of the neutralization, by confirming the existent order, of every
emancipatory step. In the shadow of its own incomplete emancipation the
bourgeois consciousness must fear to be annulled by a more advanced consciousness; not being the whole freedom, it senses that it can produce only
a caricature of freedom — hence its theoretical expansion of its autonomy
into a system similar to its own coercive mechanisms.

Out of itself, the bourgeois *ratio* undertook to produce the order it had
negated outside itself. Once produced, however, that order ceased to be an

order and was therefore insatiable. Every system was such an order, such an absurdly rational product: a posited thing posing as being-in-itself. Its origin had to be placed into formal thought divorced from content; nothing else would let it control the material. The philosophical systems were antinomical from the outset. Their rudiments entwined with their own impossibility; it was precisely in the early history of the modern systems that each was condemned to annihilation at the hands of the next. To prevail as a system, the *ratio* eliminated virtually all qualitative definitions it referred to, thus coming into an irreconcilable conflict with the objectivity it violated by pretending to grasp it. The *ratio* came to be removed from objectivity – the farther removed, the more completely objectivity was subjected to its axioms, and finally to the one axiom of identity. The pedantries of all systems, down to the architectonic complexities of Kant – and even of Hegel, despite the latter's program – are the marks of an a priori inescapable failure, noted with incomparable honesty in the fractures of the Kantian system; Molière was the first to show pedantry as a main feature of the ontology of the bourgeois spirit.

Whenever something that is to be conceived flees from identity with the concept, the concept will be forced to take exaggerated steps to prevent any doubts of the unassailable validity, solidity, and acribia of the thought product from stirring. Great philosophy was accompanied by a paranoid zeal to tolerate nothing else, and to pursue everything else with all the cunning of reason, while the other kept retreating farther and farther from the pursuit. The slightest remnant of nonidentity sufficed to deny an identity conceived as total. The excrescences of the systems, ever since the Cartesian pineal gland and the axioms and definitions of Spinoza, already crammed with the entire rationalism he would then deductively extract – by their untruth, these excrescences show the untruth, the mania, of the systems themselves.

Idealism as Rage

The system in which the sovereign mind imagined itself transfigured, has its primal history in the pre-mental, the animal life of the species. Predators get hungry, but pouncing on their prey is difficult and often dangerous; additional impulses may be needed for the beast to dare it. These impulses and the unpleasantness of hunger fuse into rage at the victim, a rage whose expression in turn serves the end of frightening and paralyzing the victim. In the advance to humanity this is rationalized by projection. The "rational animal" with an appetite for his opponent is already fortunate enough to have a superego and must find a reason. The more completely his actions follow the law of self-preservation, the less can he admit the primacy of that law to himself and to others; if he did, his laboriously attained status of a *zoon politikon* would lose all credibility.

The animal to be devoured must be evil. The sublimation of this anthropological schema extends all the way to epistemology. Idealism – most explicitly Fichte – gives unconscious sway to the ideology that the not-I, *l'autrui*, and finally all that reminds us of nature is inferior, so the unity of the self-preserving thought may devour it without misgivings. This justifies the principle of the thought as much as it increases the appetite. The system is the belly turned mind, and rage is the mark of each and every idealism. It disfigures even Kant's humanism and refutes the aura of higher and nobler things in which he knew how to garb it. The view of man in the middle is akin to misanthropy: leave nothing unchallenged. The august inexorability of the moral law was this kind of rationalized rage at nonidentity; nor did the liberalistic Hegel do better with the superiority of his bad conscience, dressing down those who refused homage to the speculative concept, the hypostasis of the mind.[10] Nietzsche's liberating act, a true turning point of Western thought and merely usurped by others later, was to put such mysteries into words. A mind that discards rationalization – its own spell – ceases by its self-reflection to be the radical evil that irks it in another.

Yet the process in which the systems decomposed, due to their own insufficiency, stands in counterpoint to a social process. In the form of the barter principle, the bourgeois *ratio* really approximated to the systems whatever it would make commensurable with itself, would identify with itself – and it did so with increasing, if potentially homicidal, success. Less and less was left outside. What proved idle in theory was ironically borne out in practice. Hence the ideological popularity of talk about a "crisis of the system" among all the types who earlier could not spout enough stentorian rancor at the "aperçu," according to the system's own, already obsolete ideal. Reality is no longer to be construed, because it would be all too thoroughly construable. Pretexts are furnished by its irrationality, intensifying under the pressure of particular rationality: there is disintegration by way of integration. If society could be seen through as a closed system, a system accordingly unreconciled to the subjects, it would become too embarrassing for the subjects as long as they remain subjects in any sense.

Angst, that supposed "existential," is the claustrophobia of a systematized society. Its system character, yesterday still a shibboleth of academic philosophy, is strenuously denied by initiates of that philosophy; they may, with impunity, pose as spokesmen for free, for original, indeed, for unacademic thinking. Criticism of the systems is not vitiated by such abuse. A proposition common to all emphatic philosophy – as opposed to the skeptical one, which refrained from emphasis – was that only as a system could philosophy be pursued; this proposition has done hardly less to cripple philosophy than have the empiricisms. The things philosophy has yet to judge are postulated before it begins. The system, the form of presenting a totality to which nothing remains extraneous, absolutizes the thought against each of its contents and evaporates the content in thoughts. It proceeds idealistically before advancing any arguments for idealism.

The Twofold Character of the System

In criticism we do not simply liquidate systems, however. At the peak of the Enlightenment, d'Alembert rightly distinguished between *l'esprit de système* and *l'esprit systématique*, and the method of the Encyclopédie took account of the distinction. Speaking for the *esprit systématique* is not only the trivial motive of a cohesion that will tend to crystallize in the incoherent anyway; it does not only satisfy the bureaucrats' desire to stuff all things into their categories. The form of the system is adequate to the world, whose substance eludes the hegemony of the human thought; but unity and unanimity are at the same time an oblique projection of pacified, no longer antagonistic conditions upon the coordinates of supremacist, oppressive thinking. The double meaning of philosophical systematics leaves no choice but to transpose the power of thought, once delivered from the systems, into the open realm of definition by individual moments.

To Hegelian logic this procedure was not altogether alien. The micro-analysis of individual categories, which simultaneously appears as their objective self-reflection, was to let each concept pass into its otherness without regard to an overlay from above; to Hegel, the totality of this movement meant the system. There is contradiction as well as kinship between this concept of the system – a concept that concludes, and thus brings to a standstill – and the concept of dynamism, of pure, autarkic, subjective generation, which constitutes all philosophical systematics. Hegel could adjust the tension between statics and dynamics only by construing his unitarian principle, the spirit, as a simultaneous being-in-itself and pure becoming, a resumption of the Aristotelian-scholastic *actus purus*; and that the implausibility of this construction – in which subjective generation and ontology, nominalism and realism, are syncopated at the Archimedean point – will prevent the resolution of that tension is also immanent in the system.

And yet, such a concept of the philosophical system towers above a merely scientific systematics that call for orderly organization and presentation of thoughts, for a consistent structure of topical disciplines, without insisting strictly, from the object's point of view, upon the inner unity of its aspects. The postulate of this unity is bound up with the presupposition that all things in being are identical with the cognitive principle; but on the other hand, once burdened as it is in idealistic speculation, that postulate legitimately recalls the affinity which objects have for each other, and which is tabooed by the scientific need for order and obliged to yield to the surrogate of its schemata. What the objects communicate in – instead of each being the atom it becomes in the logic of classification – is the trace of the objects' definition in themselves, which Kant denied and Hegel, against Kant, sought to restore through the subject.

To comprehend a thing itself, not just to fit and register it in its system of reference, is nothing but to perceive the individual moment in its imma-nent connection with others. Such anti-subjectivism lies under the crackling shell of absolute idealism; it stirs in the tendency to unseal current issues by resorting to the way they came to be. What the conception of the system recalls, in reverse, is the coherence of the nonidentical, the very thing infringed by deductive systematics. Criticism of systems and asystematic thought are superficial as long as they cannot release the cohesive force which the idealistic systems had signed over to the transcendental subject.

The Antinomical Character of Systems

The ego principle that founds the system, the pure method before any content, has always been the *ratio*. It is not confined by anything outside it, not even by a so-called mental order. Idealism, attesting the positive infinity of its prin-ciple at every one of its stages, turns the character of thought, the historic evo-lution of its independence, into metaphysics. It eliminates all heterogeneous being. This defines the system as pure becoming, a pure process, and eventu-ally as that absolute engendering which Fichte – in this respect the authentic systematizer of philosophy – declared thinking to be. Kant had already held that the emancipated *ratio*, the *progressus ad infinitum*, is halted solely by recog-nizing nonidentities in form, at least. The antinomy of totality and infinity – for the restless *ad infinitum* explodes the self-contained system, for all its being owed to infinity alone – is of the essence of idealism.

It imitates a central antinomy of bourgeois society. To preserve itself, to remain the same, to "be," that society too must constantly expand, progress, advance its frontiers, not respect any limit, not remain the same.[11] It has been demonstrated to bourgeois society that it would no sooner reach a ceiling, would no sooner cease to have noncapitalist areas available outside itself, than its own concept would force its self-liquidation. This makes clear why, Aristotle notwithstanding, the modern concept of dynamics was inappropriate to Antiquity, as was the concept of the system. To Plato, who chose the aporetical form for so many of his dialogues, both concepts could be imputed only in retrospect. The reprimand which Kant gave the old man for that reason is not, as he put it, a matter of plain logic; it is historical, modern through and through. On the other hand, systematics is so deeply ingrained in the modern consciousness that even Husserl's anti-systematic efforts – which began under the name of ontology, and from which "fundamental ontology" branched off later – reverted irresistibly to a system, at the price of formalization.

Thus intertwined, the system's static and dynamic characters keep clashing. No matter how dynamically a system may be conceived, if it is in fact to be a closed system, to tolerate nothing outside its domain, it will become a positive infinity – in other words, finite and static. The fact that it sustains itself in this manner, for which Hegel praised his own system, brings it to a standstill. Bluntly put, closed systems are bound to be finished. Eccentricities like the one constantly held up to Hegel – of world history being perfected in the Prussian state – are not mere aberrations for ideological purposes, nor are they irrelevant vis-à-vis the whole. Their necessary absurdity shatters the asserted unity of system and dynamics. By negating the concept of the limit and theoretically assuring itself that there always remains something outside, dynamics also tends to disavow its own product, the system.

An aspect under which it might well be fruitful to treat the history of modern philosophy is how it managed to cope with the antagonism of statics and dynamics in its systems. The Hegelian system in itself was not a true becoming; implicitly, each single definition in it was already preconceived. Such safeguards condemn it to untruth. Unconsciously, so to speak, consciousness would have to immerse itself in the phenomena on which it takes a stand. This would, of course, effect a qualitative change in dialectics. Systematic unanimity would crumble. The phenomenon would not remain a case of its concept, as it does to Hegel, despite all pronouncements to the contrary. The thought would be burdened with more toil and trouble than Hegel defines as such, because the thought he discusses always extracts from its objects only that which is a thought already. Despite the program of self-yielding, the Hegelian thought finds satisfaction in itself; it goes rolling along, however often it may urge the contrary. If the thought really yielded to the object, if its attention were on the object, not on its category, the very objects would start talking under the lingering eye.

Hegel had argued against epistemology that one becomes a smith only by smithing, by the actual cognition of things that resist cognition – of things which are, so to speak, atheoretical. There we have to take him at his word; nothing else would return to philosophy what Hegel calls the "freedom to the object" – what philosophy had lost under the spell of the concept 'freedom," of the subject's sense-determining autonomy. But the speculative power to break down the gates of the insoluble is the power of negation. The systematic trend lives on in negation alone. The categories of a critique of systems are at the same time the categories in which the particular is understood. What has once legitimately transcended particularity in the system has its place outside the system. The interpretive eye which sees more in a phenomenon than it is – and solely because of what it is – secularizes metaphysics. Only a philosophy in fragment form would give their proper place to the monads, those illusory idealistic drafts. They would be conceptions, in the particular, of the totality that is inconceivable as such.

Argument and Experience

The thought, to which a positive hypostasis of anything outside actual dialectics is forbidden, overshoots the object with which it no longer simulates being as one. It grows more independent than in the conception of its absoluteness, in which sovereignty and complaisance mingle, each inwardly depending on the other. This may have been the end to which Kant exempted the intelligible sphere from all immanence. An aspect of immersion in particularity, that extreme enhancement of dialectical immanence, must also be the freedom to step out of the object, a freedom which the identity claim cuts short. Hegel would have censured that freedom; he relied upon complete mediation by the objects. In cognitive practice, when we resolve the insoluble, a moment of such cogitative transcendence comes to light in the fact that for our micrological activity we have exclusively macrological means.

The call for binding statements without a system is a call for thought models, and these are not merely monadological in kind. A model covers the specific, and more than the specific, without letting it evaporate in its more general super-concept. Philosophical thinking is the same as thinking in models; negative dialectics is an ensemble of analyses of models. Philosophy would be debasing itself all over again, into a kind of affirmative solace, if it were to fool itself and others about the fact that it must, from without, imbue its objects with whatever moves them within it. What is waiting in the objects themselves needs such intervention to come to speak, with the perspective that the forces mobilized outside, and ultimately every theory that is brought to bear on the phenomena, should come to rest in the phenomena. In that sense, too, philosophical theory means that its own end lies in its realization.

There is no lack of related intentions in history. The French Enlightenment got a formally systematic touch from its supreme concept, that of reason; yet the constitutive entanglement of its idea of reason with that of an objectively rational arrangement of society deprived the idea of a pathos which it was not to recover until the realization of reason as an idea was renounced, until it was absolutized into the spirit. Encyclopedic thinking – rationally organized and yet discontinuous, unsystematic, loose – expressed the self-critical spirit of reason. That spirit represented something which later departed from philosophy, due as much to its increasing distance from practical life as to its absorption in the academic bustle: it represented mundane experience, that eye for reality of which thought, too, is a part.

The free spirit is nothing else. The element of the *homme de lettres*, disparaged by a petty bourgeois scientific ethos, is indispensable to thought; and no less indispensable, of course, is the element abused by a philosophy garbed as science: the meditative contraction – the argument, which came to merit so much skepticism. Whenever philosophy was substantial, both elements would coincide. At a distance, dialectics might be characterized as the elevation to self-consciousness of the effort to be saturated with dialectics. Otherwise the argument deteriorates into the technique of conceptless specialists amid the concept, as it is now spreading academically in the so-called "analytical philosophy," which robots can learn and copy.

The immanently argumentative element is legitimate where the reality that has been integrated in a system is received in order to oppose it with its own strength. The free part of thought, on the other hand, represents the authority which already knows about the emphatic untruth of that real-systematic context. Without this knowledge there would be no eruption; without adopting the power of the system, the outbreak would fail. That the two elements will not merge without a rift is due to the real power of the system, which includes even what potentially excels it. The untruth of the immanent context itself, however, shows in the overwhelming experience that the world – though organized as systematically as if it were Hegel's glorified realization of reason – will at the same time, in its old unreason, perpetuate the impotence of the seemingly almighty spirit. The immanent critic of idealism defends idealism by showing how much it is defrauded of its own self – how much the first cause, which according to idealism is always the spirit, is in league with the blind predominance of merely existing things. The doctrine of the absolute spirit immediately aids that predominance.

A scientific consensus tends to admit that experience also implies theory. It holds, however, that experience is a "standpoint," hypothetically at best.

Conciliatory representatives of scientivism demand that what they call "decent" or "clean" science should account for premises of the sort. Precisely this demand is incompatible with the mind's experience. Any standpoint it were asked to have would be that of the diner regarding the roast. Experience lives by consuming the standpoint; not until the standpoint is submerged in it would there be philosophy. Until then, theory in mental experience embodies that discipline which already pained Goethe in relation to Kant. If experience were to trust solely to its dynamics and good fortune, there would be no stopping.

Ideology lies in wait for the mind which delights in itself like Nietzsche's Zarathustra, for the mind which all but irresistibly becomes an absolute to itself. Theory prevents this. It corrects the naïve self-confidence of the mind without obliging it to sacrifice its spontaneity, at which theory aims in its turn. For the difference between the so-called subjective part of mental experience and its object will not vanish by any means, as witness the necessary and painful exertions of the knowing subject. In the unreconciled condition, nonidentity is experienced as negativity. From the negative, the subject withdraws to itself, and to the abundance of its ways to react. Critical self-reflection alone will keep it from a constriction of this abundance, from building walls between itself and the object, from the supposition that its being-for-itself is an in-and-for-itself. The less identity can be assumed between subject and object, the more contradictory are the demands made upon the cognitive subject, upon its unfettered strength and candid self-reflection.

Theory and mental experience need to interact. Theory does not contain answers to everything; it reacts to the world, which is faulty to the core. What would be free from the spell of the world is not under theory's jurisdiction. Mobility is of the essence of consciousness; it is no accidental feature. It means a doubled mode of conduct: an inner one, the immanent process which is the properly dialectical one, and a free, unbound one like a stepping out of dialectics. Yet the two are not merely disparate. The unregimented thought has an elective affinity to dialectics, which as criticism of the system recalls what would be outside the system; and the force that liberates the dialectical movement in cognition is the very same that rebels against the system. Both attitudes of consciousness are linked by criticizing one another, not by compromising.

Notes

1 Cf. Immanuel Kant, *Critique of Pure Reason*, trans. Norman Kemp Smith (London: Macmillan, 1929), A838/B866.

2   Cf. F. A. Trendelenburg, *Logische Untersuchungen*, vol. I (Leipzig, 1870), pp. 43ff, 167ff.

3   Cf. Benedetto Croce, *Lebendiges und Totes in Hegels Philosophie*, trans. K. Büchler (Heidelberg, 1909), pp. 66ff, 68ff, 72ff, 82ff.

4   Cf. G. W. F. Hegel, *Science of Logic*, trans. A. V. Miller (London: George Allen and Unwin, 1969), p. 413.

5   Cf. Theodor W. Adorno, *Against Epistemology*, trans. Willis Domingo (Oxford: Blackwell, 1982).

6   G. W. F. Hegel, *The Encyclopaedia Logic*, trans. T. F. Geraets, W. A. Suchting, H. S. Harris (Indianapolis: Hackett, 1991), p. 40.

7   "Moreover, if skepticism even nowadays is frequently considered an irresistible enemy of all positive knowledge, and thus of philosophy insofar as it is a matter of positive cognition, we have to counter by saying that it is indeed only finite, abstractly intellectual thought that need fear skepticism and cannot withstand it, while philosophy contains the skeptical as one of its own elements, namely, as dialectics. But then philosophy will not halt at the merely negative result of dialectics, as is the case in skepticism. Skepticism misconceives its result, holding on to pure (i.e., abstract) negation. As dialectics has the negative for its result, this negative, being a result, is simultaneously positive, since it contains sublimated within itself that from which it results and without which it is not. This is the basic definition of the third form of logic, namely, of speculation or positive reason." (Ibid., p. 131.)

8   Kant, *Critique of Pure Reason*, Axvi.

9   Walter Benjamin, *Briefe*, vol. 2 (Frankfurt-am-Main: Suhrkamp, 1966), p. 686.

10 "The thought or conception which has before it only a definite being, existence, is to be relegated to the aforementioned beginning of science that was made by Parmenides, who purified and exalted his conceiving – and thus the conceiving of subsequent times as well – into the pure thought of being as such, and thus created the element of science." (Hegel, *Science of Logic*, p. 88.)

11 Cf. Karl Marx, Frederick Engels, *Collected Works* Vol. 35 (*Capital*, Vol. I) (London: Lawrence and Wishart, 1996), pp. 565ff; *Collected Works* Vol. 6 (*Communist Manifesto*), p. 487.

The Melancholy Science

Minima Moralia is the most personal of Adorno's works. As a meditation on experience it draws inevitably on events from Adorno's own life. *Minima Moralia*, however, is not simply autobiography in that through personal or particular experience it attempts to understand what it means to be an individual under the generative conditions of late capitalism. The title of the book inverts Aristotle's *Magna Moralia*, a book which, interestingly, states that 'The good of man in society is the subject of our discourse' (1182b). In this extract – the Dedication to his old friend and colleague, Max Horkheimer – Adorno refers obliquely to Aristotle's project, noting that it was once the concern of philosophy to pursue the question of the good life. But life is now debased (damaged, as the subtitle of the book puts it) by the reified social conditions in which the individual is constitutively subordinated to the requirements of production. Adorno sees the task of *Minima Moralia* (again by inverting another famous philosophical title) as the melancholy science. In Nietzsche's *Gay Science*, as the demon of the eternal recurrence demands, reality is to be affirmed and embraced without reservation. Given Adorno's views about the essential falseness of society it follows that affirmation is an inappropriate response to the experience of society. Instead society is to be subjected to critical reflection. Adorno takes his own claim about the ideological nature of society very seriously in admitting that if he is correct then achieving an objective and critical perspective from within society is no easy matter. By engaging in an analysis of society which takes its route through subjective experience we risk an analysis which is already enmeshed in false consciousness. Analysis presupposes the perspective of an autonomous subject who can gain distance from social conditions. But autonomy is semblance. It is confirmed neither by empirical evidence nor by the more radical insight that the individual is essentially the product of society. The melancholy science is hesitant and even evasive as it attempts to reveal something about modern life. This is reflected in the structure of the book. Other works of Adorno's may appear to follow no traditional structure (though in fact they are not without structure) but *Minima Moralia* is avowedly fragmentary as the form most appropriate to the very idea of a melancholy science.

Dedication, *Minima Moralia: Reflections from Damaged Life* [1951] (London: NLB, 1974), pp. 15–18. Translated by E. F. N. Jephcott.

Dedication

The melancholy science from which I make this offering to my friend relates to a region that from time immemorial was regarded as the true field of philosophy, but which, since the latter's conversion into method, has lapsed into intellectual neglect, sententious whimsy and finally oblivion: the teaching of the good life. What the philosophers once knew as life has become the sphere of private existence and now of mere consumption, dragged along as an appendage of the process of material production, without autonomy or substance of its own. He who wishes to know the truth about life in its immediacy must scrutinize its estranged form, the objective powers that determine individual existence even in its most hidden recesses. To speak immediately of the immediate is to behave much as those novelists who drape their marionettes in imitated bygone passions like cheap jewellery, and make people who are no more than component parts of machinery act as if they still had the capacity to act as subjects, and as if something depended on their actions. Our perspective of life has passed into an ideology which conceals the fact that there is life no longer.

But the relation between life and production, which in reality debases the former to an ephemeral appearance of the latter, is totally absurd. Means and end are inverted. A dim awareness of this perverse *quid pro quo* has still not been quite eradicated from life. Reduced and degraded essence tenaciously resists the magic that transforms it into a façade. The change in the relations of production themselves depends largely on what takes place in the 'sphere of consumption', the mere reflection of production and the caricature of true life: in the consciousness and unconsciousness of individuals. Only by virtue of opposition to production, as still not wholly encompassed by this order, can men bring about another more worthy of human beings. Should the appearance of life, which the sphere of consumption itself defends for such

bad reasons, be once entirely effaced, then the monstrosity of absolute production will triumph.

Nevertheless, considerations which start from the subject remain false to
the same extent that life has become appearance. For since the overwhelming objectivity of historical movement in its present phase consists so far only
in the dissolution of the subject, without yet giving rise to a new one, individual experience necessarily bases itself on the old subject, now historically
condemned, which is still for-itself, but no longer in-itself. The subject still
feels sure of its autonomy, but the nullity demonstrated to subjects by the
concentration camp is already overtaking the form of subjectivity itself. Subjective reflection, even if critically alerted to itself, has something sentimental
and anachronistic about it: something of a lament over the course of the
world, a lament to be rejected not for its good faith, but because the lamenting subject threatens to become arrested in its condition and so to fulfil in
its turn the law of the world's course. Fidelity to one's own state of consciousness and experience is forever in temptation of lapsing into infidelity,
by denying the insight that transcends the individual and calls his substance
by its name.

Thus Hegel, whose method schooled that of *Minima Moralia*, argued
against the mere being-for-itself of subjectivity on all its levels. Dialectical
theory, abhorring anything isolated, cannot admit aphorisms as such. In the
most lenient instance they might, to use a term from the *Preface* to the *Phenomenology of Mind*, be tolerated as 'conversation'. But the time for that is
past. Nevertheless, this book forgets neither the system's claim to totality,
which would suffer nothing to remain outside it, nor that it remonstrates
against this claim. In his relation to the subject Hegel does not respect the
demand that he otherwise passionately upholds: to be in the matter and not
'always beyond it', to 'penetrate into the immanent content of the matter'.[1]
If today the subject is vanishing, aphorisms take upon themselves the duty
'to consider the evanescent itself as essential'. They insist, in opposition to
Hegel's practice and yet in accordance with his thought, on negativity: 'The
life of the mind only attains its truth when discovering itself in absolute deso-
lation. The mind is not this power as a positive which turns away from the
negative, as when we say of something that it is null, or false, so much for
that and now for something else; it is this power only when looking the
negative in the face, dwelling upon it.'[2]

The dismissive gesture which Hegel, in contradiction to his own insight,
constantly accords the individual, derives paradoxically enough from his necessary entanglement in liberalistic thinking. The conception of a totality harmonious through all its antagonisms compels him to assign to individuation,
however much he may designate it a driving moment in the process, an infe-

rior status in the construction of the whole. The knowledge that in prehistory the objective tendency asserts itself over the heads of human beings,
indeed by virtue of annihilating individual qualities, without the reconciliation of general and particular – constructed in thought – ever yet being
accomplished in history, is distorted in Hegel: with serene indifference he
opts once again for liquidation of the particular. Nowhere in his work is the
primacy of the whole doubted. The more questionable the transition from
reflective isolation to glorified totality becomes in history as in Hegelian
logic, the more eagerly philosophy, as the justification of what exists, attaches
itself to the triumphal car of objective tendencies. The culmination of
the social principle of individuation in the triumph of fatality gives philosophy occasion enough to do so. Hegel, in hypostasizing both bourgeois
society and its fundamental category, the individual, did not truly
carry through the dialectic between the two. Certainly he perceives, with
classical economics, that the totality produces and reproduces itself precisely
from the interconnection of the antagonistic interests of its members. But the
individual as such he for the most part considers, naively, as an irreducible
datum – just what in his theory of knowledge he decomposes. Nevertheless,
in an individualistic society, the general not only realizes itself through
the interplay of particulars, but society is essentially the substance of the
individual.

For this reason, social analysis can learn incomparably more from individual experience than Hegel conceded, while conversely the large historical categories, after all that has meanwhile been perpetrated with their help,
are no longer above suspicion of fraud. In the hundred and fifty years since
Hegel's conception was formed, some of the force of protest has reverted to
the individual. Compared to the patriarchal meagreness that characterizes his
treatment in Hegel, the individual has gained as much in richness, differentiation and vigour as, on the other hand, the socialization of society has enfeebled and undermined him. In the period of his decay, the individual's
experience of himself and what he encounters contributes once more to
knowledge, which he had merely obscured as long as he continued unshaken
to construe himself positively as the dominant category. In face of the totalitarian unison with which the eradication of difference is proclaimed as a
purpose in itself, even part of the social force of liberation may have tem-
porarily withdrawn to the individual sphere. If critical theory lingers there,
it is not only with a bad conscience.

All this is not meant to deny what is disputable in such an attempt. The
major part of this book was written during the war, under conditions enforc-
ing contemplation. The violence that expelled me thereby denied me full
knowledge of it. I did not yet admit to myself the complicity that enfolds all

those who, in face of unspeakable collective events, speak of individual matters at all.

In each of the three parts the starting-point is the narrowest private sphere, that of the intellectual in emigration. From this follow considerations of broader social and anthropological scope; they concern psychology, aesthetics, science in its relation to the subject. The concluding aphorisms of each part lead on thematically also to philosophy, without ever pretending to be complete or definitive: they are all intended to mark out points of attack or to furnish models for a future exertion of thought.

The immediate occasion for writing this book was Max Horkheimer's fiftieth birthday, February 14th, 1945. The composition took place in a phase when, bowing to outward circumstances, we had to interrupt our work together. This book wishes to demonstrate gratitude and loyalty by refusing to acknowledge the interruption. It bears witness to a *dialogue intérieur*: there is not a motif in it that does not belong as much to Horkheimer as to him who found the time to formulate it.

The specific approach of *Minima Moralia*, the attempt to present aspects of our shared philosophy from the standpoint of subjective experience, necessitates that the parts do not altogether satisfy the demands of the philosophy of which they are nevertheless a part. The disconnected and non-binding character of the form, the renunciation of explicit theoretical cohesion, are meant as one expression of this. At the same time this ascesis should atone in some part for the injustice whereby one alone continued to perform the task that can only be accomplished by both, and that we do not forsake.

Notes

1 G. W. F. Hegel, *The Phenomenology of Mind*, trans. J. B. Baillie (London: George Allen and Unwin, 1966), p. 112.
2 Ibid., p. 93.

5

Meditations on Metaphysics: After Auschwitz

When the Nuremberg laws were passed in 1933, Adorno, along with all other Jews and part Jewish academics, had his *venia legendi* withdrawn. Realizing the precariousness of his future under the new regime he left Germany, spending three years at Oxford, registered as an advanced student, before moving on to various parts of the United States of America. It was only in 1949 that Adorno finally returned to Germany, helping to restore the study of critical theory at the University of Frankfurt. Even abroad he felt the effect of the Nazi's policy of anti-Semitism. During the early parts of his exile he feared for the safety of his parents before they too were able to escape (to Switzerland). Most painful of all, however, was the loss of his close friend Walter Benjamin who, in his panic-stricken flight from the Nazis, committed suicide. That the terror of those times left their mark on Adorno is evinced by his many references to the Holocaust as the ultimate catastrophe and indictment of human reason. His reading of the Holocaust is not that it was purely the product, as most historians argue, of a confluence of history and culture peculiar to Germany. Rather, the Holocaust was the absolute manifestation of the administered world in which the individual was finally reduced to a thing.

It is worth noting that Adorno's reaction to the evils of the Nazis did not change his mind about the basic function of philosophy, nor even add to it particularly. 'The Actuality of Philosophy' (of 1931) can be seen as the embryonic form of what was to become negative dialectics. So what, then, are we to make of the philosophical significance of the experience of the Holocaust for Adorno? In the following extract Adorno notes the problem of metaphysics by which he means the sustainability of Hegel's optimistic story of the self-fulfilment of *Geist*. It is clear that metaphysical speculation of that sort is grotesque in light of the Holocaust. Yet in 1931 Adorno had for purely philosophical reasons rejected the possibility of Hegelian metaphysics anyway. We might say that the Holocaust, which Adorno particularizes through the eternally disturbing images of Auschwitz, gave him reason to reflect on the very morality of his continued commitment to the philosophical enterprise. This existential implication provides Adorno's consideration of what might otherwise be purely philosophical questions with a deeply personal quality (though Adorno's mature works prior to the advent of the Third Reich were never dispassionate). The moral issue manifests itself through an ambivalence, the pain of which is obvious from Adorno's agonized language: he undertakes a philosophical treatment of the catastrophe, yet it is precisely the activity of reflection which distances us from the experiences themselves. However painful, though, philosophy owes it to those who were murdered to undertake that task. In Adorno's later works we find frequent references to the experience of guilt employed incongruously in the context of epistemology. But the events of the Holocaust confirmed for Adorno that the abstract business of philosophy is embedded in real social relations – in the basic rationality assumed to be nothing more than common sense – and the consequences of philosophy are therefore not necessarily merely theoretical.

'Meditations on Metaphysics', *Negative Dialectics* [1966] (London: Routledge, 1973), pp. 361–5.
Translated by E. B. Ashton.

We cannot say any more that the immutable is truth, and that the mobile, transitory is appearance. The mutual indifference of temporality and eternal ideas is no longer tenable even with the bold Hegelian explanation that temporal existence, by virtue of the destruction inherent in its concept, serves the eternal represented by the eternity of destruction. One of the mystical impulses secularized in dialectics was the doctrine that the intramundane and historic is relevant to what traditional metaphysics distinguished as transcendence – or at least, less gnostically and radically put, that it is relevant to the position taken by human consciousness on the questions which the canon of philosophy assigned to metaphysics. After Auschwitz, our feelings resist any claim of the positivity of existence as sanctimonious, as wronging the victims; they balk at squeezing any kind of sense, however bleached, out of the victims' fate. And these feelings do have an objective side after events that make a mockery of the construction of immanence as endowed with a meaning radiated by an affirmatively posited transcendence.

Such a construction would affirm absolute negativity and would assist its ideological survival – as in reality that negativity survives anyway, in the principle of society as it exists until its self-destruction. The earthquake of Lisbon sufficed to cure Voltaire of the theodicy of Leibniz, and the visible disaster of the first nature was insignificant in comparison with the second, social one, which defies human imagination as it distills a real hell from human evil. Our metaphysical faculty is paralyzed because actual events have shattered the basis on which speculative metaphysical thought could be reconciled with experience. Once again, the dialectical motif of quantity recoiling into quality scores an unspeakable triumph. The administrative murder of millions made of death a thing one had never yet to fear in just this fashion. There is no chance any more for death to come into the individuals' empirical life as somehow conformable with the course of that life. The last, the poorest possession left to the individual is expropriated. That in the concentration camps it was no longer an individual who died, but a specimen – this is a fact bound to affect the dying of those who escaped the administrative measure.

Genocide is the absolute integration. It is on its way wherever men are leveled off – "polished off," as the German military called it – until one exterminates them literally, as deviations from the concept of their total nullity. Auschwitz confirmed the philosopheme of pure identity as death. The most far out dictum from Beckett's *Endgame*, that there really is not so much to be feared any more, reacts to a practice whose first sample was given in the concentration camps, and in whose concept – venerable once upon a time – the destruction of nonidentity is ideologically lurking. Absolute negativity is in plain sight and has ceased to surprise anyone. Fear used to be tied to the *principium individuationis* of self-preservation, and that principle, by its own consistency, abolishes itself. What the sadists in the camps foretold their victims, "Tomorrow you'll be wiggling skyward as smoke from this chimney," bespeaks the indifference of each individual life that is the direction of history. Even in his formal freedom, the individual is as fungible and replaceable as he will be under the liquidators' boots.

But since, in a world whose law is universal individual profit, the individual has nothing but this self that has become indifferent, the performance of the old, familiar tendency is at the same time the most dreadful of things. There is no getting out of this, no more than out of the electrified barbed wire around the camps. Perennial suffering has as much right to expression as a tortured man has to scream; hence it may have been wrong to say that after Auschwitz you could no longer write poems. But it is not wrong to raise the less cultural question whether after Auschwitz you can go on living – especially whether one who escaped by accident, one who by rights should have been killed, may go on living. His mere survival calls for the coldness, the basic principle of bourgeois subjectivity, without which there could have been no Auschwitz; this is the drastic guilt of him who was spared. By way of atonement he will be plagued by dreams such as that he is no longer living at all, that he was sent to the ovens in 1944 and his whole existence since has been imaginary, an emanation of the insane wish of a man killed twenty years earlier.

Thinking men and artists have not infrequently described a sense of being not quite there, of not playing along, a feeling as if they were not themselves at all, but a kind of spectator. Others often find this repulsive; it was the basis of Kierkegaard's polemic against what he called the esthetic sphere. A critique of philosophical personalism indicates, however, that this attitude toward immediacy, this disavowal of every existential posture, has a moment of objective truth that goes beyond the appearance of the self-preserving motive. "What does it really matter?" is a line we like to associate with bourgeois callousness, but it is the line most likely to make the individual aware, without dread, of the insignificance of his existence. The inhuman part of it, the ability to keep one's distance as a spectator and to rise above things, is in the final analysis the human part, the very part resisted by its ideologists.

It is not altogether implausible that the immortal part is the one that acts in this fashion. The scene of Shaw on his way to the theater, showing a beggar his identification with the hurried remark, "Press," hides a sense of that beneath the cynicism. It would help to explain the fact that startled Schopenhauer: that affections in the face of death, not only other people's but our own, are frequently so feeble. People, of course, are spellbound without exception, and none of them are capable of love, which is why everyone feels loved too little. But the spectator's posture simultaneously expresses doubt that this could be all – when the individual, so relevant to himself in his delusion, still has nothing but that poor and emotionally animal–like ephemerality.

Spellbound, the living have a choice between involuntary ataraxy – an esthetic life due to weakness – and the bestiality of the involved. Both are wrong ways of living. But some of both would be required for the right *désinvolture* and sympathy. Once overcome, the culpable self-preservation urge has been confirmed, confirmed precisely, perhaps, by the threat that has come to be ceaselessly present. The only trouble with self-preservation is that we cannot help suspecting the life to which it attaches us of turning into something that makes us shudder: into a specter, a piece of the world of ghosts, which our waking consciousness perceives to be nonexistent. The guilt of a life which purely as a fact will strangle other life, according to statistics that eke out an overwhelming number of killed with a minimal number of rescued, as if this were provided in the theory of probabilities – this guilt is irreconcilable with living. And the guilt does not cease to reproduce itself, because not for an instant can it be made fully, presently conscious.

This, nothing else, is what compels us to philosophize. And in philosophy we experience a shock: the deeper, the more vigorous its penetration, the greater our suspicion that philosophy removes us from things as they are – that an unveiling of the essence might enable the most superficial and trivial views to prevail over the views that aim at the essence. This throws a glaring light on truth itself. In speculation we feel a certain duty to grant the position of a corrective to common sense, the opponent of speculation. Life feeds the horror of a premonition: what must come to be known may resemble the down-to-earth more than it resembles the sublime; it might be that this premonition will be confirmed even beyond the pedestrian realm, although the happiness of thought, the promise of its truth, lies in sublimity alone.

If the pedestrian had the last word, if it were the truth, truth would be degraded. The trivial consciousness, as it is theoretically expressed in positivism and unreflected nominalism, may be closer than the sublime consciousness to an *adaequatio rei atque cogitationis*; its sneering mockery of truth may be truer than a superior consciousness, unless the formation of a truth concept other than that of *adaequatio* should succeed. The innervation that metaphysics might win only by discarding itself applies to such other truth, and it is not the last among the motivations for the passage to materialism. We can trace the leaning to it from the Hegelian Marx to Benjamin's rescue of induction; Kafka's work may be the apotheosis of the trend. If negative dialectics calls for the self-reflection of thinking, the tangible implication is that if thinking is to be true – if it is to be true today, in any case – it must also be a thinking against itself. If thought is not measured by the extremity that eludes the concept, it is from the outset in the nature of the musical accompaniment with which the SS liked to drown out the screams of its victims.

Part II

The Concepts of Philosophy

6

The Essay as Form

Some of the earlier pieces in this reader show us clearly enough Adorno's efforts to give philosophical relevance to the idea of a dialectical consciousness. As understood by Adorno, dialectical consciousness is an openness to experience, and contrasts with an identity or positivist consciousness which preconceives the order of things. But Adorno believes that it is not sufficient for us simply to know the differences between the two forms of consciousness if the dialectical version is to be realized. At the level of knowledge it would remain a merely theoretical matter. To put this another way, false consciousness can have available to it information about its status, but it is only through praxis – a movement of consciousness – that it can be transformed. As we can see elsewhere, Adorno recommends the experience of modernist art for this process of transformation. He also turns to considerations of whether the genre of philosophy might contain a possibility for the praxis of dialectical consciousness. Conventional philosophical texts, he argues, formally confirm what is contentually proposed in that both the form of the text and the order of experience are decided in advance. The great architectonics of the tradition assume that their subject matter should be abstract entities and purified concepts and that the form in which these are to be presented – an apparently strict and objective process of deduction – confirms the nature of the content. 'The Essay as Form' argues for a new approach to writing philosophy, advocating a form, the essay, that is not pre-structured. Of course, the history of philosophy offers many examples of the essay, but not all correspond to this ideal. Adorno's view of the essay is that it is the form of open-ended enquiry guided by nothing but the subject matter, setting itself no prior criteria of relevance. In this way the essay embodies an intellectual freedom excluded in conventional presentations. As such it is a praxis, though one which hardly seems to amount to a political programme, but nevertheless one of the few possibilities now available, as Adorno's thoughts on reification make clear. This leads Adorno to the further claim that the essay is especially suited to the task of interpretation. The essay illuminates the object by being open to it. Here, as elsewhere on the same question. Adorno provides no formal criteria which would enable us to know what constitutes a good interpretation. Instead he seems to suggest that the experience of illumination by itself indicates an objective interpretation, Adorno sharply and impressively sets the possibilities of the essay against the limitations on intellectual experience expounded by Descartes' four rules in the *Discourse*. (Descartes, interestingly, is also found in the Skoteinos essay of *Hegel: Three Studies* where once again Adorno is attempting to establish a freer, though rational, approach to the understanding of experience.) Many of Adorno's writings exhibit the dialectic of the essay form. These texts thereby achieve what is arguably an attenuated unity of theory and praxis. 'The Essay as Form' can certainly be regarded as Adorno's clearest exposition of his all-pervasive views on the relation between form and content.

'The Essay as Form' [1958], *New German Critique*, no. 32 (Spring–Summer, 1984), pp. 151–71.
Translated by Bob Hullot-Kentor and Frederic Will.

"Destined, to see the illuminated, not the light."

Goethe, *Pandora*

That in Germany the essay is decried as a hybrid; that it is lacking a convincing tradition; that its strenuous requirements have only rarely been met: all this has been often remarked upon and censured. "The essay form has not yet, today, travelled the road to independence which its sister, poetry, covered long ago; the road of development from a primitive, undifferentiated unity with science, ethics, and art."[1] But neither discontent with this situation, nor discontent with the mentality that reacts to the situation by fencing up art as a preserve for the irrational, identifying knowledge with organized science and excluding as impure anything that does not fit this antithesis: neither discontent has changed anything in the customary national prejudice. The bestowal of the garland "writer" still suffices to exclude from academia the person one is praising. Despite the weighty perspicacity that Simmel and the young Lukács, Kassner and Benjamin entrusted to the essay, to the speculative investigation of specific, culturally predetermined objects,[2] the academic guild only has patience for philosophy that dresses itself up with the nobility of the universal, the everlasting, and today – when possible – with the primal; the cultural artifact is of interest only to the degree that it serves to exemplify universal categories, or at the very least allows them to shine through – however little the particular is thereby illuminated. The stubbornness with which this stereotypical thought survives would be as puzzling as its emotional rootedness if it were not fed by motives that are stronger than the painful recollection of how much cultivation is missing from a culture that historically scarcely recognizes the *homme de lettres*. In Germany the essay provokes resistance because it is reminiscent of the intellectual freedom that, from the time of an unsuccessful and lukewarm Enlightenment, since Leibniz's day, all the way to the present has never really emerged, not even under the conditions of formal freedom; the German Enlightenment was always ready to proclaim, as its essential concern, subordination under whatever higher courts. The essay, however, does not permit its domain to be prescribed. Instead of achieving something scientifically, or creating something artistically, the effort of the essay reflects a childlike freedom that catches fire, without scruple, on what others have already done. The essay mirrors what is loved and hated instead of presenting the intellect, on the model of a boundless work ethic, as *creatio ex nihilo*. Luck and play are essential to the essay. It does not begin with Adam and Eve but with what it wants to discuss; it says what is at issue and stops where it feels itself complete – not where nothing is left to say. Therefore it is classed among the oddities. Its concepts are neither deduced from any first principle nor do they come full circle and arrive at a final principle. Its interpretations are not philologically hardened and sober, rather – according to the predictable verdict of that vigilant calculating reason that hires itself out to stupidity as a guard against intelligence – it overinterprets. Due to a fear of negativity *per se*, the subject's effort to break through what masks itself as objectivity is branded as idleness. Everything is supposedly much simpler. The person who interprets instead of unquestioningly accepting and categorizing is slapped with the charge of intellectualizing as if with a yellow star; his misled and decadent intelligence is said to subtilize and project meaning where there is nothing to interpret. Technician or dreamer, those are the alternatives. Once one lets oneself be terrorized by the prohibition of going beyond the intended meaning of a certain text, one becomes the dupe of the false intentionality that men and things harbor of themselves. Understanding then amounts to nothing more than unwrapping what the author wanted to say, or, if need be, tracking down the individual psychological reactions that the phenomenon indicates. But just as it is scarcely possible to figure out what someone at a certain time and place felt and thought, such insights could not hope to gain anything essential. The author's impulses are extinguished in the objective substance they grasp. The objective abundance of significations encapsulated within each spiritual phenomenon, if it is to reveal itself, requires from the person receiving them precisely that spontaneity of subjective fantasy that is chastised in the name of objective discipline. Nothing can be interpreted out of a work without at the same time being interpreted into it. The criteria of this process are the compatibility of the interpretation with the text and with itself and its power to release the object's expression in the unity of its elements. The essay thereby acquires an aesthetic autonomy that is easily criticized as simply borrowed from art, though it distinguishes itself from art through its conceptual character and its claim to truth free from aesthetic semblance. Lukács failed to recognize this when he called the essay an art form in a letter to Leo Popper that serves as the introduction to *Soul and Form*.[3] Neither is the positivist maxim superior to Lukács' thesis, namely the maxim which maintains that what is written about art may claim nothing of art's mode of presentation, nothing, that is, of its autonomy of form. The positivist tendency to set up every possible examinable object in rigid opposition to the knowing subject remains – in this as in every other instance – caught up with the rigid separation of form and content: for it is scarcely possible to speak of the aesthetic unaesthetically, stripped of any similarity with its object, without becoming narrow-minded and *a priori* losing touch with the aesthetic object. According to a positivist procedure the content, once rigidly modelled on the protocol sentence, should be indifferent to its presentation. Presentation should be conventional, not demanded by the matter itself. Every impulse of expression – as far as the instinct of scientific purism is concerned – endangers an objectivity that is said to spring forth after the subtraction of the subject; such expression would thus endanger the authenticity of the material, which is said to prove itself all the better the less it relies on form, even though the measure of form is precisely its ability to render content purely and without addition. In its allergy to forms, as pure accidents, the scientific mind approaches the stupidly dogmatic mind. Positivism's irresponsibly bungled language fancies itself to be responsibly objective and adequate to the matter at hand; the reflection on the spiritual becomes the privilege of the spiritless.

None of these offspring of resentment are simply untruth. If the essay disdains to begin by deriving cultural products from something underlying them, it embroils itself only more intently in the culture industry and it falls for the conspicuousness, success and prestige of products designed for the market place. Fictional biographies and all the related commercial writing are no mere degeneration but the permanent temptation of a form whose suspicion toward false profundity is no defense against its own turning into skillful superficiality. The essay's capitulation is already evident in Sainte-Beuve, from whom the genre of the modern essay really stems. Such works – along with products like the biographical sketches of Herbert Eulenberg,[4] the German model for a flood of cultural trash-literature, all the way to the films about Rembrandt, Toulouse-Lautrec, and the Holy Bible – have promoted the neutralizing transformation of cultural artifacts into commodities, a transformation which, in recent cultural history, has irresistably seized up all that which in the eastern bloc is shamelessly called "the cultural heritage." This process is perhaps most striking in the instance of Stefan Zweig, who in his youth wrote several discerning essays, and who finally, in his book on Balzac, stooped so low as to describe the psychology of the creative artist. Such writing does not criticize basic abstract concepts, mindless dates, worn-out clichés, but implicitly and thereby with the greater complicity, it presupposes them. The detritus of an hermeneutic psychology is fused with common categories drawn from the *Weltanschauung* of the cultural philistines, categories like those of personality and the irrational. Such essays mistake themselves for that kind of feuilleton journalism with which the enemies of form confuse the form of the essay. Torn from the discipline of academic unfreedom intellectual (*geistige*) freedom itself becomes unfree and sets itself to work in the service of the socially performed needs of its customers. The moment of irresponsibility, in itself an aspect of every truth that does not exhaust itself in responsibility toward the status quo, will account for itself when faced with the needs of the established consciousness; bad essays are no less conformist than bad dissertations. Responsibility, however, respects not only authorities and committees but the object itself.

The bad essay chats about people instead of opening up the matter at hand; in this the essay form is somewhat complicitous. The separation of knowledge from art is irreversible. Only the naiveté of the literary entrepreneur takes no notice of this separation; he thinks of himself as at least an organizational genius, and simply chews up good art-works into bad ones. With the objectification of the world in the course of progressing demythologization, science and art have separated from each other. A consciousness in which perception and concept, image and sign would be one is not, if it ever existed, to be recreated with a wave of the wand; its restitution would be a return to chaos. Only as the completion of the mediating process would such a consciousness be thinkable, as a utopia just as that on which idealist philosophers since Kant had bestowed the name of creative intuition, and which failed them whenever actual knowledge appealed to it. When philosophy supposes that by borrowing from art it can do away with objectifying thought and its history – with what is usually termed the antithesis of subject and object – and indeed expects that being itself would speak out of a poetic montage of Parmenides and Jungnickel,[5] it only approximates a washed-out pseudo-culture. With peasant cunning legitimated as primordiality, it refuses to honor the obligation of conceptual thought to which it has subscribed as soon as it has employed concepts in statements and judgments. At the same time its aesthetic element remains a second-hand thinned-out cultural reminiscence of Hölderlin or Expressionism, or possibly of *art nouveau*, simply because no thought can entrust itself to language as boundlessly and blindly as the idea of a primal utterance deceptively suggests. Out of the violence that image and concept do to one another in such writings springs the jargon of authenticity in which words tremble as though possessed, while remaining secretive about that which possesses them. The ambitious transcendence of language beyond its meaning results in a meaninglessness that can easily be seized upon by a positivism to which one thinks oneself superior; and yet, one falls victim to positivism precisely through that meaninglessness that positivism criticizes and which one shares with it. The playing chips of both are the same. Under the spell of such developments, language, where in the sciences it still dares to stir, approximates pseudo-art; and only that scientist proves, negatively, his fidelity to the aesthetic who in general resists language and instead of degrading the word to a mere paraphrase of his calculations prefers the charts that uninhibitedly admit the reification of consciousness and so produces a sort of form for reification without resorting to any apologetic borrowing from art. Of course art was always so interwoven with the dominant tendency of the Enlightenment that it has, since antiquity, incorporated scientific discoveries in its technique. Yet quantity becomes quality. When technique is made absolute in the art-work; when construction becomes total, eliminating what motivates it and what resists it, expression; when art claims to be science and makes scientific criteria its standard, it sanctions a crude preartistic manipulation of raw material as devoid of meaning as all the talk about "Being" (*Seyn*) in philosophical seminars. It allies itself with that reification against which it is the function of functionless art, even today, to raise its own however mute and objectified protest.

But although art and science have separated from each other in history, their opposition is not to be hypostatized. The disgust for anachronistic eclecticism does not sanctify a culture organized according to departmental specialization. In all of their necessity these divisions simply attest institutionally to the renunciation of the whole truth. The ideals of purity and cleanliness bear the marks of a repressive order; these ideals are shared by the bustle of authentic philosophy aiming at eternal values, a sealed and flawlessly organized science, and by a conceptless, intuitive art. Spirit must pass a competency test to assure that it will not overstep the offical culture or cross its officially sanctioned borders. The presupposition is that all knowledge can potentially be converted into science. Theories of knowledge that distinguish pre-scientific from scientific consciousness have therefore grasped this distinction as one of degree only. The fact that this convertibility has remained a mere assertion and that living consciousness has never really been transformed into scientific consciousness, points to the precariousness of the transition itself, to a qualitative difference. The simplest reflection on the life of consciousness would reveal just how little acts of knowledge, which are not just arbitrary premonitions, can be completely caught by the net of science. The work of Marcel Proust, no more lacking than Bergson's in scientific-positivistic elements, is a single effort to express necessary and compelling perceptions about men and their social relations which science can simply not match, while at the same time the claim of these perceptions to objectivity would be neither lessened nor left up to vague plausibility. The measure of such objectivity is not the verification of asserted theses through repeated testing, but individual experience, unified in hope and disillusion. Experience, reminiscing, gives depth to its observations by confirming or refuting them. But their individually grasped unity, in which the whole surely appears, could not be divided up and reorganized under the separated *personae* and apparatuses of psychology and sociology. Under the pressure of the scientific spirit and of an ever-present desire latent in every artist, Proust attempted, by means of a scientifically modelled technique, a sort of experimentation, to save or reproduce a form of knowledge that was still considered valid in the days of bourgeois individualism when the individual consciousness still trusted itself and was not yet worried about organizational censure: the knowledge of an experienced man, that extinct *homme de lettres*, whom Proust once again conjures up as the highest form of the dilettante. No one would have thought to dismiss as unimportant, accidental or irrational the observations of an experienced man because they are only his own and as such do not lend themselves readily to scientific generalization. Those of his discoveries which slip through the meshes of science certainly elude science itself. Science, as cultural science (*Geisteswissenschaft*), negates what it promises to culture: to open up its artifacts from within. The young writer who wants to learn at college what an art-work is, what linguistic form, aesthetic quality, even aesthetic technique are, will only haphazardly learn anything at all about the matter; at best he will pick up information ready culled from whatever modish philosophy and more or less arbitrarily slapped on to the content of works currently under discussion. If he turns, however, to philosophical aesthetics he is beleagured with highly abstract propositions that have neither a connection with the works he wants to understand, nor with the content after which he is groping. The division of labor within the *kosmos noetikos* (intelligible world) into art and science is not, however, altogether responsible for this situation; the internal boundaries between art and science will not be obviated by good will or over-arching planning. Rather, the spirit irretrievably modeled on the pattern of the control of nature and material production forgoes both recollection of any surpassed phase that would promise any other future and any transcendence vis-à-vis the frozen relations of production; this cripples the technical intelligence's own specialized procedure precisely with regard to its specific objects.

With regard to scientific procedure and its philosophic grounding as method, the essay, in accordance with its idea, draws the fullest consequences from the critique of the system. Even the empiricist doctrines that grant priority to open, unanticipated experience over firm, conceptual ordering remain systematic to the extent that they investigate what they hold to be the more or less constant pre-conditions of knowledge and develop them in as continuous a context as possible. Since the time of Bacon, who was himself an essayist, empiricism – no less than rationalism – has been "method." Doubt about the unconditional priority of method was raised, in the actual process of thought, almost exclusively by the essay. It does justice to the consciousness of non-identity, without needing to say so, radically un-radical in refraining from any reduction to a principle, in accentuating the fragmentary, the partial rather then the total. "Perhaps the great Sieur de Montaigne felt something like this when he gave his writings the wonderfully elegant and apt title of *Essays*. The simple modesty of this word is an arrogant courtesy. The essayist dismisses his own proud hopes which sometimes lead him to believe that he has come close to the ultimate: he had, after all, no more to offer than explanations of the poems of others, or at best of his own ideas. But he ironically adapts himself to this smallness – the eternal smallness of the most profound work of the intellect in face of life – and even emphasizes it with ironic modesty."[6] The essay does not obey the rules of the game of organized science and theory that, following Spinoza's principle, the order of things is identical with that of ideas. Since the airtight order of concepts is not identical with existence, the essay does not strive for closed, deductive or inductive, construction. It revolts above all against the doctrine – deeply rooted since Plato – that the changing and ephemeral is unworthy of philosophy; against that ancient injustice toward the transitory, by which it is once more anathematized, conceptually. The essay shys away from the violence of dogma, from the notion that the result of abstraction, the temporally invariable concept indifferent to the individual phenomenon grasped by it, deserves ontological dignity. The delusion that the *ordo idearum* (order of ideas) should be the *ordo rerum* (order of things) is based on the insinuation that the mediated is unmediated. Just as little as a simple fact can be thought without a concept, because to think it always already means to conceptualize it, it is equally impossible to think the purest concept without reference to the factual. Even the creations of phantasy that are supposedly independent of space and time, point toward individual existence – however far they may be removed from it. Therefore the essay is not intimidated by the depraved profundity which claims that truth and history are incompatible. If truth has in fact a temporal core, then the full historical content becomes an integral moment in truth; the *a posteriori* becomes concretely the *a priori*, as only generally stipulated by Fichte and his followers. The relation to experience – and from it the essay takes as much substance as does traditional theory from its categories – is a relation to all of history; merely individual experience, in which consciousness begins with what is nearest to it, is itself mediated by the all-encompassing experience of historical humanity; the claim that social-historical contents are nevertheless supposed to be only indirectly important compared with the immediate life of the individual is a simple self-delusion of an individualistic society and ideology. The depreciation of the historically produced, as an object of theory, is therefore corrected by the essay. There is no salvaging the distinction of a first philosophy from a mere philosophy of culture that assumes the former and builds on it, a distinction with which the taboo on the essay is rationalized theoretically. The intellectual process which canonizes a distinction between the temporal and the timeless is losing its authority. Higher levels of abstraction invest thought neither with a greater sanctity nor with metaphysical content; rather, the metaphysical content evaporates with the progress of abstraction, for which the essay attempts to make reparation. The usual reproach against the essay, that it is fragmentary and random, itself assumes the givenness of totality and thereby the identity of subject and object, and it suggests that man is in control of totality. But the desire of the essay is not to seek and filter the eternal out of the transitory; it wants, rather, to make the transitory eternal. Its weakness testifies to the non–identity that it has to express, as well as to that excess of intention over its object, and thereby it points to that utopia which is blocked out by the classification of the world into the eternal and the transitory. In the emphatic essay, thought gets rid of the traditional idea of truth.

The essay simultaneously suspends the traditional concept of method. Thought acquires its depth from penetrating deeply into a matter, not from referring it back to something else. In this the essay becomes polemical by treating what is normally held to be derived, without however pursuing its ultimate derivation. The essay freely associates what can be found associated in the freely chosen object. It does not insist stubbornly on a realm transcending all mediations – and they are the historical ones in which the whole of society is sedimented – rather the essay seeks truth contents as being historical in themselves. It does not concern itself with any supposed primeval condition in order to contravene society's false sociality, which, just because it tolerates nothing not stamped by it, ultimately tolerates nothing indicative of its own omnipresence and necessarily cites, as its ideological complement, that nature which its own praxis eliminates. The essay silently abandons the illusion that thought can break out of *thesis* into *physis*, out of culture into nature. Spellbound by what is fixed and admittedly deduced, by artifacts, the essay honors nature by confirming that it no longer exists for human beings. The essay's Alexandrianism replies to the fact that by their very existence the lilac and the nightingale, wherever the universal net allows them to survive, only want to delude us that life still lives. The essay abandons the main road to the origins, the road leading to the most derivative, to being, the ideology that simply doubles that which already exists; at the same time the essay does not allow the idea of immediacy, postulated by the very concept of mediation, to disappear entirely. All levels of the mediated are immediate to the essay, before its reflection begins.

As the essay denies any primeval givens, so it refuses any definition of its concepts. Philosophy has completed the fullest critique of definition from the most diverse perspectives, including those of Kant, Hegel and Nietzsche. But science has never adopted this critique. While the movement beginning with Kant, a movement against the scholastic residues in modern thought, replaces verbal definition with an understanding of concepts as part of the process in which they are temporally embodied, the individual sciences insist stubbornly on the pre-critical job of definition – and do so for the sake of the undisturbed security of their operation. In this regard the neopositivists, who identify philosophy with scientific method, agree with Scholasticism. The essay, in contrast, takes the anti-systematic impulse into its own procedure, and introduces concepts directly, "immediately," as it receives them. They gain their precision only through their relation to one another. In this, however, the essay gets some support from the concepts themselves. For it is a mere superstition of a science exclusively concerned with the appropriation of raw materials to believe that concepts are in themselves undetermined, that they are first determined by their definition. Science requires the image of the concept as a *tabula rasa*, in order to secure its claim to domination; the claim to be the sole power at the head of the table. Actually, all concepts are already implicitly concretized through the language in which they stand. The essay begins with such meanings and, itself being essentially language, it forces these meanings on farther; it wants to help language, in its relation to concepts, to grasp these concepts reflectively in the way that they are already unconsciously named in language. That effort is already envisaged by the procedure of meaning-analysis in phenomenology; only there the relation of concepts to language is fetishized. The essay remains as skeptical of this as it is of definition. Without apology the essay draws on itself the reproach that it does not know beyond a doubt just what is to be understood as the real content of concepts. For the essay perceives that the longing for strict definitions has long offered, through fixating manipulations of the meanings of concepts, to eliminate the irritating and dangerous elements of things that live within concepts. Yet the essay can neither do without general concepts – even language that does not fetishize the concept cannot do without concepts – nor does it treat them arbitrarily. It therefore takes the matter of presentation more seriously than do those procedures that separate out method from material and are indifferent to the way they represent their objectified contents. The *how* of expression should rescue, in precision, what the refusal to outline sacrifices, without, however, betraying the intended matter to the arbitrariness of previously decreed significations. In this Benjamin was an unequaled master. Such precision, however, cannot remain atomistic. Not less, but more than the process of defining, the essay urges the reciprocal interaction of its concepts in the process of intellectual experience. In the essay, concepts do not build a continuum of operations, thought does not advance in a single direction, rather the aspects of the argument interweave as in a carpet. The fruitfulness of the thoughts depends on the density of this texture. Actually, the thinker does not think, but rather transforms himself into an arena of intellectual experience, without simplifying it. While even traditional thought draws its impulses from such experience, such thought by its form eliminates the remembrance of these impulses. The essay, on the other hand, takes them as its model, without simply imitating them as reflected form; it mediates them through its own conceptual organization; it proceeds, so to speak, methodically unmethodically.

The way in which the essay appropriates concepts is most easily comparable to the behavior of a man who is obliged, in a foreign country, to speak that country's language instead of patching it together from its elements, as he did in school. He will read without a dictionary. If he has looked at the same word thirty times, in constantly changing contexts, he has a clearer grasp of it than he would if he looked up all the word's meanings; meanings that are generally too narrow, considering they change depending on the context, and too vague in view of the nuances that the context establishes in every individual case. Just as such learning remains exposed to error, so does the essay as form; it must pay for its affinity with open intellectual experience by the lack of security, a lack which the norm of established thought fears like death. It is not so much that the essay ignores indisputable certainty, as that it abrogates the ideal. The essay becomes true in its progress, which drives it beyond itself, and not in a hoarding obsession with fundamentals. Its concepts receive their light from a *terminus ad quem* hidden to the essay itself. and not from an obvious *terminus a quo*. In this the very method of the essay expresses the utopian intention. All of its concepts are presentable in such a way that they support one another, that each one articulates itself according to the configuration that it forms with the others. In the essay discreetly separated elements enter into a readable context; it erects no scaffolding, no edifice. Through their own movement the elements crystallize into a configuration. It is a force field, just as under the essay's glance every intellectual artifact must transform itself into a force field.

The essay gently defies the ideals of *clara et distincta perceptio* and of absolute certainty. On the whole it could be interpreted as a protest againt the four rules that Descartes' *Discourse on Method* sets up at the beginning of modern Western science and its theory. The second of these rules, the decomposition of the object into "as many parts as possible and as might be necessary for its adequate solution,"[7] formulates that analysis of elements under whose sign traditional theory equates a conceptual order with the structure of being. But the object of the essay, the artifact, refuses any analysis of its elements and can only be constructed from its specific idea; it is not accidental that Kant treated art-works and organisms analogously, although at the same time he insisted, against all romantic obscurantism, on distinguishing them. The whole is to be hypostatized into a first principle just as little as is the product of analysis, the elements. In opposition to both, the essay is informed by the idea of that interaction which in fact tolerates the question of elements as little as that of the elementary. Neither are the specific elements to be developed purely out of the whole, nor vice versa. The artifact is a monad, yet it is not; its elements, as such of a conceptual kind, point beyond the specific object in which they gather themselves. But the essay does not follow these elements to that point where they legitimize themselves, on the far side of the specific object; otherwise it would turn into a bad kind of infinity. Rather, the essay comes so close to the here and now of the object, up to the point where that object, instead of being simply an object, dissociates itself into those elements in which it has its life.

The third Cartesian rule, "to conduct my thoughts in such an order that, by commencing with the simplest and easiest to know, I might ascend by little and little, step by step, to the knowledge of the more complex,"[8] is sharply contravened by the form of the essay in that it begins with the most complex, not the most simple, which is in every instance the habitual. The essay as form will be a good guide for the person who is beginning to study philosophy, and before whose eyes the idea of philosophy somehow stands. He will hardly begin by reading the easiest writers, whose common sense[9] will skim the surface where depth is called for; he will rather go for the allegedly difficult writers, who shed light on what is simple and illuminate it as a "stance of the mind toward objectivity." The naiveté of the student, to whom the difficult and formidable seems good enough, is wiser than the adult pedantry that admonishes thought with a threatening finger to understand the simple before risking that complexity which alone entices it. Such a postponement of knowledge only prevents knowledge. In opposition to the cliché of the "understandable," the notion of truth as a network of causes and effects, the essay insists that a matter be considered, from the very first, in its whole complexity; it counteracts that hardened primitiveness that always allies itself with reason's current form. Whereas science treats the difficulties and complexities of an antagonistic and monadologically split reality according to the expectation of this society by reducing them to simplifying models and then belatedly differentiates them with fabricated material, the essay shakes off the illusion of a simple, basically logical world that so perfectly suits the defense of the status quo. Its differentiation is no supplement, but its medium. Established thought readily ascribes that differentiation to the mere psychology of the author and then thinks that it has adequately dealt with it. The pompous scientific objections to over-sophistication actually do not aim at the impertinently unreliable method but at the irritating aspects of the object which the essay reveals.

The fourth Cartesian rule that one "should in every case institute such exhaustive enumerations and such general surveys" that one "is sure of leaving nothing out" – this ultimate principle of systematic thought – reappears unchanged in Kant's polemic against Aristotle's "rhapsodic" thought. This rule corresponds to the particular objection to the essay that, in the words of the schoolmaster, it is not exhaustive, while it is clear that every object, and above all a cultural object, encloses endlessly many aspects, the choice among which can only be determined by the intention of the knower. The "general survey" would only be possible if it were determined in advance that the object in question can be fully grasped by the concepts which treat it; that nothing is left over that could not be anticipated by these concepts. Following that assumption, the rule requiring the exhaustive enumeration of the individual elements claims that the object can be presented in an airtight deductive system: a supposition of a philosophy of identity. As a practical technique of thought, as for example in its insistence on definition, the Cartesian rule has outlived the rationalistic theorem on which it was founded: a comprehensive general view and a continuity of presentation is urged even upon empirically open scientific procedure. In this fashion the intellectual conscience that should, in Descartes' philosophy, keep watch over the necessity of knowledge is transformed into the arbitrariness of a "frame of reference."[10] In order to satisfy a methodological need and to support the plausibility of the whole, it becomes an axiomatic doctrine that is being set up as the gateway to thought while no longer being able to demonstrate its own validity or proof.

Or, in the German version, it becomes a "project" (*Entwurf*) that, with the pathos-laden claim of reaching into being, simply suppresses its subjective conditions. The insistence on the continuity of thought's process tends to prejudice the inner coherence of the object, its own harmony. A continuous presentation would contradict material that is full of antagonisms as long as it did not simultaneously define continuity as discontinuity. Unconsciously and far from theory, the need arises in the essay as form to annul the theoretically outmoded claims of totality and continuity, and to do so in the concrete procedure of the intellect. If the essay struggles aesthetically against that narrow-minded method that will leave nothing out, it is obeying an epistemological motive. The romantic conception of the fragment as an artifact that is not complete in itself but openly striding into infinity by way of self-reflection, advocates this anti-idealist motive even in the midst of idealism. Even in its manner of delivery the essay refuses to behave as thought it had deduced its object and had exhausted the topic. Self-relativization is immanent in its form; it must be constructed in such a way that it could always, and at any point, break off. It thinks in fragments just as reality is fragmented and gains its unity only by moving through the fissures, rather than by smoothing them over. The unanimity of the logical order deceives us about the antagonistic nature of that on which it was jauntily imposed. Discontinuity is essential to the essay; its concern is always a conflict brought to a standstill. While the essay adjusts concepts to one another by virtue of their function in the parallelogram of the forces of the materials, it shrinks back from the over-arching concept under which particular concepts should be subordinated; what the over-arching concept merely pretends to accomplish, the essay's method recognizes as insoluble while nevertheless attempting to accomplish it. The word "essay" – in which thought's utopia of hitting the bull's eye unites with the consciousness of its own fallibility and provisional nature – indicates something, like most historically surviving terminologies, about the form, the importance of which is magnified by the fact that it results not programmatically but as a characteristic of the form's groping intention. The essay must let the totality light up in one of its chosen or haphazard features but without asserting that the whole is present. It corrects the isolated and accidental aspects of its insights by allowing them to multiply, confirm, and restrict themselves – whether in the essay's proper progress or in its mosaic-like relation to other essays; and it does so not by abstracting characteristic features from its insights. "Thus the essay distinguishes itself from a scientific treatise. He writes essayistically who writes while experimenting, who turns his object this way and that, who questions it, feels it, tests it, thoroughly reflects on it, attacks it from different angles, and in his mind's eye collects what he sees, and puts into words what the object allows to be seen under the conditions established in the course of writing."[11] The discontent with this procedure, the feeling that it could all go on indefinitely, has its truth and untruth. Its truth, because in fact the essay comes to no final conclusions and makes explicit its inability to do so by parodying its own *a priori*; it is then saddled with the guilt that is actually incurred by those forms that erase every trace of arbitrariness. Yet that discontent with the essay is at the same time untrue because, as a constellation, the essay is not arbitrary in the way that it seems to a philosophical subjectivism which translates the exigencies of the object into those of its conceptual organization. The essay is determined by the unity of its object, together with that of theory and experience which have migrated into the object. The essay's openness is not vaguely one of feeling and mood, but obtains its contour from its content. It resists the idea of the master-work that reflects the idea of creation and totality. Its form follows the critical thought that man is no creator, that nothing human is creation. The essay, always directed towards artifacts, does not present itself as a creation; nor does it long for something all-embracing, the totality of which would resemble creation. Its totality, the unity of a form thoroughly constructed in itself, is that of non-totality; one that even as form does not assert the thesis of the identity of thought and thing, the thesis which in its own content the essay rejects. Freedom from the pressure of identity occasionally provides the essay (and this is lacking in official thought) with an aspect of ineffaceability, of inextinguishable color. In Simmel certain foreign words – *cachet, attitude* – betray this intention, without it being treated theoretically as such.

The essay is both more open and more closed than traditional thought would like. It is more open in so far as, through its inner nature, it negates anything systematic and satisfies itself all the better the more strictly it excludes the systematic; residues of the systematic in the essay such as the infiltration of literary studies with ready-made, wide-spread philosophical commonplaces, by which these studies try to make themselves respectable, are of no more value than psychological banalities. On the other hand, the essay is more closed in that it labors emphatically on the form of its presentation. The consciousness of the non-identity between presentation and presented material forces the form to make unlimited efforts. In that respect alone the essay resembles art; otherwise, on account of the concepts which appear in it and which import not only their meaning but also their theoretical aspects, the essay is necessarily related to theory. To be sure, the essay relates itself to theory as cautiously as to the concept. It neither deduces itself rigidly from theory – the cardinal fault of all Lukács' later essayistic work – nor is it a down-payment on future syntheses. Disaster threatens intellectual experience the more strenuously it ossifies into theory and acts as if it held the philosopher's stone in hand. And yet, intellectual experience itself strives by its own nature toward such objectification. This antinomy is mirrored by the essay. Just as it absorbs concepts and experiences, so it absorbs theories. However, its relation to them is not that of a standpoint. If this lack of a standpoint is no longer naive and dependent on the prominence of its objects; if the essay rather uses the relationship to its objects as a weapon against the spell of beginnings, it parodically practices the otherwise only feeble polemic of thought against mere standpoint philosophy. The essay swallows up the theories that are close by; its tendency is always toward the liquidation of opinion, even that from which it takes its own impulse. The essay remains what it always was, the critical form *par excellence*; specifically, it constructs the immanent criticism of cultural artifacts, and it confronts that which such artifacts are with their concept; it is the critique of ideology. "The essay is the form of the critical category of our mind. For whoever criticizes must necessarily experiment; he must create conditions under which an object is newly seen, and he must do so in a fashion different from that of a creative author. Above all the fragility of the object must be probed, tested; this is precisely the meaning of the small variation that an object undergoes in the hands of its critic."[12] If the essay is accused of lacking a standpoint and of tending toward relativism because it recognizes no standpoint lying outside of itself, then the accusation implicitly contains the conception of truth as something "ready-made," a hierarchy of concepts, an image of truth that Hegel destroyed in his dislike of standpoints: in this the essay touches its polar opposite, the philosophy of absolute knowledge. The essay would like to cure thought of its arbitrariness by taking arbitrariness reflectively into its own procedure instead of masking it as spontaneity.

Hegelian philosophy, to be sure, remained trapped in the inconsistency that it criticized the abstract, over-arching concept, the mere "result," in the name of an internally discontinuous process, while at the same time, in the ideal-ist tradition, speaking about dialectical method. Therefore the essay is more dialectical than the dialectic as it articulates itself. The essay takes Hegelian logic at its word: neither may the truth of the totality be played off imme-diately against individual judgments, nor may truth be reduced to individual judgments; rather, the claim of the particular to truth is taken literally to the point where there is evidence of its untruth. The risked, anticipatory, and incompletely redeemed aspect of every essayistic detail draws in other details as negation; the untruth in which the essay knowingly entangles itself is the element of its truth. Untruth certainly also resides in the essay's basic form, in its relation to what is culturally preformed and derived as though it were something in-itself. But the more energetically the essay suspends the concept of some first principle, the more it refuses to spin culture out of nature, the more fundamentally it recognizes the unremittingly natural essence of culture itself. Up to the present day, a blind natural interconnectedness, myth, perpetuates itself in culture. It is precisely this upon which the essay reflects: its proper theme is the interrelation of nature and culture. It is not by coincidence that, rather than "reducing" the artifact, the essay immerses itself in cultural phenomena as in a second nature, a second immediacy, in order through persistence to remove the illusion of immediacy. The essay deceives itself as little as the philosophy of origins about the difference between culture and that which underlies it. Yet for the essay, culture is not some epiphenomenon superimposed on being that must be eliminated, but rather what lies underneath is itself artificial (*thesei*), false society. Thus, for the essay, origins have no priority over the super-structure. The essay owes its freedom in its choice of objects, its sovereignty vis-à-vis all priorities[13] of fact or theory to the circumstance that for it all objects are equally near the center, to the principle that casts a spell over everything. The essay refuses to glorify concern for the primal as something more primal than concern for the mediated, because to the essay primacy itself is an object of reflection, something negative. It corresponds to a situation in which the primal, as a standpoint of the mind within the falsely socialized world, becomes a lie. It covers a wide territory from the enshrinement as primal words of historical concepts extracted from historical languages, to academic instruction in "creative writing;"[14] from craft-shop primitiveness to recorders and finger-painting:[15] in every instance the pedagogical necessity sets itself up as a metaphysical virtue. Thought is not exempt from Baudelaire's rebellion of poetry against nature as a social reservation. Even the paradises of thought are only artificial, and in them the essay indulges. Since, according to Hegel's dictum, there is nothing between heaven and earth that is not mediated, thought may only hold true to the idea of immediacy by way of the mediated, but it becomes the prey of the mediated the instant it grasps directly for the unmediated. Cunningly, the essay settles itself into texts, as though they were simply there and had authority; without the illusion of the primal, it gets under its feet a ground, however dubious, comparable to earlier theological exegesis of holy writings. The essay's impulse, however, is the exact opposite of the theological; it is critical: through confrontation of texts with their own emphatic concept, with the truth that each text intends even in spite of itself, to shatter the claim of culture and move it to remember its untruth – the untruth of that ideological façade which reveals culture's bondage to nature. Under the glance of the essay second nature becomes conscious of itself as first nature.

If the truth of the essay gains its momentum by way of its untruth, its truth is not to be sought in mere opposition to what is ignoble and proscribed in it, but in these very things: in its mobility, its lack of that solidity which science demands, transferring it, as it were, from property-relationships to the intellect. Those who believe they must defend the intellect against the charge of a lack of solidity are the enemies of intellect: intellect itself, once emancipated, is mobile. As soon as it wants more than simply the administrative repetition and manipulated presentation of what already exists, it is somehow exposed; truth abandoned by play would be nothing more than tautology. Thus historically the essay is related to rhetoric, which the scientific mentality, since Descartes and Bacon, has always wanted to do away with; that is, until, appropriately in the age of science, rhetoric decayed and became a science *sui generis*, the science of communication. Of course rhetoric has always been a form of thought which accommodated itself to communicative language. It directed itself to the unmediated: the substitute-satisfaction of its audience. Yet the essay preserves in the very autonomy of its presentation, through which it distinguishes itself from the scientific mode of communication, traces of the communicative with which science dispenses. The pleasures which rhetoric wants to provide to its audience are sublimated in the essay into the idea of the pleasure of freedom vis-à-vis the object, freedom that gives the object more of itself than if it were mercilessly incorporated into the order of ideas. The scientific consciousness, which is directed against any anthropomorphic idea whatsoever, was always closely bound up with the reality principle and similarly hostile to happiness. While happiness is supposedly the goal of all domination over nature, it always appears to the reality principle as regression to mere nature. This can be seen even in the highest philosophies, including Kant's and Hegel's. Reason, in whose absolute idea these philosophies have their pathos, is denounced by them as something both pert and disrespectful as soon as it challenges the established system of values. Against this inclination the essay rescues a sophistic element. The hostility to happiness of official critical thought can be felt particularly in Kant's transcendental dialectic: it wants to eternalize the boundary between understanding and speculation, and, according to its characteristic metaphor, to prevent any "roaming around in intelligible worlds." While self-critical reason should, according to Kant, keep both feet planted on the ground, indeed should ground itself, it follows its innermost principle and seals itself off against anything new as well as against curiosity, the pleasure principle of thought, that is also upbraided by existential ontology. What in the content of his thought Kant projects as the goal of reason, utopia, the production of humanity, is disbarred by the form of his thought, the theory of knowledge; it forbids reason to go beyond the realm of experience, which, caught in the machinery of mere material and unchangeable categories, is reduced to that which always was. But the object of the essay is the new as something genuinely new, as something not translatable back into the staleness of already existing forms. By reflecting the object without doing violence to it, the essay silently laments the fact that truth has betrayed happiness and thus itself; this lament incites the rage against the essay. In the essay the persuasive aspect of communication, analogously to the functional transformation of many traits in autonomous music, is alienated from its original goal and converted into the pure articulation of presentation in itself; it becomes a compelling construction that does not want to copy the object, but to reconstruct it out of its conceptual *membra disjecta*. But the objectionable transitions in rhetoric, in which association, ambiguity of words, neglect of logical synthesis all make it easy for the auditor, yoking him to the speaker's will: all these are fused in the essay with its truth-content. Its transitions disavow rigid deduction in the interest of establishing internal cross-connections, something for which discursive logic has no use. It uses equivocation neither out of slovenliness nor in ignorance of their proscription by science, but to clarify what usually remains obscure to the critique of equivocation and its mere discrimination of meanings: whenever a word means a variety of things, the differences are not entirely distinct, for the unity of the word points to some unity, no matter how hidden, in the thing itself; however, it is obviously not the case that this unity, as claimed by contemporary restorative philosophies, can itself be taken simply as a unity of linguistic affinities. Here as well the essay verges on the logic of music, the stringent and yet aconceptual art of transition; it aims at appropriating for expressive language something that it forfeited under the domination of a discursive logic which cannot be circumvented, but may be outwitted in its own form by the force of an intruding subjective expression. For the essay is not situated in simple opposition to discursive procedure. It is not unlogical; rather it obeys logical criteria in so far as the totality of its sentences must fit together coherently. Mere contradictions may not remain, unless they are grounded in the object itself. It is just that the essay develops thoughts differently from discursive logic. The essay neither makes deductions from a principle nor does it draw conclusions from coherent individual observations. It co-ordinates elements, rather than subordinating them; and only the essence of its content, not the manner of its presentation, is commensurable with logical criteria. If, thanks to the tension between presentation and what is presented, the essay – compared with forms which indifferently convey a ready-made content – is more dynamic than traditional thought, it is at the same time, as a constructed juxtaposition of elements, more static than traditional thought. In that alone rests the essay's affinity to the visual image; except that the essay's static quality is itself composed of tensions which, as it were, have been brought to a standstill. The slightly yielding quality of the essayist's thought forces him to greater intensity than discursive thought can offer; for the essay, unlike discursive thought, does not proceed blindly, automatically, but at every moment it must reflect on itself. This reflexion, however, does not only extend to the essay's relation to established thought, but also to its relation to rhetoric and communication. Otherwise the essay, while fancying itself meta-scientific, would become vainly pre-scientific.

The relevance of the essay is that of anachronism. The hour is more unfavorable to it than ever. It is being crushed between an organized science, on one side, in which everyone presumes to control everyone and everything else, and which excludes, with the sanctimonious praise of "intuitive" or "stimulating," anything that does not conform to the status quo; and, on the other side, by a philosophy that makes do with the empty and abstract residues left aside by the scientific apparatus, residues which then become, for philosophy, the objects of second-degree operations. The essay, however, has to do with that which is blind in its objects. Conceptually it wants to blow open what cannot be absorbed by concepts, or what, through contradictions in which concepts entangle themselves, betrays the fact that the network of their objectivity is a purely subjective rigging. It wants to polarize the opaque, to unbind the powers latent in it. It strives to concretize content as determined by space and time; it constructs the interwovenness of concepts in such a way that they can be imagined as themselves interwoven in the object. It frees itself from the stipulation of those attributes which since the definition in the *Symposium* have been ascribed to ideas; the notion that ideas "exist eternally and neither come into being nor pass away, neither change nor wane;" "A being eternally created in itself and for itself;" and yet the essay remains idea, in that it does not capitulate under the burden of mere being, does not bow down before what merely is. It does not measure what is by some eternal standard, rather by an enthusiastic fragment from Nietzsche's later life: "If we affirm one single moment, we thus affirm not only ourselves but all existence. For nothing is self-sufficient, neither in ourselves nor in things: and if our soul has trembled with happiness and sounded like a harpstring just once, all eternity was needed to produce this one event – and in this single moment of affirmation all eternity was called good, redeemed, justified, and affirmed."[16] This with the exception that the essay mistrusts such justification and affirmation. For the happiness that Nietzsche found holy, the essay has no other name than the negative. Even the highest manifestations of the intellect that express happiness are always at the same time caught in the guilt of thwarting happiness as long as they remain mere intellect. Therefore the law of the innermost form of the essay is heresy. By transgressing the orthodoxy of thought, something becomes visible in the object which it is orthodoxy's secret purpose to keep invisible.

Notes

1   George Lukács, *Soul and Form*, trans. Anna Bostock (Cambridge, Mass.: MIT, 1974), p. 13.
2   Ibid., p. 10. "The essay is always concerned with something already formed, or at best, with something that has been; it is part of its essence that it does not draw something new out of an empty vacuum, but only gives a new order to such things as once lived. And because he only newly orders them, not forming something new out of the formless, he is bound to them; he must always speak 'the truth' about them, find, that is, the expression for their essence."
3   Lukács, "On the Nature and Form of the Essay," in *Soul and Form*, pp. 1–18.
4   [Herbert Eulenberg (1876–1949), author of *Schattenbilder* (*Silhouttes*), a conection of biographical miniatures of notables published in 1910. Translator's note.]
5   [Ludwig Heinrich Jungnickel (b. 1881 in Vienna), painter and handicraft artist well known for his animal woodcuts. This and the following passage refer to Heidegger. Translator's note.]
6   Lukács, p. 9.
7   René Descartes, *A Discourse On Method*, trans. John Veitch (New York: E. P. Dutton, 1951), p. 15.
8   Ibid.
9   [In English.]
10 [In English.]
11 Max Bense, "Über den Essay und seine Prosa," *Merkur* 1:3 (1947), 418.
12 Ibid., 420.
13 [In English.]
14 [In English.]
15 [In English.]
16 Friedrich Nietzsche, *The Will To Power*, trans. W. Kaufmann and R. J. Hollingdale (London: Weidenfeld and Nicolson, 1968), pp. 532–3.

7

Metacritique of Epistemology

The *Metacritique of Epistemology* – or *Against Epistemology* as its English translation is titled – is ostensibly a book about phenomenology. Its subtitle is *Husserl and the Phenomenological Antinomies*. It was the final product of many years' concern with Husserl about whom Adorno had previously written a doctoral dissertation and a *Habilitationsschrift*. During his time at Oxford Adorno extensively revised his Husserl material, eventually publishing it in the form whose Introduction is reprinted here. He was particularly satisfied with this Introduction. His editor, Rolf Tiedemann, notes that Adorno 'would allude to the Introduction [to the *Metacritique*] above all the work which next to the article, "The Essay as From". . . , came closest to encompassing a programme for his philosophy'.* Adorno did not regard this Introduction as important merely because it shed new light on Husserl – though undoubtedly he believed that too – but in essence because through the 'occasion' of Husserl, as Adorno put it, he had shown the deficiencies of the entire conception and project of modern philosophy. It is easy to understand why Adorno was pleased with this piece. It introduces the reader to an impressive range of concepts with a clarity that Adorno was seldom to match, even in the later *Negative Dialectics*. The most important of these concepts are those of mediation (*Vermittlung*) and immediacy (*Unmittlebarkeit*). The term mediation denotes several sorts of relations all of which are alike in holding that nothing can be independently

* Theodor W. Adorno, trans. Willis Domingo, *Against Epistemology: A Metacritique* (Oxford: Basil Blackwell, 1982), p. 241 (Editorial Postscript).

constituted. In the specific field of modern philosophy, with its foundational-ist impulse – termed 'first philosophy' by Adorno, or *prima philosophia*, as he usually puts it – certain preferred concepts, he argues, are absolutized. Adorno holds that these concepts are intelligible only by reference to other concepts. For instance, universality could hardly be intelligible without particularity since it is both a definitionally contrasting concept and also, in reality, one which if effective is supposed to apply to particulars (e.g. every particular human being is mortal.) To elevate the universal can therefore be exposed as a philosophical strategy which deliberately excludes key mediating concepts. But *prima philosophia* negates these other concepts in order to achieve the exclusivity required for a foundational position. Adorno maintains that certain concepts are interrelated in a way which undermines possible exclusivity.

Husserl is taken as the instance *par excellence* of *prima philosophia* in that he articulates a comprehensive system which aims to found all knowledge and experience exclusively by reference to subjectivity. In this way subjectivity becomes the certainty which is achieved only by radically differentiating it from the other of subjectivity. This, however, not only affects what we understand by the other of subjectivity, it also radically circumscribes the concept of sub-jectivity itself. This immediate subject, which is severed from any non-I (be it society, culture, other people), is conceived as something ahistorical and self-realizable. From the original assumption of immediacy, essential to the opera-tions of *prima philosophia*, certain inevitable further assumptions follow. First, there is the notion of systematicity which results from the explanation of ex-perience from within the possibilities of the original concept. Second, there follows the assumption of method in which the material of experience must be made compatible with the foundational principle. Adorno further specifies that inherent in the idea of immediacy is an identity claim, that is, that reality is identical in some way with the primary concepts. To this end nonidentity – a term which covers particularity in experience – is deliberately excluded by the conceptual schemes of philosophy.

Adorno's argument is ultimately that because traditional philosophies, such as subjective idealism, empiricism, and phenomenology, have failed to appreciate the mediated basis of knowledge, they are composed of funda-mentally contradictory claims: they are antinomical, containing concepts which cannot, in experience, be reduced to the required univocity. As the ter-minology puts it, traditional philosophies contain an immanent dialectic which undermines their claims to completeness or identity. Whilst it is clear that this analysis is firmly within the tradition of pure philosophy, Adorno effectively connects it with critical theory by arguing that immediacy is the product of the identity consciousness which reifies the world. The Introduction to the *Metacritique* is certainly a challenging piece, but it rewards its reader with a radical yet rational way of reading the central principles of modern philosophy.

Introduction, *Against Epistemology: A Metacritique* [1956] (Oxford: Basil Blackwell, 1982), pp. 3–29.
Translated by Willis Domingo.

Θνατὰ χρὴ τὸν Θνατόν, οὐκ ἀ Θάνατα τὸν Θνατὸν φρονεῖν.
A mortal must think mortal and not immortal thoughts.

Epicharmus, Fragment 20★

Procedure and Object

The attempt to discuss Husserl's pure phenomenology in the spirit of the dialectic risks the initial suspicion of caprice. Husserl's programme deals with a 'sphere of being of absolute origins',[1] safe from that 'regulated, methodically cultivated spirit of contradiction', which Hegel called his procedure in conversations with Goethe.[2] The dialectic, as Hegel once conceived it and which was later turned against him, is, however congenial, qualitatively different from the positive philosophies, among which in the name of the system his is included. Though Hegel's logic, like Kant's, may be 'fastened' to the transcendental subject, and be completed (*vollkommener*) Idealism, yet it refers beyond itself – as does everything complete according to Goethe's dialectical dictum. The power of the uncontradictable, which Hegel wields like no other – and whose force later bourgeois philosophy, including Husserl's, only gropingly and in fragments rediscovered for itself – is the power of contradiction. This power turns against itself and against the idea of absolute knowledge. Thought, by actively beholding, rediscovers itself in every entity, without tolerating any restrictions. It breaches, as just such a restriction, the requirement to establish a fixed ultimate to all its determinations. It thus also undermines the primacy of the system and its own content.

    The Hegelian system must indeed presuppose subject–object identity, and thus the very primacy of spirit which it seeks to prove. But as it unfolds concretely, it confutes the identity which it attributes to the whole. What is antithetically developed, however, is not, as one would no doubt currently have it, the structure of being in itself, but rather antagonistic society. For it is no coincidence that all the stages of the *Phenomenology of Spirit* – which appears as self-movement on the part of the concept – refer to the stages of antagonistic society. What is compelling about both the dialectic and the system and is inseparable from their character of immanence or 'logicality', is made to approximate real compulsion by their own principle of identity. Thought submits to the real compulsion of societal debt relations and, deluded, claims this compulsion as its own. Its closed circle brings about the unbroken illusion of the natural and, in the end, the metaphysical illusion of being. Dialectic, however, constantly brings this appearance back to nothing.

In the face of this, Husserl appealed to the end, in the name of his serried complete presentation of phenomenology, to that Cartesian illusion which applies to the absolute foundations of philosophy. He would like to revive *prima philosophia* by means of reflection on a spirit divested of every trace of the entity pure and simple. The metaphysical conception which characterized the beginning of the era appeared in the end as most exceedingly sublimated and disabused. As a result, however, it just appeared all the more unavoidable and consistent, naked and bare: The development of a doctrine of being under the conditions of nominalism and the reduction of concepts to the thinking subject. But this phenomenological conception just rejects dialectical analysis and Hegel's negativity as the enemy. The doctrine that everything is mediated, even supporting immediacy, is irreconcilable with the urge to 'reduction'[3] and is stigmatized as logical nonsense. Hegel's scepticism about the choice of an absolutely first (*absolut Ersten*), as the doubt-free and certain point of departure for philosophy, is supposed to amount to casting philosophy into the abyss. In the schools deriving from Husserl this theme quickly enough turned against all labour and effort of the concept, and thus bore the brunt of inhibiting thought in the middle of thinking.

Whoever does not let himself be intimidated by this, seems from the outset to miss his measure. He seems to pander to the fruitless transcendent critique which repays the empty claim to an overarching 'standpoint' with being nonbinding and with the fact that it never did enter into the controversy, but prejudged it 'from above', as Husserl would have said.

Immanent Critique

Yet Husserl's methodological objection remains far too formal in regard to the dialectic, which utterly refuses to be committed to the distinction between matter and method. Dialectic's very procedure is immanent critique. It does not so much oppose phenomenology with a position or 'model' external and alien to phenomenology, as it pushes the phenomenological model, with the latter's own force, to where the latter cannot afford to go. Dialectic exacts the truth from it through the confession of its own untruth.

Genuine refutation must penetrate the power of the opponent and meet him on the ground of his strength; the case is not won by attacking him somewhere else and defeating him where he is not.[4]

The contradiction in the idea of an ontology gained from an historically irrevocable nominalism is evident to a consciousness armed against academic consensus. This contradiction is that there should be found, openly or disguised, a doctrine of being disposed before all subjectivity and lifted above its critique, but with reference back to that very subjectivity which had denied the doctrine of being as dogmatic. The thought of dialectic, however, does not leave this contradiction abstract, but uses it as the motor of conceptual movement to the binding decision concerning what has been phenomenologically asserted. No stratum can be uncovered as the authentic first with the hammer of original being from under the constituents of pure phenomenology. And the phenomenological claim cannot thereby be somewhere surpassed. Rather, ostensible originary concepts – in particular those of epistemology, as they are presented in Husserl – are totally and necessarily mediated in themselves, or – to use the accepted scientific term – 'laden with presuppositions'.

The concept of the absolutely first must itself come under critique. Were it to turn out that the givenness with which epistemology deals, postulates the mechanism of reification, while in philosophy of immanence, to which that term belongs, reified existence refers back to the structure of the given, it does not reciprocally follow that the reified has primacy over the given. Indeed the hierarchical schema of supporting first and what is derived from it rather loses validity. Any attempt to pass justification on to a privileged category gets entangled in antinomy. This is expressed in immanent method by the analysis of the reified running into the given and vice versa. That, however, is no objection to a procedure which does not appropriate the norm of reducibility, just against the method which obeys the canon of such reducibility. If critique of the first does not seek to set off in quest of the absolutely first (*Allerersten*), then it must not plead against phenomenology what the latter and many of its successors have in mind, namely providing an immanent philosophical foundation for transcendent being. The issue is the very concept and legitimacy of such a foundation and not the content thesis, however constantly it may change, of what the final ground may be. The character of philosophical compulsion must be broken by taking it strictly and calling it by name. No other newer and yet older constraint (*Bann*) should be devised in its place.

Mediating the First

An emphatic use of the concept of the first itself is implied in the fact that the content of what is asserted as first is less essential than the question of the first as such, and that perchance the conflict over dialectical or ontological beginnings – whether to begin with a first principle at all, that of being or spirit – remains irrelevant before the critique of representation. That use lies in the identity hypothesis. Everything should just arise out of the principle which is taken as the philosophically first, regardless of whether this principle is called being or thought, subject or object, essence or facticity. The first of the philosophers makes a total claim: It is unmediated and immediate. In order to satisfy their own concept, mediations would always just be accounted for as practically addenda to thought and peeled off the first which is irreducible in itself.

But every principle which philosophy can reflect upon as its first must be universal, unless philosophy wants to be exposed to its contingency. And every universal principle of a first, even that of facticity in radical empiricism, contains abstraction within it. Even empiricism could not claim an individual entity here and now or fact as first, but rather only the principle of the factical in general. The first and immediate is always, as a concept, mediated and thus not the first. Nothing immediate or factical, in which the philosophical thought seeks to escape mediation through itself, is allotted to thinking reflection in any other way than through thoughts.

This was both noted and explained by the pre-Socratic metaphysics of being in Parmenides' verse that thought and being are the same. And thus certainly the genuinely Eleatic doctrine of being as absolute was already denied. With the principle of νοεῖν, that reflection was thrust into the process which had to destroy the pure identity of εἶναι though remaining confined to it as the most abstract concept, the ineradicable opposite of the most abstract thought.

The criteria which have been bestowed on the 'true being' of things are the criteria of non-being, of nothingness; the 'true world' has been constructed out of contradiction into the actual world: indeed an apparent world, insofar as it is merely a moral–optical illusion.[5]

All ontology ever since was idealistic.[6] It was idealistic at first unknowingly, then for itself as well, and finally against the despairing will of theoretical reflection, which wants as an in-itself to break out of the self-established realm of spirit into the in-itself. In contrast, the distinctions, which sustain the official history of philosophy, including that of the psychological and the transcendental, pale into irrelevance.

Husserl's sincerity conceded that in the *Cartesian Meditations*. Yet he constantly reiterates that even pure descriptive psychology is in no sense transcendental phenomenology, despite the strict parallelism between the two disciplines.

To be sure, pure psychology of consciousness is a precise parallel to transcendental phenomenology of consciousness. Nevertheless the two must at first be kept strictly separate, since failure to distinguish them, which is characteristic of transcendental psychologism, makes a genuine philosophy impossible.[7]

But what is at issue are the nuances. This admission weighs all the heavier in that Husserl himself must furnish the criterion that allowed the contrast between the pure ego which in the end he promoted, the homeland of the transcendental, and the immanence of consciousness in traditional scientific style. In the latter the data of consciousness could be a part of the world – existence (*Dasein*) – but not in the former. But to the question as to what else they may be, he imparts the information 'actuality phenomena'.[8] Nonexistent (*ohne Dasein*) phenomena can, however, hardly be in question.

Mathematicization

Since the philosophical first must always already contain everything, spirit confiscates what is unlike itself and makes it the same, its property. Spirit inventories it. Nothing may slip through the net. The principle must guarantee completeness.

The accountability of the stock becomes axiomatic. Availability establishes the bond between philosophy and mathematics that has lasted ever since Plato amalgamated both the Eleatic and the Heraclitean tradition with that of the Pythagoreans. His later doctrine that Ideas are numbers is no simple orgy of exotic speculation. One may almost always read off what is central from the eccentricities in thought. The metaphysics of numbers exemplarily effects the hypostasis of order with which spirit so thoroughly weaves a cover over dominated things, until it seems as though the fabric were itself what is concealed. Socrates in Plato's middle period already feels it 'necessary to take refuge in concepts, and use them in trying to investigate the true essence of things'.[9]

But the thicker the veil before spirit, the more reified spirit, as master, itself becomes – as occurs with numbers. In the concept of the first, which presides in the original texts of western philosophy and becomes thematic in the concept of being in Aristotelian metaphysics, number and computability are also thought. In itself the first already belongs in the number series. Wherever a πρῶτον is discussed, a δεύτερον must present itself and let itself be counted. Even the Eleatic concept of the supposedly isolated One is comprehensible only in its relation to the Many that it negates. We object to the second part of Parmenides' poem on account of its incompatibility with the thesis of the One. Yet without the Idea of the Many, that of the One could never be specified. In numbers is reflected the opposition of organizing and retentive spirit to what it faces. First spirit reduces it to indeterminacy, in order to make it the same as itself, and then determines it as the Many. Of course, spirit does not yet say it is identical with or reducible back to itself. But the two are already similar. As a set of unities the Many forfeits its particular qualities till it reveals itself as the abstract repetition of the abstract centre.

The difficulty of defining the concept of number arises from the fact that its peculiar essence is the mechanism of concept construction, which must then help in defining number. Concepts themselves involve subsumption and thus contain numerical ratio. Numbers are an arrangement for making the non-identical, dubbed 'the Many', commensurable with the subject, the model of unity. They bring the manifold of experience to its abstraction. The Many mediates between logical consciousness as unity and the chaos which the world becomes as soon as the former confronts the latter. If, however, unity is already contained in the Many in itself as the element without which the Many cannot be considered, then conversely the One demands the idea of counting and plurality. Surely the thought of plurality has not yet restored what the subject faces to unity through synthesis. The idea of the unity of the world belongs to a later stage, that of the philosophy of identity. The continuity of the number series, however, remained since Plato the model of all continuous systems and of their claim to completeness. The Cartesian rule, respected by all philosophy which presents itself as science, not to skip intermediate steps, can already be inferred from it. In dogmatic anticipation of later philosophical identity claims, it already imprints a uniformity on what is to be thought, though it is uncertain whether continuity actually belongs there. The identity of spirit with itself and the subsequent synthetic unity of apperception, is projected on things by the method alone, and thus becomes more ruthless as it tries to be more sober and stringent.

That is the original sin of *prima philosophia*. Just in order to enforce continuity and completeness, it must eliminate everything which does not fit from whatever it judges. The poverty of philosophical systematics which in the end reduces philosophical systems to a bogey, is not at first a sign of their decay, but is rather teleologically posited by the procedure itself, which in Plato already demanded without opposition that virtue must be demonstrable through reduction to its schema, like a geometrical figure.[10]

Concept of Method

Plato's authority, as well as the inculcation of mathematical habits of thought as the only kind which are binding, hardly permit one to become fully conscious of the monstrousness of the fact that a concrete social category, like that of virtue – which was expressly located by Gorgias in a social context, namely that of lordship[11] – should in such a way be reduced to its skeleton as if that were its essence. In the triumph of mathematics as in every triumph resounds, as in the oracles' decree, something of mythical mockery: Whoever heeds it has already forgotten the best. Mathematics is tautology, also by the limitation of its total dominance to what it itself has already prepared and formed. In the *Meno* Socrates' desideratum that virtue be reduced to its unchangeable but also abstract features, extracted from Gorgias' context, is expressed as self-evident and thus unfounded and dogmatic – indeed without opposition. And this is perhaps not without reason, for the monstrousness can thus be obfuscated.

But this desideratum, which can still be detected behind every analysis of meaning in pure phenomenology, is already the methodological desideratum in the pregnant sense of a mode of procedure of spirit, which can always be reliably and constantly used because it divests itself of any relation to things, i.e. the object of knowledge – a relation which Plato still wanted to be held in respect.[12] Such a concept of method is one of self-implication and of recourse to the self-mastering subject, the as yet unconscious preliminary form of epistemology. It was hardly ever more than reflection of method. Yet it completes a pattern which belongs constitutively to the concept of a $\pi\varrho\dot{\omega}\tau\eta$ $\varphi\iota\lambda o\sigma o\varphi\acute{\iota}\alpha$. Since this cannot be represented as other than methodical, so method, the regulated 'way', is always the law-like consequence of a successor to something earlier. Methodical thinking also demands a first, so that the way does not break off and end up being arbitrary. For it was devised against that. The procedure was so planned from the beginning that nothing outside its sequence of stages could disturb it. Hence the imperviousness of method to everything from Cartesian doubt right up to Heidegger's respectful destruction of the philosophical legacy. Only specific and never absolute doubt has ever become dangerous to the ideologists. Absolute doubt joins of itself in the parade through the goal of method, which is once again to be produced out of method itself. This corresponds in Husserl's epistemology to the distinction between the $\dot{\varepsilon}\pi o\chi\acute{\eta}$ and sophistry or scepticism.[13] Doubt simply shifts judgement to preparing for assuming the vindication of precritical consciousness scientifically in secret sympathy with conventional sensibility (*Menschenverstand*).

At the same time, however, method must constantly do violence to unfamiliar things, though it exists only so that they may be known. It must model the other after itself. This is the original contradiction in the construction of freedom from contradiction in the philosophy of origins. The τέλος of cognition which, as methodical, is protected from aberration, autarchic and takes itself to be unconditioned, is pure logical identity. But it thereby substitutes itself for things as the absolute. Without the act of violence of method, society and spirit, substructure and superstructure would have hardly been possible. And that subsequently grants it the irresistibility which metaphysics reflects back as trans-subjective being. The philosophy of origins, which as method first matured the very idea of truth, was also, however, originally a ψεῦδος. Its thought paused for breath only in moments of historical hiatus such as that between the relaxation of the force of scholasticism and the beginning of the new bourgeois–scientific impulse. In Montaigne, e.g., the timid freedom of the thinking subject is bound to scepticism about the omnipotence of method, namely science.[14]

Socially, however, the split of method from things in its constitution appears as the split between mental (*geistiger*) and physical labour. In the work process the universality of the advance of method was the fruit of specialization. Spirit, which has been narrowed to a special function, misunderstands itself as absolute, for the sake of its peculiar privilege.

The break in Parmenides' poem is already a sign of the discrepancy between method and matter (*Sache*), although a concept of method is still missing. The absurdity of two sorts of truth, which enter unmediated beside one another, though one of them is supposed to be mere appearance, flagrantly expresses the absurdity of the earliest manifestations of 'rationalization'. Truth, being and unity, the highest Eleatic terms, are pure determinations of thought and Parmenides recognizes them as such. They are also, however – as he and his successors still conceal – instructions as to how to think, viz. 'method'. Natorp's ahistorical neo-Kantianism had a better grasp of this aspect of ancient philosophy than the far too respectful immersion in its archaic venerability. Things confront both methodical procedure and Parmenides' original utterances as just disturbing content. They are a simple fraud which method rejects. Parmenides' δόξα is the surplus of the world of sense over thought; only thought is true being. It is not so much that the pre-Socratics authentically pose original questions which have grown dumb through the guilt of later desecration. Rather, in them and even Plato the break and alienation are expressed purely and undisguisedly. That is their value, one of thoughts which have not yet veiled the unholy to which they give witness. The advancing *ratio*, however, has as an advancing mediation ever more ingeniously hidden that break without ever coming to master it. Thus it continually strengthened the untruth of the origin. Plato's doctrine of χωρισμός already thought both spheres together, as opposed to the yawning and conceptually unrestricted contradiction of the Eleatics, though in their glaring contradiction. This was a first mediation before all μέθεξις, and Plato's later work, like all of Aristotle's, strives strenuously to fill the gap. For while this is built into philosophies of origin as their proper condition, yet they cannot possibly tolerate it. It admonishes them of their impossibility in that their objectivity is derived from subjective arbitrariness. Their inclusiveness *is* the break.

Hence the fanatical intolerance of the method and its total arbitrariness, against any arbitrariness as deviation. Its subjectivity sets up the law of objectivity. The lordship of spirit believes only itself to be without bounds. As regained unity, however, it merely assures disunion. It is truly an absolute, the appearance of reconciliation, disattached from that to which it was to be reconciled, and in such absoluteness all the more an image of the hopeless debit structure. Indeed the continuous texture, which spirit nevertheless cannot do without, inflicts disaster on philosophies of origin, and also takes the condition of their freedom from them. The process of demythologization, which spirit merging into second mythology undergoes, reveals the untruth of the very idea of the first. The first must become ever more abstract to the philosophy of origin. The more abstract it becomes, the less it comes to explain and the less fitting it is as a foundation. To be completely consistent, the first immediately approaches analytic judgements into which it would like to transform the world. It approaches tautology and says in the end nothing at all. The idea of the first consumes itself in its development, and that is its truth, which would not have been gained without the philosophy of the first.

Promoting the Subject

By furnishing the principle from which all being proceeds, the subject promotes itself. Thus little has changed from Husserl back to the market cries and self-publicity of those pre-Socratics who, like unemployed medicine men, roam around and whose dishonesty echoes in Plato's rage against the Sophists. Husserl's writings are full of wonder for the 'prodigious expanses'[15] which open up to him. In the *Cartesian Meditations* he says, 'A science whose peculiar nature is unprecedented comes into our field of vision'[16] or

Once we have laid hold of the phenomenological task of describing consciousness concretely, veritable infinities of facts – never explored prior to phenomenology – become disclosed.[17]

Heidegger strikes the same note in his pronunciamento that being is 'the most unique of all'.[18] Since long ago the spokesman for *prima philosophia* has beat his breast as he who has everything in the bag and knows all. He makes a claim to sovereignty over the many (which he binds to himself through scorn) such as Plato still acknowledged as part of a demand for philosopher kings. Even at its highest level, viz. Hegel's doctrine of absolute knowledge, *prima philosophia* has not been cured of this. Hegel just let slip what otherwise poor sages mostly kept to themselves, i.e. that philosophy itself is true being. Plato, on the other hand, was contented, outside of utopia, with reserving a favourable place for philosophers in immortality.[19] The open or secret pomp and the totally unobvious need for absolute spiritual security – for why, indeed, should the playful luck of spirit be diminished by the risk of error? – are the reflex to real powerlessness and insecurity. They are the self-deafening roar through positivity of those who neither contribute to the real reproduction of life nor actually participate in its real mastery. As middlemen, they only commend and sell to the master his means of lordship, spirit objectified (*versachlicht*) into method. What they do not have they want at least in the mirage of their own domain, that of spirit. Irrefutability replaces mastery for them and merges with the service which they in fact carry out, their contribution to the mastery of nature. Punishment immediately overtakes their subjectivism, deluded from the very beginning, for its restrictiveness. For the sake of mastery, subjectivism must master and negate itself. Just to avoid mistake – since that is how they promote themselves – they abase themselves and at best would like to eliminate themselves. They use their subjectivity to subtract the subject from truth and their idea of objectivity is as a residue. All *prima philosophia* up to Heidegger's claims about 'destruction'[20] was essentially a theory of residue. Truth is supposed to be the leftover, the dregs, the most thoroughly insipid. The content of even Husserl's phenomenological residuum is utterly meagre and empty and is convicted of that as soon as philosophy, as in the sociological excurses of the *Cartesian Meditations*,[21] ventures the slightest step to free itself from the prison of the residuum and return to free life.

For *philosophia perennis* behaves towards undiminished experience as do Unitarians towards religion, and culture to what its neutralized concept administers. Huxley is ironically correct when he passes thinkers in review and picks out his *philosophia perennis* from what they have in common. The resulting flimsy quintessence extracts what had already been implied, where true being was pathetically awarded for the first time to the general concept. Only in freedom is spirit capable of filling and reconciling itself with what it let go. An element of uncertainty comes over spirit whenever it does not descend to mere protestation. Freedom itself is never given and is constantly menaced. The absolutely certain as such, however, is always unfreedom. The requirement to indulge in certainty works, like all compulsion, at its own destruction. Under the banner of doubt-free certainty the scientific spirit obliterates all doubt-free certainty.

But that does not upset the leading idea of something left over. The absolutist Husserl, who wishes to methodically extract the 'phenomenological residuum',[22] shares that idea and even its terminology with raging nominalists and relativists like Pareto, who contrasts residues and derivatives.[23]

The most divergent tendencies of traditional theory[24] are agreed that, in accord with the practice of natural science, whatever conceals pure things, viz. 'interfering factors', should be eliminated. Such factors, however, are a constant subjective supplement in things. But the more fundamentally the operation is carried through, the more compellingly it leads to pure thoughts and thus to the very humans it strives to eliminate. The path to freedom from anthropomorphism, which first philosophy enters under the standard of demythologization, leads to the apotheosis of ἄνθρπος as a second mythology. Not least because it was reminiscent of psychology, did proud philosophy since Husserl reject psychology. Dread of psychology leads philosophy in quest of the residuum to sacrifice everything for which it exists. What innocent parsons in distant provinces may still preach – namely that infinity is worth no more than a penny – is implied in all *prima philosophia*, not least of all that of Max Scheler who so thoroughly despised the petite bourgeoisie. But, since Plato hypostatized eternal ideas, the fact that the temporal has ensconced from metaphysics, and the residua of the temporal been reified, is due to metaphysics thriving in deficiency, the continual fear of forfeiting the insignificant. Metaphysics disconcertedly constructs its infinity along the lines of the temporal, viz. property relations constructed by men and which, alienated, rule over them. Husserl's programme of philosophy as a rigorous science and its idea of absolute security are no exception. His Cartesianism builds fences around whatever *prima philosophia* believes it holds the title deeds of the invariable and *a priori* for, i.e. around what (in the French of the *Cartesian Meditations*) 'm'est spécifiquement propre, à moi ego'.[25] Thus *prima philosophia* itself becomes property. Accordingly, *prima philosophia* is unaware of the function of invariants for cognition and whether it is dealing with something essential or indifferent. Thus Husserl expects a healthy reform of psychology in the construction of an intentional, i.e. pure *a priori* psychology, without discussing whether, in the richness of its insight, empirical and certainly not unvarying psychology furnishes much more than the other which can be fearless because it risks nothing.

Persistence as Truth

With the imposition of the persisting (*das Bleibende*) as the true, the onset of truth becomes the onset of deception. It is a fallacy that what persists is truer than what perishes. The order, which remodels the world into disposable property, is passed off as the world itself. The invariance of the concept, which would not be unless the temporal determinacy of what is grasped under concepts were ignored, is confused with the unchangeability of being in itself.

The grotesque manœuvre of that phenomenological practitioner[26] who deals with what is called the problem of immortality in his jargon, by unblushingly acknowledging the destruction of every soul, but then consoling himself because the pure concept of every such soul, its individual εἶδος, is incorruptible – this helpless trick brings to light simply through its clumsiness what is hidden in the cavernous depths of great speculation.

Heraclitus, whom Hegel and Nietzsche both praised,[27] had already compared essence and the past. Ever since the first authentic formulation of the theory of Ideas,[28] the past has always been ascribed to appearance, the kingdom of δόξα and illusion. Infinity was reserved for essence. Only Nietzsche protested.

The other idiosyncrasy of the philosophers is no less dangerous; it consists in confusing the last and the first. They place that which comes at the end – unfortunately! for it ought not to come at all! – namely, the 'highest concepts', which means the most general, the emptiest concepts, the last smoke of evaporating reality, in the beginning, as the beginning. This again is nothing but their way of showing reverence: the higher may not grow out of the lower, may not have grown at all. Moral: whatever is of the first rank must be *causa sui*. Origin out of something else is considered an objection, a questioning of value. All the highest concepts, the entity, the unconditional, the good, the true, the perfect – all these cannot have become and must therefore be *causa sui*. All these, moreover, cannot be unlike each other or in contradiction to each other. . . . That which is last, thinnest, and emptiest is put first, as cause in itself, as *ens realissimum*.[29]

But what Nietzsche views as the sacrilege of 'sick web-spinners'[30] that, for the sake of life, never should have 'come about', was perpetrated with the wildness of life itself. The calamity which he explains out of that πρῶτον ψεῦδος as a sickness of spirit, arises from real lordship. Victory was codified by the victor setting himself up as better. After a successful act of violence, the subjugated should believe that what survives has more right on its side than what perishes. The dues the survivor has to pay for this, namely that thought transfigures him into truth, is his own life. He must be dead in order to be consecrated to infinity.

You ask me which of the philosophers' traits are really idiosyncrasies? For example, their lack of historical sense, their hatred of the very idea of becoming, their Egyptticism. They think that they show their respect for a subject when they de-historicize it, *sub specie aeterni* – when they turn it into a mummy. All that philosophers have handled for thousands of years have been concept-mummies: nothing real escaped their grasp alive. When these honourable idolaters of concepts worship something, they kill it and stuff it; they threaten the life of everything they worship. Death, change, old age, as well as procreation and growth, are to their minds objections – even refutations. Whatever is does not become; whatever becomes is not. Now they all believe, desperately even, in the entity. But since they never grasp it, they seek for reasons why it is kept from them.[31]

But at the same time Nietzsche undervalued what he saw through. Thus he stayed in a contradiction out of which the self-reflection of thought still has to emerge.

Formerly, alteration, change, any becoming at all, were taken as proof of mere appearance, as an indication that there must be something which led us astray. Today, conversely, precisely insofar as the prejudice of reason forces us to posit unity, identity, permanence, substance, cause, thinghood, being, we see ourselves caught in error, compelled into error. So certain are we, on the basis of rigorous examination, that this is where the error lies.[32]

The metaphysics of the persisting draws its epistemological foundation from the constancy of the thing over its appearances. So the enlightened critique which Nietzsche revives (for it is in essence Hume's) disintegrated the hypostasis of the thing set up by that metaphysics. But even that cannot succeed without a hitch. Opposing the solid to the chaotic and mastering nature would never succeed without a moment of solidity in the subjugated. Or else it would constantly expose the subject as a lie. Just sceptically disputing that moment as a whole and localizing it in the subject, is no less subjective hubris than the absolutization of the schemata of conceptual order. In both cases subject and object are already congealed in ὑποκείμενον. Sheer chaos, from which reflective spirit disqualifies the world for the sake of its own total power, is just as much spirit's product as the cosmos which it establishes to revere.

The Elementary

Philosophical concepts represent the solid and supporting as the elementary. It should be simpler than what is supported – something even Descartes never doubted. But since the ὑποκείμενον is truer than that which is raised above it, primitiveness and truth are brought together.

That is perhaps the most disastrous consequence of the assumption of immediacy, with which the subject desperately deceives itself about itself as mediation. A tendency to regression, a hatred of the complicated, is steadily at work in theory of origins, thus guaranteeing its affinity with lordship. Progress and demythologization have neither exposed nor extinguished this tendency, but rather have let it appear even more crassly wherever possible. The enemy, the other, the non-identical is always also what is distinguished and differentiated from the subject's universality. Philosophers have defamed it wherever reflection behaves radically and with obvious vigour, from Plato's curse against ostensibly effeminate musical keys to Heidegger's invective against 'idle talk' (*Gerede*). Ever since they began to question what was at the beginning, the act which cuts the Gordian knot lay on their lips. Even Hegel warded off that tendency of traditional philosophy with the motif of the nullity of the individuated. To its greater glory, the pure concept abuses the more highly developed individual as impure and decay. No progress of scientific and philosophical rationality without such retrenchment.

Totalitarian systems have not contrived that saying out of the historical nowhere, but rather brutally executed what ideology for thousands of years had prepared spiritally as the lordship of spirit. The word 'elementary', however, includes both the scientifically simple and the mythologically original. The equivocation is as little an accident as most. Fascism sought to actualize philosophy of origins. The oldest, what has existed the longest, should immediately and literally rule. Hence the first's inclination to usurpation lurches glaringly into the light. Blood and earth, the original forces which the fascists concretized, and which in industrial society are entirely chimerical, became child's play even in Hitler's Germany. The identity of originality and lordship came down to whoever had the power being presumably not just the first, but also the original. Absolute identity as a political programme turns into absolute ideology which no one any longer believes.

The Regressive

First philosophy has in no sense been pure lordship. Its initial goal is liberation from the context of nature, and rationality has never entirely given up the memory of autonomy and its actualization. But as soon as it was absolutized, it almost constantly approached the feared dissolution. The philoso-

phy of origins – which through self-consistency, the flight before the conditioned, turns to the subject and pure identity·– also fears that it will lose
itself in the determinacy of the purely subjective, which, as isolated moment,
has precisely never reached pure identity and bears its defect as well as its
opposite. Great philosophy has not escaped this antinomy. Thought, which
regards itself as the ground of being, is always on the point of prohibiting
itself as a disturbing factor in being. Even idealistic speculation has only apparently transgressed this prohibition, that is, so to speak, desubjectivized the
subject. The self-concealed abstraction mechanism immanently inclines to the
same ontology as it works against. By dint of this tendency, troubled philosophy of origins has fled from subjective reflection back into Platonism and
must also strive despairingly to reduce such recidivism to a common denominator with the irrevocable subjective-critical motif.

That goes back to Kant. He wished to both refute the conclusion of the
first as immediacy and to verify the first in the form of the *constituens*. He
liquidated the question of being, and yet taught *prima philosophia*, 'founda-
tionalism' in every respect. Even Hegel's heroic struggles against this were
ineffective. Subject–object was still disguised subject.

The problem of being today does *not* stand before us once again, free from
the ruins of millennia, as authentic in the face of such transcendental subjectivity – though the apologists of this question would like that. Rather, its
absolute in-itself is merely absolute delusion about its own subjective mediacy,
which is immanent to the question of being itself. The movement of thought
which aims at knowledge of origins announces its own bankruptcy with its
both dogmatic and empty positing of being. It celebrates origin at the
expense of knowledge.

The irrationality, in which the philosophically absolutized *ratio* perishes,
confesses to the arbitrariness of whatever seeks to eliminate the arbitrary. It
does so not just in talk about existential projects but already in Husserl, who
decreed that phenomenological reductions should produce his 'sphere of
being of absolute origins', as if their execution were arbitrary. This is, in
express contradiction to the concept of obligation (*Nötigung*) from Kantian
ethics, for example, and Kant's derivation of the Copernican revolution as
altogether necessary and needed by reason for mastering those contradictions
in which reason is no less necessarily entangled. Today the more total the
claim of ontology, which stretches out to mythos over all reflective thought,
the more dependent it becomes on mere 'attitude' (*Einstellung*), which in
Husserl functions as practically an existential of cognition.

While such philosophizing straightforwardly emulates mathematics in its
handling of the so-called constitution problem, since mathematics can

proceed arbitrarily, in the name of the most rigorous stringency, and posit and vary manifolds at will, the arbitrariness of the absolute soon fulfils its political function. The form of total philosophy is appropriate to the total state in that it links the arbitrariness of speech, in which the necessity of words vanishes, with the dictatorial command of unprotesting recognition. Authority and usurpation return to being immediately one.

Philosophy of Origins and Epistemology

The philosophy of origins took shape scientifically as epistemology. The latter wished to raise the absolutely first to the absolutely certain by reflecting on the subject – not to be excluded from any concept of the first. But the drive to identity is also strengthened in the course of such reflection. Thoughts – which are no longer, in Husserl's words, 'straightforwardly' (*geradehin*) executed, but rather turned back upon themselves – seal themselves off more and more from whatever does not emanate from them and their jurisdiction, the immanence of the subject. The fact that in immanence the world is produced, or rather the validity of judgements about the world is verified, is to begin with no more problematic than judgement unconcerned with mediation. So it was only very gradually established as a principle in the progress of reflection.

Arbitrariness, the complement of compulsion, already lurks in the assumption that such a recourse is the sufficient condition of truth, even though it be motivated step by step by scientific contemplation. Epistemology falls into this arbitrariness by its own process. The qualification of the absolutely first in subjective immanence founders because immanence can never completely disentangle the moment of non-identity within itself, and because subjectivity, the organ of reflection, clashes with the idea of an absolutely first as pure immediacy. Though the idea of philosophy of origins aims monistically at pure identity, subjective immanence, in which the absolutely first wishes to remain with itself undisturbed, will not let itself be reduced to that pure identity with itself. What Husserl calls the 'original foundation' (*Urstiftung*) of transcendental subjectivity is also an original lie. Hence immanence itself is constantly being polarized into subjective and objective moments in epistemological analysis. Emil Lask showed quite emphatically how that was so. Husserl's noetico-noematic structure is likewise one of dualistic immanence, though that did not make him conscious of the contradiction thereby perpetuated.

The return of subject and object within subjectivity and the duality of the one is detailed in two types of epistemology, each of which lives on the unrealizability of the other. These fall roughly into the rationalist and empiricist sort. As complementary enemies, they are not so radically distinguished in their internal structure and their conclusions as traditional history of philosophy suggests. The metacritique of epistemology should deal with both. Empiricism has never defended as conclusively as rationalism and its idealistic successors the idea of the absolutely first and absolute identity. It seems less entangled and thus abandons itself with far diminished energy to the process which leads through entanglement up to the bounds of the qualifications of immanence itself. Thought capitulates into empiricism too early and with too little resistance. By humbly deferring to sheer existence, thought fails to come to grips with it and thus abandons the moment of freedom and spontaneity.

Logically consistent critical and self-reflective thought grasps, in the very jurisdiction of immanence, incomparably more about essence – viz. about the life process of society – than a procedure that resigns itself to registering facts, and really lays down its arms before even beginning. Though empiricism as an epistemology tracks down the conditions of all knowledge in factical-psychological consciousness which it regards as an underlying principle, this consciousness and what is given in it could always be different, according to empirical ground rules. Such consciousness contradicts the idea of the first which is nevertheless the only motivation for analysis of consciousness, even the empiricist analysis of the 'human understanding',[33] as philosophical method. The isolated subjective antipode within consciousness, however, or 'spirit', which withdraws from the isolated objective encounterability of the entity or the 'given', thus withdraws from determination just as much as its opposite. Both spirit and its 'actions' defy analysis. It does not let itself be established in the way that epistemology as scientific method should demand, while what can be established itself is already formed according to the model of that facticity to which spirit should present the antipode. But spirit can as little be separated from the given as the given from spirit. Neither is a first. Since both are essentially mediated by one another, both are equally unsuitable as original principles. Were one of them to want to discover the original principle itself in such mediacy (*Vermitteltsein*), then it would confuse a relational with a substantial concept and reclaim the *flatus vocis* as origin.

Mediacy is not a positive assertion about being but rather a directive to cognition not to comfort itself with such positivity. It is really the demand to arbitrate dialectic concretely. Expressed as a universal principle, mediacy, just as in Hegel, always amounts to spirit. If it turns into positivity, it becomes untrue. Mastering such aporia is the perennial effort of epistemologies, though none will succeed. Every one of them stands under Anaximander's curse, whose philosophy of being was one of the earliest but practically prophesied the coming destiny of them all.

The metacritique of epistemology requires constructive reflection upon its structure as one of guilt and punishment (*Schuld und Strafe*), necessary error and futile correction. With growing demythologization, philosophical concepts become ever more spiritual *and* more mythical. The Introduction to Hegel's *Phenomenology of Spirit* and its hitherto unredeemed programme anticipates something of that need. Certainly the immanent critique of epistemology itself is not exempt from the dialectic. While philosophy of immanence – the equivocation between logical and epistemological immanence indicates a central structure – can only be ruptured immanently, i.e. in confrontation with its own untruth, its immanence itself is untruth. Immanent critique must transcendently know of this untruth just to begin. Hegel's *Phenomenology* corresponds to this by both passively following the movement of the concept and actively directing this movement, thus transforming the object.

The concept of immanence sets the limits on immanent critique. If an assertion is measured by its presuppositions, then the procedure is immanent, i.e. it obeys formal-logical rules and thought becomes a criterion of itself. But it is not decided as a necessity of thought in the analysis of the concept of being that not all being is consciousness. The inclusiveness of such an analysis is rather thereby halted. To think non-thinking (*Nichtdenken*) is not a seamless consequence of thought. It simply suspends claims to totality on the part of thought. Immanence, however, in the sense of that equivocation of conscious and logical immanence, it nothing other than such totality. Dialectic negates both together. Epistemology is true as long as it accounts for the impossibility of its own beginning and lets itself be driven at every stage by its inadequacy to the things themselves. It is, however, untrue in the pretension that success is at hand and that states-of-affairs would ever simply correspond to its constructions and aporetic concepts. In other words, it is untrue according to the measure of scientificity which is its own.

That the critique of such untruth may itself remain imprisoned in the abstractions which it undoes, as a superfluous concern of the erudite, cannot be maintained after the materialistic dialectic, whose aim is to stand the philosophy of consciousness on its head, degenerates to the same dogmatics and dispatches philosophy of consciousness by sheer decree, without ever having confronted the logic of the matter. Before that succeeds, idealism will rise easily from the dead.

System and Debit

Despite its static-descriptive tenor and apparent reluctance to speculate, Husserl's epistemology is also roped into a debit structure. Its very system resembles, in modern terms, a credit system. Its concepts form a constellation in which everyone must redeem the liabilities of another, even though the presentation conceals the litigation pending between them. Husserlian expressions like fulfilment (*Erfüllung*) – i.e. of a contract; evidence – judicial exhibits; judgement – of a trial – all unwittingly construe epistemology analogously to a legal contest. In the end, the similarity grows even stronger at every possible locus through archaizing supplements from the language of law, such as 'demesne' (*Domäne*), and 'endowment' (*Stiftung*).[34]

The most enlightened epistemology still participates in the myth of the first in the figure of a contract which is never fulfilled and therefore in itself endless, self-repeating without respite. Its metacritique presents it with its promissory note and forces from it the external insight, gained from society, that equivalence is not truth and that a fair trade-off is not justice. The real life process of society is not something sociologically smuggled into philosophy through associates. It is rather the core of the contents of logic itself.

Opposing Forces in Epistemology

Epistemology, the quest for the pure realization of the principle of identity through seamless reduction to subjective immanence, turns, despite itself, into the medium of non-identity. As advancing demythologization, it does not simply consolidate the jurisdiction of the concept, purified of everything heterogeneous, but rather also works at breaking through that jurisdiction. Its posthumous realization and the writing of its inner history is the true awakening. Individual epistemological conditions are thus not absolutely false – they become that only when they seek absolute truth – but neither are they concerned with states-of-affairs. Each of them is necessitated only by the demand for non-contradiction. What must be eliminated is the illusion that this non-contradictoriness, the totality of consciousness, is the world, and not the self-contemplation of knowledge. The last thing the critique of epistemology – whose canon is the mediacy of the concept – is supposed to do is proclaim unmediated objectivism. That is the job of contemporary ontologies or the thought bureaucrats of the Eastern bloc.

Criticizing epistemology also means . . . retaining it. It must be confronted with its own claim to being absolute, be it Kantian and its question of how metaphysics as science is possible, or Husserl's ideal of philosophy as rigorous science. The usurpation of universality which epistemology perpetrates also requires that the universality of thought be satisfied. This implies the disintegration of the privilege on which the philosophical spirit has survived by ascribing universality to itself. Cognition, which measures itself by the ideal of universality, can no longer be monopolized by the medicine men and sages who compel it. Wisdom is just as anachronistic as − according to Valéry's insight − virtue. The more consistent the procedures of epistemology, the less it expands. Thus it prepares the end of the fetishism of knowledge. The fetishizing spirit becomes its own enemy. And this has seldom been as penetrating or prototypical as in Husserl. If philosophy of immanence codifies the ὕβρις of spirit that wants to be everything, then it has precisely already discovered the moment of reflection and mediation. And thus it has also determined both knowledge as labour and the bearer of knowledge, the logical-general subject, as society. Every concept of dialectic would be null without the moment of subjective reflection. What is not reflected in itself does not know contradiction. And the perversion of dialectical materialism into the state religion of Russia and a positive ideology is theoretically based on the defamation of that element as idealistic.

Though philosophy of immanence may, with reason, tend to lapse into dogma, ontology or replica realism, it does also develop the antidote. Idealism was the first to make clear that the reality in which men live is not unvarying and independent of them. Its shape is human and even absolutely extra-human nature is mediated through consciousness. Men cannot break through that. They live in social being, not in nature. Ideology, however, is idealism which merely humanizes reality. In this it is one with naive realism as its reflective justification. It thus immediately revokes what is in 'nature', even transcendental nature.

The Drive for System

The structure of immanence as absolutely self-contained and all-inclusive is necessarily always already system, irrespective of whether it has been expressly deduced from the unity of consciousness or not. Nietzsche's mistrust of *prima philosophia* was thus also essentially directed against system builders. 'I mistrust all systematizers and I avoid them. The will to a system is a lack of integrity.'[35] Just as newer authors infer the thought of the system of right from didactic requirements, such as for a self-contained presentation convincing to hearers,[36] so philosophical systems may indeed be referred to a related need.

The two first system builders in the grand manner were also the first directors of organized schools. As the system leaves nothing out, so behaves the teacher, speaker and demagogue to his listeners. His irrational authority is mediated through *ratio*. The claim to leadership is mediated through logical-argumentative compulsion. Even Plato's Socrates finished off his interlocutors with the far from Attic-elegant proof of their ignorance. The soft echo of discomfort at this reverberates through Alcibiades' panegyric at the end of the *Symposium*. The more problematic wisdom becomes, the more untiringly it must stress its stringency. Therefore, the logic of consistency commends itself since it permits the exercise of the compulsion to thought while ignoring the experience of the object – and thus 'formally' and incontestably. While Plato's philosophy denounced the rhetoricians, who dealt formally with objects about which they understood nothing, he *also* applied himself to an advocate's formalism, in the method of conditioning concepts, which surpassed sophistic formalism only in logical consistency. In the contest Socrates must almost always be in the right against those designated as his opponents, even though and because he 'knows nothing'. Not by chance does it remain in suspense in Agathon's speech, or occasionally in the *Phaedrus*, whether Plato is parodying a rhetorical showpiece or presenting a stage of the truth, or, in the end, both. The bombastic character of several pre-Socratic sayings certainly follows from the concomitant exclusiveness of the total knowledge they ascribe to themselves, the inclusiveness of the system.

That is perhaps the darkest secret of first philosophy. Its great discovery, the emphatic distinction between essence and appearance, has equally the aspect of 'I know and you don't', however much callous and self-alienated life requires that distinction as its corrective.

Notes

* [Fragment *263 (123[b] Ahr), p. 140, *Poetarum Graecorum Fragmenta*, ed. U. von Wilamowitz-Moellendorf, vol. VI, fasc. prior.; *Comicorum Graecorum Fragmenta*, ed. Georg Kaibel, *Doriensum Comoedia Mimi Phlyaces*, vol. 1, fasc. prior. (Berlin: Weidmann, 1899). Source of fragment, Arist. *Rhet.* II, p. 1394b 25. Trans.]

1 Edmund Husserl, *Ideas, General Introduction to Pure Phenomenology*, trans. W. R. Boyce-Gibson (London: Collier-Macmillan, 1962), p. 154.

2   *Eckermann's Conversations with Goethe*, trans. R. O. Moon (London: Morgan, Laird and Co., no date), p. 527.

3   Cf. Husserl, *Ideas*, pp. 103 and 140ff.

4   G. W. F. Hegel, *Science of Logic*, trans. A. V. Miller (London: George Allen and Unwin, New York: Humanities Press, 1969), p. 581.

5   *Nietzsche, The Portable Nietzsche*, ed. and trans. Walter Kaufmann, *Twilight of the Idols* (New York: Viking, 1968), p. 484.

6   Ibid., p. 483.

7   Edmund Husserl, *Cartesian Meditations, an Introduction to Phenomenology*, trans. Dorion Cairns (The Hague: Nijhoff, 1969), p. 70.

8   Ibid., p. 71; '*Wirklichkeitsphänomenon*'.

9   Plato, *Phaedo*, p. 99; cf. also ibid., p. 100.

10 Cf. Plato, *Meno*, passim, esp. pp. 86–7.

11 Ibid., p. 73.

12 Cf. Plato, *Phaedrus*, pp. 265–6.

13 Cf. Husserl, *Ideas*, p. 99.

14 Cf. in Montaigne, *Essais* (Rat, Paris) o.J. II, ch. XII ('Apologie de Raimon Sebond'), pp. 113ff.

15 Edmund Husserl, *Formal and Transcendental Logic*, trans. Dorion Cairns (The Hague: Nijhoff, 1969), p. 157 and 217ff.

16 Husserl, *Cartesian Meditations*, p. 68.

17 Ibid., p. 79.

18 Martin Heidegger, *Introduction to Metaphysics*, trans. Ralph Mannheim (New Haven and London: Yale, 1968), p. 79.

19 Plato, *Phaedo*, passim, esp. p. 82.

20 Cf. Martin Heidegger, *Being and Time* trans. John MacQuarrie and Edward Robinson, (Oxford: Blackwell, 1962), p. 41.

21 Husserl, *Cartesian Meditations* in §58, pp. 159ff.

22 Cf. Husserl, *Ideas*, p. 136ff.

23 Vilfredo Pareto, *Traité de la sociologie générale* (Paris, 1932), pp. 56 and 459; cf. *The Mind and Society; a Treatise on General Sociology*, ed. Arthur Livingston, trans. Andrew Bongiorno and Arthur Livingston (New York: Dover, 1963).

24 Cf. Max Horkheimer *Critical Theory, Selected Essays*, trans. Matthew J. O'Connell, et al. (New York: Herder and Herder, 1972).

25 Husserl, *Cartesian Meditations*, p. 78.

26 [Max Scheler. Trans.]

27 Cf. G. W. F. Hegel, *Lectures on the History of Philosophy* I, trans. E. S. Haldane (Lincoln: University of Nebraska Press, 1995), pp. 278ff.; cf. Nietzsche, *Twilight of the Idols*, pp. 480–1.

28 Plato, *Symposium*, pp. 210e ff.

29 Nietzsche, *Twilight of the Idols*, pp. 481–2.

30 Ibid. p. 482.

31 Ibid. pp. 479–80.

32 Ibid. p. 482.

33 [In English in the text. Trans.]
34 [In Husserl these are usually translated as 'domain' and 'foundation' respectively. Trans.]
35 Ibid. p. 470.
36 Cf. Helmut Coing, *Geschichte und Bedeutung des Systemgedankens in der Rechtswissenschaft*, in *Frankfurter Universitätsreden*, Heft 17, 1956, p. 36.

8

Subject and Object

This essay was first published in 1969, the year of Adorno's death, and is the last of the many pieces Adorno wrote on the problems of epistemology. With specific reference to the subject–object problem, it carries on the programme announced in the Introduction to the *Metacritique of Epistemology*. These days it is a commonplace for philosophers to berate the separation of subject and object. However it is far from easy to construct an alternative subject–object model. Of course, such unfashionable and historically unsustainable positions as naïve realism and idealism are available. But the sense of fatigue and irresolvability surrounding the subject–object problem has seen philosophy move away from what John Ruskin once described as 'two of the most objectionable words . . . coined by the troublesomeness of metaphysics'. Adorno, however, continued to develop a subject–object theory for two main reasons. First, subject–object theory remains within rational philosophy. For him that contrasts with philosophies which attempt the allegedly more radical analysis of pre-conceptuality (that is, the moment before experience has been divided into subject and object). Second, the correct subject-object theory provides a powerful framework against which the effectiveness of various philosophical theories may be judged. (Adorno believes that his framework can reveal latent idealism in certain positions which deliberately avoid subject–object analysis.) 'Subject and Object' brings Adorno's thoughts on these matters to their most sophisticated whilst also fulfilling the formal openness of philosophical reflection proposed in 'The Essay as Form'. In addition to being an outstanding metaphilosophical consideration of epistemology, 'Subject and Object' is one of the finest products of the critical theory reading of philosophy. Skilfully interweaving epistemology and critical theory, it effectively reveals parallels between the activities of philosophy and the processes of exchange society without, at the same time, merely reducing the problems of philosophy (in the traditional Marxist manner) to the problems of society. In the course of his analysis of subject and object Adorno employs the notions of true and false in a unique way, inverting them when moving from descriptive to normative judgments. For example, naïve realism (which holds that mind and world are entirely separate) is true in that it accurately reflects an alienated and reified society, and false in that it threatens to prescribe such limited relations as the essence of the subject's engagement with the object. Its falseness is thereby directly connected by Adorno with its ideological function in the sense that it will perpetuate at the level of ideas what is in fact at the level of socially constructed exchange relations. Unlike other philosophers confronted by an epistemology which separates us from objects (Lukács and Heidegger being the ones Adorno has in mind), Adorno does not appeal to an undifferentiated unity, a unity which is the product, in his view, of romantic yearnings. Nor does he accept the solution offered by idealism in which subject and object are reconciled under identity. Under the descriptive/normative schema he argues that idealism is true in that it reflects the abstraction of subjectivity from a world in which it might be constitutively immersed, but false in that its very hypostatization masks its real lack of freedom.

Against these positions Adorno offers a range of arguments based on what he calls a 'dialectical' primacy or priority of the object. These arguments, whilst not adding up to a unified position, nevertheless raise difficulties for the spirit/transcendental theories of subjectivity. First, subjectivity is not a private achievement, but, rather, the result of the process of engagement with objects. Second, the very reality of the subject, as a socially engaged entity, is possible only because the subject is itself an object of a certain kind. Adorno further argues that the primacy of the object is dialectical in that the object too is not to be defined as the contrary of subjects. Its apparently subjective qualities – meanings – are essential to what it is as an object.

'Subject and Object' [1969], in *The Essential Frankfurt School Reader* (Oxford: Basil Blackwell, 1978), pp. 497–511, edited by Andrew Arato and Eike Gebhardt. Translated by Andrew Arato and Eike Gebhardt.

To engage in reflections on subject and object poses the problem of stating what we are to talk about. The terms are patently equivocal. "Subject," for instance, may refer to the particular individual as well as to general attributes, to "consciousness in general" in the language of Kant's *Prolegomena*. The equivocation is not removable simply by terminological clarification, for the two meanings have reciprocal need of each other; one is scarcely to be grasped without the other. The element of individual humanity – what Schelling calls "egoity" – cannot be thought apart from any concept of the subject; without any remembrance of it, "subject" would lose all meaning. Conversely, as soon as we reflect upon the human individual as an individual at all, in the form of a general concept – as soon as we cease to mean only the present existence of some particular person – we have already turned it into a universal similar to that which came to be explicit in the idealist concept of the subject. The very term "particular person" requires a generic concept, lest it be meaningless. Even in proper names, a reference to that universal is still implied. They mean one who is called by that name, not by any other; and "one" stands elliptically for "one human being."

If on the other hand we tried to define the two terms so as to avoid this type of complication, we would land in an aporia that adds to the problematics of defining, as modern philosophy since Kant has noted time and again, for in a way, the concepts of subject and object – or rather, the things they intend – have priority before all definition. Defining means that something objective, no matter what it may be in itself, is subjectively captured by means of a fixed concept. Hence the resistance offered to defining by subject and object. To determine their meanings takes reflection on the very thing which definition cuts off for the sake of conceptual flexibility. Hence the advisability, at the outset, of taking up the words "subject" and "object" as the well-honed philosophical language hands them to us as a historical sediment – not, of course, sticking to such conventionalism but continuing with critical analysis. The starting point would be the allegedly naive, though already mediated, view that a knowing subject, whatever its kind, was confronting a known object, whatever its kind. The reflection, which in philosophical terminology goes by the name of *intentio obliqua*, is then a re-relation of that ambiguous concept of the object to a no less ambiguous concept of the subject. The second reflection reflects the first, more closely determining those vague subject and object concepts for their content's sake.

The separation of subject and object is both real and illusory. True, because in the cognitive realm it serves to express the real separation, the dichotomy of the human condition, a coercive development. False, because the resulting separation must not be hypostasized, not magically transformed into an invariant. This contradiction in the separation of subject and object is imparted to epistemology. Though they cannot be thought away, as separated, the *pseudos* of the separation is manifested in their being mutually mediated – the object by the subject, and even more, in different ways, the subject by the object. The separation is no sooner established directly, without mediation, than it becomes ideology, which is indeed its normal form. The mind will then usurp the place of something absolutely independent – which it is not; its claim of independence heralds the claim of dominance. Once radically parted from the object, the subject reduces it to its own measure; the subject swallows the object, forgetting how much it is an object itself.

The picture of a temporal or extratemporal original state of happy identity between subject and object is romantic, however – a wishful projection at times, but today no more than a lie. The undifferentiated state before the subject's formation was the dread of the blind web of nature, of myth; it was in protest against it that the great religions had their truth content. Besides, to be undifferentiated is not to be one; even in Platonic dialectics, unity requires divers items of which it is the unity. For those who live to see it, the new horror of separation will transfigure the old horror of chaos – both are the ever-same. The fear of yawning meaninglessness makes one forget a fear which once upon a time was no less dreadful: that of the vengeful gods of which Epicurean materialism and the Christian "fear not" wanted to relieve mankind. The only way to accomplish this is through the subject. If it were liquidated rather than sublated in a higher form, the effect would be regression – not just of consciousness, but a regression to real barbarism.

Fate, myth's bondage to nature, comes from total social tutelage, from an age in which no eyes had yet been opened by self-reflection, an age in which subject did not yet exist. Instead of a collective practice conjuring that age to return, the spell of the old undifferentiatedness should be obliterated. Its prolongation is the sense of identity of a mind that repressively shapes its Other in its own image. If speculation on the state of reconciliation were permitted, neither the undistinguished unity of subject and object nor their antithetical hostility would be conceivable in it; rather, the communication of what was distinguished. Not until then would the concept of communication, as an objective concept, come into its own. The present one is so infamous because the best there is, the potential of an agreement between people and things, is betrayed to an interchange between subjects according to the requirements of subjective reason. In its proper place, even epistemologically, the relationship of subject and object would lie in the realization of peace among men as well as between men and their Other. Peace is the state of distinctness without domination, with the distinct participating in each other.

In epistemology, "subject" is mostly understood to mean the "transcendental subject." According to idealist doctrine, it will either construct the objective world with raw material along Kantian lines or, since Fichte, engender that world itself. The critics of idealism were not the first to discover that this transcendental subject constituting the substance of experience was abstracted from living individuals. It is evident that the abstract concept of the

transcendental subject — its thought forms, their unity, and the original productivity of consciousness — presupposes what it promises to bring about:
actual, live individuals. This notion was present in the idealist philosophies.
Kant, in his chapter on psychological paralogisms, did try to develop a
constitutive-hierarchic difference in principle between transcendental and
empirical subject; but his successors, notably Fichte and Hegel, as well as
Schopenhauer, resorted to logical subtleties to cope with the immense
difficulty of the circle. They frequently had recourse to the Aristotelian motif
that what comes first for our consciousness — in this case, the empirical
subject — is not the First in itself, that as its condition or its origin it postulates the transcendental subject. Even Husserl's polemics against psychologism,
along with the distinction of genesis and validity, continues the line of that
mode of argument. It is apologetic. The conditioned is to be justified as
unconditional, the derived as primary. That nothing can be true except the
First — or, as Nietzsche critically phrased it, what has not come into being —
is a *topos* of the entire Western tradition; we find it repeated here. There is
no mistaking the ideological function of the thesis. The more individuals are
really degraded to functions of the social totality as it becomes more systematized, the more will man pure and simple, man as a principle with the
attributes of creativity and absolute domination, be consoled by exaltation of
his mind.

Yet for all that, the question of the transcendental subject's reality weighs
heavier than appears in its sublimation as pure mind, fully so in the critical
retraction of idealism. In a sense (although idealism would be the last to admit
this) the transcendental subject is more real — that is to say, more determinant for the real conduct of men and for the resulting society — than those
psychological individuals from which the transcendental one was abstracted.
They have little to say in the world, having on their part turned into
appendages of the social apparatus and ultimately into ideology. The living
human individual, as he is forced to act in the role for which he has been
marked internally as well, is the *homo oeconomicus* incarnate, closer to the transcendental subject than to the living individual for which he immediately
cannot but take himself. To this extent, idealistic theory was realistic and did
not need to feel embarrassed when charged with idealism by opponents.
What shows up faithfully in the doctrine of the transcendental subject is the
priority of the relations — abstractly rational ones, detached from the human
individuals and their relationships — that have their model in exchange. If the
exchange form is the standard social structure, its rationality constitutes
people; what they are for themselves, what they seem to be to themselves, is
secondary. They are deformed beforehand by the mechanism that has been
philosophically transfigured as transcendental. The supposedly most evident

of things, the empirical subject, would really have to be viewed as not yet in existence; in this perspective, the transcendental subject is "constitutive."

This alleged origin of all objects is objectified in rigid timelessness, quite in keeping with Kant's doctrine of the firm and immutable forms of transcendental consciousness. Its solidity and invariance, which according to transcendental philosophy bring forth all objects or at least prescribe their rule, are the reflective form of the reification of humans that has been objectively accomplished in the social relationship. The fetish character, a socially necessary semblance, has historically turned into the *prius* of what according to its concept would have it be the *posterius*. The philosophical problem of constitution has reversed into its mirror image; but in this very reversal, it tells the truth about the historic stage that has been reached — in a truth, of course, which a second Copernican turn might theoretically negate again. True, it has its positive aspect as well: society, as prior, keeps its members and itself alive. The particular individual has the universal to thank for the possibility of his existence — witness thought, which is a general relation, and thus a social one. It is not just as fetish that thought takes priority over the individual. Only in idealism, one side is hypostasized, the side which is incomprehensible except in relation to the other. But the datum, the irremovable *skandalon* of idealism, will demonstrate time and again the failure of the hypostasis.

It is not the old *intentio recta* that is restored by insight into the object's primacy; not the trustful bondage to the outside world as it is and as it appears this side of critique; not an anthropological state devoid of the self-consciousness that crystallizes only in the context of re-relating knowledge to the knower. The crude confrontation of subject and object in naive realism is indeed historically necessary and not removable by any act of will. At the same time it is a product of the wrong abstraction, already a piece of reification. Once we have seen through this, we would be unable without self-reflection to drag further a consciousness objectified to itself, a consciousness externalized precisely as such and virtually recoiling outward. The turn to the subject, though aiming at its primacy from the start, does not simply vanish with its revision; not the least reason why the revision occurs is the subjective interest of freedom. Rather, by primacy of the object is meant that the subject, for its part an object in a qualitatively different sense, in a sense more radical than the object, which is not known otherwise than through consciousness, is as an object also a subject.

What is known through consciousness must be something; mediation aims at the mediated. But the subject, the epitome of mediation, is the How — never the What, as opposed to the object — that is postulated by any comprehensible idea of its concept. Potentially, even if not actually, objectivity can be conceived without a subject; not so subjectivity without an object. No matter how we define the subject, some entity cannot be juggled out of it. If it is not something – and "something" indicates an irreducible objective moment – the subject is nothing at all; even as *actus purus*, it still needs to refer to something active. The object's primacy is the *intentio obliqua* of the *intentio obliqua*, not the warmed-over *intentio recta*. It is the corrective of the subjective reduction, not the denial of a subjective share. The object, too, is mediated; but according to its own concept, it is not so thoroughly dependent on the subject as the subject is on objectivity. Idealism has ignored such differences and has thus coarsened a spiritualization that serves abstraction as a disguise. Yet this occasions a revision of the stand toward the subject which prevails in traditional theory. That theory glorifies the subject in ideology and slanders it in epistemological practice. If one wants to reach the object, on the other hand, its subjective attributes or qualities are not to be eliminated, for precisely that would run counter to the primacy of the object.

If the subject does have an objective core, the object's subjective qualities are so much more an element of objectivity. For it is only as something definite that the object becomes anything at all. In the attributes that seem to be attached to it by the subject alone, the subject's own objectivity comes to the fore: all of them are borrowed from the objectivity of the *intentio recta*. Even according to idealist doctrine, the subjective attributes are not mere attachments; they are always called for by the *definiendum* as well, and it is there that the object's primacy is upheld. Conversely, the supposedly pure object lacking any admixture of thought and visuality is the literal reflection of abstract subjectivity: nothing else but abstraction makes the Other like itself. Unlike the undefined substrate of reductionism, the object of undiminished experience is more objective than that substrate. The qualities which the traditional critique of knowledge eliminates from the object and credits to the subject are due, in subjective experience, to the object's primacy; this is what we were deceived about by the ruling *intentio obliqua*. Its inheritance went to a critique of experience that realized its historical conditionality, and eventually that of society. For society is immanent in experience, not an *allo genos*. Nothing but the social self-reflection of knowledge obtains for knowledge the objectivity that will escape it as long as it obeys the social coercions that hold sway in it, and does not become aware of them. Social critique is a critique of knowledge, and vice versa.

Primacy of the object can be discussed legitimately only when that primacy – over the subject in the broadest sense of the term – is somehow definable, when it is more than the Kantian thing-in-itself as the unknown cause of the phenomenon. Despite Kant, of course, even the thing-in-itself bears a minimum of attributes merely by being distinct from the categorially predicated; one such attribute, a negative one, would be that of acausality. It suffices to set up an antithesis to the conventional view that conforms with subjectivism. The test of the object's primacy is its qualitative alteration of opinions held by the reified consciousness, opinions that go frictionlessly with subjectivism. Subjectivism does not touch the substance of naive realism; it only seeks to state formal criteria of its validity, as confirmed by the Kantian formula of empirical realism. One argument for primacy of the object is indeed incompatible with Kant's doctrine of constitution: that in modern natural science, the ratio peers over the very wall it has built, that it grabs a snippet of what differs with its well-honed categories. Such broadening of the ratio shatters subjectivism. But what defines the prior object as distinct from its subjective trappings is comprehensible in the conditionality of what conditions it, in that which in turn defines the categorial apparatus it is to be defined by, according to the subjectivist pattern. The categorial attributes without which there is no objectivity as yet, according to Kant, are posited also, and thus, if you will, they are really "merely subjective." The *reductio ad hominem* thus becomes the downfall of anthropocentrism. That even man as a *constituens* is man-made – this disenchants the creativity of the mind. But since primacy of the object requires reflection on the subject and subjective reflection, subjectivity – as distinct from primitive materialism, which really does not permit dialectics – becomes a moment that lasts.

Ever since the Copernican turn, what goes by the name of phenomenalism – that nothing is known save by a knowing subject – has joined with the cult of the mind. Insight into the primacy of the object revolutionizes both. What Hegel intended to place within subjective brackets has the critical consequence of shattering them. The general assurance that innervations, insights, cognitions are "merely subjective" ceases to convince as soon as subjectivity is grasped as the object's form. Phenomenality is the subject's magical transformation into the ground of its own definition, its positing as true being. The subject itself is to be brought to objectivity; its stirrings are not to be banished from cognition.

But the illusion of phenomenalism is a necessary one. It attests to the all but irresistibly blinding context which the subject produces as a false consciousness, and whose member it is at the same time. Such irresistibility is the foundation of the ideology of the subject. Awareness of a defect – of the limits of knowledge – becomes a virtue, so as to make the defect more bearable. A collective narcissism was at work. But it could not have prevailed with such stringency, could not have brought forth the most potent philosophies, if the fundament had not contained a kernel, albeit a distorted one, of truth.

What transcendentalism praised in creative subjectivity is the subject's unconscious imprisonment in itself. Its every objective thought leaves the subject
harnessed like an armored beast in the shell it tries in vain to shed; the only
difference is that to such animals it did not occur to brag of their captivity
as freedom.

We may well ask why human beings did so. Their mental imprisonment
is exceedingly real. That as cognitive beings they depend on space, on time,
on thought forms, marks their dependence on the species. Those constituents
were its precipitation; they are no less valid for that reason. The a priori and
society are intertwined. The universality and necessity of those forms, their
Kantian glory, is none other than that which unites mankind. It needed them
to survive. Captivity was internalized; the individual is no less imprisoned in
himself than in the universal, in society. Hence the interest in the reinter-
pretation of captivity as freedom. The categorial captivity of individual consciousness repeats the real captivity of every individual.

The very glance that allows consciousness to see through that captivity is
determined by the forms it has implanted in the individual. Their imprisonment in themselves might make people realize their social imprisonment; pre-
venting this realization was and is a capital interest of the status quo. It was
for the sake of the status quo, something hardly less necessary than the forms
themselves, that philosophy was bound to lose its way. Idealism was that ideological even before starting to glorify the world as an absolute idea. The
primal compensation already includes the notion that reality, exalted into a
product of the supposedly free subject, would vindicate itself as free.

Identitarian thought, the covering image of the prevailing dichotomy, has
ceased in our era of subjective impotence to pose as absolutization of the
subject. What is taking shape instead is the type of seemingly antisubjectivist,
scientifically objective identitarian thought known as reductionism. (The early
Russell used to be called a "neo-realist.") It is at present the characteristic
form of the reified consciousness — false, because of its latent and thus much
more fatal subjectivism. The residue is made to the measure of the ordering
principles of subjective reason, and being abstract itself, it agrees with the
abstractness of that reason. The reified consciousness that mistakes itself for
nature is naive: having evolved, and being very much mediated in itself, it
takes itself — to speak in Husserl's terms — for a "sphere of Being of absolute
origins" and the Other it has equipped for the desired matter. The ideal of
depersonalizing knowledge for objectivity's sake keeps nothing but the *caput
mortuum* of objectivity.

Once we concede the object's dialectical primacy, the hypothesis of an
unreflected practical science of the object as residual after deducting the

subject will collapse. The subject is then no longer a deductible addendum to objectivity. By the elimination of one of its essential elements, objectivity is falsified, not purified. And indeed, the notion that guides objectivity's residual concept has its primal image in something posited and man-made – by no means in the idea of that in-itself for which it substitutes the cleansed object. It is the model of profit, rather, that stays on the balance sheet after all costs of production have been subtracted. Profit, however, is the subjective interest, limited and reduced to the form of calculation. What counts for the sober realism of profit thinking is anything but "the matter"; the matter is submerged in the yield. But cognition would have to be guided by what exchange has not maimed, or – for nothing is left unmaimed – by what the exchange processes are hiding. The object is no more a subjectless residuum than what the subject posits. The two contradictory definitions fit into each other: the residue, with which science can be put off as its truth, is the product of their subjectively organized manipulative procedures.

Defining what the object is would in turn be part of such arrangements. The only way to make out objectivity is to reflect, at each historic and each cognitive step, on what is then presented as subject and object, as well as on the mediations. In that sense, the object is indeed "infinitely given," as Neo-Kantianism taught. At times, the subject as unlimited experience will come closer to the object than the filtered residuum shaped to fit the requirements of subjective reason. According to its present polemical value in the philosophy of history, unreduced subjectivity can function more objectively than objectivistic reductions. Not the least respect in which all knowledge under the spell has been hexed is that traditional epistemological theses put the case upside down: Fair is foul, and foul is fair. The objective content of individual experience is not produced by the method of comparative generalization; it is produced by dissolving what keeps that experience, as being biased itself, from yielding to the object without reservations – as Hegel put it: with the freedom that would relax the cognitive subject until it truly fades into the object to which it is akin, on the strength of its own objective being.

The subject's key position in cognition is empirical, not formal; what Kant calls formation is essentially deformation. The preponderant exertion of knowledge is destruction of its usual exertion, that of using violence against the object. Approaching knowledge of the object is the act in which the subject rends the veil it is weaving around the object. It can do this only where, fearlessly passive, it entrusts itself to its own experience. In places where subjective reason scents subjective contingency, the primacy of the object is shimmering through – whatever in the object is not a subjective admixture. The subject is the object's agent, not its constituent; this fact has consequences for the relation of theory and practice.

Even after the second reflection of the Copernican turn, there remains some truth in Kant's most questionable theorem: in the distinction between the transcendent thing in itself and the constituted object. For then the object would be the nonidentical, free from the subjective spell and comprehensible through its self-criticism – if it is there at all, if indeed it is not what Kant outlined in his concept of the idea. Such nonidentity would come quite close to Kant's thing in itself, even though he insisted on the vanishing point of its coincidence with the subject. It would not be a relic of a disenchanted *mundus intelligibilis*; rather, it would be more real than the *mundus sensibilis* insofar as Kant's Copernican turn abstracts from that nonidentity and therein finds its barrier.

But then the object, along Kantian lines, is what has been "posited" by the subject, the web of subjective forms cast over the unqualified Something; and finally it is the law that combines the phenomena, disintegrated by their subjective re-relation, into an object. The attributes of necessity and generality that Kant attaches to the emphatic concept of the law have the solidity of things and are impenetrably equal to that social world with which the living collide. It is that law, according to Kant, which the subject prescribes to nature; in his conception, it is the highest peak of objectivity, the perfect expression of the subject as well as of its self-alienation: at the peak of its formative pretension, the subject passes itself off as an object. Paradoxically, however, this is not wrong at all: in fact, the subject is an object as well; it only forgets in its formal hypostasis how and whereby it was constituted. Kant's Copernican turn hits the exact objectification of the subject, the reality of reification. Its truth content is the by no means ontological but historically amassed block between subject and object. The subject erects that block by claiming supremacy over the object and thereby defrauding itself of the object. As truly nonidentical, the object moves the farther from the subject the more the subject "constitutes" the object.

The block on which Kantian philosophy racks its brain is at the same time a product of that philosophy. And yet, due to the *chorismos* of any material, the subject as pure spontaneity and original apperception, seemingly the absolutely dynamic principle, is no less reified than the world of things constituted after the model of natural science. For by that *chorismos* the claimed absolute spontaneity is brought to a halt – in itself, though not for Kant; it is a form supposed to be the form of something, but one which due to its own character cannot interact with any Something. Its abrupt divorcement from the activity of individual subjects, an activity that has to be devalued as contingent–psychological, destroys Kant's inmost principle, original apperception. His apriorism deprives pure action of the very temporality without which simply nothing can be understood by "dynamics." Action recoils into a second-class Being – explicitly, as everyone knows, in the late Fichte's turn away from the 1794 theory of science. Kant codifies such objective ambiguities in the concept of the object, and no theorem about the object has the right to ignore it. Strictly speaking, primacy of the object would mean that there is no object as the subject's abstract opposite, but that as such it seems necessary. The necessity of that illusion ought to be removed.

No more, to be sure, "is there" really a subject. Its hypostasis in idealism leads to absurdities. They may be summarized like this: that the definition of the subject involves what it is posited against – and by no means only because as a *constituens* it presupposes a *constitutum*. The subject itself is an object insofar as existence is implied by the idealist doctrine of constitution – there must be a subject so that it can constitute anything at all – insofar as this had been borrowed in turn, from the sphere of facticity. The concept of what "is there" means nothing but what exists, and the subject as existent comes promptly under the heading of "object." As pure apperception, however, the subject claims to be the downright Other of all existents. This, too, is the negative appearance of a slice of truth: that the reification which the sovereign subject has inflicted on everything, including itself, is mere illusion. The subject moves into the chasm of itself whatever would be exempt from reification – with the absurd result, of course, of thereby issuing a permit for all other reification.

By idealism, the idea of true life is wrongly projected inwards. The subject as productive imagination, as pure apperception, finally as free action, encodes that activity in which human life is really reproduced, and in that activity it logically anticipates freedom. This is why so little of the subject will simply vanish in the object or in anything supposed to be higher, in Being as it may be hypostasized. The self-positing subject is an illusion and at the same time historically very real. It contains the potential of sublating its own rule.

The difference between subject and object cuts through both the subject and the object. It can no more be absolutized than it can be put out of mind. Actually, everything in the subject is chargeable to the object; whatever part of it is not objective will semantically burst the "is." According to its own concept, the pure subjective form of traditional epistemology always exists only as a form of something objective, never without such objectivity; without that, it is not even thinkable. The solidity of the epistemological I, the identity of self-consciousness, is visibly modeled after the unreflected experience of the enduring identical object; even Kant essentially relates it to that experience. He could not have claimed the subjective forms as conditions of objectivity, had he not tacitly granted them an objectivity borrowed from the one to which he opposes the subject. But in the extreme into which subjectivity contracts, from the point of that extreme's synthetic unity, what is combined is always only what goes together anyway. Otherwise, synthesis would be nothing but arbitrary classification. True, without a subjectively performed synthesis, such going together is equally inconceivable. Even the subjective a priori can be called objectively valid only insofar as it has an objective side; without that side the object constituted by the a priori would be a pure tautology for the subject. Finally, due to its being insoluble, given, and extraneous to the subject, the object's content – to Kant, the material for cognition – is also something objective in the subject.

It is accordingly easy to look on the subject as nothing – as was not so very far from Hegel's mind – and on the object as absolute. Yet this is another transcendental illusion. A subject is reduced to nothing by its hypostasis, by making a thing of what is not a thing. It is discredited because it cannot meet the naively realistic innermost criterion of existence. The idealist construction of the subject founders on its confusion with something objective as inherently existent – the very thing it is not; by the standard of the existent, the subject is condemned to nothingness. The subject is the more the less it is, and it is the less the more it credits itself with objective being. As an element, however, it is ineradicable. After an elimination of the subjective moment, the object would come diffusely apart like the fleeting stirrings and instants of subjective life.

The object, though enfeebled, cannot be without a subject either. If the object lacked the moment of subjectivity, its own objectivity would become nonsensical. A flagrant instance is the weakness of Hume's epistemology. It was subjectively directed while believing it might do without a subject. To be judged, then, is the relation between individual and transcendental subject. The individual one is a component of the empirical world, as has, since Kant, been stated in countless variations. But its function, its capacity for experience – which the transcendental subject lacks, for no purely logical construct could have any sort of experience – is in truth far more constitutive than the function ascribed by idealism to the transcendental subject, which is itself a precritical and profoundly hypostasized abstraction from the individual consciousness. Nevertheless, the concept of transcendentality reminds us that thinking, by dint of its immanent moments of universality, transcends its own inalienable individuation. The antithesis of universal and particular, too, is both necessary and deceptive. Neither one exists without the other – the particular only as defined and thus universal; the universal only as the definition of something particular, and thus itself particular. Both of them are and are not. This is one of the strongest motives of nonidealist dialectics.

The subject's reflection upon its own formalism is reflection on society, and results in a paradox: on the one hand, as the late Durkheim intended, the form-giving constitutive elements have social sources, but on the other hand, as current epistemology can boast, they are objectively valid; in Durkheim's argumentations, they are already presumed in every proposition that demonstrates their contingency. The paradox is likely to be at one with the subject's objective imprisonment in itself. The cognitive function, without which there would be neither difference nor unity on the subject's part, had emerged from a source. It consists essentially in those form-givers; as far as there is cognition, it has to be carried out along their lines even where it looks beyond them. They define the concept of cognition. Yet they are not absolute; they have come to be like the cognitive function itself, and their disappearance is not beyond the realm of the possible. To predicate them as absolute would absolutize the cognitive function, the subject; to relativize them would be a dogmatic retraction of the cognitive function.

Against this, we are told that the argument involves a silly sociologism: that God made society and society made man, followed by God in man's image. But the priority thesis is absurd only as long as the individual or its earlier biological form is hypostasized. In the history of evolution, a more likely presumption would be the temporal *prius*, or at least the contemporaneousness of the species. That "the" human being antedated the species is either a Biblical reminiscence or sheer Platonism. Nature on its lower levels teems with unindividuated organisms. If, as more recent biologists claim, humans are actually born so much more ill-equipped than other creatures, it probably was only in association, by rudimentary social toil, that they could stay alive; the *principium individuationis* would be secondary to that, a hypothetical kind of biological division of labor. That any single human should have emerged first, archetypically, is improbable. By the faith in such an emergence, the *principium individuationis*, historically fully developed already, is mythically projected backwards, or onto the firmament of eternal ideas. The species might individuate itself by mutation, in order then, by individuation, to reproduce itself in individuals along lines of biological singularity.

Man is a result, not an *eidos*; the cognitions of Hegel and Marx penetrate to the inmost core of the so-called questions of constitution. The ontology of "the" human being, the model for the construction of the transcendental subject, is oriented towards the evolved individual, as shown linguistically by the ambiguity in the article "the," which in German covers both the individual and the member of the species. Thus nominalism, the opponent of ontology, is far ahead of ontology in featuring the primacy of the species, of society. Society, to be sure, joins with nominalism in a prompt denial of the species (perhaps because it reminds them of animal life) – a denial which ontology performs by raising the individual to the form of unity and to Being-in-itself as opposed to the Many, and nominalism by unreflectingly proclaiming the individual, after the model of the human individual, as true Being. Nominalism denies society in concepts by disparaging it as an abbreviation for individuals.

Part III

Sociology

9

The Concept of Enlightenment

During the period of the Institute of Social Research's location in the United States of America Adorno collaborated with Max Horkheimer to produce *Dialectic of Enlightenment*. It appeared in its first form in 1944 in a privately published edition. The times in which it was written perhaps explain the occasionally febrile quality of the analysis. As exiles, Adorno and Horheimer saw their culture collapse into a coolly administered genocide. But *Dialectic of Enlightenment* is not simply a critique of National Socialism. Rather, Adorno and Horkheimer understand Nazi Germany as the culmination of a kind of irrevocably reductive world view inherent in the very idea of enlightenment, and it is this latter idea that the book examines. The argument is that the emancipatory promise of enlightenment thinking – that it would free human beings from dogmatism – has degenerated to an invariant dogma of its own. Methods used for undermining the occult-filled forces of the old world are applied to all experience. But some experience – such as intellectual reflections on the possibility and future of society – are incompatible with the method. In the end these reflections are dismissed by the supposedly more realistic rationality of the method. Enlightenment, in this way, becomes the other of itself by generating a new unfreedom, a limitation on critical thought. In this respect the development of enlightenment exhibits a dialectical structure: it has manifested its own inner contradiction. That dialectic would lead to a revision of the authority of enlightenment rationality were it not for the inability of individuals to recognize the contradiction. Because of the pervasive false consciousness, enlightenment rationality is mistaken for a natural feature of human thought. Initially a critique of the mythic world, enlightenment calcified, abandoned its critical self-reflection and now assumes the same role once played by myth in ancient societies: it cannot be questioned and, at the same time, it can hardly be justified.

Dialectic of Enlightenment is perhaps the classic critique of so-called instrumental rationality. What is sometimes confusing about the book though is the extension of the term 'enlightenment'. As a term employed during the critique of instrumental rationality, it certainly seems to refer to the great cultural revolution in Europe from the seventeenth century onwards. However, the book also discusses primitive phases (the early steps away from the shaman, for example). The analysis of instrumental rationality in 'The Concept of Enlightenment' falls into a number of closely connected ideas. First, *method* as the presupposition of enlightenment is identified as the means by which quality is reduced to quantity. Experience must conform to the method. In so far as it does not it is supposedly irrational. Second, enlightenment has turned *against nature* in that nature, as a dynamic quality, cannot be accommodated within its system. The result is a world split in two according to what can fit within (e.g. the rational, calculative self) and what must be relegated to without. Third, Adorno and Horkheimer appear to postulate the rather romantic notion of a state of nature lost by the reifications of instrumental rationality. It is in this context that the idea of *mimesis* is employed. *Mimesis* represents the ideal relation between human beings and their environment, a relationship of reciprocity in which neither side loses its identity, whilst at the same time each finds its identity only through its relation with the other. *Mimesis* serves as a regulative idea in the critique of enlightenment rationality. It is, in effect, utopian, positing an ideal against which current arrangements can be assessed. As such, *mimesis* is not given any positive theoretical justification. Fourth, enlightenment, contrary to its original ideals, has assumed a power in the *control of knowledge* in that certain questions are excluded in advance by the methodology which identifies itself with rationality.

'The Concept of Enlightenment', *Dialectic of Enlightenment* [1947] (London: Verso, 1979), pp. 3–32 (abridged). Translated by John Cumming.

In the most general sense of progressive thought, the Enlightenment has always aimed at liberating men from fear and establishing their sovereignty. Yet the fully enlightened earth radiates disaster triumphant. The program of the Enlightenment was the disenchantment of the world; the dissolution of myths and the substitution of knowledge for fancy. Bacon, the "father of experimental philosophy,"[1] had defined its motives. He looked down on the masters of tradition, the "great reputed authors" who first "believe that others know that which they know not; and after themselves know that which they know not. But indeed facility to believe, impatience to doubt, temerity to answer, glory to know, doubt to contradict, end to gain, sloth to search, seeking things in words, resting in part of nature; these and the like have been the things which have forbidden the happy match between the mind of man and the nature of things; and in place thereof have married it to vain notions and blind experiments: and what the posterity and issue of so honorable a match may be, it is not hard to consider. Printing, a gross invention; artillery, a thing that lay not far out of the way; the needle, a thing partly known before: what a change have these three things made in the world in these times; the one in the state of learning, the other in the state of war, the third in the state of treasure, commodities, and navigation! And those, I say, were but stumbled upon and lighted upon by chance. Therefore, no doubt, the sovereignty of man lieth hid in knowledge; wherein many things are reserved, which kings with their treasure cannot buy, nor with their force command; their spials and intelligencers can give no news of them, their seamen and discoverers cannot sail where they grow: now we govern nature in opinions, but we are thrall unto her in necessity: but if we would be led by her in invention, we should command her by action."[2]

Despite his lack of mathematics, Bacon's view was appropriate to the scientific attitude that prevailed after him. The concordance between the mind of man and the nature of things that he had in mind is patriarchal: the human mind, which overcomes superstition, is to hold sway over a disenchanted nature. Knowledge, which is power, knows no obstacles: neither in the enslavement of men nor in compliance with the world's rulers. As with all the ends of bourgeois economy in the factory and on the battlefield, origin is no bar to the dictates of the entrepreneurs: kings, no less directly than businessmen, control technology; it is as democratic as the economic system with which it is bound up. Technology is the essence of this knowledge. It does not work by concepts and images, by the fortunate insight, but refers to method, the exploitation of others' work, and capital. The "many things" which, according to Bacon, "are reserved," are themselves no more than instrumental: the radio as a sublimated printing press, the dive bomber as a more effective form of artillery, radio control as a more reliable compass. What men want to learn from nature is how to use it in order wholly to dominate it and other men. That is the only aim. Ruthlessly, in despite of itself, the Enlightenment has extinguished any trace of its own self-consciousness. The only kind of thinking that is sufficiently hard to shatter myths is ultimately self-destructive. In face of the present triumph of the factual mentality, even Bacon's nominalist credo would be suspected of a metaphysical bias and come under the same verdict of vanity that he pronounced on scholastic philosophy. Power and knowledge are synonymous.[3] For Bacon as for Luther, "knowledge that tendeth but to satisfaction, is but as a courtesan, which is for pleasure, and not for fruit or generation." Not "satisfaction, which men call truth," but "operation," "to do the business," is the "right mark": for ". . . what is the true end, scope, or office of knowledge, which I have set down to consist not in any plausible, delectable, reverend or admired discourse, or any satisfactory arguments, but in effecting and working, and in discovery of particulars not revealed before, for the better endowment and help of man's life."[4] There is to be no mystery – which means, too, no wish to reveal mystery.

The disenchantment of the world is the extirpation of animism. Xenophanes derides the multitude of deities because they are but replicas of the men who produced them, together with all that is contingent and evil in mankind; and the most recent school of logic denounces – for the impressions they bear – the words of language, holding them to be false coins better replaced by neutral counters. The world becomes chaos, and synthesis salvation. There is said to be no difference between the totemic animal, the dreams of the ghost-seer, and the absolute Idea. On the road to modern science, men renounce any claim to meaning. They substitute formula for concept, rule and probability for cause and motive. Cause was only the last philosophic concept which served as a yardstick for scientific criticism: so to speak because it alone among the old ideas still seemed to offer itself to scientific criticism, the latest secularization of the creative principle. Substance and quality, activity and suffering, being and existence: to define these concepts in a way appropriate to the times was a concern of philosophy after Bacon – but science managed without such categories. They were abandoned as *idola theatri* of the old metaphysics, and assessed as being even then memorials of the elements and powers of the prehistory for which life and death disclosed their nature in myths and became interwoven in them. The categories by which Western philosophy defined its everlasting natural order marked the spots once occupied by Oncus and Persephone, Ariadne and Nereus. The pre-Socratic cosmologies preserve the moment of transition. The moist, the indivisible, air, and fire, which they hold to be the primal matter of nature, are already rationalizations of the mythic mode of apprehension. Just as the images of generation from water and earth, which came from the Nile to the Greeks, became here hylozoistic principles, or elements, so all the equivocal multitude of mythical demons were intellectualized in the pure form of ontological essences. Finally, by means of the Platonic ideas, even the patriarchal gods of Olympus were absorbed in the philosophical *logos*. The Enlightenment, however, recognized the old powers in the Platonic and Aristotelian aspects of metaphysics, and opposed as superstition the claim that truth is predicable of universals. It asserted that in the authority of universal concepts, there was still discernible fear of the demonic spirits which men sought to portray in magic rituals, hoping thus to influence nature. From now on, matter would at last be mastered without any illusion of ruling or inherent powers, of hidden qualities. For the Enlightenment, whatever does not conform to the rule of computation and utility is suspect. So long as it can develop undisturbed by any outward repression, there is no holding it. In the process, it treats its own ideas of human rights exactly as it does the older universals. Every spiritual resistance it encounters serves merely to increase its strength.[5] Which means that enlightenment still recognizes itself even in myths. Whatever myths the resistance may appeal to, by virtue of the very fact that they become arguments in the process of opposition, they acknowledge the principle of dissolvent rationality for which they reproach the Enlightenment. Enlightenment is totalitarian.

Enlightenment has always taken the basic principle of myth to be anthropomorphism, the projection onto nature of the subjective.[6] In this view, the supernatural, spirits and demons, are mirror images of men who allow themselves to be frightened by natural phenomena. Consequently the many mythic figures can all be brought to a common denominator, and reduced to the human subject. Oedipus' answer to the Sphinx's riddle: "It is man!" is the Enlightenment stereotype repeatedly offered as information, irrespective of whether it is faced with a piece of objective intelligence, a bare schematization, fear of evil powers, or hope of redemption. In advance, the Enlightenment recognizes as being and occurrence only what can be apprehended in unity: its ideal is the system from which all and everything follows. Its rationalist and empiricist versions do not part company on that point. Even though the individual schools may interpret the axioms differently, the structure of scientific unity has always been the same. Bacon's postulate of *una scientia universalis*,[7] whatever the number of fields of research, is as inimical to the unassignable as Leibniz's *mathesis universalis* is to discontinuity. The multiplicity of forms is reduced to position and arrangement, history to fact, things to matter. According to Bacon, too, degrees of universality provide an unequivocal logical connection between first principles and observational judgments. De Maistre mocks him for harboring "*une idole d'échelle*."[8] Formal logic was the major school of unified science. It provided the Enlightenment thinkers with the schema of the calculability of the world. The mythologizing equation of Ideas with numbers in Plato's last writings expresses the longing of all demythologization: number became the canon of the Enlightenment. The same equations dominate bourgeois justice and commodity exchange. "Is not the rule, '*Si inaequalibus aequalia addas, omnia erunt inaequalia*,' an axiom of justice as well as of the mathematics? And is there not a true coincidence between commutative and distributive justice, and arithmetical and geometrical proportion?"[9] Bourgeois society is ruled by equivalence. It makes the dissimilar comparable by reducing it to abstract quantities. To the Enlightenment, that which does not reduce to numbers, and ultimately to the one, becomes illusion; modern positivism writes it off as literature. Unity is the slogan from Parmenides to Russell. The destruction of gods and qualities alike is insisted upon.

Yet the myths which fell victim to the Enlightenment were its own products. In the scientific calculation of occurrence, the computation is annulled which thought had once transferred from occurrence into myths. Myth intended report, naming, the narration of the Beginning; but also presentation, confirmation, explanation: a tendency that grew stronger with the recording and collection of myths. Narrative became didactic at an early stage. Every ritual includes the idea of activity as a determined process which magic can nevertheless influence. This theoretical element in ritual won independence in the earliest national epics. The myths, as the tragedians came upon them, are already characterized by the discipline and power that Bacon celebrated as the "right mark." In place of the local spirits and demons there appeared heaven and its hierarchy; in place of the invocations of the magician and the tribe the distinct gradation of sacrifice and the labor of the unfree mediated through the word of command. The Olympic deities are no longer directly identical with elements, but signify them. In Homer, Zeus represents the sky and the weather, Apollo controls the sun, and Helios and Eos are already shifting to an allegorical function. The gods are distinguished from material elements as their quintessential concepts. From now on, being divides into the *logos* (which with the progress of philosophy contracts to the monad, to a mere point of reference), and into the mass of all things and creatures without. This single distinction between existence proper and reality engulfs all others. Without regard to distinctions, the world becomes subject to man. In this the Jewish creation narrative and the religion of Olympia are at one: ". . . and let them have dominion over the fish of the sea, and over the fowl of the air, and over the cattle, and over all the earth, and over every creeping thing that creepeth upon the earth."[10] "O Zeus, Father Zeus, yours is the dominion of the heavens, and you oversee the works of man, both wicked and just, and even the wantonness of the beasts; and righteousness is your concern."[11] "For so it is that one atones straightaway, and another later; but should one escape and the threatening decree of the gods not reach him, yet it will certainly be visited at last, if not upon him then upon his children or another generation."[12] Only he who always submits survives in the face of the gods. The awakening of the self is paid for by the acknowledgement of power as the principle of all relations. In view of the unity of this *ratio*, the divorcement between God and man dwindles to the degree of irrelevancy to which unswervable reason has drawn attention since even the earliest critique of Homer. The creative god and the systematic spirit are alike as rulers of nature. Man's likeness to God consists in sovereignty over existence, in the countenance of the lord and master, and in command.

Myth turns into enlightenment, and nature into mere objectivity. Men pay for the increase of their power with alienation from that over which they exercise their power. Enlightenment behaves toward things as a dictator toward men. He knows them in so far as he can manipulate them. The man of science knows things in so far as he can make them. In this way their potentiality is turned to his own ends. In the metamorphosis the nature of things, as a substratum of domination, is revealed as always the same. This identity constitutes the unity of nature. It is a presupposition of the magical invocation as little as the unity of the subject. The shaman's rites were directed to the wind, the rain, the serpent without, or the demon in the sick man, but not to materials or specimens. Magic was not ordered by one, identical spirit: it changed like the cultic masks which were supposed to accord with the various spirits. Magic is utterly untrue, yet in it domination is not yet negated by transforming itself into the pure truth and acting as the very ground of the world that has become subject to it. The magician imitates demons; in order to frighten them or to appease them, he behaves frighteningly or makes gestures of appeasement. Even though his task is impersonation, he never conceives of himself as does the civilized man for whom the unpretentious preserves of the happy hunting-grounds become the unified cosmos, the inclusive concept for all possibilities of plunder. The magician never interprets himself as the image of the invisible power; yet this is the very image in which man attains to the identity of self that cannot disappear through identification with another, but takes possession of itself once and for all as an impenetrable mask. It is the identity of the spirit and its correlate, the unity of nature, to which the multiplicity of qualities falls victim. Disqualified nature becomes the chaotic matter of mere classification, and the all-powerful self becomes mere possession – abstract identity. In magic there is specific representation. What happens to the enemy's spear, hair or name, also happens to the individual; the sacrificial animal is massacred instead of the god. Substitution in the course of sacrifice marks a step toward discursive logic. Even though the hind offered up for the daughter, and the lamb for the first-born, still had to have specific qualities, they already represented the species. They already exhibited the non-specificity of the example. But the holiness of the *hic et nunc*, the uniqueness of the chosen one into which the representative enters, radically marks it off, and makes it unfit for exchange. Science prepares the end of this state of affairs. In science there is no specific representation: and if there are no sacrificial animals there is no god. Representation is exchanged for the fungible – universal interchange-ability. An atom is smashed not in representation but as a specimen of matter, and the rabbit does not represent but, as a mere example, is virtually ignored by the zeal of the laboratory. Because the distinctions in functional science are so fluid that everything is subsumed in the same matter, the scientific object is petrified, and the fixed ritual of former times appears flexible because it attributed the other to the one. The world of magic retained distinctions whose traces have disappeared even in linguistic form.[13] The multitudinous affinities between existents are suppressed by the single rela-tion between the subject who bestows meaning and the meaningless object, between rational significance and the chance vehicle of significance. On the magical plane, dream and image were not mere signs for the thing in question, but were bound up with it by similarity or names. The relation is one not of intention but of relatedness. Like science, magic pursues aims, but seeks to achieve them by mimesis – not by progressively distancing itself from the object. It is not grounded in the "sovereignty of ideas," which the primitive, like the neurotic, is said to ascribe to himself;[14] there can be no "over-evaluation of mental processes as against reality" where there is no radical distinction between thoughts and reality. The "unshakable confidence in the possibility of world domination,"[15] which Freud anachronistically ascribes to magic, corresponds to realistic world domination only in terms of a more skilled science. The replacement of the milieu-bound practices of the medicine man by all-inclusive industrial technology required first of all the autonomy of ideas in regard to objects that was achieved in the reality-adjusted ego.

As a linguistically expressed totality, whose claim to truth suppresses the older mythic belief, the national religion or patriarchal solar myth is itself an Enlightenment with which the philosophic form can compare itself on the same level. And now it has its requital. Mythology itself set off the unending process of enlightenment in which ever and again, with the inevitability of necessity, every specific theoretic view succumbs to the destructive criticism that it is only a belief – until even the very notions of spirit, of truth and, indeed, enlightenment itself, have become animistic magic. The principle of fatal necessity, which brings low the heroes of myth and derives as a logical consequence from the pronouncement of the oracle, does not merely, when refined to the stringency of formal logic, rule in every rationalistic system of Western philosophy, but itself dominates the series of systems which begins with the hierarchy of the gods and, in a permanent twilight of the idols, hands down an identical content: anger against insufficient righteousness. Just as the myths already realize enlightenment, so enlightenment with every step becomes more deeply engulfed in mythology. It receives all its matter from the myths, in order to destroy them; and even as a judge it comes under the mythic curse. It wishes to extricate itself from the process of fate and retribution, while exercising retribution on that process. In the myths everything that happens must atone for having happened. And so it is in enlightenment: the fact becomes null and void, and might as well not have happened. The doctrine of the equivalence of action and reaction asserted the power of repetition over reality, long after men had renounced the illusion that by repetition they could identify themselves with the repeated reality and thus escape its power. But as the magical illusion fades away, the more relentlessly in the name of law repetition imprisons man in the cycle – that cycle whose objectification in the form of natural law he imagines will ensure his action as a free subject. The principle of immanence, the explanation of every event as repetition, that the Enlightenment upholds against mythic imagination, is the principle of myth itself. That arid wisdom that holds there is nothing new under the sun, because all the pieces in the meaningless game have been played, and all the great thoughts have already been thought, and because all possible discoveries can be construed in advance and all men are decided on adaptation as the means to self-preservation – that dry sagacity merely reproduces the fantastic wisdom that it supposedly rejects: the sanction of fate that in retribution relentlessly remakes what has already been. What was different is equalized. That is the verdict which critically determines the limits of possible experience. The identity of everything with everything else is paid for in that nothing may at the same time be identical with itself. Enlightenment dissolves the injustice of the old inequality – unmediated lordship and mastery – but at the same time perpetuates it in universal mediation, in the relation of any one existent to any other. It does what Kierkegaard praises his Protestant ethic for, and what in the Heraclean epic cycle is one of the primal images of mythic power; it excises the incommensurable. Not only are qualities dissolved in thought, but men are brought to actual conformity. The blessing that the market does not enquire after one's birth is paid for by the barterer, in that he models the potentialities that are his by birth on the production of the commodities that can be bought in the market. Men were given their individuality as unique in each case, different to all others, so that it might all the more surely be made the same as any other. But because the unique self never wholly disappeared, even after the liberalistic epoch, the Enlightenment has always sympathized with the social impulse. The unity of the manipulated collective consists in the negation of each individual: for individuality makes a mockery of the kind of society which would turn all individuals to the one collectivity. The horde which so assuredly appears in the organization of the Hitler Youth is not a return to barbarism but the triumph of repressive equality, the disclosure through peers of the parity of the right to injustice. The phony Fascist mythology is shown to be the genuine myth of antiquity, insofar as the genuine one saw retribution, whereas the false one blindly doles it out to the sacrifices. Every attempt to break the natural thralldom, because nature is broken, enters all the more deeply into that natural enslavement. Hence the course of European civilization. Abstraction, the tool of enlightenment, treats its objects as did fate, the notion of which it rejects: it liquidates them. Under the leveling domination of abstraction (which makes everything in nature repeatable), and of industry (for which abstraction ordains repetition), the freed themselves finally came to form that "herd" (*Trupp*) which Hegel[16] has declared to be the result of the Enlightenment.

The distance between subject and object, a presupposition of abstraction, is grounded in the distance from the thing itself which the master achieved through the mastered. The lyrics of Homer and the hymns of the Rig-Veda date from the time of territorial dominion and the secure locations in which a dominant warlike race established themselves over the mass of vanquished natives.[17] The first god among the gods arose with this civil society in which the king, as chieftain of the arms-bearing nobility, holds down the conquered to the earth, whereas physicians, soothsayers, craftsmen and merchants see to social intercourse. With the end of a nomadic existence, the social order is created on a basis of fixed property. Mastery and labor are divided. A proprietor like Odysseus "manages from a distance a numerous, carefully gradated staff of cowherds, shepherds, swineherds and servants. In the evening, when he has seen from his castle that the countryside is illumined by a thousand fires, he can compose himself for sleep with a quiet mind: he knows that his upright servants are keeping watch lest wild animals approach, and to chase thieves from the preserves which they are there to protect."[18] The universality of ideas as developed by discursive logic, domination in the conceptual sphere, is raised up on the basis of actual domination. The dissolution of the magical heritage, of the old diffuse ideas, by conceptual unity, expresses the hierarchical constitution of life determined by those who are free. The individuality that learned order and subordination in the subjection of the world, soon wholly equated truth with the regulative thought without whose fixed distinctions universal truth cannot exist. Together with mimetic magic, it tabooed the knowledge which really concerned the object. Its hatred was extended to the image of the vanquished former age and its imaginary happiness. The chthonic gods of the original inhabitants are banished to the hell to which, according to the sun and light religion of Indra and Zeus, the earth is transformed.

Heaven and hell, however, hang together. Just as the name of Zeus, in non-exclusive cults, was given to a god of the underworld as well as to a god of light;[19] just as the Olympian gods had every kind of commerce with the chthonic deities: so the good and evil powers, salvation and disaster, were not unequivocally distinct. They were linked together like coming up and passing away, life and death, summer and winter. The gloomy and indistinct religious principle that was honored as *mana* in the earliest known stages of humanity, lives on in the radiant world of Greek religion. Everything unknown and alien is primary and undifferentiated: that which transcends the confines of experience; whatever in things is more than their previously known reality. What the primitive experiences in this regard is not a spiritual as opposed to a material substance, but the intricacy of the Natural in contrast to the individual. The gasp of surprise which accompanies the experience of the unusual becomes its name. It fixes the transcendence of the unknown in relation to the known, and therefore terror as sacredness. The dualization of nature as appearance and sequence, effort and power, which first makes possible both myth and science, originates in human fear, the expression of which becomes explanation. It is not the soul which is transposed to nature, as psychologism would have it; *mana*, the moving spirit, is no projection, but the echo of the real supremacy of nature in the weak souls of primitive men. The separation of the animate and the inanimate, the occupation of certain places by demons and deities, first arises from this preanimism, which contains the first lines of the separation of subject and object. When the tree is no longer approached merely as tree, but as evidence for an Other, as the location of *mana*, language expresses the contradiction that something is itself and at one and the same time something other than itself, identical and not identical.[20] Through the deity, language is transformed from tautology to language. The concept, which some would see as the sign-unit for whatever is comprised under it, has from the beginning been instead the product of dialectical thinking in which everything is always that which it is, only because it becomes that which it is not. That was the original form of objectifying definition, in which concept and thing are separated. The same form which is already far advanced in the Homeric epic and confounds itself in modern positivist science. But this dialectic remains impotent to the extent that it develops from the cry of terror which is the duplication, the tautology, of terror itself. The gods cannot take fear away from man, for they bear its petrified sound with them as they bear their names. Man imagines himself free from fear when there is no longer anything unknown. That determines the course of demythologization, of enlightenment, which compounds the animate with the inanimate just as myth compounds the inanimate with the animate. Enlightenment is mythic fear turned radical. The pure immanence of positivism, its ultimate product, is no more than a so to speak universal taboo. Nothing at all may remain outside, because the mere idea of outsideness is the very source of fear. The revenge of the primitive for death, when visited upon one of his kin, was sometimes appeased by reception of the murderer into his own family;[21] this, too, signified the infusion of alien blood into one's own, the generation of immanence. The mythic dualism does not extend beyond the environs of existence. The world permeated by *mana* and even the world of Indian and Greek myth know no exits, and are eternally the same. Every birth is paid for with death, every fortune with misfortune. Men and gods may try in their short space to assess fate in other terms than the blind course of destiny, but in the end existence triumphs over them. Even their justice, which is wrested from fatality, bears the marks of fatality: it corresponds to the look which men – primitives, Greeks and barbarians alike – cast from a society of pressure and misery on the circumambient world. Hence, for mythic and enlightened justice, guilt and atonement, happiness and unhappiness were sides of an equation. Justice is subsumed in law. The shaman wards off danger by means of its image. Equivalence is his instrument; and equivalence regulates punishment and reward in civilization. The mythic representations can also be traced back in their entirety to natural conditions. Just as the Gemini – the constellation of Castor and Pollux – and all other symbols of duality refer to the inevitable cycle of nature, which itself has its ancient sign in the symbol of the egg from which they came, so the balance held by Zeus, which symbolizes the justice of the entire patriarchal world, refers back to mere nature. The step from chaos to civilization, in which natural conditions exert their power no longer directly but through the medium of the human consciousness, has not changed the principle of equivalence. Indeed, men paid for this very step by worshipping what they were once in thrall to only in the same way as all other creatures. Before, the fetishes were subject to the law of equivalence. Now equivalence itself has become a fetish. The blindfold over Justitia's eyes does not only mean that there should be no assault upon justice, but that justice does not originate in freedom. [. . .]

For enlightenment is as totalitarian as any system. Its untruth does not consist in what its romantic enemies have always reproached it for: analytical method, return to elements, dissolution through reflective thought; but instead in the fact that for enlightenment the process is always decided from the start. When in mathematical procedure the unknown becomes the unknown quantity of an equation, this marks it as the well-known even before any value is inserted. Nature, before and after the quantum theory, is that which is to be comprehended mathematically; even what cannot be made to agree, indissolubility and irrationality, is converted by means of mathematical theorems. In the anticipatory indentification of the wholly conceived and mathematized world with truth, enlightenment intends to secure itself against the return of the mythic. It confounds thought and mathematics. In this way the latter is, so to speak, released and made into an absolute instance. "An infinite world, in this case a world of idealities, is conceived as one whose objects do not accede singly, imperfectly, and as if by chance to our cognition, but are attained by a rational, systematically unified method – in a process of infinite progression – so that each object is ultimately apparent according to its full inherent being . . . In the Galilean mathematization of the world, however, *his selfness* is idealized under the guidance of the new mathematics: in modern terms, it becomes itself a mathematical multiplicity."[22] Thinking objectifies itself to become an automatic, self-activating process; an impersonation of the machine that it produces itself so that ultimately the machine can replace it. Enlightennment[23] has put aside the classic requirement of thinking about thought – Fichte is its extreme manifestation – because it wants to avoid the precept of dictating practice that Fichte himself wished to obey. Mathematical procedure became, so to speak, the ritual of thinking. In spite of the axiomatic self-restriction, it establishes itself as necessary and objective: it turns thought into a thing, an instrument – which is its own term for it. But this kind of mimesis, in which universal thought is equalized, so turns the actual into the unique, that even atheism itself is subjected to the ban on metaphysics. For positivism, which represents the court of judgment of enlightened reason, to digress into intelligible worlds is no longer merely forbidden, but meaningless prattle. It does not need – fortunately – to be atheistic, because objectified thinking cannot even raise the problem. The positivist censor lets the established cult escape as willingly as art – as a cognition-free special area of social activity; but he will never permit that denial of it which itself claims to be knowledge. For the scientific mind, the separation of thought from business for the purpose of adjusting actuality, departure from the privileged area of real existence, is as insane and self-destructive as the primitive magician would consider stepping out of the magic circle he has prepared for his invocation; in both cases the offense against the taboo will actually result in the malefactor's ruin. The mastery of nature draws the circle into which the criticism of pure reason banished thought. Kant joined the theory of its unceasingly laborious advance into infinity with an insistence on its deficiency and everlasting limitation. His judgment is an oracle. There is no form of being in the world that science could not penetrate, but what can be penetrated by science is not being. According to Kant, philosophic judgment aims at the new; and yet it recognizes nothing new, since it always merely recalls what reason has always deposited in the object. But there is a reckoning for this form of thinking that considers itself secure in the various departments of science – secure from the dreams of a ghost-seer: world domination over nature turns against the thinking subject himself; nothing is left of him but that eternally same *I think* that must accompany all my ideas. Subject and object are both rendered ineffectual. The abstract self, which justifies record-making and systematization, has nothing set over against it but the abstract material which possesses no other quality than to be a substrate of such possession. The equation of spirit and world arises eventually, but only with a mutual restriction of both sides. The reduction of thought to a mathematical apparatus conceals the sanction of the world as its own yardstick. What appears to be the triumph of subjective rationality, the subjection of all reality to logical formalism, is paid for by the obedient subjection of reason to what is directly given. What is abandoned is the whole claim and approach of knowledge: to comprehend the given as such; not merely to determine the abstract spatio-temporal relations of the facts which allow them just to be grasped, but on the contrary to conceive them as the superficies, as mediated conceptual moments which come to fulfillment only in the development of their social, historical, and human significance. The task of cognition does not consist in mere apprehension, classification, and calculation, but in the determinate negation of each immediacy. Mathematical formalism, however, whose medium is number, the most abstract form of the immediate, instead holds thinking firmly to mere immediacy. Factuality wins the day; cognition is restricted to its repetition; and thought becomes mere tautology. The more the machinery of thought subjects existence to itself, the more blind its resignation in reproducing existence. Hence enlightenment returns to mythology, which it never really knew how to elude. For in its figures mythology had the essence of the *status quo*: cycle, fate, and domination of the world reflected as the truth and deprived of hope. In both the pregnancy of the mythical image and the clarity of the scientific formula, the everlastingness of the factual is confirmed and mere existence pure and simple expressed as the meaning which it forbids. The world as a gigantic analytic judgment, the only one left over from all the dreams of science, is of the same mold as the cosmic myth which associated the cycle of spring and autumn with the kidnapping of Persephone. The uniqueness of the mythic process, which tends to legitimize factuality, is deception. Originally the carrying off of the goddess was directly synonymous with the dying of nature. It repeated itself every autumn, and even the repetition was not the result of the buried one but the same every time. With the rigidification of the consciousness of time, the process was fixed in the past as a unique one, and in each new cycle of the seasons an attempt was made ritually to appease fear of death by recourse to what was long past. But the separation is ineffective.

Through the establishment of a unique past, the cycle takes on the character of inevitability, and dread radiates from the age-old occurrence to make every event its mere repetition. The absorption of factuality, whether into legendary prehistory or into mathematical formalism, the symbolical relation of the contemporary to the mythic process in the rite or to the abstract category in science, makes the new appear as the predetermined, which is accordingly the old. Not existence but knowledge is without hope, for in the pictorical or mathematical symbol it appropriates and perpetuates existence as a schema.

In the enlightened world, mythology has entered into the profane. In its blank purity, the reality which has been cleansed of demons and their conceptual descendants assumes the numinous character which the ancient world attributed to demons. Under the title of brute facts, the social injustice from which they proceed is now as assuredly sacred a preserve as the medicine man was sacrosanct by reason of the protection of his gods. It is not merely that domination is paid for by the alienation of men from the objects dominated: with the objectification of spirit, the very relations of men — even those of the individual to himself — were bewitched. The individual is reduced to the nodal point of the conventional responses and modes of operation expected of him. Animism spiritualized the object, whereas industrialism objectifies the spirits of men. Automatically, the economic apparatus, even before total planning, equips commodities with the values which decide human behavior. Since, with the end of free exchange, commodities lost all their economic qualities except for fetishism, the latter has extended its arthritic influence over all aspects of social life. Through the countless agencies of mass production and its culture the conventionalized modes of behavior are impressed on the individual as the only natural, respectable, and rational ones. He defines himself only as a thing, as a static element, as success or failure. His yardstick is self-preservation, successful or unsuccessful approximation to the objectivity of his function and the models established for it. Everything else, idea and crime, suffers the force of the collective, which monitors it from the classroom to the trade union. But even the threatening collective belongs only to the deceptive surface, beneath which are concealed the powers which manipulate it as the instrument of power. Its brutality, which keeps the individual up to scratch, represents the true quality of men as little as value represents the things which he consumes. The demonically distorted form which things and men have assumed in the light of unprejudiced cognition, indicates domination, the principle which effected the specification of *mana* in spirits and gods and occurred in the jugglery of magicians and medicine men. The fatality by means of which prehistory sanctioned the incomprehensibility of death is transferred to wholly comprehensible real existence. The noontide panic fear in which men suddenly became aware of nature as totality has found its like in the panic which nowadays is ready to break out at every moment: men expect that the world, which is without any issue, will be set on fire by a totality which they themselves are and over which they have no control.

The mythic terror feared by the Enlightenment accords with myth. Enlightenment discerns it not merely in unclarified concepts and words, as demonstrated by semantic language-criticism, but in any human assertion that has no place in the ultimate context of self-preservation. Spinoza's "*Conatus sese conservandi primum et unicum virtutis est fundamentum*"[24] contains the true maxim of all Western civilization, in which the religious and philosophical differences of the middle class are reconciled. The self (which, according to the methodical extirpation of all natural residues because they are mytho-logical, must no longer be either body or blood, or soul, or even the natural I), once sublimated into the transcendental or logical subject, would form the reference point of reason, of the determinative instance of action. Whoever resigns himself to life without any rational reference to self-preservation would, according to the Enlightenment – and Protestantism – regress to pre-history. Impulse as such is as mythic as superstition; to serve the god not pos-tulated by the self is as idiotic as drunkenness. Progress has prepared the same fate for both adoration and descent into a state of directly natural being, and has anathematized both the self-abandonment of thought and that of plea-sure. The social work of every individual in bourgeois society is mediated through the principle of self; for one, labor will bring an increased return on capital; for others, the energy for extra labor. But the more the process of self-preservation is effected by the bourgeois division of labor, the more it requires the self-alienation of the individuals who must model their body and soul according to the technical apparatus. This again is taken into account by enlightened thought: in the end the transcendental subject of cognition is apparently abandoned as the last reminiscence of subjectivity and replaced by the much smoother work of automatic control mechanisms. Subjectivity has given way to the logic of the allegedly indifferent rules of the game, in order to dictate all the more unrestrainedly. Positivism, which finally did not spare thought itself, the chimera in a cerebral form, has removed the very last insu-lating instance between individual behavior and the social norm. The tech-nical process, into which the subject has objectified itself after being removed from the consciousness, is free of the ambiguity of mythic thought as of all meaning altogether, because reason itself has become the mere instrument of the all-inclusive economic apparatus. It serves as a general tool, useful for the manufacture of all other tools, firmly directed toward its end, as fateful as the precisely calculated movement of material production, whose result for mankind is beyond all calculation. At last its old ambition, to be a pure organ of ends, has been realized. The exclusiveness of logical laws originates in this unique functional significance, and ultimately in the compulsive nature of self-preservation. And self-preservation repeatedly culminates in the choice between survival and destruction, apparent again in the principle that of two contradictory propositions only one can be true and only one false. The formalism of this principle, and of the entire logic in which form it is established, derives from the opacity and complexity of interests in a society in which the maintenance of forms and the preservation of individuals coincide only by chance. The derivation of thought from logic ratifies in the lecture room the reification of man in the factory and the office. In this way the taboo encroaches upon the anathematizing power, and enlightenment upon the spirit which it itself comprises. Then, however, nature as true self-preservation is released by the very process which promised to extirpate it, in the individual as in the collective destiny of crisis and armed conflict. If the only norm that remains for theory is the ideal of unified science, practice must be subjected to the irrepressible process of world history. The self that is wholly comprehended by civilization resolves itself in an element of the inhumanity which from the beginning has aspired to evade civilization. The primordial fear of losing one's own name is realized. For civilization, pure natural existence, animal and vegetative, was the absolute danger. One after the other, mimetic, mythic and metaphysical modes of behavior were taken as superseded eras, any reversion to which was to be feared as implying a reversion of the self to that mere state of nature from which it had estranged itself with so huge an effort, and which therefore struck such terror into the self. In every century, any living reminiscence of olden times, not only of nomadic antiquity but all the more of the pre-patriarchal stages, was most rigorously punished and extirpated from human consciousness. The spirit of enlightenment replaced the fire and the rack by the stigma it attached to all irrationality, because it led to corruption. Hedonism was moderate, finding the extreme no less odious than did Aristotle. The bourgeois ideal of naturalness intends not amorphous nature, but the virtuous mean. Promiscuity and asceticism, excess and hunger, are directly identical, despite the antagonism, as powers of disintegration. By subjecting the whole of life to the demands of its maintenance, the dictatorial minority guarantees, together with its own security, the persistence of the whole. From Homer to modern times, the dominant spirit wishes to steer between the Scylla of a return to mere reproduction and the Charybdis of unfettered fulfillment; it has always mistrusted any star other than that of the lesser evil. The new German pagans and warmongers want to set pleasure free once more. But under the pressure of labor, through the centuries, pleasure has learned self-hatred, and therefore in the state of totalitarian emancipation remains mean and disabled by self-contempt. It remains in the grip of the self-preservation to which it once trained reason – deposed in the meantime. At the turning points of Western civilization, from the transition to Olympian religion up to the Renaissance, Reformation, and bourgeois atheism, whenever new nations and classes more firmly repressed myth, the fear of uncomprehended, threatening nature, the consequence of its very materialization and objectification, was reduced to animistic superstition, and the subjugation of nature was made the absolute purpose of life within and without. If in the end self-preservation has been automated, so reason has been abandoned by those who, as administrators of production, entered upon its inheritance and now fear it in the persons of the disinherited. The essence of enlightenment is the alternative whose ineradicability is that of domination. Men have always had to choose between their subjection to nature or the subjection of nature to the Self. With the extension of the bourgeois commodity economy, the dark horizon of myth is illumined by the sun of calculating reason, beneath whose cold rays the seed of the new barbarism grows to fruition. Under the pressure of domination human labor has always led away from myth – but under domination always returns to the jurisdiction of myth.

Notes

1   Voltaire, *Lettres Philosophiques*, XII, *Œuvres Complètes* (Paris: Garnier, 1879), vol. XXII, p. 118.

2   Bacon, "In Praise of Human Knowledge" (*Miscellaneous Tracts upon Human Knowledge*) *The Works of Francis Bacon*, ed. Basil Montagu (London, 1825), vol. I, pp. 254ff.

3   Cf. Bacon, *Novum Organum, Works*, vol. XIV, p. 31.

4   Bacon, "Valerius Terminus: Of the Interpretation of Nature" (*Miscellaneous Tracts upon Human Knowledge*), *Works*, vol. I, p. 281.

5   Cf. G. W. F. Hegel, *The Phenomenology of Spirit* trans. A. V. Millar (Oxford: O.U.P., 1977), pp. 328ff.

6   Xenophanes, Montaigne, Hume, Feuerbach, and Salomon Reinach are at one here. See, for Reinach: *Orpheus*, trans. F. Simmons (London and New York: Heinemann, 1909), pp. 9ff.

7   Bacon, *De Augmentis Scientiarum, Works*, vol. VIII. p. 152.

8   *Les Soirées de Saint-Pétersbourg* (5ième entretien), *Œuvres Complètes* (Lyon, 1891), vol. IV, p. 256.

9   Bacon, *Advancement of Learning, Works*, vol. II, p. 126.

10   Genesis I. 26 (AV).

11   Archilochos, fr. 87; quoted by Deussen, *Allgemeine Geschichte der Philosophie*, vol. II, pt. 1 (Leipzig, 1911), p. 18.

12 Solon, fr. 13.25, quoted by Deussen, p. 20.

13 See, for example: Robert H. Lowie, *An Introduction to Cultural Anthropology* (New York: Farrar and Rinehart, 1940), pp. 344ff.

14 Cf. Freud, *Complete Psychological Works* Vol XIII, trans. James Strachey (*Totem and Taboo*) (London: Hogarth Press, 1955), p. 86.

15 Ibid., p. 89.

16 Hegel, *Phenomenology of Spirit*, p. 342.

17 Cf. W. Kirfel, *Geschichte Indiens*, in *Propyläenweltgeschichte*, vol. III, pp. 261ff; and G. Glotz, *Histoire Grecque*, vol. I, in: *Histoire Ancienne* (Paris, 1938), pp. 137ff.

18 Glotz, p. 140.

19 See Kurt Eckermann, *Jahrbuch der Religionsgeschichte und Mythologie* (Halle, 1845), vol. I, p. 241; and O. Kern, *Die Religion der Griechen* (Berlin, 1926), vol. I, pp. 181ff.

20 This is how Hubert and Mauss interpret "sympathy," or *mimesis: "L'un est le tout, est dans l'un, la nature triomphe de la nature."* H. Hubert and M. Mauss, "*Théorie générale de la Magie,*" in *L'Année Sociologique*, 1902–3, p. 100.

21 Cf. Edward Westermarck, *Ursprung der Moralbegriffe* (Leipzig: Klinkhardt, 1913), vol. I, p. 402.

22 Edmund Husserl, *The Crisis of European Sciences and Transcendental Phenomenology*, trans. David Carr (Evanston, Ill.: Northwestern, 1970) pp. 22–3.

23 Cf. Arthur Schopenhauer, *Parerga und Paralipomena*, vol. II, S. 356; *Werke* (Munich, 1913), ed. Deussen, vol. V, p. 671.

24 *Ethica*, Pars. IV. Propos, XXII. Coroll.

10

Sociology and Empirical Research

In 1961 some of the leading German-speaking social theorists of the time assembled in Tübingen for what promised to be a decisive engagement between what were loosely seen as the two dominant sociological theories: critical theory and critical rationalism. The latter was labelled 'positivism' by its opponents, and the debate between the two sides was subsequently to become known as the positivist dispute. Adorno was the principal for critical theory, responding to the other side's main representative, Karl Popper. The debate was notably dissatisfying, Popper in the course of his paper denying that he was positivist and Adorno choosing not to reply to Popper's paper in the form expected by the latter. However, the debate assumed an energy which was to take it beyond the Tübingen conference with the eventual publication in 1969 of the book *The Positivist Dispute in German Sociology* which contained the conference proceedings and some additional articles. Adorno, controversially, was chosen to write the introduction to the book. Furthermore, an earlier piece – the most incisive of his contributions to the debate about sociological methods – 'Sociology and Empirical Research' was included. The key issue in this piece is that of the methods appropriate for the investigation of society, or, as Adorno puts it, the self-reflection of sociological method. Before that issue can be resolved, however, the question of what sort of phenomenon society is has to be addressed.

Adorno argues that society is a totality in which each element is determined by its mediation within that totality. Clearly this has a metaphysical sound to it and for that reason empirical methodology or positivism, Adorno claims, has dismissed it as speculative. Instead, empirical methodology takes society at face value and interprets it as nothing more than a totality of facts. On that basis it proceeds to investigate society by means of opinion surveys without suspecting that those opinions might be the result of hidden processes which constitute the individual. Furthermore, the methodology has an inherent circularity, Adorno argues, in that it sets out to investigate society apparently in the spirit of objectivity, but its method predetermines what its findings are going to look like in that it can yield only disparate facts about atomic individuals. As such it is ideological in the classic sense that it perpetuates as natural one view of society, namely, society as a collective of social atoms. According to Adorno, the phenomenon of society is dialectical in that it is internally contradictory and antagonistic and therefore not amenable to the form of analysis proposed in positivism. The contradiction is that between the definition of society as a collective of autonomous individuals and the reality that society dominates individuals and moulds them to those purposes which contribute to the preservation of society. Adorno notes that society was originally a philosophical construct, albeit formerly misunderstood by philosophy as essence or spirit. Of course the difficulty Adorno faces is that of proposing an alternative methodology, even if his critique of positivism is taken to be correct. He turns to an idea suggested as early as 'The Actuality of Philosophy', that of interpretation. The essence of Adorno's form of interpretation, in the case of society, is to assemble disparate social phenomena in a way that might illuminate the subterranean structures of society. Adorno warns that we cannot simply import certain notions from above (like the class-structure or exchange system) but rather the reality or otherwise of these phenomena will be confirmed by their ability to allow us access to the structures which explain the real life processes of the apparently atomic individual.

'Sociology and Empirical Research' [1957], in *The Positivist Dispute in German Sociology* (London: Heinemann, 1976), pp. 66–86, edited by Glyn Adey and David Frisby.
Translated by Glyn Adey and David Frisby.

1

The modes of procedure assembled under the name of sociology as an academic discipline are united in an extremely abstract sense, namely, in that all of them in some way deal with society. But neither their object nor their method is uniform. Some apply to societal totality and its laws of movement, others, in pointed opposition, apply to individual social phenomena which one relates to a concept of society at the cost of ostracization for being speculative. Accordingly, the methods vary. In the former case, insight into the societal context is supposed to follow from structural basic conditions, such as the exchange relationship. In the latter, such an endeavour, even though it may in no way desire to justify the factual from the standpoint of an autocratic mind, is dismissed as philosophical residue in the development of science, and is to give way to the mere establishment of what is the case. Historically divergent models underlie both conceptions. The theory of society originated in philosophy whilst, at the same time, it attempts to reformulate the questions posed by the latter by defining society as the substratum which traditional philosophy called eternal essences or spirit. Just as philosophy mistrusted the deceit of appearances and sought after interpretation, so the more smoothly the façade of society presents itself, the more profoundly does theory mistrust it. Theory seeks to give a name to what secretly holds the machinery together. The ardent desire for thought, to which the senselessness of what merely exists was once unbearable, has become secularized in the desire for disenchantment. It seeks to raise the stone under which the monster lies brooding. In such knowledge alone meaning has been preserved for us. Sociological research into facts opposes such a desire. Disenchantment of the kind that Max Weber accepted, is merely a special case of sorcery for such research, and reflection upon that which governs secretly and would have to be changed, is viewed as a mere waste of time on the way towards the alteration of the manifest. This is especially the case since what nowadays generally bears the name empirical social science has taken, more or less avowedly since Comte's positivism, the natural sciences as its model. The two tendencies refuse to be reduced to a common denominator. Theoretical reflections upon society as a whole cannot be completely realized by empirical findings; they seek to evade the latter just as spirits evade para-psychological experimental arrangements. Each particular view of society as a whole necessarily transcends its scattered facts. The first condition for construction of the totality is a concept of the object [Sache], around which the disparate data are organized. From the living experience, and not from one already established according to the societally installed control mechanisms, from the memory of what has been conceived in the past, from the unswerving consequence of one's own reflection, this construction must always bring the concept to bear on the material and reshape it in contact with the latter. But if theory is not to fall prey to the dogmatism over whose discovery scepticism – now elevated to a prohibition on thought – is always ready to rejoice, then theory may not rest here. It must transform the concepts which it brings, as it were, from outside into those which the object has of itself, into what the object, left to itself, seeks to be, and confront it with what it is. It must dissolve the rigidity of the temporally and spatially fixed object into a field of tension of the possible and the real: each one, in order to exist, is dependent upon the other. In other words, theory is indisputably critical. But, for this reason, hypotheses derived from it − forcasts of what can be regularly expected − are not completely sufficient for it. What can merely be expected is itself a piece of societal activity, and is incommensurable with the goal of criticism. The cheap satisfaction that things actually come about in the manner which the theory of society had suspected, ought not to delude the theory, that, as soon as it appears as a hypothesis, it alters its inner composition. The isolated observation through which it is verified belongs, in turn, to the context of delusion which it desires to penetrate. The concretization and certainty gained must be paid for with a loss in penetrating force; as far as the principle is concerned it will be reduced to the phenomenon against which it is tested. But if, conversely, one wishes to proceed in accordance with general scientific custom from individual investigations to the totality of society then one gains, at best, classificatory higher concepts, but not those which express the life of society itself. The category 'a society based on the division of labour in general' is higher and more general than 'capitalistic society' − but it is not more substantial. Rather, it is less substantial and tells us less about the life of the people and what threatens them. This does not mean, however, that a logically lower category such as 'urbanism' would say more. Neither upwards nor downwards do sociological levels of abstraction correspond simply to the societal knowledge value. For this reason, one can expect so little from their systematic standardization by means of a model such as Parsons' 'functional' model. But still less can be expected from the promises repeatedly made, and postponed since sociological prehistory, of a synthesis of the theoretical and the empirical, which falsely equate theory with formal unity and refuse to admit that a theory of society, purged of the substantive contents, displaces all its emphases. It should be remembered how indifferent recourse to the 'group' is as opposed to recourse to industrial society. Societal theory formation, based on the model of classificatory systems, substitutes the thinnest conceptual residue for what gives society its law. The empirical and the theoretical cannot be registered on a continuum. Compared with the presumption of insight into the essence of modern society, empirical contributions are like drops in the ocean. But according to the empirical rules of the game, empirical proofs for central structural laws remain, in any case, contestable. It is not a matter of smoothing out such divergences and harmonizing them. Only a harmonistic view of society could induce one to such an attempt. Instead, the tensions must be brought to a head in a fruitful manner.

2

Nowadays, in the train of disappointment with both cultural-scientific [*Geisteswissenschaftlich*] and formal sociology, there is a predominant tendency to give primacy to empirical sociology. Its immediate practical utilizability, and its affinity to every type of administration, undoubtedly play a role here. But the reaction against either arbitrary or empty assertions made about society from above is legitimate. Nevertheless, empirical procedures do not merit simple priority. It is not merely the case that there exist other procedures besides these. Disciplines and modes of thought are not justified by their mere existence but rather their limit is prescribed for them by the object [*Sache*]. Paradoxically, the empirical methods, whose power of attraction lies in their claim to objectivity, favour the subjective – and this is explained by their origins in market research. At most, this preference abstracts from statistical data of the census type – such as sex, age, marital status, income, education and the like, and also opinions and attitudes – the behavioural modes of human subjects. So far, at any rate, only within this compass has what is specific to them asserted itself. As inventories of so-called objective states of affairs they could only be distinguished with some difficulty from pre-scientific information for administration purposes. In general, the objectivity of empirical social research is an objectivity of the methods, not of what is investigated. From surveys of varying numbers of individuals, statements are derived by means of statistical processing which are generalizable and independent of individual fluctuations in accordance with the laws of the theory of probability. But even if their validity be objective, in most cases the mean values remain objective statements about human subjects, and, in fact, they remain statements about how human subjects see themselves and reality. The empirical methods – questionnaire, interview and whatever combination and supplementation of these is possible – have ignored societal objectivity, the embodiment of all the conditions, institutions and forces within which human beings act, or at most, they have taken them into account as accidentals. At fault here are not only those interested in commissioning research who consciously or unconsciously prevent the elucidation of such conditions and who in America are careful to make sure – even when distributing research projects on mass communications for instance – that only reactions within the dominant 'commercial system' are recorded and that the structure and implications of the system itself are not analysed. Moreover, even the empirical means are objectively fashioned to this end. This involves the largely pre-ranked questioning of many individuals and its statistical evaluation which, in advance, tend to recognize widely-held – and, as such, preformed – views as justification for judgment on the object itself. In these views, objectivities may also be reflected but certainly not entirely, and often in a distorted from. In any case, as the most cursory glance at the manner in which working people function in their jobs will demonstrate, the weight of subjective opinions, attitudes and modes of behaviour is secondary compared with such objectivities. No matter how positivistic the modes of procedure, they are implicitly based upon the notion – derived from the ground rules of democratic elections and all-too unhesitatingly generalized – that the embodiment of the contents of man's consciousness or unconsciousness which form a statistical universe possesses an immediate key role for the societal process. Despite their objectification, in fact on account of it, the methods do not penetrate the objectification of the object, or in particular, the constraint of economic objectivity. For them, all opinions possess virtually the same validity, and they capture such elementary differences as that of the weight of opinions in proportion to societal power purely through additional refinements such as the selection of key groups. The primary becomes the secondary. Such shifts within the method are not, however, indifferent to what is investigated. For all the aversion of empirical sociology to the philosophical anthropologies which became fashionable in the same period, it shares with them a standpoint; namely, the belief that already in the here and now it is man as such who is central, instead of determining socialized human beings in advance as a moment of societal totality – in fact, predominantly as the object of the latter. The reified nature [*Dinghaftigkeit*] of the method, its inherent tendency to nail down the facts of the case, is transferred to its objects, that, to the subjective facts which have been ascertained, as if they were things in themselves and not hypostatized entities. The method is likely both to fetishize its object and, in turn, to degenerate into a fetish. Not for nothing – and quite rightly as far as the logic of scientific procedures under discussion is concerned – in discussions of empirical social research do questions of method outweigh substantive questions. As a criterion, the dignity of the objects to be examined is frequently replaced by the objectivity of the findings which are to be ascertained by means of a method. In the empirical scientific process, the selection of the research objects and the starting point of the investigation are guided, if not by practical administrative considerations and not so much by the essential nature of what is investigated, but rather by the available methods which, at most, must be developed further. This explains the undoubted irrelevance of so many empirical studies. The procedure of operational or instrumental definition generally current in empirical techniques – which will define a category such as 'conservatism' by means of certain numerical values of the answers to questions within the investigation itself – sanctions the primacy of the method over the object, and ultimately sanctions the arbitrariness of the scientific enterprise itself. The pretence is made to examine an object by means of an instrument of research, which through its own formulation, decides what the object is; in other words, we are faced with a simple circle. The gesture of scientific honesty, which refuses to work with concepts that are not clear and unambiguous, becomes the excuse for superimposing the self-satisfied research enterprise over what is investigated. With the arrogance of the uninstructed, the objections of the great philosophical tradition to the practice of definition are forgotten.[1] What this tradition rejected as scholastic residue is dragged along in an unreflected manner by individual disciplines in the name of scientific exactitude. But as soon as there is any extrapolation from the instrumentally defined concepts even to the conventionally common concepts – and this is almost inevitable – research is guilty of the impurity which it intended to eradicate with its definitions.

3

It is in the nature of society itself that the natural scientific model cannot be happily and unreservedly transferred to it. But although the ideology suggests otherwise, and this is rationalized by the reactionary opposition to new techniques in Germany, this is not because the dignity of man, for the gradual abolition of which mankind is a avidly working, would be excluded from methods which regard him as a part of nature. Instead, it is more true to say that mankind commits a flagrant sin in so far as man's claim to domination represses the remembrance of his natural being and thus perpetuates blind natural spontaneity (*Naturwüchsigkeit*) than when human beings are reminded of their natural instincts (*Naturhaftigkeit*). 'Sociology is not a cultural science (*Geisteswissenschaft*).'[2] Insofar as the obduracy of society continually reduces human beings to objects and transforms their condition into 'second nature', methods which find it guilty of doing just this are not sacrilegious. The lack of freedom in the methods serves freedom by attesting wordlessly to the predominant lack of freedom. The enraged, indignant protests and the subtler defensive gestures provoked by Kinsey's investigations are the most powerful argument for Kinsey. Wherever human beings are, in fact, reduced under the pressure of conditions to the 'amphibious' mode of reaction,[3] as they are in their capacity as compulsive consumers of the mass media and other regimented joys, opinion research, which infuriates lixiviated humanism, is better suited to them than, for instance, an 'interpretative' sociology. For, the substratum of understanding, namely human behaviour, which is in itself unified and meaningful, has already been replaced in the human subjects themselves by mere reaction. A social science which is both atomistic, and ascends through classification from the atoms to generalities, is the Medusan mirror to a society which is both atomized and organized according to abstract classificatory concepts, namely those of administration. But in order to become true, this *adaequatio rei atque cogitationis* requires self-reflection. Its legitimation is solely critical. In that moment in which one hypostatizes that state which research methods both grasp and express as the immanent reason of science, instead of making it the object of one's thought, one contributes intentionally or otherwise to its perpetuation. Then, empirical social research wrongly takes the epiphenomenon – what the world has made of us – for the object itself. In its application, there exists a presupposition which should not be deduced from the demands of the method but rather the state of society, that is, historically. The hypostatized method postulates the reified consciousness of the people tested. If a questionnaire inquires into musical taste and, in so doing, offers a choice between the categories 'classical' and 'popular', then it rightly believes that it has ascertained that the audience in question listens in accordance with these categories. Similarly, one automatically recognizes, without reflection, when one turns on the radio, whether one has found a popular music programme, or what is considered serious music, or the background music to a religious act. But as long as the societal conditions for such forms of reaction are not met, the correct finding is also misleading. It suggests that the division of musical experience into 'classical' and 'popular' is final and even natural. But the societally relevant question only arises with this division, with its perpetuation as something self-evident, and necessarily implies the question whether the perception of music under the a priori sectors most acutely affects the spontaneous experience of the perceived. Only the insight into the genesis of the existing forms of reaction and their relationship to the meaning of that experienced would permit one to decipher the phenomenon registered. The predominant empiricist habit, however, would reject any discussion of the objective meaning of the particular work of art, and would discuss such meaning as a mere subjective projection by the listeners and relegate the structure to the mere 'stimulus' of a psychological experimental arrangement. In this manner, it would, from the outset, exclude the possibility of discussing the relationship between the masses and the products forced upon them by the culture industry. Ultimately, the products themselves would be defined through the reactions of the masses whose relation to the products was under discussion. But it is all the more urgent today to proceed beyond the isolated study since, with the hold of the media on the population growing stronger, the pre-formation of their consciousness also increases so that there is scarcely a gap left which might permit an awareness of this very pre-formation. Even such a positivistic sociologist as Durkheim, who in his rejection of *Verstehen* was in agreement with social research, had good reason for associating the statistical laws, to which he also adhered, with the 'contrainte sociale'[4] and even for recognizing in the latter the criterion of society's general law-like nature. Contemporary social research denies this connection and thereby also sacrifices the connection between its generalizations and concrete, societal determinations of structure. But if such perspectives are pushed aside and considered to be the task of special investigations which must be carried out at some point, then scientific mirroring indeed remains a mere duplication, the reified apperception of the hypostatized, thereby distorting the object through duplication itself. It enchants that which is mediated into something immediate. As a corrective, it is not then sufficient simply to distinguish descriptively between the 'collective realm' and the 'individual realm', as Durkheim intended, but rather the relationship between the two realms must be mediated and must itself be grounded theoretically. The opposition between quantitative and qualitative analysis is not absolute. It is not the last word in the matter. It is well known that whoever quantifies must always first abstract from qualitative differences in the elements, and everything that is societally individual contains the general determinations for which the quantitative generalizations are valid. The proper categories of the latter are always qualitative. A method which does not do justice to this fact and rejects qualitative analysis as incompatible with the essence of the collective realm distorts what it should investigate. Society is one. Even where the major societal forces have not yet made their influence felt, the 'undeveloped' spheres are functionally inter-related with those spheres which have advanced towards rationality and uniform socialization (*Vergesellschaftung*). Sociology, which disregards this and remains content with such weak and inadequate concepts as induction and deduction,[5] supports what exists in the over-zealous attempt to say what exists. Such sociology becomes ideology in the strict sense – a necessary illusion. It is illusion since the diversity of methods does not encompass the unity of the object and conceals it behind so called factors into which the object is broken up for the sake of convenience; it is necessary since the object, society, fears nothing more than to be called by name, and therefore it automatically encourages and tolerates only such knowledge of itself that slides off its back without any impact. The conceptual dichotomy of induction and deduction is the scientistic substitute for dialectics. But just as a binding theory of society must have fully immersed itself in its material, so the fact to be processed must itself throw light on the societal totality by virtue of the process which apprehends it. If, however, the method has already rendered it a *factum brutum*, then no light can subsequently

penetrate it. In the rigid opposition and complementation of formal sociology and the blind establishment of facts, the relationship between the general
and the particular disappears. But society draws its life from this relationship,
which therefore provides sociology with its only humanly worthy object. If
one subsequently adds together what has been separated, then the material
relationship is stood upon its head by the gradation of the method. The eager-
ness to quantify immediately even the qualitative findings is not fortuitous.
Science wishes to rid the world of the tension between the general and the
particular by means of its consistent system, but the world gains its unity from
inconsistency.

4

This inconsistency is the reason why the object of sociology – society and
its phenomena – does not possess the type of homogeneity which so-called
classical natural science was able to count upon. In sociology one cannot
progress to the same degree from partial assertions about societal states of
affairs to their general, even if restricted, validity, as one was accustomed to
infer the characteristics of lead in general from the observation of the characteristics of one piece of lead. The generality of social-scientific laws is not
at all that of a conceptual sphere into which the individual parts can be
wholly incorporated, but rather always and essentially relates to the relationship of the general to the particular in its historical concretion. In negative
terms, this attests to the lack of homogeneity of the state of society – the
'anarchy' of all history up till now – whilst, in positive terms, it attests to the
moment of spontaneity which cannot be apprehended by the law of large
numbers. Anyone who contrasts the human world with the relative regular-
ity and constancy of the objects in the mathematical natural sciences, or at
least in the 'macro-realm', does not transfigure this world. The antagonistic
character of society is central and this is conjured away by mere generalization. Homogeneity, rather than its absence, requires clarification insofar as it
subjects human behaviour to the law of large numbers. The applicability of
this law contradicts the *principium individuationis* namely that, despite everything, it cannot be overlooked that human beings are not merely members
of a species. Their modes of behaviour are mediated through their intellect.
The latter certainly contains a moment of the general which can very easily
recur in the statistical generality. Yet it is also specified by means of the interests of particular individuals which diverge in bourgeois society and, even
given uniformity, tend to be opposed to one another, not to mention the
irrationality in individuals, reproduced under the societal constraints. It is only

the unity of the principle of an individualistic society which unites the dispersed interests of the individuals in the formula of their 'opinion'. The currently widespread talk about the social atom certainly does justice to the powerlessness of the individual confronted with the totality, yet it remains merely metaphorical when compared with the natural scientific concept of the atom. Even in front of the television screen, the similarity of the smallest social units, that is the similarity of individuals, cannot be seriously asserted with the strictness possible in the case of physical-chemical matter. Yet empirical social research proceeds as if it took the idea of the social atom at its face value. That it is to some extent successful, is a critical reflection upon society. The general law-like nature of society, which disqualifies statistical elements, testifies that the general and the particular are not reconciled, that precisely in individualistic society the individual is blindly subjected to the general and is himself disqualified. Talk about society's 'character mask' once recorded this state of affairs, but contemporary empiricism has forgotten it. The communal social reaction is essentially that of social pressure. It is only on this account that empirical research, with its conception of the collective realm, is able to brush individuation aside in such a high-handed manner, since the latter has remained ideological up to the present, and since human beings are not yet human beings. In a liberated society, statistics would become, in a positive manner, what today it can only be in negative terms: an administrative science, but really a science for the administration of objects – namely, consumer-goods – and not of people. Yet despite its awkward basis in the social structure, empirical social research should retain its capacity for self-criticism to the extent that the generalizations which it achieves should not immediately be attributed to reality, to the standardized world, but instead they should always be attributed to the method as well. For even through the generality of the question put to individuals or their restricted selection – the cafeteria – the method prepares in advance what is to be ascertained – the opinions to be investigated – in such a manner that it becomes an atom.

5

Insight into the heterogeneity of sociology as a scientific construct, that is, insight into the heterogeneity of the categorial, and not merely graded and easily bridgeable, divergence between disciplines such as social theory, the analysis of objective social conditions and institutions, and subjectively orientated social research in the narrower sense, does not imply that one should simply accept the sterile division between the disciplines. The formal demand for the unity of a science is certainly not to be respected when the science itself bears the marks of an arbitrary division of labour and cannot set itself up as if it could discern without difficulty the much-favoured totalities, whose social existence is, in any case, questionable. But the critical amalgamation of divergent sociological methods is required for concrete reasons, for the cognitive goal. In view of the specific nexus of social theory formation and specific social interests, a corrective of the type offered by the research methods is salutary no matter how entangled with particular interests the latter may be by virtue of their 'administrative' structure. Numerous stalwart assertions of social theories – and here we shall only mention for the purpose of illustration, Max Scheler's assertion about the typical lower-class forms of consciousness[6] – can be tested and refuted with the aid of strict investigations. On the other hand, social research is dependent upon confrontation with theory and with knowledge of objective social structures, otherwise it would degenerate into irrelevancy or willingly comply with apologetic slogans such as those of the family, which occasionally gain popularity. Isolated social research becomes untrue as soon as it wishes to extirpate totality as a mere crypto-metaphysical prejudice, since totality cannot, in principle, be apprehended by its methods. Science then pledges itself to the mere phenomena. If one taboos the question of being as an illusion, as something which cannot be realized with the aid of the method, then the essential connections – what actually matters in society – are protected a priori from knowledge. It is futile to ask whether these essential connections are 'real', or merely conceptual structures. The person who attributes the conceptual to social reality need not fear the accusation of being idealistic. What is implied here is not merely the constitutive conceptuality of the knowing subject but also a conceptuality which holds sway in reality (Sache) itself. Even in the theory of the conceptual mediation of all being, Hegel envisaged something decisive in real terms. The law which determines how the fatality of mankind unfolds itself is the law of exchange. Yet, in turn, this does not represent a simple immediacy but is conceptual. The act of exchange implies the reduction of the products to be exchanged to their equivalents, to something abstract, but by no means – as traditional discussion would maintain – to something material. This mediating conceptuality is, however, not a general formulation of average expectations, nor is it an abbreviating addition on the part of a science which creates order. Instead, society obeys this conceptuality tel quel, and it provides the objectively valid model for all essential social events. This conceptuality is independent both of the consciousness of the human beings subjected to it and of the consciousness of the scientists. Confronted with physical reality and all the hard data, one might call this conceptual entity illusion, since the exchange of equivalents proceeds both justly and unjustly. It is not an illusion to which organizing science sublimates reality but rather it is immanent to reality. Moreover, talk about the unreality of social laws is only justified critically, namely with regard to the commodity's fetish character. Exchange value, merely a mental configuration when compared with use value, dominates human needs and replaces them; illusion dominates reality. To this extent, society is myth and its elucidation is still as necessary as ever. At the same time, however, this illusion is what is most real, it is the formula used to bewitch the world. The critique of this illusion has nothing to do with the positivistic scientific critique according to which one cannot regard the objective nature of exchange as valid. This validity is unremittingly corroborated by reality itself. But if sociological empiricism claims that the law is not something that exists in real terms, then it involuntarily denotes something of the social illusion in the object – an illusion which sociological empiricism wrongly attributes to the method. It is then precisely the alleged anti–idealism of the scientific mentality which benefits the continued existence of ideology. The latter is supposed to be inaccessible to science since it is not, of course, a fact. Yet nothing is more powerful than the conceptual mediation which conjures up before human beings the being-for-another (*das Füranderesseiende*) as an in-itself, and prevents them from becoming conscious of the conditions under which they live. As soon as sociology opposes recognition of what is known as its 'fact' and remains content simply to register and order it – in so doing, mistaking the rules distilled for the law which governs the facts and in accordance with which they develop – then it has already succumbed to justification, even if it does not suspect that it has done so. In the social sciences, one cannot therefore proceed from the part to the whole as one can in the natural sciences, since it is something conceptual, totally different in its logical extension and in the unity of features of any individual elements, which constitutes the whole. Nevertheless, because of its mediated conceptual nature, this whole has nothing in common with 'totalities' and forms, which necessarily must always be conceptualized as being immediate. Society has more in common with the system than with the organism. An empirical research devoid of theory which gets by with mere hypotheses is blind to society as a system, its authentic object, since its object does not coincide with the sum of all the parts. It does not subsume the parts nor is it made up, like a geographical map, of their juxtaposition of 'country and people'. No social atlas in the literal and figurative sense represents society. Insofar as society is more than the immediate life of its members and the related subjective and objective facts, research which exhausts itself in the investigation of such immediacy misses its mark. For all the hypostatization of the method, even by virtue of such hypostatization as the idolization of what can be simply observed, it produces an illusion of being alive, an illusion of neighbourliness, as it were, from countenance to countenance. A dissolution of such an illusion would not be the last of the tasks for social knowledge if it had not already been dissolved. Today, however, it is repressed. In this respect, the transfiguring metaphysics of existence and the rigid description of what is the case are equally guilty. Moreover, to a considerable extent, the practice of empirical sociology does not even comply with its own admission that hypotheses are necessary. Whilst the necessity of the latter is reluctantly conceded, each hypothesis is met with suspicion since it might become a 'bias' and lead to an infringement of impartial research.[7] This view is based upon a 'residual theory of truth', upon the notion that truth is what remains after the allegedly mere subjective addition, a sort of cost price, has been deducted. Since Georg Simmel and Freud, psychology has realized that the conclusiveness of the experience of objects, if the latter in turn are essentially subjectively mediated like society, is increased and not decreased by the degree of subjective participation of the knowing subject. But this insight has not yet been incorporated into the social sciences. As soon as individual common sense is suspended in favour of the responsible behaviour of the scientist, people seek salvation in procedures which are as free from hypotheses as possible. Empirical social research ought to dismiss completely the superstition that research must begin like a *tabula rasa*, where the data that are assembled in an unconditioned manner are prepared. In so doing, it ought to recall epistemological controversies which are indeed fought out long ago, but are forgotten all too willingly by short-winded consciousness in its reference to the urgent requirements of the research process. Scepticism with regard to its own ascetic ideals befits a sceptical science. The readily-quoted statement that a scientist needs 10% inspiration and 90% perspiration is secondary and leads to a prohibition on thought. For a long time, the abstinent work of the scholar has mainly consisted in renouncing for poor pay those thoughts which he did not have in any case. Nowadays, since the better paid executive has succeeded the scholar, lack of intellect is not only celebrated as a virtue on the part of the modest well-adapted person who is incorporated into the team, but, in addition, it is institutionalized through the establishment of levels of research which hardly recognize the spontaneity of individuals as anything other than as indices of friction. But the antithesis of grandiose inspiration and solid research work is, as such, of secondary importance. Thoughts do not come flying along but rather they crystallize in protracted subterranean processes, even if they emerge suddenly. The abruptness of what research technicians condescendingly call intuition marks the penetration of living experience through the hardened crust of the *communis opinio*. It is the long drawn-out breath of opposition to the latter, and by no means the privilege of highly gifted moments, which permits unregimented thought that contact with being which is often inexorably sabotaged by the distended apparatus that intervenes. Conversely, scientific assiduity is always both the operation and exertion of the concept, the opposite of the mechanical, doggedly unconscious procedure with which it is equated. Science should be the recognition of the truth and untruth of what the phenomenon under study seeks to be. There is no knowledge which is not, at the same time, critical by virtue of its inherent distinction between true and false. Only a sociology which set the petrified antitheses of its organization in motion would come to its senses.

6

The categorial difference between the discipline is confirmed by the fact that what should be fundamental, namely the combination of empirical investigations with theoretically central questions, has − despite isolated attempts − not yet been achieved. The most modest demand and yet, in terms of immanent critique, the most plausible demand for empirical social research in accordance with its own rules of 'objectivity', would be to confront all its statements directed at the subjective consciousness and unconsciousness of human beings and groups of human beings with the objective factors of their existence. What seems merely accidental or mere 'background study' to the domain of social research provides the precondition for the possibility of social research ever reaching the essential. Inevitably, in these given factors, it will first emphasize what is connected with the subjective opinions, feelings and behaviour of those studied, although these connections, in particular, are so wide-ranging that such a confrontation ought not really to content itself with the knowledge of individual institutions but instead should have recourse to the structure of society. The categorial difficulty is not removed by means of a comparison between certain opinions and certain conditions. But even with this weighty reservation, the results of opinion research acquire a different value as soon as they can be measured against the real nature of what opinions are concerned with. The differences which thereby emerge between social objectivity and the consciousness of the subjectivity, no matter in what form this consciousness may be generally distributed, mark a place at which empirical social research reaches knowledge of society − the knowledge of ideologies, of their genesis and of their function. Such knowledge would be the actual goal, although not of course the only goal, of empirical social research. Taken in isolation, however, the latter does not have the weight of social knowledge. The laws of the market, in whose system it remains in an unreflected manner, remain a façade. Even if a survey provided the statistically overwhelming evidence that workers no longer consider themselves to be workers and deny that there still exists such a thing as the proletariat, the non-existence of the proletariat would in no way have been proved. But rather, such subjective findings would have to be compared with objective findings, such as the position of those questioned in the production process, their control or lack of control over the means of production, their societal power or powerlessness. The empirical findings concerning the human subjects would certainly still retain their significance. One would not simply have to ask within the content of the theory of ideology how such modes of consciousness come about, but also whether something essential has changed in social objectivity through their very existence. In the latter, the nature and self-consciousness of human beings, no matter how this is produced and reproduced, can only be neglected by erroneous dogma. Even the existence of such consciousness, whether as an element of the affirmation of what exists or as a potential for something different, is a moment in societal totality. Not only theory but also its absence becomes a material force when it seizes the masses. Empirical social research is not only a corrective in that it prevents blindly superimposed constructions, but also in the relationship between appearance and essence. If the task of a theory of society is to relativize critically the cognitive value of appearance, then conversely it is the task of empirical research to protect the concept of essential laws from mythologization. Appearance is always also an appearance of essence and not mere illusion. Its changes are not indifferent to essence. If no one in fact knows any more that he is a worker then this affects the inner composition of the concept of the worker even if its objective definition – through separation from the means of production – is still fulfilled.

7

Empirical social research cannot evade the fact that all the given factors investigated, the subjective no less than the objective relations, are mediated through society. The given, the facts which, in accordance with its methods, it encounters as something final, are not themselves final but rather are conditioned. Consequently, empirical social research cannot confuse the roots of its knowledge – the givenness of facts which is the concern of its method – with the real basis, a being in-itself of facts, their immediacy as such, their fundamental character. It can protect itself against such a confusion in that it is able to dissolve the immediacy of the data through refinement of the method. This accounts for the significance of motivational analyses although they remain under the spell of subjective reaction. They can indeed seldom rest upon direct questions; and correlations indicate functional connections but do not elucidate causal dependencies. Consequently, the development of indirect methods is, in principle, the opportunity for empirical social research to reach beyond the mere observation and preparation of superficial facts. The cognitive problem of its self-critical development remains, namely that the facts ascertained do not faithfully reflect the underlying societal conditions but rather they simultaneously constitute the veil by means of which these conditions, of necessity, disguise themselves. For the findings of what is called – not without good reason – 'opinion research' Hegel's formulation in his *Philosophy of Right* concerning public opinion is generally valid: it deserves to be respected and despised in equal measure.[8] It must be respected since even ideologies, necessary false consciousness, are a part of social reality with which anyone who wishes to recognize the latter must be acquainted. But it must be despised since its claim to truth must be criticized. Empirical social research itself becomes ideology as soon as it posits public opinion as being absolute. This is the fault of an unreflectedly nominalistic concept of truth which wrongly equates the 'volonté de tous' with truth in general, since a different truth cannot be ascertained. This tendency is particularly marked in American empirical social research. But it should not be dogmatically confronted with the mere assertion of a 'volonté générale' as a truth in-itself, for instance in the form of postulated 'values'. Such a procedure would be loaded with the same arbitrariness as the installation of popular opinion as objectively valid. Historically, since Robespierre, the establishment of the 'volonté générale' by decree has possibly caused even more harm than the concept-free assumption of a 'volonté de tous'. The only way out of the fateful alternative was provided by immanent analysis; the analysis of the consistency or inconsistency of opinion in itself and of its relationship to reality (*Sache*), not however the abstract antithesis of the objectively valid and of opinion. Opinion should not be rejected with Platonic arrogance, but rather its untruth is to be derived from the truth: from the supporting societal relationship and ultimately from the latter's own untruth. On the other hand, however, average opinion does not represent an approximate value of truth, but instead the socially average illusion. In the latter, there participate what unreflective social research imagines to be its *ens realissimum*: those questioned, the human subjects. Their own nature, their being as subjects, depends upon the objectivity, upon the mechanisms which they obey, and which constitute their concept. This can only be determined, however, if one perceives in the facts themselves the tendency which reaches out beyond them. That is the function of philosophy in empirical social research. If it is not realized or suppressed, if merely the facts are reproduced then such a reproduction is at the same time a corruption of facts into ideology. .

Notes

1 Cf. Immanuel Kant, *Critique of Pure Reason*, trans. N. Kemp Smith (London: Macmillan/New York: St. Martin's, 1933), pp. 586f; *Hegel's Science of Logic*, trans. A. V. Miller (London: George Allen and Unwin/New York Humanities Press, 1969), pp. 795ff; and numerous passages in Nietzsche.

2 'Sociology and Empirical Social Research', in *Aspects of Sociology* (London/Boston: Beacon Press, 1973), p. 124 (amended translation).

3 M. Horkheimer and T. W. Adorno, *Dialectic of Enlightenment* (New York: Seabury Press, 1972/London: NLB, 1973), p. 36.

4 Cf. Emile Durkheim, *Les Règles de la méthode sociologique* (Paris: PUF, 1950), pp. 6ff.

5 Cf. Erich Reigrotzki, *Soziale Verflechtungen in der Bundesrepublik* (Tübingen: Mohr, 1956), p. 4.

6 Cf. 'Ideologie und Handeln', in Max Horkheimer and Theodor W. Adorno, *Sociologica II, Reden und Vorträge, Frankfurter Beiträge zur Soziologie*, vol. 10, 2nd edn (Frankfurt: Suhrkamp, 1967), pp. 41ff.

7 Cf. René König, 'Beobachtung und Experiment in der Sozialforschung', in *Praktische Sozialforschung* (Cologne: Verlag für Politik und Wirtschaft, 1956), II, p. 27.

8 Cf. *Hegel's Philosophy of Right*, trans. T. M. Knox (Oxford/New York: Oxford University Press, 1952), §318, p. 205.

Part IV

Art, Culture and Society

11

Cultural Criticism and Society

There is hardly a more important essay for understanding the very activity of critical theory than 'Cultural Criticism and Society'. In a complex, and indeed demanding, piece Adorno outlines the idea of immanent criticism through an analysis of the position of the critic both within and towards her object, culture. The essay achieves an impressive argumentative tension by contrasting immanent criticism, which Adorno eventually recommends, with conventional cultural criticism, identified here as transcendent criticism. In the latter the critic sees both her position and artistic phenomena as wholly independent of society and its norms, a perspective which, Adorno argues, is ideological. In order to give substance to these charges Adorno outlines his theory of ideology. This theory emerges from Adorno's materialist transformation of Hegel's concept of *Geist*, entailing that society and culture are, as one commentator puts it, 'two extreme poles of a self-producing social totality.'* For instance, in so far as the work of the critic functions as an advertisement for consumable culture it parallels the economic world of exchange. This theory differs substantially from the classic Marxist version which holds that base (economic life) causes superstructure (culture and social institutions).

Ideologically the transcendent critic thinks of culture as the collection of societally independent entities, the superior examples of which represent the ideal of harmony. Against this ideology Adorno argues that cultural phenomena are the indirect expression of the lamentable condition of human society. In order to retrieve their social meaning immanent criticism is required. It ana-

---

* Michael Rosen, *On Voluntary Servitude: False Consciousness and the Theory of Ideology* (Cambridge: Polity Press, 1996), p. 227.

lyzes phenomena by attempting to uncover the ways in which they fail to fulfil their aims and that failure will somehow intimate social truths. In line with this position Adorno puts forward a criterion of 'successful' art: it is that which explicitly embodies contradictions by deliberately failing to live up to its own 'pretensions'. (Beckett's *Endgame* is such an example.) In that way successful art contains the truth that society is contradictory. Other cultural phenomena (non-art and unsuccessful art), it seems, are unintentionally contradictory. In addition to the topic of immanent criticism, 'Cultural Criticism and Society' considers the ideas of the autonomy of art and the division of labour. (Cf. 'The Autonomy of Art' (below) for further discussion.)

'Cultural Criticism and Society' [1951], in *Prisms* (Cambridge, Mass.: MIT Press, 1981), pp. 17–34.
Translated by Samuel and Shierry Weber.

To anyone in the habit of thinking with his ears, the words 'cultural criticism' (*Kulturkritik*) must have an offensive ring, not merely because, like 'automobile', they are pieced together from Latin and Greek. The words recall a flagrant contradiction. The cultural critic is not happy with civilization, to which alone he owes his discontent. He speaks as if he represented either unadulterated nature or a higher historical stage. Yet he is necessarily of the same essence as that to which he fancies himself superior. The insufficiency of the subject – criticized by Hegel in his apology for the *status quo* – which in its contingency and narrowness passes judgment on the might of the existent, becomes intolerable when the subject itself is mediated down to its innermost make-up by the notion to which it opposes itself as independent and sovereign. But what makes the content of cultural criticism inappropriate is not so much lack of respect for that which is criticized as the dazzled and arrogant recognition which criticism surreptitiously confers on culture. The cultural critic can hardly avoid the imputation that he has the culture which culture lacks. His vanity aids that of culture: even in the accusing gesture, the critic clings to the notion of culture, isolated, unquestioned, dogmatic. He shifts the attack. Where there is despair and measureless misery, he sees only spiritual phenomena, the state of man's consciousness, the decline of norms. By insisting on this, criticism is tempted to forget the unutterable, instead of striving, however impotently, so that man may be spared.

The position of the cultural critic, by virtue of its difference from the prevailing disorder, enables him to go beyond it theoretically, although often enough he merely falls behind. But he incorporates this difference into the very culture industry which he seeks to leave behind and which itself needs the difference in order to fancy itself culture. Characteristic of culture's pretension to distinction, through which it exempts itself from evaluation against the material conditions of life, is that it is insatiable. The exaggerated claims of culture, which in turn inhere in the movement of the mind, remove it ever further from those conditions as the worth of sublimation becomes increasingly suspect when confronted both by a material fulfillment near enough to touch and by the threatening annihilation of uncounted human beings. The cultural critic makes such distinction his privilege and forfeits his legitimation by collaborating with culture as its salaried and honoured nuisance. This, however, affects the substance of criticism. Even the implacable rigour with which criticism speaks the truth of an untrue consciousness remains imprisoned within the orbit of that against which it struggles, fixated on its surface manifestations. To flaunt one's superiority is, at the same time, to feel in on the job. Were one to study the profession of critic in bourgeois society as it progressed towards the rank of cultural critic, one would doubtless stumble on an element of usurpation in its origins, an element of which a writer like Balzac was still aware. Professional critics were first of all 'reporters': they oriented people in the market of intellectual products. In so doing, they occasionally gained insights into the matter at hand, yet remained continually traffic agents, in agreement with the sphere as such if not with its individual products. Of this they bear the mark even after they have discarded the role of agent. That they should have been entrusted with the roles of expert and then of judge was economically inevitable although accidental with respect to their objective qualifications. Their agility, which gained them privileged positions in the general competition – privileged, since the fate of those judged depends largely on their vote – invests their judgments with the semblance of competence. While they adroitly slipped into gaps and won influence with the expansion of the press, they attained that very authority which their profession already presupposed. Their arrogance derives from the fact that, in the forms of competitive society in which all being is merely there *for* something else, the critic himself is also measured only in terms of his marketable success – that is, in terms of his *being for* something else. Knowledge and understanding were not primary, but at most by-products, and the more they are lacking, the more they are replaced by Oneupmanship and conformity. When the critics in their playground – art – no longer understand what they judge and enthusiastically permit themselves to be degraded to propagandists or censors, it is the old dishonesty of trade fulfilling itself in their fate. The prerogatives of information and position permit them to express their opinion as if it were objectivity. But it is solely the objectivity of the ruling mind. They help to weave the veil.

The notion of the free expression of opinion, indeed, that of intellectual freedom itself in bourgeois society, upon which cultural criticism is founded, has its own dialectic. For while the mind extricated itself from a theological-feudal tutelage, it has fallen increasingly under the anonymous sway of the *status quo*. This regimentation, the result of the progressive societalization of all human relations, did not simply confront the mind from without; it immigrated into its immanent consistency. It imposes itself as relentlessly on the autonomous mind as heteronomous orders were formerly imposed on the mind which was bound. Not only does the mind mould itself for the sake of its marketability, and thus reproduce the socially prevalent categories. Rather, it grows to resemble ever more closely the *status quo* even where it subjectively refrains from making a commodity of itself. The network of the whole is drawn ever tighter, modelled after the act of exchange. It leaves the individual consciousness less and less room for evasion, preforms it more and more thoroughly, cuts it off *a priori* as it were from the possibility of differencing itself as all difference degenerates to a nuance in the monotony of supply. At the same time, the semblance of freedom makes reflection upon one's own unfreedom incomparably more difficult than formerly when such reflection stood in contradiction to manifest unfreedom, thus strengthening dependence. Such moments, in conjunction with the social selection of the 'spiritual and intellectual leaders', result in the regression of spirit and intellect. In accordance with the predominant social tendency, the integrity of the mind becomes a fiction. Of its freedom it develops only the negative moment, the heritage of the planless-monadological condition, irresponsibility. Otherwise, however, it clings ever more closely as a mere ornament to the material base which it claims to transcend. The strictures of Karl Kraus against freedom of the press are certainly not to be taken literally. To invoke seriously the censors against hack-writers would be to drive out the devil with Beelzebub. Nevertheless, the brutalization and deceit which flourish under the aegis of freedom of the press are not accidental to the historical march of the mind. Rather, they represent the stigma of that slavery within which the liberation of the mind – a false emancipation – has taken place. This is nowhere more striking than where the mind tears at its bonds: in criticism. When the German fascists defamed the word and replaced it with the inane notion of 'art appreciation', they were led to do so only by the rugged interests of the authoritarian state which still feared the passion of a Marquis Posa in the impertinence of the journalist. But the self-satisfied cultural barbarism which clamoured for the abolition of criticism, the incursion of the wild horde into the preserve of the mind, unawares repaid kind in kind. The bestial fury of the Brownshirt against 'carping critics' arises not merely from his envy of a culture which excludes him and against which he blindly rebels; nor is it merely his resentment of the person who can speak out the negative moment which he himself must repress. Decisive is that the critic's sovereign gesture suggests to his readers an autonomy which he does not have, and arrogates for itself a position of leadership which is incompatible with his own principle of intellectual freedom. This is innervated by his enemies. Their sadism was idiosyncratically attracted by the weakness, cleverly disguised as strength, of those who, in their dictatorial bearing, would have willingly excelled the less clever tyrants who were to succeed them. Except that the fascists succumbed to the same naivete as the critics, the faith in culture as such, which reduced it to pomp and approved spiritual giants. They regarded themselves as physicians of culture and removed the thorn of criticism from it. They thus not only degraded culture to the Official, but in addition, failed to recognize the extent to which culture and criticism, for better or for worse, are intertwined. Culture is only true when implicitly critical, and the mind which forgets this revenges itself in the critics it breeds. Criticism is an indispensable element of culture which is itself contradictory: in all its untruth still as true as culture is untrue. Criticism is not unjust when it dissects – this can be its greatest virtue – but rather when it parries by not parrying.

The complicity of cultural criticism with culture lies not in the mere mentality of the critic. Far more, it is dictated by his relation to that with which he deals. By making culture his object, he objectifies it once more. Its very meaning, however, is the suspension of objectification. Once culture itself has been debased to 'cultural goods', with its hideous philosophical rationalization, 'cultural values', it has already defamed its *raison d'être*. The distillation of such 'values' – the echo of commercial language is by no means accidental – places culture at the will of the market. Even the enthusiasm for foreign cultures includes the excitement over the rarity in which money may be invested. If cultural criticism, even at its best with Valéry, sides with conservativism, it is because of its unconscious adherence to a notion of culture which, during the era of late capitalism, aims at a form of property which is stable and independent of stock-market fluctuations. This idea of culture asserts its distance from the system in order, as it were, to offer universal security in the middle of a universal dynamic. The model of the cultural critic is no less the appraising collector than the art critic. In general, cultural criticism recalls the gesture of bargaining, of the expert questioning the authenticity of a painting or classifying it among the Master's lesser works. One devaluates in order to get more. The cultural critic evaluates and hence is inevitably involved in a sphere stained with 'cultural values', even when he rants against the mortgaging of culture. His contemplative stance towards culture necessarily entails scrutinizing, surveying, balancing, selecting: this piece suits him, that he rejects. Yet his very sovereignty, the claim to a more profound knowledge of the object, the separation of the idea from its object through the independence of the critical judgment threatens to succumb to

the thinglike form of the object when cultural criticism appeals to a collection of ideas on display, as it were, and fetishizes isolated categories such as
mind, life and the individual.

But the greatest fetish of cultural criticism is the notion of culture as such.
For no authentic work of art and no true philosophy, according to their very
meaning, has ever exhausted itself in itself alone, in its being-in-itself. They
have always stood in relation to the actual life-process of society from which
they distinguished themselves. Their very rejection of the guilt of a life which
blindly and callously reproduces itself, their insistence on independence and
autonomy, on separation from the prevailing realm of purposes, implies, at
least as an unconscious element, the promise of a condition in which freedom
were realized. This remains an equivocal promise of culture as long as its
existence depends on a bewitched reality and, ultimately, on control over the
work of others. That European culture in all its breadth – that which reached
the consumer and which today is prescribed for whole populations by man-
agers and psychotechnicians – degenerated to mere ideology resulted from a
change in its function with regard to material *praxis*: its renunciation of inter-
ference. Far from being culture's 'sin', the change was forced upon culture by
history. For it is only in the process of withdrawing into itself, only indirectly
that is, that bourgeois culture conceives of a purity from the corrupting traces
of a totalitarian disorder which embraces all areas of existence. Only in so
far as it withdraws from a *praxis* which has degenerated into its opposite,
from the ever-changing production of what is always the same, from the
service of the customer who himself serves the manipulator – only in so far
as it withdraws from Man, can culture be faithful to man. But such concentration on substance which is absolutely one's own, the greatest example of
which is to be found in the poetry and theoretical writings of Paul Valéry,
contributes at the same time to the impoverishment of that substance. Once
the mind is no longer directed at reality, its meaning is changed despite the
strictest preservation of meaning. Through its resignation before the facts of
life and, even more, through its isolation as one 'field' among others, the mind
aids the existing order and takes its place within it. The emasculation of
culture has angered philosophers since the time of Rousseau and the 'ink-
splattering age' of Schiller's *Robbers*, to Nietzsche and finally, to the preach-
ers of commitment for its own sake. This is the result of culture's becoming
self-consciously cultural, which in turn places culture in vigorous and consistent opposition to the growing barbarism of economic hegemony. What
appears to be the decline of culture is its coming to pure self-consciousness.
Only when neutralized and reified, does Culture allow itself to be idolized.
Fetishism gravitates towards mythology. In general, cultural critics become
intoxicated with idols drawn from antiquity to the dubious, long-evaporated

warmth of the liberalist era, which recalled the origins of culture in its decline. Cultural criticism rejects the progressive integration of all aspects of consciousness within the apparatus of material production. But because it fails to see through the apparatus, it turns towards the past, lured by the promise of immediacy. This is necessitated by its own momentum and not merely by the influence of an order which sees itself obliged to drown out its progress in dehumanization with cries against dehumanization and progress. The isolation of the mind from material production heightens its esteem but also makes it a scapegoat in the general consciousness for that which is perpetrated in practice. Enlightenment as such — not as an instrument of actual domination — is held responsible. Hence, the irrationalism of cultural criticism. Once it has wrenched the mind out of its dialectic with the material conditions of life, it seizes it unequivocally and straightforwardly as the principle of fatality, thus undercutting the mind's own resistance. The cultural critic is barred from the insight that the reification of life results not from too much enlightenment but from too little, and that the mutilation of man which is the result of the present particularistic rationality is the stigma of the total irrationality. The abolition of this irrationality, which would coincide with the abolition of the divorce between mental and physical work, appears as chaos to the blindness of cultural criticism: whoever glorifies order and form as such, must see in the petrified divorce an archetype of the Eternal. That the fatal fragmentation of society might some day end is, for the cultural critic, a fatal destiny. He would rather that everything end than for mankind to put an end to reification. This fear harmonizes with the interests of those interested in the perpetuation of material denial. Whenever cultural criticism complains of 'materialism', it furthers the belief that the sin lies in man's desire for consumer goods, and not in the organization of the whole which withholds these goods from man: for the cultural critic, the sin is satiety, not hunger. Were mankind to possess the wealth of goods, it would shake off the chains of that civilized barbarism which cultural critics ascribe to the advanced state of the human spirit rather than to the retarded state of society. The 'eternal values' of which cultural criticism is so fond reflect the perennial catastrophe. The cultural critic thrives on the mythical obduracy of culture.

Because the existence of cultural criticism, no matter what its content, depends on the economic system, it is involved in the fate of the system. The more completely the life-process, including leisure, is dominated by modern social orders — those in the East, above all — the more all spiritual phenomena bear the mark of the order. Either, they may contribute directly to the perpetuation of the system as entertainment or edification, and are enjoyed as exponents of the system precisely because of their socially preformed character. Familiar, stamped and approved by Good Housekeeping as it were, they insinuate themselves into a regressive consciousness, present themselves as 'natural', and permit identification with powers whose preponderance leaves no alternative but that of false love. Or, by being different, they become rarities and once again marketable. Throughout the liberalist era, culture fell within the sphere of circulation. Hence, the gradual withering away of this sphere strikes culture to the quick. With the elimination of trade and its irrational loopholes by the calculated distributive apparatus of industry, the commercialization of culture culminates in absurdity. Completely subdued, administered, thoroughly 'cultivated' in a sense, it dies out. Spengler's denunciation: that mind and money go together, proves correct. But because of his sympathy with direct rule, he advocated a structure of existence divested of all economic as well as spiritual mediations. He maliciously threw the mind together with an economic type which was in fact obsolete. What Spengler failed to understand was that no matter to what extent the mind is a product of that type, it implies at the same time the objective possibility of overcoming it. Just as culture sprang up in the marketplace, in the traffic of trade, in communication and negotiation, as something distinct from the immediate struggle for individual self-preservation, just as it was closely tied to trade in the era of mature capitalism, just as its representatives were counted among the class of 'third persons' who supported themselves in life as middlemen, so culture, considered 'socially necessary' according to classical rules, in the sense of reproducing itself economically, is in the end reduced to that as which it began, to mere communication. Its alienation from human affairs terminates in its absolute docility before a humanity which has been enchanted and transformed into clientele by the suppliers. In the name of the consumer, the manipulators suppress everything in culture which enables it to go beyond the total immanence in the existing society and allow only that to remain which serves society's unequivocal purpose. Hence, 'consumer culture' can boast of being not a luxury but rather the simple extension of production. Political slogans, designed for mass manipulation, unanimously stigmatize, as 'luxury', 'snobbism', and 'highbrow', everything cultural which displeases the commissars. Only when the established order has become the measure of all things does its mere reproduction in the realm of consciousness become truth. Cultural criticism points to this and rails against 'superficiality' and 'loss of substance'. But by limiting its attention to the entanglement of culture in commerce, such criticism itself becomes superficial. It follows the pattern of reactionary social critics who pit 'productive' against 'predatory' capital. In fact, all culture shares the guilt of society. It ekes out its existence only by virtue of injustice already perpetrated in the sphere of production, much as does commerce (cf, *Dialektik der Aufklärung*).

Consequently, cultural criticism shifts the guilt: such criticism is ideology as long as it remains mere criticism of ideology. Totalitarian regimes of both kinds, seeking to protect the *status quo* from even the last traces of insubordination which they ascribe to culture even at its most servile, can conclusively convict culture and its introspection of servility. They suppress the mind, in itself already grown intolerable, and so feel themselves to be purifiers and revolutionaries. The ideological function of cultural criticism bridles its very truth which lies in its opposition to ideology. The struggle against deceit works to the advantage of naked terror. 'When I hear the word "culture", I reach for my gun,' said the spokesman of Hitler's Imperial Chamber of Culture.

Cultural criticism is, however, only able to reproach culture so penetratingly for prostituting itself, for violating in its decline the pure autonomy of the mind, because culture originates in the radical separation of mental and physical work. It is from this separation, the original sin as it were, that culture draws its strength. When culture simply denies the separation and feigns harmonious union, it falls back behind its own notion. Only the mind which, in the delusion of being absolute, removes itself entirely from the merely existent, truly defines the existent in its negativity. As long as even the least part of the mind remains engaged in the reproduction of life, it is its sworn bondsman. The anti-philistinism of Athens was both the most arrogant contempt of the man who need not soil his hands for the man from whose work he lives, and the preservation of an image of existence beyond the constraint which underlies all work. In projecting its own uneasy conscience on to its victims as their 'baseness', such an attitude also accuses that which they endure: the subjugation of men to the prevailing form in which their lives are reproduced. All 'pure culture' has always been a source of discomfort to the spokesmen of power. Plato and Aristotle knew why they would not permit the notion to arise. Instead, in questions concerning the evaluation of art, they advocated a pragmatism which contrasts curiously with the *pathos* of the two great metaphysicians. Modern bourgeois cultural criticism has, of course, been too prudent to follow them openly in this respect. But such criticism secretly finds a source of comfort in the divorce between 'high' and 'popular' culture, art and entertainment, knowledge and non-committal *Weltanschauung*. Its anti-philistinism exceeds that of the Athenian upper class to the extent that the proletariat is more dangerous than the slaves. The modern notion of a pure, autonomous culture indicates that the antagonism has become irreconcilable. This is the result both of an uncompromising opposition to being-for-something else, and of an ideology which in its hybris enthrones itself as being-in-itself.

Cultural criticism shares the blindness of its object. It is incapable of allowing the recognition of its frailty to arise, a frailty set in the division of mental and physical work. No society which contradicts its very notion – that of mankind – can have full consciousness of itself. A display of subjective ideology is not required to obstruct this consciousness, although in times of historical upheaval it tends to contribute to the objective blindness. Rather, the fact that every form of repression, depending on the level of technology, has been necessary for the survival of society, and that society as it is, despite all absurdity, does indeed reproduce its life under the existing conditions, objectively produces the semblance of society's legitimation. As the epitome of the self-consciousness of an antagonistic society, culture can no more divest itself of this semblance than can cultural criticism, which measures culture against culture's own ideal. The semblance has become total in a phase in which irrationality and objective falsity hide behind rationality and objective necessity. Nevertheless, by virtue of their real force, the antagonisms reassert themselves in the realm of consciousness. Just because culture affirms the validity of the principle of harmony within an antagonistic society, albeit in order to glorify that society, it cannot avoid confronting society with its own notion of harmony and thereby stumbling on discord. The ideology which affirms life is forced into opposition to life by the immanent drive of the ideal. The mind which sees that reality does not resemble it in every respect but is instead subject to an unconscious and fatal dynamic, is impelled even against its will beyond apologetics. The fact that theory becomes real force when it moves men is founded in the objectivity of the mind itself which, through the fulfilment of its ideological function must lose faith in ideology. Prompted by the incompatibility of ideology and existence, the mind, in displaying its blindness also displays its effort to free itself of ideology. Disenchanted, the mind perceives naked existence in its nakedness and delivers it up to criticism. The mind either damns the material base, in accordance with the ever-questionable criterion of its 'pure principle', or it becomes aware of its own questionable position, by virtue of its incompatibility with the base. As a result of the social dynamic, culture becomes cultural criticism, which preserves the notion of culture while demolishing its present manifestations as mere commodities and means of brutalization. Such critical consciousness remains subservient to culture in so far as its concern' with culture distracts from the true horrors. From this arises the ambivalent attitude of social theory towards cultural criticism. The procedure of cultural criticism is itself the object of permanent criticism, both in its general presuppositions – its immanence in the existing society – and in its concrete judgments. For the subservience of cultural criticism is revealed in its specific content, and only in this may it be grasped conclusively. At the same time, a dialectical theory which does not wish to succumb to 'Economism', the sentiment which holds that the transformation of the world is exhausted in the increase of production, must absorb cultural criticism, the truth of which consists in bringing untruth to consciousness of itself. A dialectical theory which is uninterested in culture as a mere epiphenomenon, aids pseudo-culture to run rampant and collaborates in the reproduction of the evil. Cultural traditionalism and the terror of the new Russian despots are in basic agreement. Both affirm culture as a whole, sight-unseen, while at the same time proscribing all forms of consciousness which are not made-to-order. They are thus no less ideological than is criticism when it calls a disembodied culture before its tribunal, or holds the alleged negativity of culture responsible for real catastrophes. To accept culture as a whole is to deprive it of the ferment which is its very truth – negation. The joyous appropriation of culture harmonizes with a climate of military music and paintings of battle-scenes. What distinguishes dialectical from cultural criticism is that it heightens cultural criticism until the notion of culture is itself negated, fulfilled and surmounted in one.

Immanent criticism of culture, it may be argued, overlooks what is decisive: the role of ideology in social conflicts. To suppose, if only methodologically, anything like an independent logic of culture is to collaborate in the hypostasis of culture, the ideological *proton pseudos*. The substance of culture, according to this argument, resides not in culture alone but in its relation to something external, to the material life-process. Culture, as Marx observed of juridical and political systems, cannot be fully 'understood either in terms of itself . . . or in terms of the so-called universal development of the mind'. To ignore this, the argument concludes, is to make ideology the basic matter and thus to establish it firmly. And in fact, having taken a dialectical turn, cultural criticism must not hypostasize the criteria of culture. Criticism retains its mobility in regard to culture by recognizing the latter's position within the whole. Without such freedom, without consciousness transcending the immanence of culture, immanent criticism itself would be inconceivable: the spontaneous movement of the object can be followed only by someone who is not entirely engulfed by it. But the traditional demand of the ideology-critique is itself subject to a historical dynamic. The critique was conceived against idealism, the philosophical form which reflects the fetishization of culture. Today, however, the definition of consciousness in terms of being has become a means of dispensing with all consciousness which does not conform to existence. The objectivity of truth, without which the dialectic is inconceivable, is tacitly replaced by vulgar positivism and pragmatism – ultimately, that is, by bourgeois subjectivism. During the bourgeois era, the prevailing theory was the ideology and the opposing *praxis* was in direct contradiction. Today, theory hardly exists any longer and the ideology drones, as it were, from the gears of an irresistible *praxis*. No notion dares to be conceived any more which does not cheerfully include, in all camps, explicit instructions as to who its beneficiaries are – exactly what the polemics once sought to expose. But the unideological thought is that which does not permit itself to be reduced to 'operational terms' and instead strives solely to help the things themselves to that articulation from which they are otherwise cut off by the prevailing language. Since the moment arrived when every advanced economic and political council agreed that what was important was to change the world and that to interpret it was *allotria*, it has become difficult simply to invoke the *Theses* against Feuerbach. Dialectics also includes the relation between action and contemplation. In an epoch in which bourgeois social science has, in Scheler's words, 'plundered' the Marxian notion of ideology and diluted it to universal relativism, the danger involved in overlooking the function of ideologies has become less than that of judging intellectual phenomena in a subsumptive, uninformed and administrative manner and assimilating them into the prevailing constellations of power which the intellect ought to expose. As with many other elements of dialectical materialism, the notion of ideology has changed from an instrument of knowledge into its strait-jacket. In the name of the dependence of superstructure on base, all use of ideology is controlled instead of criticized. No one is concerned with the objective substance of an ideology as long as it is expedient.

Yet the very function of ideologies becomes increasingly abstract. The suspicion held by earlier cultural critics is confirmed: in a world which denies the mass of human beings the authentic experience of intellectual phenomena by making genuine education a privilege and by shackling consciousness, the specific ideological content of these phenomena is less important than the fact that there should be anything at all to fill the vacuum of the expropriated consciousness and to distract from the open secret. Within the context of its social effect, the particular ideological doctrine which a film imparts to its audience is presumably far less important than the interest of the homeward bound movie-goer in the names and marital affairs of the stars. Vulgar notions such as 'amusement' and 'diversion' are more appropriate than pretentious explanations which designate one writer as a representative of the lower-middle class, another of the upper-middle. Culture has become ideological not only as the quintessence of subjectively devised manifestations of the objective mind, but even more as the sphere of private life. The illusory importance and autonomy of private life conceals the fact that private life drags on only as an appendage of the social process. Life transforms itself into the ideology of reification – a death mask. Hence, the task of criticism must be not so much to search for the particular interest-groups to which cultural phenomena are to be assigned, but rather to decipher the general social tendencies which are expressed in these phenomena and through which the most powerful interests realize themselves. Cultural criticism must become social physiognomy. The more the whole divests itself of all spontaneous elements, is socially mediated and filtered, is 'consciousness', the more it becomes 'culture'. In addition to being the means of subsistence, the material process of production finally unveils itself as that which it always was, from its origins in the exchange-relationship as the false consciousness which the two contracting parties have of each other: ideology. Inversely, however, consciousness becomes at the same time increasingly a mere transitional moment in the functioning of the whole. Today, ideology means society as appearance. Although mediated by the totality behind which stands the rule of partiality, ideology is not simply reducible to a partial interest. It is, as it were, equally near the centre in all its pieces.

The alternatives – either calling culture as a whole into question from outside under the general notion of ideology, or confronting it with the norms which it itself has crystallized – cannot be accepted by critical theory. To insist on the choice between immanence and transcendence is to revert to the traditional logic criticized in Hegel's polemic against Kant. As Hegel argued, every method which sets limits and restricts itself to the limits of its object thereby goes beyond them. The position transcending culture is in a certain sense presupposed by dialectics as the consciousness which does succumb in advance to the fetishization of the intellectual sphere. Dialectics means intransigence towards all reification. The transcendent method, which aims at totality, seems more radical than the immanent method, which presupposes the questionable whole. The transcendent critic assumes an as it were Archimedean position above culture and the blindness of society, from which consciousness can bring the totality, no matter how massive, into flux. The attack on the whole draws strength from the fact that the semblance of unity and wholeness in the world grows with the advance of reification; that is, with division. But the summary dismissal of ideology which in the Soviet sphere has already become a pretext for cynical terror, taking the form of a ban on 'objectivism', pays that wholeness too high an honour. Such an attitude buys up culture *en bloc* from society, regardless of the use to which it is put. If ideology is defined as socially necessary appearance, then the ideology today is society itself in so far as its integral power and inevitability, its overwhelming existence-in-itself, surrogates the meaning which that existence has exterminated. The choice of a standpoint outside the sway of existing society is as fictitious as only the construction of abstract utopias can be. Hence, the transcendent criticism of culture, much like bourgeois cultural criticism, sees itself obliged to fall back upon the idea of 'naturalness', which itself forms a central element of bourgeois ideology. The transcendent attack on culture regularly speaks the language of false escape, that of the 'nature boy'. It despises the mind and its works, contending that they are, after all, only man-made and serve only to cover up 'natural' life. Because of this alleged worthlessness, the phenomena allow themselves to be manipulated and degraded for purposes of domination. This explains the inadequacy of most socialist contributions to cultural criticism: they lack the experience of that with which they deal. In wishing to wipe away the whole as if with a sponge, they develop an affinity to barbarism. Their sympathies are inevitably with the more primitive, more undifferentiated, no matter how much it may contradict the level of intellectual productive forces. The blanket rejection of culture becomes a pretext for promoting what is crudest, 'healthiest', even repressive; above all, the perennial conflict between individual and society, both drawn in like manner, which is obstinately resolved in favour of society according to the criteria of the administrators who have appropriated it. From there it is only a step to the official reinstatement of culture. Against this struggles the immanent procedure as the more essentially dialectical. It takes seriously the principle that it is not ideology in itself which is untrue but rather its pretension to correspond to reality. Immanent criticism of intellectual and artistic phenomena seeks to grasp, through the analysis of their form and meaning, the contradiction between their objective idea and that pretension. It names what the consistency or inconsistency of the work itself expresses of the structure of the existent. Such criticism does not stop at a general recognition of the servitude of the objective mind, but seeks rather to transform this knowledge into a heightened perception of the thing itself. Insight into the negativity of culture is binding only when it reveals the truth or untruth of a perception, the consequence or lameness of a thought, the coherence or incoherence of a structure, the substantiality or emptiness of a figure of speech. Where it finds inadequacies it does not ascribe them hastily to the individual and his psychology, which are merely the façade of the failure, but instead seeks to derive them from the irreconcilability of the object's moments. It pursues the logic of its aporias, the insolubility of the task itself. In such antinomies criticism perceives those of society. A successful work, according to immanent criticism, is not one which resolves objective contradictions in a spurious harmony, but one which expresses the idea of harmony negatively by embodying the contradictions, pure and uncompromised, in its inner-most structure. Confronted with this kind of work, the verdict 'mere ideology' loses its meaning. At the same time, however, immanent criticism holds in evidence the fact that the mind has always been under a spell. On its own it is unable to resolve the contradictions under which it labours. Even the most radical reflection of the mind on its own failure is limited by the fact that it remains only reflection, without altering the existence to which its failure bears witness. Hence immanent criticism cannot take comfort in its own idea. It can neither be vain enough to believe that it can liberate the mind directly by immersing itself in it, nor naïve enough to believe that unflinching immersion in the object will inevitably lead to truth by virtue of the logic of things if only the subjective knowledge of the false whole is kept from intruding from the outside, as it were, in the determination of the object. The less the dialectical method can today presuppose the Hegelian identity of subject and object, the more it is obliged to be mindful of the duality of the moments. It must relate the knowledge of society as a totality and of the mind's involvement in it to the claim inherent in the specific content of the object that it be apprehended as such. Dialectics cannot, therefore, permit any insistence on logical neatness to encroach on its right to go from one *genus* to another, to shed light on an object in itself hermetic by casting a glance at society, to present society with the bill which the object does not redeem. Finally, the very opposition between knowledge which penetrates from without and that which bores from within becomes suspect to the dialectical method, which sees in it a symptom of precisely that reification which the dialectic is obliged to accuse. The abstract categorizing and, as it were, administrative thinking of the former corresponds in the latter to the fetishism of an object blind to its genesis, which has become the prerogative of the expert. But if stubbornly immanent contemplation threatens to revert to idealism, to the illusion of the self-sufficient mind in command of both itself and of reality, transcendent contemplation threatens to forget the effort of conceptualization required and content itself instead with the prescribed label, the petrified invective, most often 'petty bourgeois', the ukase dispatched from above. Topological thinking, which knows the place of every phenomenon and the essence of none, is secretly related to the paranoic system of delusions which is cut off from experience of the object. With the aid of mechanically functioning categories, the world is divided into black and white and thus made ready for the very domination against which concepts were once conceived. No theory, not even that which is true, is safe from perversion into delusion once it has renounced a spontaneous relation to the object. Dialectics must guard against this no less than against enthrallment in the cultural object. It can subscribe neither to the cult of the mind nor to hatred of it. The dialectical critic of culture must both participate in culture and not participate. Only then does he do justice to his object and to himself.

The traditional transcendent critique of ideology is obsolete. In principle, the method succumbs to the very reification which is its critical theme. By transferring the notion of causality directly from the realm of physical nature to society, it falls back behind its own object. Nevertheless, the transcendent method can still appeal to the fact that it employs reified notions only in so far as society itself is reified. Through the crudity and severity of the notion of causality, it claims to hold up a mirror to society's own crudity and sever- ity, to its debasement of the mind. But the sinister, integrated society of today no longer tolerates even those relatively independent, distinct moments to which the theory of the causal dependence of superstructure on base once referred. In the open-air prison which the world is becoming, it is no longer so important to know what depends on what, such is the extent to which everything is one. All phenomena rigidify, become insignias of the absolute rule of that which is. There are no more ideologies in the authentic sense of false consciousness, only advertisements for the world through its duplication and the provocative lie which does not seek belief but commands silence. Hence, the question of the causal dependence of culture, a question which seems to embody the voice of that on which culture is thought only to depend, takes on a backwoods ring. Of course, even the immanent method is eventually overtaken by this. It is dragged into the abyss by its object. The materialistic transparency of culture has not made it more honest, only more vulgar. By relinquishing its own particularity, culture has also relinquished the salt of truth, which once consisted in its opposition to other particularities. To call it to account before a responsibility which it denies is only to confirm cultural pomposity. Neutralized and ready-made, traditional culture has become worthless today. Through an irrevocable process its heritage, hypo- critically reclaimed by the Russians, has become expendable to the highest degree, superfluous, trash. And the hucksters of mass culture can point to it with a grin, for they treat it as such. The more total society becomes, the greater the reification of the mind and the more paradoxical its effort to escape reification on its own. Even the most extreme consciousness of doom threatens to degenerate into idle chatter. Cultural criticism finds itself faced with the final stage of the dialectic of culture and barbarism. To write poetry after Auschwitz is barbaric. And this corrodes even the knowledge of why it has become impossible to write poetry today. Absolute reification, which pre- supposed intellectual progress as one of its elements, is now preparing to absorb the mind entirely. Critical intelligence cannot be equal to this chal- lenge as long as it confines itself to self-satisfied contemplation.

12

Lyric Poetry and Society

'Lyric Poetry and Society' is the most lucid introduction provided by Adorno to the idea and practice of the sociology of art. Lyric poetry offers a serious challenge to any sociological analysis. After all, of the many literary forms it might be regarded as the least socially engaged. In essence lyric poetry is the vehicle for personal feelings and subjective experiences. Its compressed expression and usual short length provides little opportunity for extended reflection on the affairs of the world. This is certainly the case with the work of the two poets critically analysed by Adorno: Eduard Mörike and Stephan George. Mörike's lyrics convey the particularly German spirit of loneliness and loss. There is also the familiar romantic sensitivity to nature. George strives to purge poetry of political and ideological content, and, pace Mörike, rejects naturalism. Both poets alike exploit the lyric form for the communication of inward states (problematized in George). Given, then, the apparently apolitical content of lyric poetry, Adorno must propose a sociology of art which cannot rely on the evident messages of the poems. His task, as he sees it, is to uncover the social totality at work within the individual lyric. This is not a reduction of what might be deemed (controversially for Adorno) the purely aesthetic qualities of the work. Rather the very integrity of a work − what, in effect constitutes it as art at all − is achieved only when the generality of things is revealed through the individual experience. Adorno uses a striking metaphor to express this, describing the poem as a 'philosophical sundial of history'. The lyric poem is not, as a conservative interpretation might see it, the veneration of a pure and innocent environment. Rather, Adorno claims, it is an implicit criticism of a world in which experience of things is reduced to reification and categorical subsumption. Furthermore, the inwardness of the perspective is the loneliness of an alienated world, a rejection of collectivity.

'Lyric Poetry and Society' contains some other issues of note. Among them is Adorno's view of language. He appears to suggest that the individual is not constituted by language or, to put it another way, is not an appendage of language (as Heidegger is accused of believing). Adorno here as elsewhere maintains that experience and language are not identical. He can hold therefore that the individual may be the user of certain forms of language which preclude the proper expression of experience. The poet, however, brings language and experience into cohesion and that is achieved by an immersion in the individuality of things. Here the language, in a uniquely poetical structure, meets the individual moments of experience. For this reason Adorno makes the interesting claim that lyric poetry is a demonstration of the philosophical thesis of subject–object mediation in which a specific relation of reciprocity underpins experience.

Some readers might feel that Adorno's interpretations of Mörike's and George's poems are not beyond dispute and even, perhaps, that the social situation of lyric poetry is not compellingly established. But in so far as Adorno provokes us into thinking of lyric poetry as achieving its position and its force by reference to social arrangements which it never names (of which, indeed, the poet might be explicitly unaware) the essay is successful on its own terms.

'Lyric Poetry and Society' [1957], *Telos*, no. 20 (Summer, 1974), pp. 56–71.
Translated by Bruce Mayo.

The announcement of a lecture on lyric poetry and society will make a good many of you uncomfortable. You will expect a sociological study of the sort which can take any subject it wants under consideration – just as fifty years ago we had psychologies, thirty years ago phenomenologies of every conceivable thing. You will fear that a discussion of conditions under which works of art have come into being, and their subsequent effects, must impertinently preempt the place belonging to the experience of those works as such; that sociological orderings and relatings will suppress all insight into the truth or falsity of the objects themselves. You will suspect an intellectual of being likely to commit the error Hegel ascribed to the "formal directorate" [*formellen Vorstand*]: that while scanning the whole he will merely stand above the particular existence of which he speaks – that is, he will not see it but merely label it. Such a method becomes most distressing when applied to lyric poetry. The tenderest, most fragile forms must be touched by, even brought together with precisely that social bustle from which the ideals of our traditional conception of poetry have sought to protect them. A sphere of expression whose very essence lies in defying the power of social organization[1] – either by refusing to see it, or in overcoming it through the pathos of distance, as in Baudelaire or Nietzsche – must be arrogantly made by the sociologist into the opposite of that which it knows itself to be. Can anyone but a philistine, you will ask, talk about lyric poetry and society?

Clearly this suspicion can only be obviated when lyric works are not misused as objects for the demonstration of social theses, when, instead, their relation to social matters exposes something of their essential quality, something of the reason for their poetic worth. Such a relation must not lead us away from the works, it must lead us more deeply into them. This is really to be expected, however, as a moment's reflection will show: for the meaning of a poem is not merely the expression of individual experiences and stirrings of emotion. Rather, these become artistic only when, precisely because of their defined aesthetic form, they participate in the generality of things. Of course, what a lyric poem expresses is not necessarily what everyone experiences. Its generality is not a *volonté de tous*, not a generality which arises through an ability to communicate just those things which others are not able to express. Rather, the descent into individuality raises the lyric poem to the realm of the general by virtue of its bringing to light things undistorted, ungrasped, things not yet subsumed – and thus the poem anticipates, in an abstract way, a condition in which no mere generalities (i.e., extreme particularities) can bind and chain that which is human. From a condition of unrestrained individuation, the lyric work strives for, awaits the realm of the general. The peculiar danger of the lyric, however, is that its own principle of individuation never guarantees the creation of compelling authenticity. It is powerless to prevent itself from remaining stuck in the accidentals of naked, isolated existence. The generality of the lyric poem's content is, nevertheless, essentially social in nature. Only he understands what the poem says who perceives in its solitude the voice of humanity; indeed, the loneliness of the lyric expression itself is latent in our individualistic and, ultimately, atomistic society – just as, by contrast, its general binding validity derives from the denseness of its individuation. For this reason the thinking through of a work of art justly requires a concrete inquiry into social content; no proper effort at understanding can satisfy itself with vague feelings of universality and inclusiveness. Such a precisely specifying cast of thought is not at odds with art and does not add merely external commentary – it is in fact required by every linguistic creation. A poem's indigenous material, its patterns and ideas, cannot be exhausted through mere static contemplation. In order to be contemplated aesthetically, they ask to be thought through, and a thought once set into motion by a poem cannot be cut off at the poem's behest.

Nevertheless, such thoughts – which amount to the social interpretation of lyric poetry, as indeed of all art works – cannot lead directly to the so-called 'social viewpoint' or to the social interests represented by the work or held by its author. Their chief task is rather to discover how the entirety of a society, as a unity containing contradictions, appears in a work; in which respects the work remains true to its society, and in which it transcends that society. Such an interpretive procedure must be – as the philosophers would have it – *immanent*. Social ideas should not be brought to works from without but should, instead, be created out of the complete organized view of things present in the works themselves. The sentence in Goethe's *Maxims and Reflections* to the effect that you do not possess what you do not understand, applies not just to our aesthetic attitude toward works of art themselves, but to aesthetic theory as well: nothing but what is in the works, and belongs to their own particular forms, provides a legitimate ground for ascertaining what the content of the works – the things which have been raised into poetry – represents in a social way. This sort of judgment requires knowledge of a work from within, to be sure, and knowledge of the society without. But knowledge has compelling authority only when it rediscovers itself in pure and utter submission to the matter at hand. We must be especially wary of the present insufferable tendency to drag out at every slightest opportunity the concept of ideology. For ideology is untruth – false consciousness, a lie. It manifests itself in the failure of art works, in their own intrinsic falsehood, and can be uncovered by criticism. To say, however, of great works of art, which fix real existence in determinate forms and thus lend its contradictions a purpose-carrying reconciliation[2] – to say of such works that they are ideological not only belies the truth which they contain: it falsifies the idea of ideology as well. Ideology, as a concept, must not be taken as meaning that all of art and philosophy amount to some particular persons' passing off some particular interests as general ones. The concept of ideology seeks rather to unmask false thought and at the same time to grasp its historical necessity. The greatness of works of art lies solely in their power to let those things be heard which ideology conceals. Whether intended or not, their success transcends false consciousness.

Let me return to your misgivings. You respond to lyric poetry as something set against society, something purely individual. You feel strongly that it should remain this way – that lyric expression, released from the heaviness of material things, should evoke images of a life free of the impositions of the everyday world, of usefulness, of the dumb drive for self-preservation. This demand, however, that of the untouched virgin word, is in itself social in nature. It implies a protest against a social condition which every individual experiences as hostile, distant, cold, and oppressive; and this social condition impresses itself on the poetic form in a negative way: the more heavily social conditions weigh, the more unrelentingly the poem resists, refusing to give in to any heteronomy, and constituting itself purely according to its own particular laws. Its detachment from naked existence becomes the measure of the world's falsity and meanness. Protesting against these conditions, the poem proclaims the dream of a world in which things would be different. The idiosyncrasy of poetic thought, opposing the overpowering force of material things, is a form of reaction against the reification of the world, against the rule of the wares of commerce over people which has been spreading since the beginning of the modern era – which, since the Industrial Revolution, has established itself as the ruling force in life. Even Rilke's "cult of things" belongs to this form of idiosyncrasy, as an attempt to bring the alien objects into subjectively pure expression and dissolve them there – to give their alienness metaphysical credit. The aesthetic weakness of this cult of things, the cryptic gesture, the mixing of religion and decorative handicraft, betrays at once the genuine power of reification that can no longer be painted over with a lyric aura, and can no longer be comprehended.

One only gives another turn to the meaning of such insight into the social nature of lyric poetry when one says that its essential character – as something immediate to us, practically second nature – is thoroughly modern. Landscape painting and its idea of "nature" has, in a similar way, developed independently only in modern times. I know that I exaggerate in saying this and that you could produce many counterexamples for me. The most compelling would be Sappho. Chinese, Japanese, Arabic poetry I leave alone, since I cannot read any of it in the original, and I suspect that translation forces it through a process of accommodation that makes adequate understanding impossible. But the ancient manifestations of what is familiar to us as the specifically lyric spirit are only isolated flashes – just as the backgrounds of older paintings sometimes suggest and anticipate the idea of landscape painting. They do not constitute its form. The great writers of early antiquity who, according to literary notions, must be counted among the lyric poets – Pindar, for one, and Alkaios, but the greater part of Walter von der Vogelweide, as well – are immensely distant from our dominant conceptions about the lyric. They lack that quality of intimacy, of non-materiality which we have justly or unjustly adopted as our criterion of lyric utterance, and only through arduous study can we overcome these conceptions.

Nevertheless, what we mean by lyric – before we stop to elaborate its meaning historically or use it to criticize the forces of individualism – has within it, in its 'purest' form, the quality of a break or rupture. The subjective being that makes itself heard in lyric poetry is one which defines and expresses itself as something opposed to the collective and the realm of objectivity. While its expressive gesture is directed toward, it is not intimately at one with nature. It has, so to speak, lost nature and seeks to recreate it through personification and through descent into the subjective being itself. Only after a transformation into human form can nature regain anew that which man's rule over her has taken away. Even lyrical creations which are untouched by conventional, material existence, by the crude world of material objects, owe their high worth to the power the subjective being within them has, in overcoming its alienation, to evoke an image of the natural world. Their pure subjectivity, apparently flawless, without breaks and full of harmony, actually witnesses to the opposite, to a suffering caused by existence foreign to the subject, as much as it shows the subject's love toward that existence. Indeed, the harmony of such creations is nothing other than the mutual correspondence of such suffering and such love. Even the "Warte nur balde Ruhest du auch"[3] has yet a gesture of consolation; its unfathomable beauty cannot be separated from that which it passes over in silence: the image of a world refusing peace. Solely because the tone of the poem sympathizes with this unstated image does it insist that there is peace nevertheless. One would almost want to take the line "Ach, ich bin des Treibens müde" from the companion poem of the same title as an aid to the interpretation of this *Wanderers Nachtlied*.[4] To be sure, the first poem's greatness moves us as it does because it does not speak of alienated or disturbing things – because no restlessness of objects stands opposed to the speaking subject within the poem; rather, the anxiety is felt as an after-trembling. A second sort of substitute immediacy and wholeness is promised: the human element, language itself, appears as if it were once again the creation, while everything beyond the bounds of the poem fades away in the echo of the soul. The excluded world becomes more than appearance, however; it rises to full truth because, through the spoken expression of benign weariness, a shadow of yearning lingers over its consolation, even the shadow of death. For the "Warte nur balde" all of life is transformed, in an enigmatic, sad smile, to the short moment before falling into sleep. The tone of peace attests that peace itself could not be achieved without the dream's shattering to pieces. The shadow has no power over the image of life returning to itself; but, as a final remembrance of its disfiguration it does lend the dream the ponderous depth which resides under its weightless song. Seeing restful nature, from which the last trace of human form has been erased, the speaking subject becomes aware of its own nothingness. Unnoticeably, silently, irony lightly touches the consolation of this poem: the seconds before the sublime happiness of sleep are the same as those which separate the shortness of life from death. After Goethe, this elevated irony then fell to spitefulness, but it was always bourgeois in character: the elevation of the freed subject always had as its shadow the debasement of the subject to a thing of the marketplace, to that which only exists for others – to the personality of which we ask, "Well now, just what are you?" Within its single moment, however, the "Nachtlied" has its authenticity; the background of disintegration rescues it from triviality, and at the same time the force of disintegration has, as yet, no power over the powerless force of the poem's consolation. It is commonly said that a perfect lyric must possess totality or universality, must comprehend the whole within its bounds, reveal infinitude in its finiteness. If this is to be more than a truism of that sort of aesthetics which subsumes everything under the concept of symbolism, then it signifies that in every lyric poem the historical relation of subject to object, of individual to society within the realm of subjective spirit thrown back on its own resources – this historical relation must have been precipitated in the poem. This precipitation will be more perfect, the more the poem eschews the relation of self to society as an explicit theme and the more it allows this relation to crystallize involuntarily from within the poem.

Now that I have made this formulation, you may reproach me with having so sublimated the relationship between poetry and society – out of fear of sociological crudity – that really nothing remains of the relationship. Precisely that which is not social in a poem should become its social aspect. You might well recall to me that caricature of Gustave Doré's which presents an arch-reactionary politician whose praise of the *ancien régime* rises to the cry: "And who, my dear sirs, do we have to thank for the Revolution of 1789 if not Louis XIV!" You could apply this to my view of poetry and society: namely, society plays the role of the executed king and poetry that of those who fought against him. Poetry, you would reply, however, may no more be explained in terms of society than the Revolution may be construed to the credit of the monarchy which it overthrew – and without whose absurdities it might not have occured at that time. Whether Doré's politician was really just the stupid, cynical propagandist, as the cartoonist has ridiculed him, is beside the point – or even whether there is more truth to the politician's unintended humor than is plain to common sense (Hegel's *Philosophy of History* would have much to contribute to this politician's vindication).

All the same, there is something wrong with the comparison. Lyric poetry is not to be deduced from society; its social content is precisely its spontaneity, which does not follow from the conditions of the moment. But philosophy (again that of Hegel) knows the speculative proposition that the individual is rendered through the general and *vice versa*. This can only mean here that resistance to social pressure is not something absolutely individual. Rather, through the individual and his spontaneity, objective historical forces rouse themselves within the poem, forces which are propelling a restricted and restricting social condition beyond itself to a more humane one. These forces, therefore, must belong to an all-embracing configuration and in no sense merely to naked individuality, blindly opposing itself to society. Now, assuming that the lyric content has in fact – by virtue of its own subjectivity – such an objective content (and indeed, without this assumption we could hardly explain the simplest feature that makes lyric poetry possible as a genre, namely, its effect on people other than the poet himself speaking in his monologue) – then it has this objectivity only if its withdrawal into itself and away from the social surface is motivated by social forces over and beyond the head of its author. This is accomplished by means of language. The specific paradox belonging to the lyric poem – this subjective, personal element transforming itself into an objective one – is bound to that specific importance with poetry gives to linguistic *form*, an importance from which the primacy of language in all literature (prose forms as well) derives. For language itself has a double aspect. Through its configurations it submits to all possible stirrings of emotion, failing in so little that one might almost think it is language which first produces feeling. On the other hand, language remains the medium of concepts and ideas, and establishes our indispensable relation to generalities and hence to social reality. The most sublime lyric works, therefore, are those in which the subject, without a trace of his material being, intones in language until the voice of language itself is heard. The *subject's* forgetting himself, his abandoning himself to language as if devoting himself completely to an object – this and the direct intimacy and spontaneity of his *expression* are the same. Thus language begets and joins both poetry and society in their innermost natures. Lyric poetry, therefore, shows itself most thoroughly integrated into society at those points where it does not repeat what society says – where it conveys no pronouncements – but rather where the speaking subject (who succeeds in his expression) comes to full accord with the language itself, i.e., with what language seeks by its own inner tendency.

On the other hand, language cannot be raised to the position of an absolute voice of existence, as some current ontological theories of linguistics would have it. The subject, whose personal expression (in contrast to the mere signification or reporting of objective content) is necessary if that level at which the voice of historical existence may be heard is to be reached – this subject is no mere trimming on the content of language; he is not external to that content. The moment of self-forgetting in which the subject submerges in language is not a sacrifice of himself to Being. It is not a moment of compulsion or force, not even of force against the speaking subject, but rather a moment of reconciliation; language itself first speaks when it speaks not as something foreign to the subject but as his own voice.

When the speaking subject, the "I," forgets himself completely, he is yet entirely present; language (as a sanctified abracadabra) would otherwise submit to the process of reification and disintegrate as it does in everyday speech.

This, however, brings us back to the actual relation between individual and society. Not only is the individual as such brought into being by society, not only are his thoughts and feelings social in nature as well: but looking at things from the other side, society exists only by virtue of its individuals, whose essence it embodies. If in the past the great philosophers professed the truth (rejected, to be sure, by our modern logical positivists) that subject and object are no rigid, isolated poles, but can only be identified within the process in which they interact, then lyric poetry is the experimental test of this philosophical proposition. In the lyric poem the subject negates both his naked, isolated opposition to society as well as his mere functioning within rationally organized society.[5]

But as organized society's ascendancy over the individual grows, the situation of lyric art becomes more precarious. The work of Baudelaire was the first to register this, in refusing to stop at the individual's suffering. Rather (an extreme consequence of European world-weariness), it went beyond the suffering of the individual and accused the entire modern epoch itself of being anti-lyrical, and by means of an heroically stylized language, it hammered out of this accusation the sparks of genuine poetry. With Baudelaire there appears for the first time a note of despair, just delicately balanced on the point of its own paradoxes. As the contradiction of poetic to communicative language grew extreme, all lyric became a precarious and desperate game; not, as narrow-minded, philistine opinion would have it, because poetry had grown incomprehensible, but because – by means of the pure self-awareness of language as a created art-language, and through its effort to attain its own absolute objectivity, without regard for communicating a narrowed, merely historical, ideologically limited objectivity – it removed itself from the objective spirit, i.e., the living language, and replaced it with an antiquated one, a poetically created surrogate. The elevated, poeticizing, subjectively brutal aspect of subsequent weaker poetry is the price that had to be paid for the attempt to keep poetry objectively alive, undisfigured, untarnished. Its false glitter is a counterpart to the demythologized world from which it extricates itself.

Certainly all this requires some qualification if it is not to be misunderstood. It was my assertion that the lyric poem is always the subjective expression of a social antagonism, as well. Since, however, the objective world which produces poetry is in itself antagonistic, the essence of lyric poetry cannot be entirely explained as the expression of a subjectivity to which language lends objectivity. The lyric subject (the more adequately it presents *itself*, the more compellingly) does not merely embody the whole. Rather it is set apart from the whole in that it owes its existence to special privilege: only the fewest individuals, given the pressures of the necessities of life, are ever allowed to grasp the general truth or shape of things in self-immersion – few, indeed, have been allowed simply to develop themselves as independent individuals, in control of the free expression of their own subjectivities. The others, however, those who not only stand as strangers before the ill-at-ease poet, as if they were only objects – indeed, they have in the most literal sense been reduced to objects, i.e., victims, of the historical process – these others have the same or greater right to grope for the sounds in which suffering and dream are wed. This inalienable right has asserted itself again and again, in ways however impure, deformed, fragmentary, intermittent – in the only ways possible for those who must bear burdens.

All individual lyric poetry is indeed grounded in a collective substratum. If poetry in fact invokes the whole, and not merely that part of luxury, refinement, and tenderness belonging to those who can afford to be tender, then the substantiality even of individual poems derives to a significant degree from their participation in this substratum; in all likelihood it is this substratum that first makes of language the medium in which the subject becomes more than just a subject. The regard which Romanticism had for folksong is only the most striking example of this, certainly not the most compelling. For Romanticism followed a program of transfusing the collective into the individual – and as a result the individual poem tended to indulge more in a technical illusion of generality than to possess such a generality, one arising out of the poem itself. In place of employing such transfusions, poets who scorn every borrowing from the communal language are often able to participate in the collective substratum because of their historical experience. I name Baudelaire, whose poetry gives a slap in the face to the *juste milieu* and even to every normal, middle-class feeling of social sympathy – who, in poems such as the *Petites vieilles* or the one on the generous-hearted servant girl in the *Tableaux parisiens*, was nevertheless truer to the masses, against whom he turned his tragic-arrogant mask, truer than all the poor-people's poetry.

Because the conception of lyric poetry which I made my starting point – the conception of individual expression – appears today to be shaken to the core by the crisis of the individual, the collective substratum of poetry is thrusting upwards at the most widely various points, first simply as a ferment of individual expression itself, then perhaps also as an anticipation of a condition that transcends naked individuality in a positive way. If the translations don't deceive us, then Garcia Lorca – whom Franco's henchmen murdered, and whom no totalitarian regime could have tolerated – was the bearer of such force; and the name of Brecht suggests itself as that of a poet to whom integrity of expression was granted without his having had to pay the price of the esoteric. I hesitate to judge whether the poetic principle of individuation was in fact transformed into another higher principle here, or whether the cause lies in regression and weakening of the ego. In many cases contemporary poetry may owe its collective force to the linguistic and spiritual rudiments of a now yet completely atomized condition, one which is in every way pre-bourgeois – that of dialect poetry. Traditional lyric poetry, however, as the strictest aesthetic negation of modern middle-class values, has continued to be bound for just that reason to bourgeois society.

Since reflections about general principles are insufficient, I would like, with the aid of some poems, to make more concrete the relation of the poet's subjectivity – which, of course, represents a far more general, collective subjectivity – to its antithetical social reality. The thematic elements (without which no verbal art can express itself, not even *poésie pure*) will need to be interpreted here just as much as the so-called formal elements. Attention must be given especially to the ways in which both interpenetrate, for only by means of such interpenetration does the lyric poem actually capture the historic moment. Incidentally, I would prefer not to take such poems as the one of Goethe, about which I made some remarks without offering an analysis. I shall, rather, choose later poems which do not possess the sort of unqualified authenticity one finds in the *Nachtlied*. Undoubtedly the poems I shall discuss do have something of the collective substratum in them, but I would direct your attention, above all, to ways in which various levels of society's inner contradictory relationships manifest themselves in the poet's speaking. I should repeat that neither the private person of the poet, his psychology, nor his so-called social viewpoint are to come into question here; what matters is the poem itself as a philosophical sundial of history.

First I wish to read to you "Auf einer Wanderung" ("On a Hike") by Mörike.

> In ein freundliches Städtchen tret' ich ein,
> In den Straßen liegt roter Abendschein,
> Aus einem offnenen Fenster eben,
> Über den reichsten Blumenflor
> Hinweg, hört man Goldglockentöne schweben,
> Und *eine* Stimme scheint ein Nachtigallenchor,
> Daß die Blüten beben,
> Daß die Lüfte leben,
> Daß in höherem Rot die Rosen leuchten vor.
> Lang' hielt ich staunend, lustbeklommen.

Wie ich hinaus vors Tor gekommen,
Ich weiß es wahrlich selber nicht,
Ach hier, wie liegt die Welt so licht!
Der Himmel wogt in purpurnem Gewühle,
Rückwärts die Stadt in goldnem Rauch;
Wie rauscht der Erlenbach, wie rauscht im Grund die Mühle!
Ich bin wie trunken, irrgeführt –
O Muse, du hast mein Herz berührt
Mit einem Liebeshauch![6]

An image promising that sort of joy which a traveller can still find on the right day in southern German villages, presents itself to the reader, but without the least compromise to the hackneyed idyll of village life, to half-timbered houses and quaint glass-roundel windows. The poem evokes a feeling of warmth and coziness in narrow corners, and at the same time it remains a work of elevated style, not disfigured by feelings of mere comfort and *Gemütlichkeit*. It does not sentimentally praise narrow simplicity at the cost of a broader view, nor the bliss of ignorance. Simple story and language help, together, to unite skillfully the heaven of things felt close at hand with that of immense expanses. The story recognizes the village only as a momentary scene, not as a place to be visited at length. The depth of feeling resulting from delight at the girl's voice heard from the window, and the greatness of all nature as well, which hears the chorus – these appear only at a point beyond the confined scene, under the open, crimson sky with its swiftly moving clouds, where golden village and roaring stream fuse into a single ideal image. This image is aided linguistically by an imponderably delicate, hardly definable, ancient and ode-like quality. As if from a great distance, the free rhythms remind us of rhymeless Greek verses, perhaps even in the sudden outbreak of pathos in the final line of the first verse, which is nevertheless evoked with the most discreet sort of word placement: "Daß in höherem Rot die Rosen leuchten vor" ("So that in heightened red the roses shine forth").[7]

Decisive is the single word "Muse" at the end. It is as if this word, one of the most abused of German classicism, shines forth for a last, final time in the light of the setting sun by being conferred on the *genius loci*, the inner spirit of the friendly village. As something about to disappear, it seems to have mastered all the power delight knows, a power which an invocation of the muse otherwise lacks when, helpless and odd, it is phrased in words of the modern idiom. The inspiration of the poem reveals itself in no other feature quite so perfectly as this: the choice of the most objectionable word at the critical moment, cautiously prepared by the latent Greek poetic gesture dissolves the urgent motion of the whole like a musical cadence. In the briefest of forms, the lyric succeeds in attaining what the German epic vainly sought, even in such conceptions as *Hermann and Dorothea*.[8]

The social significance of this success accords with the stage of historical experience which reveals itself in the poem. German classicism had undertaken in the name of universal humanity to eliminate the accidental elements from subjective feelings, elements which threaten feelings in a society whose interpersonal relationships are no longer direct, but mediated through the market. It strove for an 'objectivizing' of the subject, such as Hegel sought in philosophy, and attempted to overcome and reconcile the contradictions of actual living in the ideal realm of spirit. The continuing existence of these contradictions in reality nevertheless had compromised a spiritual solution: compared to the senseless, competitive life of business interests, slaving to outdo one another, without any deeper purpose (what the artist manages to call "prosaic" life); compared to a world in which the fates of individual lives are determined by blind laws, "art" – whose form implies that it speaks for a fulfilled humanity – became a mere empty word. The concept of man envisioned by classicism therefore retreated into the realm of private isolated existence and its images; only here did it seem that the 'human' could be preserved. Necessarily the idea of humanity as something whole, complete, and self-determining was renounced by the middle classes, in politics as much as in aesthetics. The stubborn limiting of oneself to things which are close at hand (which itself obeys an external compulsion) made such ideals as comfort and *Gemütlichkeit* so suspect. Meaning itself became bound to the accidents of individual fortune and happiness; it acquired, or rather usurped, the dignity that it would otherwise attain only in conjunction with the happiness of the whole.

The social force in Mörike's genius, however, consists in his having combined both experiences, that of classical elevated style and that of the romantic, private miniature – and that in doing so he perceived the boundaries of both possibilities with incomparable tact, and skillfully balanced them against each other. No expression of feeling rises beyond what can be attained at the moment. The often-cited organic quality of his work is probably nothing other than this historical–philosophical tact, possessed to such a degree by hardly any other German poet. The presumed pathological traits of Mörike, which psychologists are ready to explain for us, even the failure of the efforts of his later years, are the negative side of his extreme insight into the nature of what is possible. The poems of this hypochondriac pastor of Cleversulzbach, who is counted as one of our naive poets, are virtuoso pieces surpassed by no master of *l'art pour l'art*. The hollow and ideological qualities of the elevated style are as apparent to him as the stuffy dullness of the petite bourgeoisie – the blindness to all notions of totality characteristic of the

Biedermeier period in which the greater part of his poetry appeared. He was inspired to create images which, for one last time, would betray themselves neither in their Biedermeier drapery nor in their homely table scenes, neither in their tones of virile confidence nor in their sloppy table manners. As if perched on a narrow ridge, there appears in him whatever persists of elevated style, echoing as a memory, together with the elements of an unmediated life, promising fulfillment at a time when historical developments had already condemned them. Both aspects of the vanishing era greet the poet on his hike, in their still lingering traces. He already experiences the paradox of lyric poetry in the arriving industrial age. As gently hovering and delicate as these, his first solutions, are the creations of the poets who followed him, even those who appear separated from him by a deep chasm – like Baudelaire, whose style Claudel described as a mixture of Racine and contemporary journalism. In industrial society the lyric idea of a self-regenerating directness and an immediacy of life – to the extent that it does not merely invoke an impotent romantic past – becomes more and more a condition in which the Possible stubbornly flashes its rays over lyric poetry's own impossibility.

The short poem of Stephan George, which I would now like to discuss briefly, appeared in a much later phase of this development. It is one of the famous songs from the *Seventh Ring*, a cycle of extremely compressed poems, poems which, despite their light rhythms, possess an over-heaviness of content, free of all the elements of *art nouveau*. The musical setting by the great composer Anton von Webern first brought this poem and its audacious boldness out of the horrible cultural conservatism of George's circle; with George, ideology and social content fell at widely separated extremes. The song is as follows:

> Im windes-weben   Ein glanz entfacht –
> War meine frage   Nun drängt der mai
> Nur träumerei.   Nun muss ich gar
> Nur lächeln war   Um dein aug und haar
> Was du gegeben.   Alle tage
> Aus nasser nacht   In sehnen leben.[9]

There is no doubt whatsoever of the poem's elevated style. The joy of things felt close at hand, which Mörike's much older poem still touches briefly, is forbidden here. It is banned by just that Nietzschean sense of "suffering distance" which George knew he was destined to carry on. Between Mörike and him lie only the repellent remains of the Romantics – the idyllic fragments have turned to decayed heart-warmers, hopelessly aged. While

George's poetry – that of the splendidly individual – presupposes as a condition of its very possibility an individualistic, bourgeois society, and the
individual who exists for himself alone, it nevertheless bans the commonly
accepted forms, no less than the themes, of bourgeois poetry. Because this
poetry, however, can speak from no other standpoint or configuration than
precisely those bourgeois frames of mind which it rejects – not a priori,
silently, but with express intention – because of this it is blocked, dammed
at the source: and so it feigns a feudal condition. This hides itself, socially,
behind what is tritely called George's aristocratic stance. It is not the pose
which angers the good burgher who cannot fondle these poems in his own
accustomed way. Rather, however anti-social this pose appears, it is brought
to fruition by the same social dialectic which denies the lyric writer his
identification with the existing order of things and its repertoire of forms,
while he remains sworn to this order in its every detail: he can speak from
no other standpoint than that of a past society, stably ruling itself from within.
From this society is taken the ideal of nobility which dictates the choice of
every word, image, and sound in the poem; and its form – in some hardly
specifiable manner conveyed, as it were, into the linguistic configuration – is
medieval. In this sense the poem, like all of George, is in fact neo-romantic.
It is not, however, real objects, not sounds which are called up, but a buried
condition of the soul. The latent force of the ideal, artistically compelled into
being, the absence of all crude archaisms, raises the song above the despon-
dent story (which it, nonetheless, offers): it can hardly be mistaken for the
cheap decorative imitations of *Minnesang* and medieval legend, nor for a
Sunday-supplement poem of the modern world; its stylization saves it from
conformism. There is as little space for the organic reconciliation of conflicts
in the poem as George's era granted for the smoothing over of real ones;
they are brought under control only by selection, by elimination of the
unmanageable.

Wherever 'near' things, i.e., things belonging to concrete, immediate experience, are still admitted in George's lyric poetry, they are allowed only at the
price of being mythologized. Nothing is allowed to remain as it is. Thus, in
one of the landscapes of the *Seventh Ring*, the child who picks berries is
transformed into a fairy-tale child, wordlessly, as if with a magic wand, in an
act of magic violence. The harmony of the song is wrung from an extreme
of dissonance; it rests on what Valéry called *refus*, a stern self-denial of every
means by which the convention of lyric poetry pretends to capture the
aura of objects. The method retains only the models, the mere formal ideas
and schemata of the lyric itself – in discarding every chance element, these
forms speak once again, tense with expression. In the Germany of Kaiser
Wilhelm the elevated poetic style is allowed to appeal to no tradition, least

of all the classical. Elevated style is attained not by pretending to rhetorical figures and rhythms, but by ascetically omitting whatever would lessen the distance from the tainted language of commerce. In order that the subject may truly resist the lonely process of reification he may not even attempt anymore to retreat to himself – to his private property. He is frightened by the traces of an individualism which has meanwhile sold itself to the literary supplements of the marketplace. The poet must, rather, by denying himself, step out of himself. He must, so to speak, make of himself a vessel for the ideal of a pure language. The great poems of George are dedicated to the preservation of such language. Educated in the romance languages, but especially in that reduction of lyric poetry to its simplest elements which Verlaine used to create an instrument for the most finely differentiated expression, the ear of George, of this follower of Mallarmé, hears its own language as if it were a foreign tongue. He overcomes his alienation from German by raising it to the alienation of language which is not spoken any more but imagined, and in whose potential he dimly perceives what might be composed. But his applications of this insight did not quite work out. The four lines, "Nun muss ich gar Um dein aug und haar Alle tage In sehnen leben" ("Now must I [gar] For your eye and hair Every day In longing live"), which I count among the most irresistable in German poetry, are like a quotation, but not from another poet. They seem to be, rather, from some corpus neglected by the language, irretrievably lost. The *Minnesänger* could have created such lines if they, if a tradition – one would almost say, if the German language itself had succeeded. It was in such a spirit that Borchardt wanted to translate Dante.

The word "gar" has grated on subtle ears; it is probably used in place of "ganz und gar" ["utterly" or "completely," a relatively fixed expression] and, to some extent, on account of the rhyme. One may easily concede that, in the way the word has been shoved into the verse, it has no proper meaning at all. But great works of art are those which succeed precisely in the most doubtful places: as, for example, the most sublime musical works are not entirely subsumed by their formal schemes, but radiate beyond them with a few superfluous notes or measures. So it is with this "gar," a "sediment of the absurd" in Goethe's words, with which language flees the subjective intention which called up the word. Probably it is this word in fact which establishes the rank of the poem, acting with the force of the *déjà vu*: through it its linguistic melody reaches out beyond mere signifying. In the age of the decline of language, George grasps in it the idea which the course of history denied language, and constructs lines which sound as if they did not come from him but had been present from the dawn of ages and would always be as they are. Their Quixotic qualities, however, the impossibility of such poetic restoration-work, the dangers of mere handicraft, contribute to the content of the poem; the chimerical longing of language for the impossible is made into an expression of the speaker's insatiable erotic longing; he frees himself from himself, relieves himself, in another.

A transformation of such tremendously exaggerated individuality to self-annihilation (and what is the Maximin-cult of the late George[10] if not a renunciation of individuality desperately trying to interpret itself in a positive way) was needed to prepare that phantasmagoria for which the German language had vainly groped in its greatest masters – in folk song. Only by means of a differentiation – which expanded to such a degree that it could no longer endure its own fragmentation, its extreme spread of differences; could endure nothing which failed to show the whole free from the disgrace of individuation, in its particularities – only by means of this extreme differentiation could the lyric Word do the bidding of language's deepest being and oppose its enforced service in the realm of economically organized purposes and goals.[11] And with that the thought of a free humanity is served, even if George's school masked this thought behind a base cult of elevation.[12] George has his truth in his poetry's breaking through the walls of individuality, in its perfection of the particular, in its sensitivity arrayed against the banal as much as, in the end, against the exquisitely choice. If its expression concentrated itself in the individual, completely saturating him with substance and experience garnered from its own loneliness, then precisely this speech becomes the voice of men between whom the barriers have fallen.

Translator's Notes

1   "Die Macht der Vergesellschaftung." Adorno implies specifically the forces organizing, rationalizing, "socializing" the structure of society. "Vergesellschaften" in its sociological sense refers to the transition from the organically human communities (*Gemeinschaften*) of earlier historical periods to the rational, purpose-oriented, impersonal *Gesellschaft* characteristic of modern industrial societies.

2   Works of art "die an Gestaltung und allein dadurch an tendenzieller Versöhnung tragender Widersprüche des realen Daseins ihr Wesen haben." This sentence, like many others, is but the tip of an iceberg. I understand it as follows: the artist is forced by the nature of art to render the fluid, evolving world of his experience in static, fixed forms; to do this, he must find common terms in the contradictions of the world which presents itself to him, so that its disparate and contradictory elements can be represented in a single, unified whole. Any discovery of unity in contradictions is necessarily the realization of their human,

historical purpose or "Tendenz" (tenor, tendency), since even the simplest acts of perception, such as the recognition of a face in a jumble of lines, require that we impose or discover the human significance in what is otherwise only a confusion of data. And the 'timelessness' which we commonly recognize as a quality of great works of art is nothing other than such a discovery of the deeper purpose latent in the historical moment itself to which the work points and out of which it arises.

3   These are the last two lines of a Goethe poem so well known to German readers that it would be superfluous for Adorno to mention the title; in Longfellow's translation (which cannot convey the auditory qualities of the poem) it reads:

> O'er all the hill-tops
> Is quiet now,
> In all the tree-tops
> Hearest thou
> Hardly a breath;
> The birds are asleep in the trees:
> Wait; soon like these
> Thou too shalt rest.

4   The other "Wanderer's Night-Song," again in Longfellow's translation:

> Thou that from the heavens art
> Every pain and sorrow stillest
> And the doubly wretched heart
> Doubly with refreshment fillest,
> I am weary with contending!
> Why this rapture and unrest?
> Peace descending
> Come, ah, come into my breast!

5   "Vergesellschafteten Gesellschaft." See note 1.

6
> I enter a village through the ancient tower
> Friendly streets glow in the red evening hour
> In an open window, now, and over
> Full beds of flowers ever higher
> Golden bell-sounds sweetly hover
> And a single voice seems a nightingale choir:
> That the flowers sway.
> That breezes play,
> And the roses' red to higher hue aspires.
> Long stood I joyous, stupified
> How I left the gate, found the way
> Beyond the town, I cannot say;
> But here – how bright the world lies!

Above, bright purple billows flow
Behind, the vaprous town in golden light
How roars the rushing stream, how roars the mill below
I reel in bliss, confused, misled –
O Muse! Throughout my heart has spread
A whisper of thy love.

7   Of course, no translation can hope to convey the qualities Adorno refers to here.
    The preceding two lines of the German poem, one might observe, establish
    momentarily a somewhat confining, though not strict, iambic diameter ("Daß"
    suggests a trimeter), which then expands in a "sudden outbreak of pathos" into
    a vaguely iambic pentameter. Stressing "Daß," one can also read this last line as
    a sextameter, which subtly echoes the sextameters one can hear in lines five and
    six.

8   An epic by Goethe depicting events in the life of a rising tavern-keeper's family,
    in the context of simple German village society, composed in Homeric verse.

9   In weaving winds   A glimmer kindled –
                 My asking seemed   Now presses May
                 Merely dreamed   Now must I e'er
                 That you gave   For your eye and hair
                 Was merely smiled   Endless days
                 In glistening night   In longing live.

10 George met the 15-year-old Maximiliam Kronberger in Munich in 1902; when
    the handsome and talented boy died in 1904 George wrote *Maximilian, ein
    Gedenkbuch* to celebrate his memory. In George's later poetry the youth is raised
    to a prophet of a rebirth of the Greek spirit.

11 "Economically organized" is, of course, a potentially misleading addition. I mean
    simply to remind the reader here that the purposes and goals against which the
    poet's language speaks are not *merely* those which become fixed in structures of
    the language he uses, but are indirectly the limited, utilitarian purposes of the
    social and economic organization in which the language is embedded. The next
    sentence asserts this relationship on the deeper level of the poem's 'timelessness':
    the true, unerring voice of Language-in-Itself ("das An-sich-Sein der Sprache")
    is a product – and producer – of the final, unchanging goals, i.e., the *telos* of
    human history (or history humanely understood).

12 George, like Rilke, lived an austere and 'pure' life, and the followers he gathered
    around him insisted on the corresponding other-worldly purity of the poetic
    tradition he tried, successfully, to found.

13

Culture Industry Reconsidered

Adorno's analysis of the culture industry first appeared in *Dialectic of Enlightenment*. The context was Adorno's (and Horkheimer's) view that society had become totally integrated, thereby purging itself of difference and the capacity for self-criticism. The culture industry was seen as an important instrument of that integration. In 'Culture Industry Reconsidered' Adorno returns to that subject, not to revise it, but to present it with a clarity sometimes lost in the virulence of *Dialectic of Enlightenment*.

Adorno notes that the term 'culture industry' is to be preferred to 'mass culture' in that the latter suggests a type of culture spontaneously chosen by the masses as suiting their needs. However, that is to miss the point that the culture industry has, Adorno argues, nothing to do with the views or needs of the masses. Rather the culture industry produces commodities which generate false needs. And the metaphor of industry is apt, he argues, as entertainment is produced through patterns of standardization and, with advertising and marketing, distributed like any other manufactured goods. The culture industry sustains itself through the illusion that it offers novelty, but ultimately what is new is merely another instance of what is commercially proven. The techniques of the culture industry – its skilful production of film, music, or television – are in no way equivalent to the techniques of art. The latter are the means by which the artist establishes the internal organization of a work. In the culture industry, however, technique is solely for the manufacture of external effect: to induce the experience of satisfaction and harmony in the consumer. The consumer sees fictitious conflicts resolved, heroic types taking control, little realizing the ideological purposes of these experiences: the perpetuation of the myth of autonomous subjectivity. The choices of the masses never enter into the picture: they are the objects of the industry, not its determining subjects. Culture, Adorno claims, was once the area of protest in which great art provoked consciousness of the difficulties of existence. Now, however, the culture industry achieves conformity. Adorno, in a striking remark, even suggests that consciousness and conformity have become identical. Adorno is not suggesting that the products of the culture industry are consolatory in the sense that they take us away from our daily misery since, as he argues through his critical theory, there is no consciousness of the misery of social arrangements. The culture industry encourages its consumers to see society as a positive and natural entity. The simplicity and rigid invariability of its products parallel the reified society and as such offer no alternative to or element of criticism of reification.

Adorno's critique of popular culture is trenchant and it has faced superficial charges of elitism and snobbery. It is clear that his account of the culture industry identifies undeniable strategies of manipulation. The more ambitious claim is that this manipulation produces social conformism. The strength of this position can only be appreciated when read alongside Adorno's thoughts on society and ideology.

'Culture Industry Reconsidered' [1963], New German Critique, no. 6 (Fall, 1975),
pp. 12–19.
Translated by Anson G. Rabinbach.

The term culture industry was perhaps used for the first time in the book *Dialectic of Enlightenment*, which Horkheimer and I published in Amsterdam in 1947. In our drafts we spoke of "mass culture." We replaced that expression with "culture industry" in order to exclude from the outset the interpretation agreeable to its advocates: that it is a matter of something like a culture that arises spontaneously from the masses themselves, the contemporary form of popular art. From the latter the culture industry must be distinguished in the extreme. The culture industry fuses the old and familiar into a new quality. In all its branches, products which are tailored for consumption by masses, and which to a great extent determine the nature of that consumption, are manufactured more or less according to plan. The individual branches are similar in structure or at least fit into each other, ordering themselves into a system almost without a gap. This is made possible by contemporary technical capabilities as well as by economic and administrative concentration. The culture industry intentionally integrates its consumers from above. To the detriment of both it forces together the spheres of high and low art, separated for thousands of years. The seriousness of high art is destroyed in speculation about its efficacy; the seriousness of the lower perishes with the civilizational constraints imposed on the rebellious resistance inherent within it as long as social control was not yet total. Thus, although the culture industry undeniably speculates on the conscious and unconscious state of the millions towards which it is directed, the masses are not primary, but secondary, they are an object of calculation; an appendage of the machinery. The customer is not king, as the culture industry would like to have us believe, not its subject but its object. The very word mass-media, specially honed for the culture industry, already shifts the accent onto harmless terrain. Neither is it a question of primary concern for the masses, nor of the techniques of communication as such, but of the spirit which sufflates them, their master's voice. The culture industry misuses its concern for the masses in order to duplicate, reinforce and strengthen their mentality, which it presumes is given and unchangeable. How this mentality might be changed is excluded throughout. The masses are not the measure but the ideology of the culture industry, even though the culture industry itself could scarcely exist without adapting to the masses.

The cultural commodities of the industry are governed, as Brecht and Suhrkamp expressed it thirty years ago, by the principle of their realization as value, and not by their own specific content and harmonious formation. The entire practice of the culture industry transfers the profit motive naked onto cultural forms. Ever since these cultural forms first began to earn a living for their creators as commodities in the marketplace they had already possessed something of this quality. But then they sought after profit only indirectly, over and above their autonomous essence. New on the part of the culture industry is the direct and undisguised primacy of a precisely and thoroughly calculated efficacy in its most typical products. The autonomy of works of art, which of course rarely ever predominated in an entirely pure form, and was always permeated by a constellation of effects, is tendentially eliminated by the culture industry, with or without the conscious will of those in control. The latter include both those who carry out directives as well as those who hold the power. In economic terms they are or were in search of new opportunities for the realization of capital in the most economically developed countries. The old opportunities became increasingly more precarious as a result of the same concentration process which alone makes the culture industry possible as an omnipresent phenomenon. Culture, in the true sense, did not simply accommodate itself to human beings; but it always simultaneously raised a protest against the petrified relations under which they lived, thereby honoring them. Insofar as culture becomes wholly assimilated to and integrated in those petrified relations, human beings are once more debased. Cultural entities typical of the culture industry are no longer *also* commodities, they are commodities through and through. This quantitative shift is so great that it calls forth entirely new phenomena.

Ultimately, the culture industry no longer even needs to directly pursue everywhere the profit interests from which it originated. These interests have become objectified in its ideology and have even made themselves independent of the compulsion to sell the cultural commodities which must be swallowed anyway. The culture industry turns into public relations, the manufacturing of "good will" per se, without regard for particular firms or saleable objects. Brought to bear is a general uncritical consensus, advertisements produced for the world, so that each product of the culture industry becomes its own advertisement.

Nevertheless, those characteristics which originally stamped the transformation of literature into a commodity are maintained in this process. More than anything in the world, the culture industry has its ontology, a scaffolding of rigidly conservative basic categories which can be gleaned, for example, from the commercial English novels of the late 17th and early 18th centuries. What parades as progress in the culture industry, as the incessantly new which it offers up, remains the disguise for an eternal sameness; everywhere the changes mask a skeleton which has changed just as little as the profit motive itself since the time it first gained its predominance over culture.

Thus, the expression "industry" is not to be taken literally. It refers to the standardization of the thing itself – such as that of the Western, familiar to every movie-goer – and to the rationalization of distribution techniques, but not strictly to the production process. Although in film, the central sector of the culture industry, the production process resembles technical modes of operation in the extensive division of labor, the employment of machines and the separation of the laborers from the means of production – expressed in the perennial conflict between artists active in the culture industry and those who control it – individual forms of production are nevertheless maintained. Each product affects an individual air; individuality itself serves to reinforce ideology, insofar as the illusion is conjured up that the completely reified and mediated is a sanctuary from immediacy and life. Now, as ever, the culture industry exists in the "service" of third persons, maintaining its affinity to the declining circulation process of capital, to the commerce from which it came into being. Its ideology above all makes use of the star system, borrowed from individualistic art and its commercial exploitation. The more dehumanized its methods of operation and content, the more diligently and successfully the culture industry propagates supposedly great personalities and operates with heart-throbs. It is industrial more in a sociological sense, in the incorporation of industrial forms of organization even where nothing is manufactured – as in the rationalization of office work – rather than in the sense of anything really and actually produced by technological rationality. Accordingly, the misinvestments of the culture industry are considerable, throwing those branches rendered obsolete by new techniques into crises, which seldom lead to changes for the better.

The concept of technique in the culture industry is only in name identical with technique in works of art. In the latter, technique is concerned with the internal organization of the object itself, with its inner logic. In contrast, the technique of the culture industry is, from the beginning, one of distribution and mechanical reproduction, and therefore always remains external to its object. The culture industry finds ideological support precisely insofar as it carefully shields itself from the full potential of the techniques contained in its products. It lives parasitically from the extra-artistic technique of the material production of goods, without regard for the obligation to the internal artistic whole implied by its functionality (*Sachlichkeit*), but also without concern for the laws of form demanded by aesthetic autonomy. The result for the physiognomy of the culture industry is essentially a mixture of streamlining, photographic hardness and precision on the one hand, and individualistic residues, sentimentality and an already rationally disposed and adapted romanticism on the other. Adopting Benjamin's designation of the traditional work of art by the concept of aura, the presence of that which is not present, the culture industry is defined by the fact that it does not strictly counterpoise another principle to that of aura, but rather by the fact that it conserves the decaying aura as a foggy mist. By this means the culture industry betrays its own ideological abuses.

It has recently become customary among cultural officials as well as sociologists to warn against underestimating the culture industry while pointing to its great importance for the development of the consciousness of its consumers. It is to be taken seriously, without cultured snobbism. In actuality the culture industry is important as a moment of the spirit which dominates today. Whoever ignores its influence out of skepticism for what it stuffs into people would be naive. Yet there is a deceptive glitter about the admonition to take it seriously. Because of its social role, disturbing questions about its quality, about truth or untruth, and about the aesthetic niveau of the culture industry's emissions are repressed, or at least excluded from the so-called sociology of communications. The critic is accused of taking refuge in arrogant esoterica. It would be advisable first to indicate the double meaning of importance that slowly worms its way in unnoticed. Even if it touches the lives of innumerable people, the function of something is no guarantee of its particular quality. The blending of aesthetics with its residual communicative aspects leads art, as a social phenomenon, not to its rightful position in opposition to alleged artistic snobbism, but rather in a variety of ways to the defense of its baneful social consequences. The importance of the culture industry in the spiritual constitution of the masses is no dispensation for reflection on its objective legitimation, its essential being, least of all by a science which thinks itself pragmatic. On the contrary: such reflection becomes necessary precisely for this reason. To take the culture industry as seriously as its unquestioned role demands, means to take it seriously critically, and not to cower in the face of its monopolistic character.

Among those intellectuals anxious to reconcile themselves with the phenomenon and eager to find a common formula to express both their reservations against it and their respect for its power, a tone of ironic toleration prevails unless they have already created a new mythos of the 20th century from the imposed regression. After all, those intellectuals maintain, everyone knows what pocket novels, films off the rack, family television shows rolled out into serials and hit parades, advice to the lovelorn and horoscope columns are all about. All of this, however, is harmless and, according to them, even democratic since it responds to a demand, albeit a stimulated one. It also bestows all kinds of blessings, they point out, for example, through the dissemination of information, advice and stress reducing patterns of behavior. Of course, as every sociological study measuring something as elementary as how politically informed the public is has proven, the information is meager or indifferent. Moreover, the advice to be gained from manifestations of the culture industry is vacuous, banal or worse, and the behavior patterns are shamelessly conformist.

The two-faced irony in the relationship of servile intellectuals to the culture industry is not restricted to them alone. It may also be supposed that the consciousness of the consumers themselves is split between the prescribed fun which is supplied to them by the culture industry and a not particularly well-hidden doubt about its blessings. The phrase, the world wants to be deceived, has become truer than had ever been intended. People are not only, as the saying goes, falling for the swindle; if it guarantees them even the most fleeting gratification they desire a deception which is nonetheless transparent to them. They force their eyes shut and voice approval, in a kind of self-loathing, for what is meted out to them, knowing fully the purpose for which it is manufactured. Without admitting it they sense that their lives would be completely intolerable as soon as they no longer clung to satisfactions which are none at all.

The most ambitious defense of the culture industry today celebrates its spirit, which might safely be called ideology, as an ordering factor. In a supposedly chaotic world it provides human beings with something like standards for orientation, and that alone seems worthy of approval. However, what its defenders imagine is preserved by the culture industry is in fact all the more thoroughly destroyed by it. The color film demolishes the genial old tavern to a greater extent than bombs ever could: the film exterminates its *imago*. No homeland can survive being processed by the films which celebrate it, and which thereby turn the unique character on which it thrives into an interchangeable sameness.

That which legitimately could be called culture attempted, as an expression of suffering and contradiction, to maintain a grasp on the idea of the good life. Culture cannot represent either that which merely exists or the conventional and no longer binding categories of order which the culture industry drapes over the idea of the good life as if existing reality were the good life, and as if those categories were its true measure. If the response of the culture industry's representatives is that it does not deliver art at all, this is itself the ideology with which they evade responsibility for that from which the business lives. No misdeed is ever righted by explaining it as such.

The appeal to order alone, without concrete specificity, is futile; the appeal to the dissemination of norms, without these ever proving themselves in reality or before consciousness, is equally futile. The idea of an objectively binding order, huckstered to people because it is so lacking for them, has no claims if it does not prove itself internally and in confrontation with human beings. But this is precisely what no product of the culture industry would engage in. The concepts of order which it hammers into human beings are always those of the status quo. They remain unquestioned, unanalyzed and undialectically presupposed, even if they no longer have any substance for those who accept them. In contrast to the Kantian, the categorical imperative of the culture industry no longer has anything in common with freedom. It proclaims: you shall conform, without instruction as to what; conform to that which exists anyway, and to that which everyone thinks anyway as a reflex of its power and omnipresence. The power of the culture industry's ideology is such that conformity has replaced consciousness. The order that springs from it is never confronted with what it claims to be or with the real interests of human beings. Order, however, is not good in itself. It would be so only as a good order. The fact that the culture industry is oblivious to this and extols order *in abstracto*, bears witness to the impotence and untruth of the messages it conveys. While it claims to lead the perplexed, it deludes them with false conflicts which they are to exchange for their own. It solves conflicts for them only in appearance, in a way that they can hardly be solved in their real lives. In the products of the culture industry human beings get into trouble only so that they can be rescued unharmed, usually by representatives of a benevolent collective; and then in empty harmony, they are reconciled with the general, whose demands they had experienced at the outset as irreconcilable with their interests. For this purpose the culture industry has developed formulas which even reach into such non-conceptual areas as light musical entertainment. Here too one gets into a 'jam,' into rhythmic problems, which can be instantly disentangled by the triumph of the basic beat.

Even its defenders, however, would hardly contradict Plato openly who maintained that what is objectively and intrinsically untrue cannot also be subjectively good and true for human beings. The concoctions of the culture industry are neither guides for a blissful life, nor a new art of moral responsibility, but rather exhortations to toe the line, behind which stand the most powerful interests. The consensus which it propagates strengthens blind, opaque authority. If the culture industry is measured not by its own substance and logic, but by its efficacy, by its position in reality and its explicit pretentions; if the focus of serious concern is with the efficacy to which it always appeals, the potential of its effect becomes twice as weighty. This potential, however, lies in the promotion and exploitation of the ego-weakness to which the powerless members of contemporary society, with its concentration of power, are condemned. Their consciousness is further developed retrogressively. It is no coincidence that cynical American film producers are heard to say that their pictures must take into consideration the level of eleven year olds. In doing so they would very much like to make adults into eleven year olds.

It is true that thorough research has not, for the time being, produced an airtight case proving the regressive effects of particular products of the culture industry. No doubt an imaginatively designed experiment could achieve this more successfully than the powerful financial interests concerned would find comfortable. In any case, it can be assumed without hesitation that steady drops hollow the stone, especially since the system of the culture industry that surrounds the masses tolerates hardly any deviation and incessantly drills the same formulas of behavior. Only their deep unconscious mistrust, the last residue of the difference between art and empirical reality in the spiritual makeup of the masses explains why they have not, to a person, long since perceived and accepted the world as it is constructed for them by the culture industry. Even if its messages were as harmless as they are made out to be – on countless occasions they are obviously not harmless, like the movies which chime in with currently popular hate campaigns against intellectuals by portraying them with the usual stereotypes – the attitudes which the culture industry calls forth are anything but harmless. If an astrologer urges his readers to drive carefully on a particular day, that certainly hurts no one; they will, however, be harmed indeed by the stupefication which lies in the claim that advice which is valid every day and which is therefore idiotic, needs the approval of the stars.

Human dependence and servitude, the vanishing point of the culture industry, could scarcely be more faithfully described than by the American interviewee who was of the opinion that the dilemmas of the contemporary epoch would end if people would simply follow the lead of prominent personalities. Insofar as the culture industry arouses a feeling of well-being that the world is precisely in that order suggested by the culture industry, the substitute gratification which it prepares for human beings cheats them out of the same happiness which it deceitfully projects. The total effect of the culture industry is one of anti-enlightenment, in which, as Horkheimer and I have noted, enlightenment, that is the progressive technical domination of nature, becomes mass deception and is turned into a means for fettering consciousness. It impedes the development of autonomous, independent individuals who judge and decide consciously for themselves. These, however, would be the precondition for a democratic society which needs adults who have come of age in order to sustain itself and develop. If the masses have been unjustly reviled from above as masses, the culture industry is not among the least responsible for making them into masses and then despising them, while obstructing the emancipation for which human beings are as ripe as the productive forces of the epoch permit.

14

The Autonomy of Art

During the final years of his life Adorno struggled to bring to completion a work which would represent what he had previously stated only diffusely, namely, a theory of aesthetics. From certain remarks we can see that Adorno even saw in this work the potential for a concept of praxis which would resolve what he took to be the key philosophical problem of non-identity: that is, the problem of explaining without reductionism subject-object interaction. The work, *Aesthetic Theory*, was not however to reach its final draft. It appeared in 1970 in its inevitably unsatisfactory form, one year after Adorno's death. Rolf Tiedemann tells us that Adorno had intended to give *Aesthetic Theory* this epigram from Friedrich von Schlegel: 'In the so-called philosophy of art one of two things is usually missing: either the philosophy or the art.' Adorno laboured intensely, and usually successfully, to avoid Schlegel's judgment. All theoretical discussions are contextualized within concrete instances, and artworks and art movements are explicated philosophically.

The central theme of *Aesthetic Theory* is the autonomy of art. Adorno argues that the great art of the bourgeois era is characterized by its apparent independence from society: it is not created for the purposes of public utility nor does it serve what Benjamin called a 'cultic function'. For these reasons bourgeois art has been criticized by other Marxist theorists who believe that art should, on the contrary, be politically committed. By its elevation, they say, bourgeois art fails to engage in a socially progressive critique of society. It thereby aligns itself with the forces of domination. In the sections from *Aesthetic Theory* reprinted here we see Adorno reject the idea of committed art in a confrontation with two western intellectuals, Bertold Brecht and Jean-Paul

Sartre. It is Adorno's contention that committed art is no better than political theory in that it has no specific aesthetic quality, merely political aspirations. Art loses its essence when it concedes heteronomy, in this case the heteronomy being political propaganda. Furthermore ideology cannot be exposed by edification. Political messages will be filtrated through false consciousness and dismissed. Rather, social contradictions need to be experienced and certain art holds open the possibility of that experience. Art is not autonomous in the sense that it is metaphysically removed from and independent of society. It is autonomous in that it is not reducible to the requirements of society, namely the presentation of a harmonious and meaningful whole. Adorno uses the metaphor of Leibniz's monad to explain the relation of autonomous art to society. The relevant parts of Leibniz's theory are that monads are unities, individual, internally dynamic, windowless in that they do not affect one another nor can anything pass on from any one of them, and finally they each reflect the universe from their individual perspective. Transposing this metaphor to the artwork, Adorno holds that each artwork is a coherent entity constituted by a dynamic force field of meanings. Furthermore, no artwork is reducible to any particular message (unlike, for example, committed art). Yet each is a cipher of society awaiting the appropriate interpretation. Art can be critical both in encouraging praxis which is contrary to socially prescribed experiences (cf. Schoenberg) and in drawing attention to the extraordinary in the ordinary (cf. Kafka or Beckett). With respect to the latter, neither Kafka nor Beckett ever address social conditions, yet their works are potentially more effective than explicitly critical ones in illuminating contemporary experience. This is achieved only by subversion of content by form. In this subversion art is at odds with itself whilst remaining as art. The significance of this – drawing attention to the extraordinary in the ordinary – is that it points, in the way that monads do (above), to the aporias of modern society. These aporias are unknown to false consciousness in that it takes its social environment as something given, natural, and essentially rational. Against this consciousness Kafka and Beckett provide in literary form the experience of contradiction which has, however indirectly, a critical relation to society. In this way alone is aesthetic resistance possible. Didactic art, by contrast, cannot provide that critical experience.

Adorno distinguishes autonomous art from the artworks of l'art pour l'art which are self-consciously positioned at a remove from a despised reality. But, this, Adorno claims, is ideological in that l'art pour l'art fails to engage reality and thereby becomes false consolation. The autonomy of art is the product of what Marx decried as a division between intellectual and physical labour. Even though Adorno argues for the superiority of autonomous art, a superiority due to its critical qualities, it is for him a historically necessary though not eternally desirable state of affairs precisely because it is a symptom of the division of labour.

There is no doubt that Adorno's distinctions are, at times, exceedingly fine. However, *Aesthetic Theory* stands among the twentieth century's best efforts to comprehend the essence of art.

Society, *Aesthetic Theory* [1970] (London: Routledge and Kegan Paul, 1984), pp. 320–52 (abridged).
Translated by C. Lenhardt.

The Dual Essence of Art: Social Fact and Autonomy

There is no doubt that art was in some sense more directly a social thing before its emancipation than after. Autonomy, art's growing independence from society, is a function of the bourgeois consciousness of freedom, which in turn is tied up with a specific social structure. Before that, art may have been in conflict with the forces and mores dominating society, but it was never 'for itself'. Such conflicts have always existed; desultorily they are reflected in Plato's condemnation of art in the *Republic*. The notion of a fundamentally oppositional art, however, did not occur to anyone at the time. In short, there has been a great deal of direct social control over art, from its inception all the way down to modern totalitarian states, the one exception being the bourgeois era. There is a sense however, in which bourgeois society can be said to have integrated art even more completely than any previous society. The pressure exerted by the growth of nominalism forced the latently present social essence of art more and more into the open: in the bourgeois novel that essence is incomparably more palpable than in the highly stylized, distanced epics of chivalry. The influx into art of experiences that are no longer forced into given genres and the need to constitute form out of these experiences, from below, as it were – these are two phenomena which indicate the growth of 'realism', measured purely in terms of aesthetic categories rather than content. No longer sublimated by the principle of stylization, the relation of content to the society from which it springs is thus rendered much more direct, and not only in literature. The so-called lower forms too had kept their distance from society in pre-bourgeois times. This holds true even of genres like ancient Athenian comedy, with its focus on bourgeois relations and everyday events; the flight by Aristophanes to no man's land is not some kind of escapist aberration, but an essential aspect of his form.

While art is always a social fact because it is a product of the social labour of spirit, this factual quality is being accentuated as art becomes bourgeoisified. Bourgeois art focuses directly on the relation between itself as an artefact and empirical society. *Don Quixote* marks the beginning of this development. Art, however, is not social only because it is brought about in such a way that it embodies the dialectic of forces and relations of production. Nor is art social only because it derives its material content from society. Rather, it is social primarily because it stands opposed to society. Now this opposition art can mount only when it has become autonomous. By congealing into an entity unto itself – rather than obeying existing social norms and thus proving itself to be 'socially useful' – art criticizes society just by being there. Pure and immanently elaborated art is a tacit critique of the debasement of man by a condition that is moving towards a total-exchange society where everything is a for-other. This social deviance of art is the determinate negation of a determinate society. To be sure, the rejection of society that we see reflected in the sublimation of autonomous art through the law of form also lends itself to ideological abuse: art's distance from this horrifying society also betrays an attitude of non-intervention. It must be kept in mind that society is not co-extensive with ideology. Any society is more than sheer negativity to be indicted by the aesthetic law of form; even in its most objectionable shape, society is still capable of producing and reproducing human life. Art has had to take this aspect (no less than that of its critical task) into account, at least until such time as it became clear that the social process was headed for self-destruction. And art has no way of separating affirmation and critique intentionally because it is non-judgmental. Freed of heteronomous control, a pure force of production, like the aesthetic, is objectively the counter image of binding force, but it is also the paradigm of those dreadful activities undertaken for their own sake.

Art will live on only as long as it has the power to resist society. If it refuses to objectify itself, it becomes a commodity. What it contributes to society is not some directly communicable content but something more mediate, i.e. resistance. Resistance reproduces social development in aesthetic terms without directly imitating it. Radical modernism preserves the immanence of art by letting society into its precincts but only in dimmed form, as though it were a dream. If it refused to do so, it would dig its own grave.

There is nothing in art that is directly social, not even when direct sociality is the artist's express aim. Not so long ago the politically committed Brecht (since he wanted to go on giving artistic expression to his political orientation) had to move farther and farther away from social reality, although reality is what his plays are all about. Jesuitic ratiocination had to be employed to construe what he wrote as being socialist realism. Thus he managed a narrow escape from the inquisition. Music is telling tales out of school, the school of art as a whole. Just as, in music, society with its contradictory dynamic crops up only as a shadow, speaking through it but in need of being identified, so it is with all the other arts. Whenever art tries to copy social reality it is all the more certain to become an as-if. Brecht's China in the *Good Woman of Setzuan* is ńo less stylized than Schiller's Messina in *The Bride of Messina*. All moral judgments about dramatic and fictional personages are null and void; they are appropriate only in relation to the real historical figures underlying those personages. Debates about whether or not a positive hero can have negative traits, and the like, are in fact as asinine as they appear to anyone who is not a student of dramatic theory. Form acts like a magnet ordering elements of real life in a manner such that they become estranged from their extra-aesthetic existence. But it is through this estrangement that their extra-aesthetic essence can be appropriated by art. At the other extreme there are the practices of the culture industry. It combines slavish respect for empirical details and illusory photographic attachment to them with ideological manipulation based on the utilization of those elements. What is social about art is not its political stance, but its immanent dynamic in opposition to society. Its historical posture repulses empirical reality, the fact that art works *qua* things are part of that reality notwithstanding. If any social function can be ascribed to art at all, it is the function to have no function. By being different from the ungodly reality, art negatively embodies an order of things in which empirical being would have its rightful place. The mystery of art is its demystifying power. Its social essence calls for a twofold reflection: on the being-for-itself of art, and on its ties with society. This dual essence of art comes out in all artistic phenomena; they change and contradict themselves.

Art's Fetish Character

Politically progressive critics have accused *l'art pour l'art*, many exponents of which were in fact in league with reactionary political interests, of fetishizing the concept of the pure, self-sufficient work of art. This indictment is valid in that works of art are products of social labour, and while they are subject to a law of form, be it an externally imposed or a self-generated one, they do tend to isolate themselves from what they are. Accordingly, every single work of art is vulnerable to the charge of false consciousness and ideology. In purely formal terms, prior to any analysis of what they express, art works are ideological because they *a priori* posit a spiritual entity as though it were independent of any conditions of material production, hence as though it were intrinsically superior to these conditions. In so doing art works cover up the age-old culpability that lies in the divorce of physical from mental labour. This divorce eventually undoes the original elevation of art to a status of superiority: it deflates art. That is why art works that claim to speak the truth are not wholly congruent with the concept of art. Theorists of *l'art pour l'art*, like Valéry, have pointed this out. But as with any culpability, works of art are not finished just because one has exposed their culpable fetishism, for in a world that is totally mediated by social reality nothing is blameless. The fetish character of art works is a condition of their truth, including their social truth. The principle of being-for-other only seems to be antagonistic to fetishism; in reality it is the principle of exchange, and therein lies concealed real domination. Freedom from repression can be represented only by what does not succumb to repression; residual use value, only by what is useless. Works of art are plenipotentiaries of things beyond the mutilating sway of exchange, profit and false human needs. Against the background of an illusory, social totality, art's illusory being-in-itself is like a mask of truth. Marx denounced the fact that Milton was paid a pittance for *Paradise Lost*, which at the time represented an unmarketable commodity, socially useless labour.[1] Marx's denunciation of productive labour is the strongest defence of art against its functionalization in bourgeois society (the logical extension of which is the undialectical ostracism of art by society).

A free society would situate itself beyond both the irrationality of its false costs and the means-ends rationality of utility. This ideal is encoded in art and is responsible for art's social explosiveness. Since magical fetishes are one of the historical roots of art, there is in art works a fetishistic quality that transcends mere commodity fetishism and which can neither be discharged nor disavowed. In social terms the emphasis on the moment of illusion in works of art is a necessary corrective and therefore a vehicle of truth. If art works down-play consistency and the fetishistic pretence of being absolutes, they *ipso facto* lose all value. If they consciously hypostatize their fetishistic properties, as has been the case since the middle of the nineteenth century, the survival of art itself is in jeopardy. Delusion is art's condition of existence; none the less, art cannot advocate delusion. This leads art into a dilemma from which only an understanding of the rationality of art's irrationality promises a way out. The sort of works that try to free themselves from fetishism by siding with dubious political interventions find themselves regularly enmeshed in a false social consciousness because they tend to over-simplify, selling out to a myopic praxis to which they contribute nothing but their own blindness.

Reception and Production

For its part, the objectification of art, which is the same as what society outside perceives as art's fetishism, is a product of the social division of labour. That is why, if we want to determine the nature of the relation between art and society, we must look not at the sphere of reception, but at the more basic sphere of production. Concern with the social explication of art has to address the production of art rather than study its impact (which in many cases diverges completely from art works and their social content, a divergence that can in turn be explained sociologically). Since time immemorial human responses to art works have been exceedingly mediate; they are not directly related to the specificity of a work but are determined by society as a whole. In short, the study of effects fails to show what is social about art. Under the aegis of positivism, this approach has even usurped the right to dictate norms for art to follow. The degree of heteronomy foisted on art by this normative turn in the positivist approach to phenomena of reception is more restrictive than that of all ideological aspects that pertain to art by virtue of its fetishization. Art and society converge in substance, not in something that is extraneous to art. That also applies to art history. The collectivization of the individual is a drain on society's productive forces. The real history of society repeats itself in art history because the productive forces of the former can dissociate themselves from society and live a life of their own in art. This explains why art is a recollection of transience. Art preserves the transient, bringing it before our eyes by changing it. This is the sociological explanation of art's temporal core. Seeking to steer clear of social praxis, art becomes a schema of social praxis just the same: every authentic work revolutionizes art.

However, while society insinuates itself into art via the aesthetic forces and relations – only to vanish there – art for its part tends to be amenable to socialization, i.e. to integration by society. This integration is not, as the progressivist cliché would have it, some posthumous benediction that says this or that artistic phenomenon was meet and proper after all. Reception tends to dull the critical edge of art, its determinate negation of society. Works are most critical when they first see the light of day; afterwards they become neutralized because, among other things, the social conditions have changed. Neutralization is the social price art pays for its autonomy. Once art works are buried in the pantheon of cultural exhibits, their truth content deteriorates. In the administered world neutralization becomes universal.

Surrealism once undertook to revolt against the fetishistic segregation of art in a sphere unto itself. But surrealism moved beyond pure protest and became art. Unlike André Masson, who valued the quality of *peinture* more highly than protest, some surrealist painters achieved a balance between scandal and social reception. In the end, somebody like Salvador Dali was able to become a kind of jet-set painter, the Laszlo or Van Dongen of a generation that prided itself on being 'sophisticated' in an era when crisis conditions seemed to have given way to stability. This gave birth to the false posthumous life of surrealism. Modern currents such as surrealism are predestined to align themselves with the world as soon as the surrealist law of form is damaged by the sudden invasion of content: that world finds unsublimated materials easy to get along with, for they have no critical bite. In an age of total neutralization of art, however, a similar fate has befallen radically abstract painting as well: the non-representational is perfectly compatible with the ideas affluent members of society have about decorating their walls. There is no telling whether this detracts from the immanent quality of modern painting as well. Reactionaries tend to think it does, but that may be false alarm. It would actually be downright idealistic to conceive the link between art and society strictly in terms of the structural problems of society. The dual essence of art – its autonomy and its being a *fait social* – comes out again and again in tangible dependencies and conflicts of both areas. At times there is direct socioeconomic intervention in the production of art, for instance when painters enter long-term agreements with art dealers who are always on the lookout for something idiosyncratic, some personalized gimmick or trademark.

The fact that German expressionism faded away as quickly as it did may have artistic reasons pertaining to the tension between the general idea of a work (to which expressionism still adhered) and the specific idea of the absolute scream. This meant that few expressionist works actually succeeded. Another reason for the premature obsolescence of expressionism is political: it declined when its revolutionary impetus failed to be realized and when the Soviet Union began to prosecute radical art. Forced to make ends meet, the authors belonging to this then neglected movement – it took forty to fifty years for expressionism to be taken note of – 'went commercial', as the American idiom goes. This could be shown in reference to most of the German expressionist writers who survived the First World War. What we can learn sociologically from the fate of the expressionists is that the bourgeois notion of having a stable occupation is more important than the need to express oneself, which supposedly inspired the expressionists. In bourgeois society artists, like other categories of mental labour, are forced to go on being artists once they have chosen 'artist' for an occupational label. Retired expressionists chose without any compunction themes that carried the promise of marketability. For them there was no aesthetic necessity to go on producing, only an economic one. Hence the objective indifference and insignificance of the post-war expressionist output.

Choice of Subject Matter; Artistic Subject; Relation to Science

Among the links that mediate art and society, subject matter is the most superficial and fallible one. I am referring to the treatment in art of overtly or covertly social phenomena. Today the notion that a sculpture portraying a coal heaver is intrinsically more relevant in social or political terms than one without such a proletarian hero is being promoted only by socialist regimes seeking to exploit art for the purpose of augmenting economic productivity. Emile Meunier's idealized coal heaver and his realism in general are perfectly congruent with a bourgeois ideology that disarmed the pro-letariat by attesting to the existence of a few beautiful people and noble physiques in its ranks. Unmitigated naturalism also often finds itself in agree-ment with the bourgeois personality type, notably its anal deformations. The naturalist is prone to derive satisfaction from the penury and deprava-tion he castigates. Zola, for example, glorified fertility like the ideologues of blood and soil, and he is known to have spouted anti-Semitic rubbish. In its material dimension an artistic indictment is often an amalgam of aggressiveness and conformism. The same goes for a choral work written in the agitprop vein around 1930; it was meant to give voice to the dissatisfaction of unemployed workers. It is one thing to show one's politi-cal colours (not the most progressive ones, in this case); it is quite another to preface the work with the instruction 'to be sung in an ugly manner', for it is an open question whether an artistic attitude of howling and crudeness denounces reality or identifies with it. Maybe denunciation is made possible only by figuration. And figuration is completely ignored by a social aesthetics that puts a premium on material and nothing else. What makes art works socially significant is content that articulates itself in formal structures.

Kafka is a good example here. Nowhere in his work did he address monopoly capitalism directly. Yet by zeroing in on the dregs of the adminis-tered world, he laid bare the inhumanity of a repressive social totality, and he did so more powerfully and uncompromisingly than if he had written novels about corruption in multinational corporations. That form is the key to understanding social content can be shown concretely in Kafka's language, the Kleistian matter-of-factness of which has often been noticed. Sensitive readers will invariably recognize the contrast that exists in Kafka between stylistic sobriety and highly imaginary happenings. This contrast effects a transfer such that the quasi-realistic description brings what seems distant and impossible into menacingly close range. But the, at least for a committed reader, overly artistic critique of the realistic features of Kafka's form does have a social dimension, for those features seem to make their peace with an ideal of order, perhaps an ideal of simple life and contentment with one's appointed station in it – all of which is social repression in disguise. The linguistic schema of describing what is thus-and-no-different is Kafka's medium of translating the spell of society into artistic appearance. He wisely refrains from naming, and thereby breaking, that spell. This spell in its tenacious omnipresence defines the space of Kafka's work; and since it is an *a priori* premise it cannot become an explicit theme for him. His language is the vehicle for expressing the intricate configuration of positivism and myth, the social relevance of which is only now becoming transparent. The old spell has taken on a new form of mythical immutability: reified consciousness. The latter both presupposes and confirms the fateful perpetuity of empirical being, and Kafka's epic style with its archaic qualities is a form of mimetic assimilation to it. While his work foreswore any attempt at transcending myth, it lays bare the universal blindness, which is society. This exposure is brought about by Kafka's language. In his narrative the bizarre is as normal as it is in social reality.

Artistic products that are nothing but regurgitations of what is happening socially, flattering themselves that this kind of metabolism with second nature passes for a genuine process of copying such products, are smitten with silence. The artistic subject as such is social, not private. In any case, it does not become social by means of forced collectivization or by choosing certain materials. In an age of repressive collectivism, the power of resistance to compact majorities resides in the lonely, exposed producer of art. This power of resistance has become a *sine qua non* of art; without it art would be socially untrue.[2] The productive artist always relates to his own immediacy in part negatively, which means he is unconsciously obeying a social universal: as he improves and corrects his work, a collective subject is looking over his shoulders, one that is itself badly in need of improvement. The notion of artistic objectivity goes hand in hand with[3] social emancipation, the latter being a situation where something frees itself on its own steam from social convention and control. Works of art cannot rest content with such vague and abstract universality as is typical of classicism. They depend on diremption, and that means that the concrete historical situation, art's other, is their condition. Their social truth depends on whether or not they open themselves to that concrete content, making it their own through assimilation. Their law of form for its part does not smooth over the cleavage but concerns itself with how to shape it. [. . .]

Art as a Mode of Behaviour

Social conflicts and class relations leave an imprint on the structure of works of art. By contrast, the political positions art works explicitly take are epiphenomenal. Frequently they work to the disadvantage of elaboration, ultimately undermining even the social truth content. In art little is achieved by political convictions alone.

It is a matter of controversy to what extent Attic tragedy, including Euripides, took sides in the divisive social conflicts that were raging at the time. Nevertheless, the thrust of the tragic form, as opposed to its mythical subject matter, was in the direction of undercutting the spell of fate and replacing it by subjectivity. Socio-politically, this attests as much to the growing emancipation from feudal-familial conditions as to the existence of an antagonism between the political powers backed by destiny and the idea of mankind growing up into adulthood. Both the historico-philosophical tendency and the antagonism combined to become the *a priori* form of ancient tragedy. The latter would hardly have attained the substantiality it did had it dealt with these matters directly in terms of content. Society is the more authentically portrayed in classical Greek tragedy the less directly it is addressed. Real partisanship, a virtue of art works no less than of human beings, dwells deep down, where social antinomies turn into the dialectic of forms. Artists articulate these antinomies in the language of the art work, thereby performing their role as social beings. In his later years even Lukács saw the need to think along these lines.

By articulating the otherwise ineffable contradictions of society, figuration takes on the features of a praxis which is the opposite of escapism, transforming art into a mode of behaviour. Art is a type of praxis and there is no need to make apologies for its failure to act directly. Art could not do so even if it wanted to. Surely the political impact even of so-called committed art is highly uncertain. The political positions artists take may play a role in defining their standpoint in relation to the prevailing consciousness, but when it comes to the growth of their work those positions have little importance. It is, for example, immaterial for the truth content of Mozart's music that he mouthed disgusting political views on the occasion of Voltaire's death. On the other hand, it would not make sense either to abstract completely from the political intentions of works of art, especially at the time of their first appearance in public. For instance, somebody who evaluates Brecht strictly in terms of his artistic merits would be as foolishly one-sided as another person who judges him only in terms of the significance of his political tenets. The immanence of society in art is not the immanence of art *in* society but the essential social relation *of* art. The social content of art resides in the principle of individuation, which for its part is social. This explains why art cannot gain insight into its social essence by itself but has to rely on interpretation to do the job.

Ideology and Truth

Some art works are ideological through and through, and still truth content is able to hold its own in them. Ideology is socially necessary illusion, which means that if it is necessary it must be a shape of truth, no matter how distorted. One of the ways in which a socially conscious aesthetics sets itself off from artlessness and philistinism is by reflecting the social critique levelled at the ideological dimension of art works, rather than simply regurgitating it.

The nineteenth-century German novelist Adalbert Stifter is a paradigmatic case of a writer whose *oeuvre* contains truth despite his overtly ideological intentions. What is overtly ideological in Stifter is, first of all, the reactionary choices he makes in terms of subject matter and of what the *fabula* is supposed to teach the reader. In addition, as far as form is concerned, he takes up an objectivistic posture with his minute and tender description of little things, thereby asserting the presence of meaning and justice in a life worth writing about. No wonder he became the idol of a noble and backward-looking bourgeoisie. Nowadays those layers that used to guarantee his semi-esoteric popularity have peeled off. But Stifter is by no means dead. The complaints about him as a harmonistic, affirmative writer have been exaggerated, especially in reference to his late works, where objectivity is reduced to a lifeless mask and where the alleged evocation of life reads more like a ritual to keep life at a distance. Through the eccentricity of ideology shines the hidden, repressed suffering of the alienated subject and thus the unreconciled nature of real life. A pale light is cast over Stifter's mature prose, as though it were allergic to blissful colours. It is almost like a pencil drawing, because social reality with its unruly, disturbing features has been excluded to make room for the poet's world view and his epical *a priori*, both of them incompatible with that reality. In Stifter's prose the discrepancy between form and the emergent capitalist society (which is contrary to the intentions of that prose) enhances expression. The ideological eccentricity of his work mediately imparts truth content to it and establishes Stifter's superiority over the average edification literature of his time, giving him that authentic quality which Nietzsche admired. He is a prime example of an artist whose poetic intentions – the meaning he imparts directly to his works – are at odds with objective content. Content in Stifter is truly the negation of meaning, and yet there would be no content at all were it not for the author's positing a falsely intentional content in the first place, a content that is subsequently superseded by the specific makeup of the work.

As in Stifter, affirmative art generally may become a cipher of despair. Conversely, pure negativity of content has always an admixture of affirmation. The brilliance radiated today by all anti-affirmative works is the appearance of an ineffable affirmation, the dawn of a non-existent that pretends it has being. Its claim to being passes away with the instant of aesthetic illusion. But what has no being none the less represents a promise, if it has the ability to appear. This relation between the existent and non-existent is the Utopian figure of art. While art is driven into a position of absolute negativity, it is never absolutely negative precisely because of that negativity. It always has an affirmative residue. The antinomial essence of this residue rubs off on art works immanently, i.e. before they even take a stance on the existent *qua* society, casting a penumbra over them. Beauty of any kind has to face the question of whether it is in fact beautiful or whether it is just a false claim resting on static affirmation. In a sense, the disgust with arts and crafts parallels the guilty conscience that art as such has whenever a musical chord is struck, a colour put before our eyes. Social criticism of art does not rely on external palpation. Instead, it springs directly from intra-aesthetic formations. The heightened sensitivity of the aesthetic sense tends to converge with the socially determined aversion to art.

Truth and ideology do not represent good and bad respectively. Art contains them both. This dualism in turn gives rise alike to ideological misuse and summary dismissal. It takes only one small step to pass from the Utopia of self-sameness in art works to the stench of those heavenly roses that art is said to scatter over our this-worldly life, like the women in Schiller's tirade. The more openly society moves towards ever greater totalization, assigning art (along with everything else) its specific function, the more completely it polarizes art into ideology and protest. This polarization is likely to be detrimental to art. Absolute protest hems art in, impinging on its *raison d'être*, whereas absolute ideology reduces art to a thin, authoritarian copy of reality.[4]

'Culpability'

Although art was resurrected in Germany after the catastrophe, it has a distinctly ideological flavour just by being there, and apart from any content or substance. There is such a great discrepancy between art and the recent atrocities (as well as impending ones) that art is condemned to cynicism. Even when it addresses them, it tends to divert attention from them. Objectification in post-war art entails a frigid attitude to reality, downgrading art's role to that of a henchman of barbarism. The opposite stance leaves art no better off: those who forsake objectification and drift with the current of immediacy are also accomplices of barbarity, regardless of the polemical commitment they display. At present, all works of art including radical ones have a conservative tinge, for they help reinforce the existence of a separate domain of spirit and culture whose practical impotence and complicity with the principle of unmitigated disaster are painfully evident. However, this conservative element – which is most pronounced in radically modern art – ought not simply to be junked. No resistance to the social totality and its omnipotence is conceivable unless spirit in its most progressive shape survives and goes on progressing. If the advancing spirit does not bequeath to mankind what the latter is poised to liquidate, the world would be mired in lasting barbarity instead of moving forward to a rational social order. Even when art is tolerated as it is in the administered world, it embodies something that goes against the total arrangement of things and is therefore suppressed.

The Greek military junta knew only too well why it banned Beckett's plays in which not a word is said about politics. This perceived social deviance of art becomes its political justification. Authentic works must wipe out any memory trace of reconciliation – in the interest of reconciliation. At the same time, the inescapable straining towards unity is necessarily tied up with the notion of reconciliation in its old form. By definition, art works are socially culpable. But the worthy ones among them try to atone for their guilt. Their chance for survival hinges on the requirement that this straining towards synthesis must have an irreconcilable component. Without any synthesis that confronts reality with the autonomous life of the art work, the spell of reality would be ubiquitous. Spell originates in the fundamental fact that spirit dissociates itself and is set to one side. The same principle works in the opposite direction: it breaks the spell by making it determinate. [. . .]

The Mediation of Art and Society

The fact that society 'appears' in works of art both in an ideological and a critical manner is apt to lead to historico-philosophical mystification. Speculative thought is easily duped into thinking there is a pre-established harmony between society and works of art, courtesy of world spirit. Their true relation is different, however.

The process that occurs in art works and which is arrested in them has to be conceived as being the same as the social process surrounding them. In Leibnizian terminology, they represent this process in a windowless fashion. The configurative totalization of elements in the art work follows immanent laws that are akin to those of society outside. Society's productive forces and relations, shorn of their facticity, crop up in art because artistic labour is social labour and because an artistic product is a social product. Artistic forces of production are not *per se* different from social ones. The difference lies in the constitutive turn, by the former, away from real society. All that art works do or bring forth has its latent model in social production. It is this affinity that determines whether or not a work has strength and validity outside the confines of its immanence.

Along with the social force of production, the decisive relation of production, namely the commodity form, as well as the antagonism between both, affect the work of art. That means works of art are absolute commodities; they are social products which have discarded the illusion of being-for-society, an illusion tenaciously retained by all other commodities. An absolute commodity rids itself of the ideology inherent in the commodity form. The latter pretends it is a being-for-other whereas in truth it is only for-itself, i.e. for the ruling interests of society. This shift from ideology to truth pertains to aesthetic substance; it does not directly pertain to the position that art occupies in society. Alas, even as an absolute commodity art has retained its commercial value, becoming a 'natural monopoly'. Offering art for sale on a market, as pottery and little statues used to be sold in a marketplace, is not some perverse use of art but simply a logical consequence of art's participation in productive relations. It is possible that completely non-ideological art is entirely unfeasible. Art surely does not become non-ideological just by being antithetical to empirical reality.

Sartre rightly pointed out that the principle of *l'art pour l'art* – which has had just as strong a hold on French art since Baudelaire as did the opposite ideal of art as a moral institution on German art – was perfectly acceptable to the bourgeoisie because it served as a means to neutralize art, whereas the German bourgeoisie appropriated art by assigning to it the role of an ally in its attempt to institute social control.[5] The ideological essence of *l'art pour l'art* lies not in the emphatic antithesis it posits between art and empirical life, but in the abstract and facile character of this antithesis. The idea of beauty advocated by *l'art pour l'art*, at least after Baudelaire, was not supposed to be a formal classicist one, and yet it too tended to filter out all contents except those that fit the dogmatic canon of beauty. In this vein, Stefan George complained in a letter to Hugo von Hofmannsthal that it was improper to let Titian die of the plague, as Hofmannsthal had suggested in a remark about the painter.[6] The concept of beauty in *l'art pour l'art* is at once strangely empty and content-laden. It is an artificial *jugendstil* happening of the sort that inspired Ibsen's formulations about vines that entwine somebody's hair or about 'dying in beauty'. Unable to determine itself, beauty is like an aerial root, becoming entangled in the fate of artificial ornamentation. What makes this idea of beauty so narrow in conception is its direct antithesis to the ugliness of society, whereas earlier on people like Baudelaire and Rimbaud had been able to extract an antithetical impetus from social content – in Baudelaire's case the imagery of Paris – converting an attitude of sheer distance into interventionist, determinate negation. The reason why neo-romantic and symbolistic beauty have become a consumer good so quickly lies in the self-sufficiency of this ideal, i.e., its prudish reserve before those social aspects that alone make form possible. Art of this kind brackets the world of commodities, denying its existence. In so doing its products become commodities themselves. They are condemned to being kitsch because latent in them there is the commodity form. No wonder they are being laughed out of court today. It would be easy to show in the 'artism' of Rimbaud the simultaneous presence of incisive social criticism and elements of sheepish conormity along the lines of Rilke's ecstatic response to the smell of an old chest. What ultimately won the day was the affirmative side of *l'art pour l'art*, a triumph that spelled the end of this aesthetic ideal.

In its relation to society art finds itself in a dilemma today. If it lets go of autonomy it sells out to the established order, whereas if it tries to stay strictly within its autonomous confines it becomes equally co-optable, living a harmless life in its appointed niche. This dilemma reflects the larger phenomenon of a social totality capable of ingesting all that comes its way. Modernism's refusal to communicate is a neccessary but not a sufficient condition of ideology-free art. Such art also requires vitality of expression – a kind of expression that is tensed so as to articulate the tacit posture of art works. Expression reveals works to be lacerations inflicted by society; expression is the social ferment that is added to their autonomous shape. A telling example of this is Picasso's *Guernica:* it is wholly incompatible with criteria of realism, gaining expression through inhuman construction; eventually this expression takes on the unambiguously sharp contours of social protest. The socially critical dimensions of art works are those that hurt, those that bring to light (through the medium of expression and in historically determinate ways) what is wrong with present social conditions. The public outcry evoked by works like *Guernica* is a response to that. [. . .]

Impact, Lived Experience; 'Tremor'

Art's dialectical relation to praxis manifests itself in the impact it has on society. That art is able to intervene politically can justly be doubted. Where it does so intervene, the kind of impact that results is peripheral or, worse, detrimental to the quality of art. Art's social impact, strictly understood, is very mediate. Its influence is due to the fact that art participates in spirit, which in turn congeals in art works, helping to determine changes in society, albeit in a subterranean, invisible fashion. Objectification is the precondition for this kind of participation in spirit. The impact works of art have operates at the level of remembrance; impact has nothing to do with translating their latent praxis into manifest praxis, the growth of autonomy having gone too far to permit any kind of immediate correspondence.

The historical genesis of works of art points back to cause and effect relations that do not simply vanish in these works. On the contrary, the process enacted by every art work – as a model for a kind of praxis wherein a collective subject is being constituted – has repercussions on society. No matter how small the importance of art's impact, and no matter how great the importance of art's shape may be, some impact emanates from this shape all the same. A critical analysis of the impact of art may therefore bring to light a great deal that would otherwise be hidden behind the thing-likeness of art works. An example here might be the ideological effect Richard Wagner had. It is perfectly proper to reflect on art works and their chemistry sociologically, as long as this does not take the form of imputing social characteristics from on high, an approach that ignores the tension between the substance of art and its impact.

Whether or not art works intervene practically (and how much) is not for them to decide but depends on historical circumstances. The comedies of Beaumarchais may not have been committed literature in the sense of Brecht and Sartre, but they did have a not inconsiderable political impact because their tangible content agreed with a historical tendency that found itself flattered by those comedies. When social impact is second-hand it is openly paradoxical: it is chalked up to spontaneity but actually hinges on overall social developments. Contrariwise, Brecht's work, intent as it was on change since the writing of *St Joan of the Stockyards* (1929), was probably politically impotent; and Brecht was certainly too astute not to have noticed that. His impact might be characterized as a form of preaching to the converted. The use of the estrangement effect would, he thought, cause the viewer to think. This demand for a reflective attitude on the one hand converges with the valid idea that art works need to be known objectively

— a stance which major autonomous works invariably presuppose on the part of the viewer, listener, reader. On the other hand, Brecht's didactic posture reflects intolerance of ambiguity, the sort of ambiguity that touches off thought and reflection. In this Brecht is authoritarian. Perhaps this authoritarianism was his response to what he perceived to be the lack of impact of his didactic plays: he wanted to be influential at all costs, if necessary by employing techniques of domination (at which he was a virtuoso), just as earlier on he had set in motion a plan to gain fame. Still, it is Brecht in large measure to whom we owe the growth in the self-consciousness of the art work, for when it is viewed as an element of political praxis its resistance to ideological mystification becomes that much stronger. Brecht's emphasis on praxis was a formative influence on his entire work and cannot simply be eliminated from its truth content, no matter how removed the latter actually is from the world of praxis.

One decisive reason why art works, at least those that refuse to surrender to propaganda, are lacking in social impact is that they have to give up the use of those communicative means that would make them palatable to a larger public. If they do not, they become pawns in the all-encompassing system of communication. If art works have any social influence at all, it is not by haranguing, but by changing consciousness in ways that are ever so difficult to pin down. Any directly propagandistic effect evaporates quickly, perhaps because even works of this genre tend to be perceived as being ultimately irrational, with the result that the mechanism that is supposed to trigger praxis is interrupted by the intervention of the aesthetic principle. Aesthetic education 'educes' the individual from the pre-aesthetic twilight zone where art and reality are intermingled, creating a sense of distance and laying bare the objective nature of the work of art. At the subjective level it puts an end to primitive modes of identification, annulling the recipient *qua* empirical-psychological personality in order to stress his relation to the art work. Subjectively, art calls for externalization (which is what Brecht's critique of sensitivity was all about). Art is practical in the sense that it defines the person who experiences art as a *zoon politikón* by forcing him to step outside of himself. In addition art is objectively practical because it forms and educates consciousness, provided it stays away from outright propaganda.

If you have a dispassionate attitude to art works, you will not be tempted into the kind of enthusiasm that is the basis of any call to action. The only subjective orientation that corresponds to the cognitive quality of art works is a cognitive one. Works of art affront prevailing needs by throwing new light on the familiar, thus meeting the objective need for a change in consciousness that might ultimately lead to a change of reality. Art cannot achieve the much desired impact by adapting to existing needs, for this would deprive human beings precisely of what art has to offer. Aesthetic needs are fairly vague and poorly articulated, and it is unlikely that the culture industry has done much to change that. That culture has failed points to the determination of subjective cultural needs by the supply side and the mechanisms of distribution. These needs do not exist in isolation.

The assertion that there is a need for art is largely ideological. People can do without art if they have to. This statement holds objectively as well as subjectively in terms of the psychological household of the consumer (who has no trouble changing his tastes in response to changes in his existence provided they are piecemeal). In a society that teaches its members not to think beyond themselves, anything that transcends the material reproduction of life is ultimately useless. And that includes art, even though society makes every effort to pound the notion of art's usefulness into their heads. At a time when, absurdly enough, material penury continues, when barbarism reproduces itself on an expanding scale and when the threat of total destruction is ever-present – at such a time any phenomenon that shows no concern for the preservation of life takes on a silly appearance. This much is valid about the present rebellion against art. On the one hand, the culture industry gobbles up all artistic products, even relatively good ones, and the artist therefore seems justified in being unconcerned. On the other hand, the objective indifference of the culture industry, its co-optative capacity, does ultimately affect art as well, making it equally indifferent. Quite undialectically and naively, Marx implied that there are distinct cultural needs forming part of a larger cultural sphere. He was unable to foresee that things would come to a point where the only way to show one's respect for culture is to decide to do without it and to boycott its festivals. Better to go hungry than to be force-fed.

The notion of cultural needs is objectionable not only for practical but also for aesthetic reasons. The idea behind the work of art is the intention to break up the interminable metabolism of need and gratification and thereby sin against those needs which remain unfulfilled. Any theory of needs, whether aesthetic or sociological, harks back to what is called 'lived experience' (*Erlebnis*), an old-fashioned and deficient concept. It presupposes an equivalence between the objective substance of lived experience – roughly, emotional expression – and the subjective lived experience of the recipient. In other words, when music gets excited the listener is supposed to be equally excited. This is nonsense: if he is knowledgeable, he will stay emotionally neutral, no matter now wildly the music may gesticulate. In this connection it is difficult to imagine anything more artless than those scientific experiments that try to quantify aesthetic effect and lived experience by measuring human pulse rates. The notion of an equivalence between objective and subjective lived experience is murky indeed. According to one widely held view, what is being re-enacted by lived experience are the feelings of the author. Far from being the decisive moment, the emotions of the producer are only a small part of the work as a whole. What is more, they are not verbatim reports of emotions – such verbatim reports are least likely to appeal to the listener or lend themselves to empathy and lived experience by him – but become radically changed when they are embedded in the context of artistic autonomy. Theories of lived experience distort, indeed deny, the interaction between the constructive and the mimetic element in art. What they do is take a particular out of context, blowing it out of proportion. The assumed equivalence simply does not exist. Re-enacting emotions means taking them out of their aesthetic context and translating them back into empirical data.

A legitimate subjective response to art is a sense of concern (*Betroffenheit*). Concern is triggered by great works. Concern is not some repressed emotion in the recipient that is brought to the surface by art but a momentary discomfiture, more precisely a tremor (*Erschütterung*), during which he gives himself over to the work. He loses his footing, as it were, discovering that the truth embodied in the aesthetic image has real tangible possibilities. This kind of immediacy (in the best sense of the term) in one's relation to works is a function of mediation, i.e. of incisive, encompassing experience. Experience congeals in an instant, and for it to do so the whole of consciousness is required rather than some one-dimensional stimulus and response. To experience the truth or untruth of art is more than a subjective 'lived experience': it signals the breaking-through of objectivity into subjective consciousness. Objectivity mediates aesthetic experience even when the subjective response is at its most intense.

Many a situation in Beethoven is a *scène à faire*[7] and therefore flawed. The onset of the reprise in the Ninth Symphony is a celebration of the unity of the original thesis and the symphonic process of development. It resounds like an overwhelming 'This is how it is'. Now, subjective tremor is a response to the fear of being overwhelmed. While the music is mainly affirmative, it also exposes untruth. Without employing discursive judgments, art works seem to point a finger at their content. And the spontaneous response of the recipient is a mimetic adaptation to the immediacy of that deictic gesture. But this is by no means all. The passage in Beethoven takes up a position by virtue of its gesture, a position which in turn is subject to a critical query, namely, whether or not the power of thusness (to the epiphany of which such instants of art are devoted) is an index of truth. This question calls for a conceptual answer by comprehensive experience; the latter ends up rendering a judgment about the non-judgmental work. 'Lived experience' is only a moment of a comprehensive notion of experience, a moment that is both fallible and suggestible. Works like the Ninth Symphony exert a mesmerizing influence; the power they have by virtue of their structure is translated into power over people. After Beethoven, art's power of suggestion, originally borrowed from society, has rebounded on to society and become propagandistic and ideological.

Antithetical to the conventional notion of lived experience, tremor is no particularistic gratification of the ego; indeed, it is not pleasurable at all. Rather, it is a reminder of the liquidation of the ego. However, by being shaken up the ego becomes aware of its limits and finitude. The experience of tremor, then, is contrary to the weakening of the ego that is promoted by the culture industry. For the culture industry the notion of tremor is just so much hot air. This may be one of the inmost causes for the desubstantialization of art. If the ego wishes to look beyond the walls of the prison that it is, it needs not distraction, but the utmost concentration. This state of concentration prevents tremor from being regressive even though it is spontaneous behaviour. In his aesthetics of the sublime Kant faithfully depicted the power of the subject as being a precondition for the sublime. The statement that the ego is being destroyed is not literally true because of the presence of art. What are called aesthetic lived experiences, however, must be real psychological phenomena; if one were to view them as illusory, they would not make sense. Lived experience is not an as-if. The ego, it is true does not actually vanish in the instant of tremor; rapture or ecstasy would achieve this kind of total disappearance, but they are incompatible with artistic experience. Momentarily the ego is perfectly able to become aware of the chance it has to leave the realm of self-preservation behind, but this ability alone does not suffice to realize that chance.

What is illusory is not the aesthetic tremor itself, but its stance towards objectivity: in its immediacy tremor senses the existence of a potential that it pretends is real. The ego is seized by a consciousness that is unmetaphorical and destructive of aesthetic illusion. This consciousness tells the ego that it is not an absolute but an illusion. From the perspective of the subject, art at this juncture can be seen to turn into a historical spokesman for repressed nature. In the last analysis art is critical of the ego principle, the internal agency of repression. The subjective experience of an opposition to the ego is a moment of art's objective truth.

To those who obsessively relate art works only to themselves, the avenue of lived experience is closed, except in the false form of a surrogate manipulated by culture. It is easy to misconceive the nature of this surrogate. The products of the culture industry – more tepid and standardized in kind than any one of its consumers – aim at identification, but chances are they will miss even this modest aim. In any event, the question as to what the culture industry does to people is probably too naive. The impact of the culture industry may well be more diffuse than is suggested by the specific form of the question. What it does do is fill empty time with more emptiness. It does not even produce false consciousness, but takes great pains to leave everything as it is.

Commitment

The aspect of objective praxis inherent in art turns into subjective intention when art's oppositon to society – because of the objective social tendencies and the critical reflection of art – becomes irreconcilable. The accepted term for this phenomenon is 'commitment'. Artistic commitment represents a higher stage of reflection than tendentious art, which only wants to mitigate irksome social ills, although commitment sometimes does not rise above this level of criticism, either. As a rule, however, commitment aims at changing the conditions underlying social ills, not the ill *per se*. In this it is akin to the aesthetic category of essence.

The polemical self-consciousness of art presupposes spiritualization. As art becomes more allergic to sensuous immediacy – once the defining charac- teristic of art – it also becomes more critical in its stance towards crude reality, including social reality (which is an extension of the natural state of things). The critical-reflexive feature of spiritualization intensifies the relation between art and its substance, and not only formally. Turning away from the older sensualist aesthetics of taste, Hegel emphasized both the spiritualization of the art work and the need to give greater weight to material substance. The earlier notion that art has a direct impact on other spiritual phenom- ena was false. After Hegel it has become possible to look at spriritualization in the context of particular works.

The concept of artistic commitment has to be used circumspectly. If it is employed as a yardstick to censor art, then it merely serves to reinforce that domination to which art stood opposed long before anybody conceived the idea of commitment. This is not an argument for doing away with notions like tendentious art and its unsophisticated descendants. While the aesthetics of taste would like to do just that, there is a sense in which such notions are legitimate, if only because we have entered a historical phase where the longing for, and the will to, change are extremely intense. All this does not annul the power of the law of form. Spiritual content is ultimately nothing else but material or stuff consumed by the work of art, regardless of any ideas the author may have about the centrality of content. Whatever is educational in Brecht's plays can be taught more convincingly by theory – if it needs teaching at all. His audiences were not exactly unfamiliar with insights like these: that the rich are better off than the poor; that the world is full of injustice; that repression continues amid formal equality; that private goodness turns into its opposite in a public context of objective evil; that – a dubious wisdom at best – goodness needs the mask of evil. The sententious directness with which Brecht translated such stale gems of wisdom into dramatic gestures gave his work its uniqueness. His didactic approach prompted him to introduce dramatic innovations designed to oust the old theatre of intrigue and psychology. In his plays 'theses' are important not for what they say but for what they do: they constitute the anti-illusory nature of Brechtian drama, thus contributing to the decomposition of a unified complex of meaning. This accounts for its quality; commitment has nothing to do with it. The only thing that commitment contributes to quality is the mimetic element. The Brechtian commitment reinforces the historical trend towards the decomposition of the work of art. Commitment brings a hidden property to the surface, thanks to the increasing mastery and artefactuality of art: what used to be an in-itself now becomes a for-itself.

The immanence of art works, i.e. their almost *a priori* distance from empirical being, would be inconceivable were it not for the implicit presupposition of a new social order brought about by self-conscious praxis. In *Romeo and Juliet*, for example, Shakespeare does not by any means expressly espouse an ideal of love free of familial meddling. And yet the drama is about precisely this: the human longing for a condition where love is no longer disfigured or prohibited by patriarchal rule, or any rule for that matter. Were it not for this tacit, imageless Utopia it would be difficult to explain the abiding attraction *Romeo and Juliet* has had for generations of theatre-goers. That it is only a tacit Utopia is no coincidence, for the same taboo that forbids cognition to flesh out Utopias holds for art too. Praxis is not the impact works have; it is the hidden potential of their truth content. That is why commitment can become an aesthetic force of production.

The conservative attacks upon tendentious and committed art for their part are just plain dreadful and stupid. Their concern is to keep culture pure. Underlying this concern is a desire to keep everything as it is, not only the fetishized culture but also the world outside. The indignation these purists display in the face of committed art is not so different from that shown at the opposite pole, where the 'committed' camp is prone to pounce on anything that smacks of ivory-tower art, as they like to call it, and which is therefore alleged to be outmoded in an age of mass communication. The common denominator of the conservatives and the exponents of commitment is the notion of message (*Aussage*). Brecht tastefully avoided using the term, but, positivist that he was, he did not shrink from invoking the principle behind it. The two views refute each other. If we look at a work like *Don Quixote*, we might say it furthered a completely irrelevant tendency, working towards the definitive abolition of the chivalric romance which had been dragged along as a genre long after feudalism had given way to the bourgeois age. Still, the book became a paradigmatic work of art, using this modest 'tendency' as a vehicle. The antagonistic literary genres Cervantes was working with, unbeknown to the author, turned into an antagonism of real world-historical ages, eventually into an authentic metaphysical expression of the crisis of immanent meaning in a disenchanted world. Similarly, a non-tendentious work like Goethe's *The Sufferings of Young Werther* probably had a considerable impact on the emancipation of bourgeois consciousness in Germany. The novel focuses on the problem of the collision between society and the individual who is driven to suicide out of a feeling of unrequited love. In this work Goethe protested effectively against petty bourgeois rigidity, without expressly naming it.

What the two censorial positions of bourgeois consciousness – that art ought not to want change and that it ought to be for everybody – have in common is that they defend the status quo, the first by vindicating the accommodation of art to the world, the second by seeing to it that art conforms to the accepted notions of public consciousness. Commitment and hermetic art, on the other hand, have in common a disaffection with the status quo. Reified consciousness abhors intervention because it seems to want to reify the reified work of art a second time. For it the objectification of the art work is not a movement against society but a vehicle for neutralizing art politically. Thus the extroverted side of the art work is falsely regarded as its essence and no attention is paid to its formation or to its truth content. No work of art can be true in social and political terms unless it is true in its own terms as well. By the same token, aesthetic authenticity is incompatible with a false political consciousness. The political and the immanent dimension are not congruent, but they art not radically divergent, either. This divergence has been grossly exaggerated by culture fetishists and praxis fetishists alike. Truth content always points beyond the immanent aesthetic makeup of art works towards some political significance. This duality of immanence and sociality is stamped on every single work of art. It is not some formula that defines abstractly what art in general is but the vital element of art in its many particular shapes. Art is social to the extent to which it is an in–itself, and vice versa. In art the dialectic of the social and the immanent operates at the level of the specific complexion of art works: nothing is tolerated that is purely internal and not susceptible to externalization; nor is anything tolerated that is purely external and not susceptible of becoming the vehicle of the internal, i.e. truth content.

Notes

1 Karl Marx. *Theories of Surplus Value* (Moscow: Progress, 1968), vol. 1, p. 389.
2 This, incidentally, is not to say that there is no room for collective forms of production like the composer workshops envisaged by Schoenberg. There is.
3 Interpolating 'verschwistert'. – Tr.
4 Reading 'sie' for 'sich'. – Tr.
5 Jean Paul Sartre, *What is Literature?* (New York: Harper and Row, 1965), p. 21.
6 See R. Boehringer (ed.), *Briefwechsel zwischen George und Hofmannsthal* (Munich and Düsseldorf: Küpper, 1953), p. 42.
7 Principal scene in a play. – Tr.

Part V

Criticism

15

The Perennial Fashion – Jazz

In the vast corpus of Adorno's writings on music – over half of the twenty volumes of his collected works deal in some way with the subject – we find few pieces specifically on the subject of jazz. These pieces are by no means pivotal for our understanding of his aesthetics of music yet they have provoked considerable and often bitter commentary. His dismissal of jazz both as a force for liberation and as an art form are absolutely unambivalent and, occasionally, acerbic. It has been interpreted variously as the contemptousness of a cultural mandarin, as elitist, even as anti-American. It is also suggested that his knowledge of jazz music was at best superficial, based on faulty generalizations, and certainly in no way applicable to the more interesting versions of jazz that are supposedly entitled to call themselves art forms. However, the essay 'The Perennial Fashion – Jazz' shows all of these arguments to be mistaken. The essay reveals evidence of a better knowledge of the area than is generally observed. Furthermore, his critique of jazz music as an art form is entirely consistent with his aesthetic theory, and, as such, no *ad hoc* polemic.

In 'The Perennial Fashion – Jazz' Adorno challenges claims that are made for the liberating qualities of jazz music: that it recaptures natural spontaneity in contrast to the allegedly staid formal conventions of serious music. The jazz performer is given licence to improvise, and that, it is argued, points to a freedom not available to the score-bound performer. However, against this claim is the evidence of the musical structure of jazz which, Adorno notes, is the repetition of formulae and the constriction of possible expression within rigid syncopation. Adorno sees these inherent limitations as intellectually regressive in that, in contrast to serious music, they contribute nothing to a transformation of consciousness. Interestingly, he notes that part of this structure might be explained by its beginnings in slave music. Adorno's suggestion that it originally 'combined the lament of unfreedom with its oppressed confirmation' is consistent with his views on the social situation of all forms of music and art. However, this original authentic expression of the slaves is now the possession of the culture industry which markets jazz as the music of the autonomous subject. Adorno's attempts to explain the attraction of this music lead him to make use of psychoanalytic theory. Jazz enthusiasm is, he believes, self-abasing and this can be explained only by certain concepts worked out in Freud, namely, regression and infantilism. The other major issue in this essay is Adorno's assessment of the avant-gardistic pretensions of jazz. Whilst there may be deliberate discordance in some jazz pieces the occasional bad note, Adorno argues, is not atonality. Far from taking a place among progressive art, jazz as a product of the culture industry is thoroughly heteronomous. Its purpose is profit and it is entirely congenial to the reified consciousness. ('Perennial Fashion – Jazz' is a useful text with which to contrast Adorno with other Neo-Marxists (particularly Marcuse), and lately postmodernists, who hold that popular culture contains the possibility of critical experience.)

'The Perennial Fashion – Jazz' [1953], in *Prisms* (Cambridge, Mass.: MIT Press, 1981), pp. 119–32. Translated by Samuel and Shierry Weber.

1

For almost fifty years, since 1914 when the contagious enthusiasm for it broke out in America, jazz has maintained its place as a mass phenomenon. Its method, all declarations of propagandistic historians notwithstanding, has remained essentially unchanged; its prehistory dates back to certain songs from the first half of the nineteenth century, such as 'Turkey in the Straw' and 'Old Zip Coon'. Jazz is music which fuses the most rudimentary melodic, harmonic, metric and formal structure with the ostensibly disruptive principle of syncopation, yet without ever really disturbing the crude unity of the basic rhythm, the identically sustained metre, the quarter-note. This is not to say that nothing has happened in jazz. The monochromatic piano has been forced to cede the dominant role it played during the ragtime period to small ensembles, generally winds. The wild antics of the first jazz bands from the South, New Orleans above all, and those from Chicago, have been toned down with the growth of commercialization and of the audience, and continued scholarly efforts to recover some of this original animation, whether called 'swing' or 'bebop', inexorably succumb to commercial requirements and quickly lose their sting. The syncopation principle, which at first had to call attention to itself by exaggeration, has in the meantime become so self-evident that it no longer needs to accentuate the weak beats as was formally required. Anyone still using such accents today is derided as 'corny', as out-of-date as 1927 evening dress. Contrariness has changed into second-degree 'smoothness' and the jazz-form of reaction has become so entrenched that an entire generation of youth hears only syncopations without being aware of the original conflict between it and the basic metre. Yet none of this alters the fact that jazz has in its essence remained static, nor does it explain the resulting enigma that millions of people seem never to tire of its monotonous attraction. Winthrop Sargeant, internationally known today as the art editor of *Life* magazine, is responsible for the best, most reliable and most sensible book on the subject; twenty-five years ago he wrote that jazz was in no way a new musical idiom but rather, 'even in its most complex manifestations a very elementary matter of incessantly repeated formulae'. This kind of unbiased observation seems possible only in America; in Europe, where jazz has not yet become an everyday phenomenon, there is the tendency, especially among those devotees who have adopted it as a *Weltanschauung*, to regard it falsely as a break-through of original, untrammelled nature, as a triumph over the musty museum-culture. However little doubt there can be regarding the African elements in jazz, it is no less certain that everything unruly in it was from the very beginning integrated into a strict scheme, that its rebellious gestures are accompanied by the tendency to blind obeisance, much like the sado-masochistic type described by analytic psychology, the person who chafes against the father-figure while secretly admiring him, who seeks to emulate him and in turn derives enjoyment from the subordination he overtly detests. This propensity accelerates the standardization, commercialization and rigidification of the medium. It is not as though scurrilous businessmen have corrupted the voice of nature by attacking it from without; jazz takes care of this all by itself. The abuse of jazz is not the external calamity in whose name the puristic defenders of 'real' unadulterated jazz furiously protest; such misuse originates in jazz itself. The Negro spirituals, antecedents of the blues, were slave songs and as such combined the lament of unfreedom with its oppressed confirmation. Moreover, it is difficult to isolate the authentic Negro elements in jazz. The white *lumpenproletariat* also participated in its prehistory, during the period preceding its thrust into the spotlight of a society which seemed to be waiting for it and which had long been familiar with its impulses through the cakewalk and tap dancing.

It is precisely this paltry stock of procedures and characteristics, however, the rigorous exclusion of every unregimented impulse, which makes the durability of this 'speciality' – one which accepts change only when forced to, and then generally only to suit the demands of advertising – so difficult to grasp. For the fact remains that jazz has established itself for a short eternity in the midst of a phase which is otherwise anything but static, and that it displays not the slightest inclination to relinquish any portion of its monopoly but instead only the tendency to adapt itself to the ear of the listener, no matter whether highly trained or undifferentiated. Yet for all of that it has not become any less fashionable. For almost fifty years the productions of jazz have remained as ephemeral as seasonal styles. Jazz is a form of manneristic interpretation. As with fashions what is important is show, not the thing itself; instead of jazz itself being composed, 'light' music, the most dismal products of the popular-song industry, is dressed up. Jazz fans, short for fanatics, sense this and therefore prefer to emphasize the music's improvisational features. But these are mere frills. Any precocious American teenager knows that the routine today scarcely leaves any room for improvisation, and that what appears as spontaneity is in fact carefully planned out in advance with machinelike precision. But even where there is real improvisation, in oppositional groups which perhaps even today still indulge in such things out of sheer pleasure, the sole material remains popular songs. Thus, the so-called improvisations are actually reduced to the more or less feeble rehashing of basic formulas in which the schema shines through at every moment. Even the improvisations conform largely to norms and recur constantly. The range of the permissible in jazz is as narrowly circumscribed as in any particular cut of clothes. In view of the wealth of available possibilities for discovering and treating musical material, even in the sphere of entertainment if absolutely necessary, jazz has shown itself to be utterly impoverished. Its use of the existing musical techniques seems to be entirely arbitrary. The ban on changing the basic beat during the course of the music is itself sufficient to constrict composition to the point where what it demands is not aesthetic awareness of style but rather psychological regression. The limitations placed on metre, harmony and form are no less stifling. Considered as a whole, the perennial sameness of jazz consists not in a basic organization of the material within which the imagination can roam freely and without inhibition, as within an articulate language, but rather in the utilization of certain well-defined tricks, formulas and clichés to the exclusion of everything else. It is as though one were to cling convulsively to the 'latest thing' and deny the image of a particular year by refusing to tear off the page of the calendar. Fashion enthrones itself as something lasting and thus sacrifices the dignity of fashion, its transience.

2

In order to understand how an entire sphere can be described by a few simple recipes as though nothing else existed, one must first free oneself of the clichés, 'vitality' and 'rhythm of the time', which are glorified by advertising, by its journalistic appendage and in the end, by the victims themselves. The fact is that what jazz has to offer rhythmically is extremely limited. The most striking traits in jazz were all independently produced, developed and surpassed by serious music since Brahms. And its 'vitality' is difficult to take seriously in the face of an assembly-line procedure that is standardized down to its most minute deviations. The jazz ideologists, especially in Europe, mistakenly regard the sum of psycho-technically calculated and tested effects as the expression of an emotional state, the illusion of which jazz evokes in the listener; this attitude is rather like regarding those film stars, whose regular or sorrowful faces are modelled on portraits of famous persons, as being therefore of the same stature as Lucrezia Borgia or Lady Hamilton if, indeed, the latter were not already their own mannequins. What enthusiastically stunted innocence sees as the jungle is actually factory-made through and through, even when, on special occasions, spontaneity is publicized as a featured attraction. The paradoxical immortality of jazz has its roots in the economy. Competition on the culture market has proved the effectiveness of a number of techniques, including syncopation, semi-vocal, semi-instrumental sounds, gliding, impressionistic harmonies and opulent instrumentation which suggests that 'nothing is too good for us'. These techniques are then sorted out and kaleidoscopically mixed into ever-new combinations without there taking place even the slightest interaction between the total scheme and the no less schematic details. All that remains is the results of the competition, itself not very 'free', and the entire business is then touched up, in particular by the radio. The investments made in 'name bands', whose fame is assured by scientifically engineered propaganda; and even more important, the money used to promote musical bestseller programmes like 'The Hit Parade' by the firms who buy radio advertising time, make every divergence a risk. Standardization, moreover, means the strengthening of the lasting domination of the listening public and of their conditioned reflexes. They are expected to want only that to which they have become accustomed and to become enraged whenever their expectations are disappointed and fulfillment, which they regard as the customer's inalienable right, is denied. And even if there were attempts to introduce anything really different into light music, they would be doomed from the start by virtue of economic concentration.

The insurmountable character of a phenomenon which is inherently con-tigent and arbitrary reflects something of the arbitrary nature of present social controls. The more totally the culture industry roots out all deviations, thus cutting off the medium from its intrinsic possibilities of development, the more the whole blaring dynamic business approaches a standstill. Just as no piece of jazz can, in a musical sense, be said to have a history, just as all its components can be moved about at will, just as no single measure follows from the logic of the musical progression – so the perennial fashion becomes the likeness of a planned congealed society, not so different from the night-mare vision of Huxley's *Brave New World*. Whether what the ideology here expresses – or exposes – is the tendency of an over-accumulating society to regress to the stage of simple reproduction is for economists to decide. The fear that marked the late writings of a bitterly disappointed Thorstein Veblen, that the play of economic and social forces was coming to rest in a nega-tive, historical state, a kind of higher-potency feudalism, may be highly unlikely, yet it remains the innermost desire of jazz. The image of the tech-nical world possesses an ahistorical aspect that enables it to serve as a mythi-cal mirage of eternity. Planned production seems to purge the life-process of all that is uncontrollable, unpredictable, incalculable in advance and thus to deprive it of what is genuinely new, without which history is hardly con-ceivable; in addition, the form of the standardized mass-produced article transforms the temporal sequence of objects into more of the same. The fact that a 1950 locomotive looks different from one made in 1850 leaves a para-doxical impression; it is for this reason that the most modern express trains are occasionally decorated with photographs of obsolete models. The surre-alists, who have much in common with jazz, have appealed to this level of experience since Apollinaire: 'ici même les automobiles ont l'air d'être anci-ennes.' Traces of this have been unconsciously assimilated by the perennial fashion; jazz, which knows what it is doing when it allies itself with tech-nique, collaborates in the 'technological veil' through its rigorously repetitive though objectless cultic ritual, and fosters the illusion that the twentieth century is ancient Egypt, full of slaves and endless dynasties. This remains illu-sion, however, for although the symbol of technology may be the uniformly revolving wheel, its intrinsic energies develop to an incalculable extent while remaining saddled by a society which is driven forward by its inner tensions, which persists in its irrationality and which grants men far more history than they wish. Timelessness is projected on technology by a world-order which knows that to change would be to collapse. The pseudo-eternity is belied, however, by the bad contingencies and inferiorities that have established themselves as universal principle. The men of the Thousand Year Reichs of today look like criminals, and the perennial gesture of mass culture is that of the asocial person. The fact that of all the tricks available, syncopation should have been the one to achieve musical dictatorship over the masses recalls the usurpation that characterizes techniques, however rational they may be in themselves, when they are placed at the service of irrational totalitarian control. Mechanisms which in reality are part and parcel of the entire present-day ideology, of the culture industry, are left easily visible in jazz because in the absence of technical knowledge they cannot be as easily identified as, for example, in films. Yet even jazz takes certain precautions. Parallel to standardization is pseudo-individualization. The more strictly the listener is curbed, the less he is permitted to notice it. He is told that jazz is 'consumer art', made specially for him. The particular effects with which jazz fills out its schema, syncopation above all, strive to create the appearance of being the outburst or caricature of untrammelled subjectivity – in effect, that of the listener – or perhaps the most subtle nuance dedicated to the greater glory of the audience. But the method becomes trapped in its own net. For while it must constantly promise its listeners something different, excite their attention and keep itself from becoming run-of-the-mill, it is not allowed to leave the beaten path; it must be always new and always the same. Hence, the deviations are just as standardized as the standards and in effect revoke themselves the instant they appear. Jazz, like everything else in the culture industry, gratifies desires only to frustrate them at the same time. However much jazz-subjects, representing the music listener in general, may play the non-conformist, in truth they are less and less themselves. Individual features which do not conform to the norm are nevertheless shaped by it, and become marks of mutilation. Terrified, jazz fans identify with the society they dread for having made them what they are. This gives the jazz ritual its affirmative character, that of being accepted into a community of unfree equals. With this in mind, jazz can appeal directly to the mass of listeners in self-justification with a diabolically good conscience. Standard procedures which prevail unquestioned and which have been perfected over long periods of time produce standard reactions. Well-meaning educators, who believe that a change in programming would be enough to bring the violated and oppressed to desire something better, or at least something different, are much too credulous. Even when they do not greatly transcend the ideological realm of the culture industry, serious changes in programme policy are angrily rejected in reality. The population is so accustomed to the drivel it gets that it cannot renounce it, even when it sees through it halfway. On the contrary, it feels itself impelled to intensify its enthusiasm in order to convince itself that its ignominy is its good fortune. Jazz sets up schemes of social behaviour to which people must in any case conform. Jazz enables them to practise those forms of behaviour, and they love it all the more for making the inescapable easier to bear. Jazz reproduces its own mass-basis, without thereby reducing the guilt of those who produce it. The eternity of fashion is a vicious circle.

3

Jazz fans, as has once again been emphatically shown by David Riesman, can be divided into two clearly distinguishable groups. In the inner circle sit the experts, or those who consider themselves such – for very often the most passionate devotees, those who flaunt the established terminology and differentiate jazz styles with ponderous pretention, are hardly able to give an account, in precise, technical musical concepts, of whatever it is that so moves them. Most of them consider themselves avant-gardistic, thus participating in a confusion that has become ubiquitous today. Among the symptoms of the disintegration of culture and education, not the least is the fact that the distinction between autonomous 'high' and commercial 'light' art, however questionable it may be, is neither critically reflected nor even noticed any more. And now that certain culturally defeatist intellectuals have pitted the latter against the former, the philistine champions of the culture industry can even take pride in the conviction that they are marching in the vanguard of the *Zeitgeist*. The organization of culture into 'levels' such as the first, second and third programmes, patterned after low, middle and highbrow, is reprehensible. But it cannot be overcome simply by the lowbrow sects declaring themselves to be highbrow. The legitimate discontent with culture provides a pretext but not the slightest justification for the glorification of a highly rationalized section of mass production, one which debases and betrays culture without at all transcending it, as the dawn of a new world-sensibility or for confusing it with cubism, Eliot's poetry and Joyce's prose. Regression is not origin, but origin is the ideology of regression. Anyone who allows the growing respectability of mass culture to seduce him into equating a popular song with modern art because of a few false notes squeaked by a clarinet; anyone who mistakes a triad studded with 'dirty notes' for atonality, has already capitulated to barbarism. Art which has degenerated to culture pays the price of being all the more readily confused with its own waste-products as its aberrant influence grows. Education, traditionally the privilege of the few, is paid its due by self-conscious illiteracy which proclaims the stupor of tolerated excess to be the realm of freedom. Rebelling feebly, they are always ready to duck, following the lead of jazz, which integrates stumbling and coming-too-soon into the collective march-step. There is a striking similarity between this type of jazz enthusiast and many of the young disciples of logical positivism, who throw off philosophical culture with the same zeal as jazz fans dispense with the tradition of serious music. Enthusiasm turns into a matter-of-fact attitude in which all feeling becomes attached to technique, hostile to all meaning. They feel themselves secure within a system so well defined that no mistake could possibly slip by, and the repressed yearning for things outside finds expression as intolerant hatred and in an attitude which combines the superior knowledge of the initiate with the pretentiousness of the person without illusions. Bombastic triviality, superficiality seen as apodictic certitude, transfigures the cowardly defence against every form of self-reflection. All these old accustomed modes of reaction have in recent times lost their innocence, set themselves up as philosophy and thus become truly pernicious.

Gathered around the specialists in a field in which there is little to understand besides rules are the vague, inarticulate followers. In general they are intoxicated by the fame of mass culture, a fame which the latter knows how to manipulate; they could just as well get together in clubs for worshipping film stars or for collecting autographs. What is important to them is the sense of belonging as such, identification, without their paying particular attention to its content. As girls, they have trained themselves to faint upon hearing the voice of a 'crooner'. Their applause, cued in by a light-signal, is transmitted directly on the popular radio programmes they are permitted to attend. They call themselves 'jitter-bugs', bugs which carry out reflex movements, performers of their own ecstasy. Merely to be carried away by anything at all, to have something of their own, compensates for their impoverished and barren existence. The gesture of adolescence, which raves for this or that on one day with the ever-present possibility of damning it as idiocy on the next, is now socialized. Of course, Europeans tend to overlook the fact that jazz fans on the Continent in no way equal those in America. The element of excess, of insubordination in jazz, which can still be felt in Europe, is entirely missing today in America. The recollection of anarchic origins which jazz shares with all of today's ready-made mass movements, is fundamentally repressed, however much it may continue to simmer under the surface. Jazz is taken for granted as an institution, housebroken and scrubbed behind the ears. What is common to the jazz enthusiast of all countries, however, is the moment of compliance, in parodistic exaggeration. In this respect their play recalls the brutal seriousness of the masses of followers in totalitarian states, even though the difference between play and seriousness amounts to that between life and death. The advertisement for a particular song played by a big name band was 'follow your leader, XY.' While the leaders in the European dictatorships of both shades raged against the decadence of jazz, the youth of the other countries has long since allowed itself to be electrified, as with marches, by the syncopated dance-steps, with bands which do not by accident stem from military music. The division into shock-troops and inarticulate following has something of the distinction between party élite and rest of the 'people'.

4

The jazz monopoly rest on the exclusiveness of the supply and the economic power behind it. But it would have been broken long ago if the ubiquitous speciality did not contain something universal to which people respond. Jazz must possess a 'mass basis', the technique must link up with a moment in the subjects – one which, of course, in turn points back to the social structure and to typical conflicts between the ego and society. What first comes to mind, in quest for that moment, is the eccentric clown or parallels with the early film comics. Individual weakness is proclaimed and revoked in the same breath, stumbling is confirmed as a kind of higher skill. In the process of integrating the asocial, jazz converges with the equally standardized schemas of the detective novel and its offshoots, which regularly distort or unmask the world so that asociality and crime become the everyday norm, but which at the same time charm away the seductive and ominous challenge through the inevitable triumph of order. Psychoanalytic theory alone can provide an adequate explanation of this phenomenon. The aim of jazz is the mechanical reproduction of a regressive moment, a castration symbolism. 'Give up your masculinity, let yourself be castrated,' the eunuchlike sound of the jazz band both mocks and proclaims, 'and you will be rewarded, accepted into a fraternity which shares the mystery of impotence with you, a mystery revealed at the moment of the iniation rite'.[1] If this interpretation of jazz – whose sexual implications are better understood by its shocked opponents than by its apologists – appear arbitrary and far-fetched, the fact remains that it can be substantiated in countless details of the music as well as of the song lyrics. In the book, *American Jazz Music*, Wilder Hobson describes an early jazz bandleader Mike Riley, a musical eccentric who must have truly mutilated the instruments. 'The band squirted water and tore clothes, and Riley offered perhaps the greatest of trombone comedy acts, an insane rendition of "Dinah" during which he repeatedly dismembered the horn and reassembled it erratically until the tubing hung down like brass burnishings in a junk shop, with a vaguely harmonic honk still sounding from one or more of the loose ends.' Long before, Virgil Thomson had compared the performances of the famed jazz trumpeter, Louis Armstrong, to those of the great *castrati* of the eighteenth century. The entire sphere is saturated with terminology which distinguishes between 'long' and 'short haired' musicians. The latter are jazz people who earn money and can afford to appear presentable; the others, the caricature of the Slavic pianist, for instance, whose long mane is exemplary, are grouped under the little esteemed stereotype of the artist who is starving and who flaunts the demands of convention. This is the manifest content of the terminology. What the shorn hair represents hardly requires elaboration. In jazz, the Philistines standing over Samson are permanently transfigured.

In truth, the Philistines. The castration symbolism, deeply buried in the practices of jazz and cut off from consciousness through the institutionalization of perennial sameness, is for that very reason probably all the more potent. And sociologically, jazz has the effect of strengthening and extending, down to the very physiology of the subject, the acceptance of a dreamless-realistic world in which all memories of things not wholly integrated have been purged. To comprehend the mass basis of jazz one must take full account of the taboo on artistic expression in America, a taboo which continues unabated despite the official art industry, and which even affects the expressive impulses of children; progressive education, which seeks to stimulate their faculties of expression as an end in itself, is simply a reaction to this. Although the artist is partially tolerated, partially integrated into the sphere of consumption as an 'entertainer', a functionary – like the better-paid waiter subject to the demands of 'service' – the stereotype of the artist remains the introvert, the egocentric idiot, frequently the homosexual. While such traits may be tolerated in professional artists – a scandalous private life may even be expected as part of the entertainment – everyone else makes himself immediately suspicious by any spontaneous artistic impulse not ordered in advance by society. A child who prefers to listen to serious music or practise the piano rather than watch a baseball game or television will have to suffer as a 'sissy' in his class or in the other groups to which he belongs and which embody far more authority than parents or teacher. The expressive impulse is exposed to the same threat of castration that is symbolized and mechanically and ritually subdued in jazz. Nevertheless, the need for expression, which stands in no necessary relation to the objective quality of art, cannot be entirely eliminated, especially during the years of maturation. Teenagers are not entirely stifled by economic life and its psychological correlative, the reality principle. Their aesthetic impulses are not simply extinguished by suppression but are rather diverted. Jazz is the preferred medium of such diversion. To the masses of young people who, year after year, chase the perennial fashion, presumably to forget it after a few years, it offers a compromise between aesthetic sublimation and social adjustment. The 'unrealistic', practically useless, imaginative element is permitted to survive at the price of changing its character; it must tirelessly strive to remake itself in the image of reality, to repeat the latter's commands to itself, to submit to them. Thus it reintegrates itself into the sphere from which it sought to escape. Art is deprived of its aesthetic dimension, and emerges as part of the very adjustment which it in principle contradicts. Viewed from this standpoint, several unusual features of jazz can be more easily understood. The role played by arrangement, for instance, which cannot be adequately explained in terms of a technical division of labour or of the musical illiteracy of the so-called composers. Nothing is permitted to remain what it intrinsically is. Everything must be fixed up, must bear the traces of a preparation which brings it closer to the sphere of the well known, thus rendering it more easily comprehensible. At the same time, this process of preparation indicates to the listener that the music is made for him, yet without idealizing him. And finally, arrangement stamps the music with the official seal of approval, which in turn testifies to the absence of all artistic ambitions to achieve distance from reality, to the readiness of the music to swim with the stream; this is music which does not fancy itself any better than it is.

The primacy of adjustment is no less decisive in determining the specific skills which jazz demands from its musicians, to a certain extent from its listeners as well, and certainly from the dancers who strive to imitate the music. Aesthetic technique, in the sense of the quintessence of means employed to objectify an autonomous subject-matter, is replaced by the ability to cope with obstacles, to be impervious to disruptive factors like syncopations and yet at the same time to execute cleverly the particular action which underlies the abstract rules. The aesthetic act is made into a sport by means of a system of tricks. To master it is also to demonstrate one's practicality. The achievement of the jazz musician and expert adds up to a sequence of successfully surmounted tests. But expression, the true bearer of aesthetic protest, is overtaken by the might against which it protests. Faced by this might it assumes a malicious and miserable tone which barely and momentarily disguises itself as harsh and provocative. The subject which expresses itself expresses precisely this: I am nothing, I am filth, no matter what they do to me, it serves me right. Potentially this subject has already become one of those Russians, accused of a crime, and who, although innocent, collaborates with the prosecutor from the beginning and is incapable of finding a punishment severe enough. If the aesthetic realm originally emerged as an autonomous sphere from the magic taboo which distinguished the sacred from the everyday, seeking to keep the former pure, the profane now takes its revenge on the descendant of magic, on art. Art is permitted to survive only if it renounces the right to be different, and integrates itself into the omnipotent realm of the profane which finally took over the taboo. Nothing may exist which is not like the world as it is. Jazz is the false liquidation of art – instead of utopia becoming reality it disappears from the picture.

Note

1   This theory is developed in the essay, 'Jazz', published in 1936 in the *Zeitschrift für Sozialforschung* (p. 252ff), and elaborated in a review of the books by Sargeant and Hobson in *Studies in Philosophy and Social Science*, 1941, p. 175. ['Jazz' is reprinted in Th. W. Adorno, *Moments Musicaux*, Frankfurt am Main, 1964, pp. 84–115. Translators' note.]

16

Arnold Schoenberg, 1874–1951

No philosopher has written so extensively or knowledgeably on music as Adorno. Many of his musicological principles were gained from a study of the music of Arnold Schoenberg. Given, however, that the latter is a pervasive presence throughout all of Adorno's theoretical writings, it is clear that his preoccupation with the work of Schoenberg transcends musicology. There is no brief way of adequately describing the influence of Schoenberg on Adorno's thought. What, in essence, Schoenberg's music represents for Adorno is that openness to the demands of material which revolutionizes form. Schoenberg did not innovate for innovation's sake. Rather he followed the requirements of the historical development of music when he began to compose in free atonality. One of Adorno's earliest essays on Schoenberg gave him the epithet 'the dialectical composer'. That is, in Schoenberg's engagement with musical material, as in experience, form (or consciousness) adjusts to the object, transforming both itself and the very idea of the object thereby. In this way Schoenberg progressively extended and changed, irrevocably, the process of music.

Adorno's appreciation of the intellectual value of Schoenberg's music has many facets. The first that we find in 'Arnold Schoenberg, 1874–1951' is that the experience of listening to Schoenberg's music has implications for a transformation of consciousness from something reified and passive to something engaged, mobile, and attentive. Second, Schoenberg's attitude to musical composition is exemplary of, to put it oddly perhaps, the subject–object relationship. The case of the unfinished *Oratorio* bears this out. Adorno believes that Schoenberg was unable to complete this work because there existed no authentic possibility of writing an oratorio under the circumstances of early twentieth-century culture. It was an anomaly which could not be resolved. Because Schoenberg remained true to the material, therefore, the work was never to be completed. Third, there is the very act of changing the conventions of music solely as a response to the logic of the tradition (for example, the strain on tonality in the later works of Brahms and Wagner, and indeed Liszt whom Adorno does not mention). This, as mentioned, is the dialectic of composition.

Adorno associates the experience of Schoenberg's music with praxis, an association which has caused an astonished reaction among orthodox and not so orthodox Marxists. Is this esoteric possibility – available one presumes only with the benefit of a privileged musical education – the only way open for emancipation? In order to see Adorno as neither a political irrelevance nor simply hilariously misguided it is important to remember his views of ideology. If it is possible to argue that ideology is all-encompassing, that consciousness no longer makes the 'dialectical' step which would be required to criticize its givens, then the traditional notion of a praxis, based on fraternal feelings and a clear vision of what is wrong, must be excluded. All that remains in the intellectual realm are rare experiences, among them Schoenberg's music, which might just provide consciousness with a critical example.

Adorno wrote numerous pieces on Schoenberg including the major 1949 publication, *Philosophy of Modern Music*, in which the progressiveness of Schoenberg is contrasted with the controversially propounded restorativeness of Igor Stravinsky. Adorno, though, as we also see in 'Arnold Schoenberg 1874–1951', was no hagiographer. He was critical of Schoenberg's move from free atonality to the twelve-tone technique, a criticism which should not surprise us if we appreciate just what the evaluation 'dialectical' means for Adorno. It means composing in such a way that the material develops freely, though not randomly. The twelve-tone row, however, devised by Schoenberg to maintain some coherence on ever more complicated material, was seen by Adorno as a technique which threatened to prejudice the dialectic inherent in the free atonal style.

During the period of Adorno's exile spent in California he was a near neighbour of Schoenberg. However, despite the enormous admiration which Adorno reserved for Schoenberg and in no equal measure for anyone else, both men seem to have had temperamental differences which inhibited close personal contact. Even though Adorno was a vigorous, supremely sophisticated and sometimes lonely champion of Schoenberg's achievements it is reported that Schoenberg himself (rather like Berg earlier in Vienna) had little regard for what he saw as Adorno's excessive intellectualizing.* The Californian experience,

---

*   Though Schoenberg for all that often articulated his thoughts on musical motivations and the responsibilities of a composer in Adorno–like ways. Cf. Arnold Schoenberg, trans. Leo Black, *Style and Idea: Selected Writings of Arnold Schoenberg* (London: Faber and Faber, 1975).

incidentally, partly found its way into literature. Thomas Mann, then thinking about what was to become the novel *Doctor Faustus*, drew upon Adorno's musical expertise in order to understand the demands of contemporary composition. Adorno, curiously enough, makes an appearance in the novel in the figure of the Devil.

'Arnold Schoenberg, 1874–1951' [1953], in *Prisms* (Cambridge, Mass.: MIT Press, 1981), pp. 147–72.
Translated by Samuel and Shierry Weber.

> Heard melodies are sweet, but those unheard
> Are sweeter; therefore, ye soft pipes, play on;
> Not to the sensual ear, but, more endear'd,
> Pipe to the spirit ditties of no tone.
>
> *Keats*

In the public mind of today Schoenberg appears as an innovator, as a reformer, even as the inventor of a system. With grudging respect it is admitted that he prepared the way for others, a way, it is true, which they had no great desire to travel; yet this concession is linked to the implication that he himself was a failure and has already become obsolete. The one-time pariah is repressed, neutralized and absorbed. Not merely his early works but those of his middle period as well – which at the time earned him the hatred of all culture-lovers – are dismissed as 'Wagnerian' or 'late Romantic', although in forty years few have learned how to perform them properly. The works he wrote after the First World War are appraised as examples of the twelve-tone technique. In recent years, it is true, numerous young composers have taken up this technique again, but more in the search of a shell behind which to take refuge than as the necessary result of their own experience, and hence without troubling to worry about the function of the twelve-tone method within Schoenberg's own work. Such repression and dressing-up is provoked by the difficulties that Schoenberg poses to a listening public which has been kneaded into shape by the culture industry. If one does not understand something, it is customary to behave with the sublime understanding of Mahler's jackass, and project one's own inadequacy on to the object, declaring it to be incomprehensible. And it is true that Schoenberg's music demands from the very beginning active and concentrated participation, the most acute attention to simultaneous multiplicity, the renunciation of the customary crutches of a listening which always knows what to expect, the intensive perception of the unique and specific, and the ability to grasp precisely the individual characteristics, often changing in the smallest space, and their history, devoid of all repetition. The purity and sovereignty with which

Schoenberg always entrusts himself to the demands of his subject-matter has restricted his influence; it is precisely because of its seriousness, richness and integrity that his music arouses resentment. The more it gives its listeners, the less it offers them. It requires the listener spontaneously to compose its inner movement and demands of him not mere contemplation but praxis. In this, however, Schoenberg blasphemes against the expectation, cherished despite all idealistic assurances to the contrary, that music will present the comfortable listener with a series of pleasurable sensations. Even schools such as Debussy's, despite the aesthetic atmosphere of art for art's sake, have met this expectation. The line dividing the young Debussy and salon music was fluid, and the technical accomplishments of the mature composer were adroitly incorporated by commercial mass music. With Schoenberg affability ceases. He proclaims the end of a conformity which had made music into the natural preserve of infantility within a society which had long been aware that it would be tolerated only as long as it allowed its inmates a quota of controlled juvenile happiness. He sins against the division of life into work and leisure; he insists on a kind of work for one's leisure that could easily call the latter into question. His passion points to a music of which the mind need not be ashamed, and which therefore shames the prevailing temper. His music strives to be mature at both its poles: it releases the threatening instinctual sphere which music otherwise presents only after it has been filtered and harmoniously falsified, and it demands great intellectual energy, the principle of an ego strong enough not to have to deny the instincts. Kandinsky, in whose *Blue Rider* he published the *Herzgewächse*, formulated the programme of the 'intellectual in art'. Schoenberg remained devoted to this, not by aiming at abstractions but by making the concrete form of music itself intelligible.

This gives rise to the most popular objection to Schoenberg – against his so-called 'intellectualism'. However, this either confuses the intrinsic force of intellectualization with reflection that remains external to the object, or it dogmatically exempts music from the demands of intellectualization which have become obligatory for all aesthetic media as a corrective against the transformation of culture into *biens culturels*. The truth is that Schoenberg was a naïve artist, above all in the often hapless intellectualizations with which he sought to justify his work. If anyone was ever guided by the tide of involuntary musical intuition it was he. Half self-taught, the language of music was self-evident to him. It was only with the greatest reluctance that he transformed it down to its most elementary levels. Although his music channeled all the energies of his ego towards objectifying its impulses, it nevertheless remained ego-alien to him for the duration of his life. He himself readily identified with the elect who resist their mission. Courage he considered the attribute of 'those who accomplish acts which exceed their confidence'. The paradoxical nature of the formula characterizes his attitude towards authority. It combines aesthetic avant-gardism with a conservative mentality. While inflicting the most deadly blows on authority through his work, he seeks to defend the work as though before a hidden authority and ultimately to make it itself the authority. In the eyes of the Viennese composer, coming from a parochial background, the norms of a closed, semi-feudal society seemed the will of God. Yet this respect was linked to an opposing element, although one no less incompatible with the notion of the intellectual. Something not integrated, not entirely civilized, indeed hostile to civilization, kept him outside the very order of which he was so uncritical. Like a man without origins, fallen from heaven, a musical Caspar Hauser, he hit the bullseye unerringly. Nothing was to be allowed to recall the natural milieu to which he nonetheless belonged, and the result was that his undeveloped nature became all the more evident. He who severed all ties so that he alone could be responsible for everything, was able precisely because of that isolation, to win contact with the collective undercurrent of music and to achieve that sovereignty which enables each one of his works to represent the entire genre. There was no greater surprise than when that hoarse and irritable speaker sang a few bars. His warm, free, sonorous voice was untroubled by the fear of singing which is burned into the civilized mind and which makes the pseudo-nonchalance of the professional singer all the more distressing. Music had taken over the role of parents; 'musically', he was borne along by the language of music, like the speaker of a dialect, and in that respect comparable to someone like Richard Strauss or the Slavic composers. From the earliest works – already manifest in *Transfigured Night* – there flows from this language a specific warmth, both in tone and in the wealth of successive and simultaneous musical figures, uninhibitedly productive, virtually oriental in their fertility. Enough is not enough. Schoenberg's intolerance of all excess ornament stems from his generosity, from his reluctance to have the listener deprived of true riches by ostentation. His generous imagination and artistic hospitality, intent on providing each guest with the best, is probably more important for him than what is generally termed, dubiously enough, 'the need for expression'. Non-Wagnerian, his music springs from creative fervour, not consuming desire, and is insatiable in its giving. As though all the artistic materials with which he could prove himself were borrowed property, he produces his own material as well as its resistances, driven incessantly by the disgust of everything he produces which is not entirely new. The flame of untrammelled, mimetic creation, which came over Schoenberg from that subterranean heritage in the end also consumed the heritage. Tradition and fresh start are as interwoven in him as the revolutionary and conservative aspect.

The reproach of 'intellectualism' is linked to the lack of melody. Yet he was supremely melodic. Instead of the established formula he constantly produced new forms. His melodic imagination scarcely ever contented itself with a single melody; instead, all simultaneous musical events are treated as melodies, which makes them more difficult to grasp. Even Schoenberg's instinctive mode of reaction is melodic; everything in him is actually 'sung', including the instrumental lines. This endows his music with its articulate character, free-moving and yet structural down to the last tone. The primacy of breathing over the beat of abstract time contrasts Schoenberg to Stravinsky and to all those who, having adjusted better to contemporary existence, fancy themselves more modern than Schoenberg. The reified mind is allergic to the elaboration and fulfilment of melody, for which it substitutes the docile repetition of mutilated melodic fragments. The ability to follow the breath of the music unafraid had already distinguished Schoenberg from older, post-Wagnerian composers like Strauss and Wolf, in whom the music seems unable to develop its substance according to its intrinsic impulses and requires literary and programmatic support, even in the songs. By contrast, the works of Schoenberg's first period, including the symphonic poem, *Pelleas and Melisande*, and the *Gurrelieder*, are already fully composed. Wagnerian methods are as little related to Schoenberg as Wagnerian expression; by reaching its goal instead of breaking off and beginning anew the musical impulse loses the moment of crazed desire, of obsessive preoccupation. Schoenberg's original expression, generous and, in the meaningful sense, jovial, recalls the humane expression of Beethoven. From the very start, of course, it is prepared to turn into the defiance of a world which rejects its gifts. Scorn and violence seek to subdue the coolness, rebelliousness; and the sentiment of one who fails to reach human beings precisely because he speaks to them as such turns to fear. This is the origin of Schoenberg's ideal of perfection. He reduces, constructs, arms his music; the rejected gift will become so perfect that it will have to be accepted. By reaction, his love had to become hard, like that of all minds since Schopenhauer who have not been content to make do with the world as it is. Kraus' verse, 'what has the world done to us?' is emphatically true of the musician.

Schoenberg's nonconformity is not a matter of temperament. The complexion of his musical intuition left him no choice but to compose coherently. His integrity was forced on him; he had to work out the tension between Brahmsian and Wagnerian elements. His expansive imagination thrived on Wagnerian material, whereas the demands of compositional consistency, the responsibility of respecting the music's intrinsic tendencies drew him to Brahmsian methods. Out of this context, the question of Brahmsian or Wagnerian style was irrelevant to Schoenberg. The Wagnerian style with its compositional limitations could not satisfy him any more than the Brahmsian with its academic character. Both practically and then theoretically he steadfastly rejected the notion of 'style', in the sense of a category existing prior to the subject–matter and oriented on external consensus; instead, he spoke of the 'idea', meaning the pure elaboration of musical thoughts. On all levels his primary concern was the What, not the How, the principles of selection and the means of presentation. Hence, the different stylistic phases of his work should not be over-interpreted. The decisive point comes very early, certainly not later than the *Songs* op. 6 and the d minor Quartet op. 7. These works provide the key to all the later ones. All subsequent innovations, which provoked such a sensation at the time, are nothing but the logical consequence for musical language of what was inherent in the individual musical events of the specific work. Dissonance and large intervals, the two most conspicuous elements of the mature Schoenberg, are secondary, mere derivatives of the inner structure of all of his music; besides, the large intervals are already present in his youth. The central problem is that of mastering the contradiction between essence and appearance. Richness and plenitude are to be made the essence, not mere ornament; the essence, in turn, will appear no longer as the rigid framework on which the music is draped but rather as concrete and evident in its most subtle traits. What he designated as the 'subcutaneous' – the fabric of individual musical events, grasped as the ineluctable moments of an internally coherent totality – breaks through the surface, becomes visible and manifests itself independently of all stereotyped forms. The inward dimension moves outward. Ordering categories, which reduce the difficulties of active listening at the cost of the pure elaboration of the work, are eliminated. This absence of all mediations introduced into the work from outside makes the musical progression seem fragmented and abrupt to the unnaïve-naïve listener, with the impression increasing in direct proportion to the actual degree of inner organization. The early song, *Lockung*, from op. 6, is the prototype of a characteristic that recurs continually, up into the twelve-tone phase. In its ten-measure introduction three sharply contrasting groups, also distinct in tempo, are juxtaposed; the first consisting of four measures, the other two of three each. None of the groups conspicuously repeats anything from the preceding ones, yet all are interrelated through intervening variation. The groups are also syntactically linked: turbulent question, insistence, and half-hearted, tentative and already transitional answer. There is an infinite amount taking place within the smallest space and yet everything is so totally formed that there is never any confusion. The second group, for instance, varies the first in retaining the diminished second and augmented fourth intervals while at the same time reducing the beat from 3/8 to 2/8, thus producing the general driven character. Amid radical change, melodic economy prevails. It is this organization of the musical structure that is the true Schoenberg, not the privileged use of striking techniques; what is crucial is the variegated alternation of distinct and contrasting figures with the general unity of motivic-thematic relations. It is music of identity in nonidentity. All the developments unfold more concentratedly and more rapidly than is deemed acceptable by the sluggish habits of culinary listening; polyphony functions with real parts, not with camouflaging counterpoint. The individual characteristics are intensified to the utmost; the articulation rejects all finished schemas, and contrast, repressed in the nineteenth century by transition, becomes, under the pressure of an emotional state polarized into extremes, the formative technique. Technically, the maturing of music means the protest against musical stupidity. Although Schoenberg's music is not intellectual, it does demand musical intelligence. Its basic principle is, to use his phrase, the 'developing variation'. Everything that appears strives to be developed logically, to be intensified and then resolved in an equilibrium. Universal responsibility and idiosyncrasy prevail against all musical traits which resemble journalistic language. Both fatuous rhetoric and the deceptive gesture that promises more than it fulfils are scorned. Schoenberg's music honours the listener by not making any con cessions to him.

Hence, it is reproached for being 'experimental'. Underlying this criticism is the notion that progress in artistic technique proceeds in a steady, so to speak organic flow. Anyone who, acting on his own, discovers something new, without overt historical aid, is thought not merely to sin against the tradition but also to succumb to vanity and impotence. But works of art, including music, require consciousness and spontaneity, and these consistently destroy the semblance of continual growth. So long as the new music still had a clear conscience, resulting from its hostility to a tradition that Mahler had labelled as 'sloppy'; so long as it did not try anxiously to prove that its intentions were really not that had, it advocated the concept of experiment. It is only the superstitious belief which fetishistically confuses the reified, rigidified – precisely what is estranged from nature – with nature itself, that sees to it that nothing new is tried in art. All the same, artistic extremism must be held responsible for either following the logic of its subject-matter, an objectivity, however concealed, or succumbing to mere private caprice or an abstract system. It receives its legitimacy from the tradition it negates. Hegel taught that wherever something new becomes visible, immediate, striking, authentic, a long process of formation has preceded it and it has now merely thrown off its shell. Only that which has been nourished with the life-blood of the tradition can possibly have the power to confront it authentically; the rest becomes the helpless prey of forces which it has failed to

overcome sufficiently within itself. Yet the bond of tradition is hardly equivalent to the simple sequence of events in history; rather, it is subterranean. 'A
tradition,' writes Freud in his late work on *Moses and Monotheism*, 'which was
founded only on communication could not produce the compulsive quality
characteristic of religious phenomena. It would be heard, evaluated, eventually dismissed like every other piece of external information, and would never
attain that privileged status necessary to liberate men from the sway of logical
thought. It must have undergone the destiny of repression, the state of
remaining in the unconscious, before it could develop a powerful enough
influence, upon its return, to force the masses under its spell'. The aesthetic
no less than the religious tradition is the recollection of something unconscious, indeed repressed. Where it does, in fact, unfold a 'potent influence', it
is the result not of a manifest, direct consciousness of continuity but rather
of unconscious recollection which explodes the continuum. Tradition is far
more present in works deplored as experimental than in those which deliberately strive to be traditional. What has long been observed in modern
French painting is no less true of Schoenberg and the Vienna School. The
manifest sound-material of Classicism and Romanticism, the tonal chords and
their normed associations, the melodic lines balanced between triad and
second-intervals, in short, the entire façade of the music of the last two-
hundred years is submitted to productive criticism. Yet what was crucial in
the great music of the tradition was not those elements as such, but rather
the specific function they assumed in the presentation of a particular compositional content. Beneath the façade there was a second, latent structure.
The latter was determined by the façade in many respects, yet was continually producing and justifying it in its problematic character. The understanding of traditional music always meant the recognition not of the façade alone,
but of that inner structure in its relation to that façade. As a result of the
emancipation of the subject, this relation became so precarious that finally
both structures split wide apart. Schoenberg's spontaneous productive power
executed an objective historical verdict – he liberated the latent structure
while disposing of the manifest one. Thus, it is precisely through his 'experiments' – through the anomalous character he gave to the appearances of
his music – that he became heir to the tradition. He heeded the norms
which were teleologically implicit in Viennese Classicism and then in Brahms,
and thus, in this historical sense as well, he honoured his obligations.
The objectification achieved under the primacy of 'total composition' had
lost its authority by the time of Brahms because it had begun to function
mechanically, had lost its hold on a resistant musical material and categorically repressed the impulse to rebel. In Schoenberg, however, each individual
musical moment, down to the initial 'idea', is incomparably more substantial.

His totality, true to the historical level of the mind, starts from the individual, not from a plan or architecture. As already had been done by Beethoven, although in rudimentary form, he includes the Romantic element in integral composition. Of course, this also has its place in Brahms, in lyrical melodies amid instrumental forms; there, however, it is neutralized, kept in a kind of equilibrium with the 'work', and this is the source of that illusoriness and resignation that characterize the Brahmsian form, which prudently smooths over oppositions rather than immersing itself in them. In Schoenberg the objectification of subjective impulses becomes crucial. He may have learned his motivic-thematic variations from Brahms, but the polyphony which gives his objectification of subjectivity its pungency belongs entirely to him; it is literally the recollection of something buried for over two hundred years. This stems from the fact that Beethoven's 'thematic work', particularly in the chamber music, incurred polyphonic obligations which it failed to meet, except for a few exceptions in his late period. Wilhelm Fischer, in his study, *On the Stylistic Development of Viennese Classicism*, arrived at this insight: 'In general, the development-section functions in Viennese Classicism as the playground for the melodic techniques of the old classical style which have been excluded from the exposition.' Yet this is true not merely of the 'baroque' principle of melodic elaboration, but to a far greater extent of polyphony, which continually appears in the development only to run aground. Schoenberg thinks Classicism's unfulfilled promise through to its conclusion and in so doing breaks down the traditional façade. He reasserted Bach's challenge, which Classicism, including Beethoven, had evaded, though without regressing behind Classicism. The Classic composers had neglected Bach out of historical necessity. The autonomy of the musical subject took priority over all other considerations and critically excluded the traditional form of objectivization, at the same time making do with a semblance of objectivization just as the unrestricted interplay of subjects seemed the best guarantee for society. Only today, when subjectivity in its immediacy can no longer be regarded as the supreme category since its realization depends on society as a whole, does the inadequacy of even Beethoven's solution, which extended the subject so as to cover the whole, become evident. The development-section, which even at its heights in Beethoven, in the *Eroica*, remains 'dramatic', not totally composed, is transformed through Schoenberg's polyphony; the subjective melodic impulse is dialectically dissolved into its objective multivocal components. It is this organization, not capricious tolerance, that distinguishes Schoenberg's counterpoint from all the others of his epoch. At the same time it overcomes the burdensome harmonic emphasis. He is supposed to have said that no one thinks about harmony with truly good counterpoint. This, however, is characteristic not only of Bach, in whom the stringency of the polyphony distracts attention from the *continuo* schema within which it operates, but of Schoenberg as well, in whom such stringency ultimately makes all chord schemas and all façades superfluous; his is music of the intellectual ear.

As 'developing variation', intellectualization becomes a technical principle. It overcomes all mere immediacy by accepting and following its inner dynamic. Schoenberg once ironically mentioned that musical theory is always concerned only with the beginning and the end and never with what comes between, namely, with the music itself. His entire work is a single effort to answer this question ignored by theory. Themes and their history, the musical progression, have equal weight, indeed, the difference between the two is liquidated. This takes place within the group of works which extends roughly from the *Songs* op. 6 to the *George Songs*, and which includes the first two Quartets, the *First Kammersymphonie* and the first movement of the *Second*. Only an obsessive concern with 'style' could consider such works 'transitional'; as compositions they are of the greatest maturity. The d minor Quartet, down to its last note, created an entirely new level of thematically coherent chamber-music composition. Its form is that of the later twelve-tone works; anyone who wants to understand them would do better to study this Quartet than to count series. Each 'idea', from the first beat on, is contrapuntal and contains within itself the potentiality of its development; each development preserves the spontaneity of the first idea. And that which still transpired successively in the First Quartet is then, within the scant dimensions and polyphony of the *First Kammersymphonie*, compressed into simultaneity. Thus, the façade, still tolerated to a degree in the Quartet, begins to disintegrate. In his last book, Schoenberg described and illustrated how, in the exposition of the *Kammersymphonie*, he followed the unconscious impulse – that is, the desideratum of the latent structure – sacrificed the usual conception of the logical 'consequence' of overt thematic references and instead drew the consequence from the inner consistency of the themes. The two, superficially independent main melodies of the first thematic complex reveal themselves to be related in the sense of the serial principle of the later twelve-tone technique; this is how far back in Schoenberg's development the technique reaches; it must be seen as an implication of the compositional procedure rather than of the mere material. The compulsion, however, to purge music of all preconceived notions leads not only to new sounds like the famous fourth-chord, but also to a new expressive dimension beyond the depiction of human emotions. A conductor has compared the resolution field at the end of the great development section with the joy of a glacier landscape. For the first time a break is made in the *Kammersymphonie* with what had been a basic stratum of music since the age of the *basso continuo*, from the *stile rappresentativo*, from the adjustment of musical language to the significative aspect of human language. For the first time Schoenberg's warmth turns into the extreme of coolness which expresses itself through the absence of all expression. Later he polemicized against those who demand 'animal warmth' of music; his dictum, which proclaims that what music has to say can be said only through music, suggests the idea of a language unlike that of human beings. The brilliant, dynamically reserved and yet barbed quality which increases throughout the *First Kammersymphonie*, anticipates fifty years beforehand and without preclassical gestures the later functionalism. Music which lets itself be driven by pure, unadulterated expression becomes highly allergic to everything representing a potential encroachment on this purity, to every tendency to ingratiate itself with the listener as well as the latter's efforts to ingratiate himself with it, to all identification and empathy. The logical consequence of the principle of expression includes the moment of its own negation as that negative form of truth which transforms love into the power of unremitting protest.

At first, and for many years thereafter, Schoenberg did not pursue this any further. The first movement of the *Second Kammersymphonie*, written at the same time, is thoroughly expressive and harmonic; with its vast wealth of qualitatively distinct and constructively employed chord intervals, it is one of the most consummate examples of total harmonization that Schoenberg's imagination wrung from the vertical dimension. The second movement, however, which was composed later in America at the urging of Fritz Stiedry, applies the experiences of the twelve-tone technique to the late tonality, thus resulting in an intermingling of expression and construction that is unique even for Schoenberg. The piece starts off playfully, like a serenade, but as it continues to condense contrapuntally the tragic knot is drawn ever more tightly until at the end it confirms the sombre tone of the first movement – and merges with it. The *Second Kammersymphonie* is technically closer to the f sharp minor Quartet op. 10 than to the *First Kammersymphonie*. This piece, as H. F. Redlich has remarked, represents in microcosm, retrospectively and prospectively, Schoenberg's entire development. The first movement, with its extraordinary abundance of intervals and thematic figures, balancing on one foot as it were, drains tonality of all it has left, exploiting it as a means of representation. The second movement, *scherzando*, unleashes all the glaring whites and the black caricatures of Strindbergian Expressionism; demons mangle the tonality. In the third movement, the lyric variations on George's 'Litany', music meditates on itself. The most essential motivic ingredients of the first two movements converge serially in the theme. Integral construction curbs the outburst of grief. The last movement, however, in song once again, sounds as though it came from another world, from the realm of freedom; it is the new music through and through, despite the f sharp major at the end, its first unadulterated manifestation, more utopian in its inspiration than any thereafter. The instrumental introduction of this 'withdrawal' has the sound of truth, as though music had been freed of all chains and was soaring above and beyond enormous abysses towards that other planet invoked in the poem. Schoenberg's encounter with George's poetry, which is diametrically opposed and yet inherently related to his work, is one of the few fortunate events in his sporadic and uncertain experiences with the non-musical life of his epoch. As long as he measured himself against George, he was protected against the literary temptations of paltry 'ur-sounds'. George's maxim: 'The strictest standard is also the supreme freedom,' could have been his own. Of course, musical quality does not depend simply on that of the poetry, but authentic vocal music will succeed only when it encounters authentic poetry. The *Georgelieder* op. 15 already testify to the manifest break in style, which is why Schoenberg introduced them at their premiere performance with a programmatic declaration. But in their substance they belong to the f sharp minor Quartet, especially to its last movement. The compositional technique, at the time thoroughly unusual and provocative, recalls once again the idea of the great song cycles, of the *Fernen Geliebten*, the *Müllerin* and the *Winterreise*. With Schoenberg, 'the first time' is always 'once again'. The brevity, pregnancy and character of each individual song is equal in stature to the architecture of the whole, with the caesura after the eighth song, the adagio climaxing in the eleventh and the intensification of the last to the finale. The piano ascetically abandons the conventional resonance and thus creates the muted charm of cosmic distance. The lyrical warmth of *Saget mir auf welchem pfade*, the unconcealed nakedness of *Wenn ich heut nicht deinen leib berühre*, the pulsating pianissimo at the climax of the almost unbearable expressive intensity of *Als wir hinter dem beblümten tore* – all this sounds as though it could not have been otherwise and had always existed. The sombre parting at the end, however, expands symphonically like the rejoicing of *Und ein liebend Herz erreichet/was ein liebend Herz geweiht* before it.

With the *Georgelieder* the phase of 'free atonality' begins. This brought Schoenberg the fame of a subversive after the public scandal which had already been caused by the *Kammersymphonie* and the *Second Quartet*. What at the time seemed a radical break may be seen today as ratification of the inevitable. Schoenberg overturned the vocabulary, from the individual sounds to the schemas of the large forms, but he continued to speak the idiom and to strive for the kind of musical texture which is inseparably tied to the means he eliminated, not merely through common genesis but through its very meaning. Such a contradiction hindered Schoenberg's further development as much as it furthered it. Even in his most advanced works he remained traditional; he excluded the material of musical language which had provided musical structure with its basis since the beginning of the seventeenth century, and yet retained the structural categories, the bearers of the 'subcutaneous' moment in his music, virtually intact. The idiom was as self-evident and beyond question to him as to Schubert, and this is at least partly responsible for the conviction inherent in his work. Yet at the same time, the familiar categories of musical structure, like theme, elaboration, tension, resolution, no longer suit the material he has set free. Purged of all prior implications, the idiom is neutralized. Actually, each instant and each tone should be equally near the centre, and this would preclude the organization of musical time-progression which prevails in Schoenberg. Occasionally, in particularly unruly pieces such as the third one of op. 11, he did compose accordingly; otherwise, however, he composed as though he were still using prestructured material. Perhaps the innermost intention of the twelve-tone technique was to endow, on its own, the material with that prestructured quality. Otherwise, the coordination of the material assumes an external, arbitrary, indeed blind character. Nowhere is this more striking than in Schoenberg's relation to musical drama. It was determined directly by Wagernian aesthetics, despite the extreme expressionism of the first two dramatic works. As late as *Moses and Aaron*, the relation of music to text is scarcely different from any post-Wagnerian opera no matter how little attention is paid to the music-dramatic scores. In Schoenberg different historical moments collide. The composer who, in immanent-musical terms, was light-years ahead of his epoch, remained a child of the nineteenth century where its *terminus ad quem*, its function, was concerned. To this extent Stravinsky's critique of Schoenberg is not simply reactionary; it defines the bounds set by Schoenberg's naïveté.

This is, of course, opposed by the antiartistic, explosive element in Schoenberg. The piano pieces op. 11 are antiornamental to the point of gesticulating destructively. Unadorned, naked expression and hostility to art are united.[1] Something in Schoenberg, perhaps allegiance to the command cited in the text of the choral pieces op. 27 – 'Thou shalt make no graven images' – seeks to eradicate the depictive-aesthetic features of music, the imageless art. At the same time, this feature characterizes the idiom in which every one of Schoenberg's musical ideas is conceived. He laboured under this contradiction to the very end. Repeatedly, even in the twelve-tone phase, he made heroic efforts to forget, to demolish concealing musical layers, but the musical idiom always maintained its opposition. Hence, his reductions are always followed by complex, richly woven works in which musical language emerges out of the effort to eliminate such language. Thus, the first atonal piano pieces were followed by the orchestral pieces op. 16, which sacrifice nothing of the emancipation of the material but which, amid their 'prose', develop anew in polyphony and thematic work. This results in 'basic figures', long before the twelve-tone technique. *Pierrot lunaire*, too, has similar elements, such as the 'moon spot', which became famous through the *tour de force* of a fugue accompanied by two simultaneous crablike canons; yet in addition, the theme of the fugue and of the woodwind canon is strictly derived from a series, whereas the canon in the strings forms an 'accompanying system', of the kind that then became virtually the rule in the twelve-tone technique. Just as free atonality developed out of the fabric of large tonal chamber music, the twelve-tone procedure in turn stemmed from free atonal composition. The fact that the orchestral pieces discover the serial principle without rigidifying it into a system ranges them among the most successful of his works. Some of them – the intricate lyric of the second, and the last, culminating in a finale of unparalleled perspectival power – are the equals of the great tonal chamber music works and of the *Georgelieder*. As compositions, the stage works, *Erwartung* and *Glückliche Hand*, are no worse. But Schoenberg's anti-artistic tendency becomes unartistic in them and so upsets the conception. It is true that he scarcely ever composed anything which was freer than *Erwartung*. It is not merely the means of presentation which emancipates itself, but the syntax as well. Webern did not exaggerate when, in the first published collection on Schoenberg, he wrote that the score is 'an unheard-of event. In it a break is made with all traditional architectonics; there is always something new coming, with the most abrupt changes in expression'. Every moment abandons itself to the spontaneous impulse, and the object – the representation of dread – conserves Schoenberg's historical innervation, which was related to the most profound elements in Expressionism immediately preceding 1914. But Schoenberg was not capable of discriminating in his choice of text. Marie Pappenheim's monodrama is second-hand Expressionism, dilettante in its language and structure, and this rubs off on the music as well. However ingenious Schoenberg is in dividing the whole into three sections, search, outbreak and concluding lament, the music still draws inner form from the text, and, in adapting itself to it, is forced to repeat continually the same gestures and configurations. It thus violates the postulate of incessant innovation. In the *Glückliche Hand*, a no less Expressionist attitude turns compositionally to the objective symphonic form, designing pastose formal surfaces; yet here, too, such objectivity is hopelessly compromised by the foolish, narcissistic subject-matter. The symphony into which Schoenberg's work ought to coalesce was never written.

The Orchestral Songs op. 22 conclude with the words, *Und bin ganz allein in dem großen Sturm* [*And am all alone in the great storm*]. At the time, Schoenberg must have experienced the height of his powers. His music expands like a giant, as though the totality, the 'great storm', were about to emerge from self-oblivious subjectivity, 'all alone'. To these years belongs *Pierrot lunaire*, the best known of all of Schoenberg's works after his abandonment of tonality. The objectivist, expansive tendencies are happily balanced by what the subject is capable of filling. A cosmos of every conceivable musical and expressive characteristic is created, yet one reflected in the mirror of isolated inwardness, in a hothouse of souls like that mentioned shortly before in the Maeterlinck song; a cosmos which is both fanciful and absurd. The restorative element – passacaglia, fugue, canon, waltz, serenade and strophic song – enters the *paradis artificiel* only ironically, as though it were denatured, and the aphoristically abbreviated themes sound like the distant echo of literal ones. This discontinuity is not to be separated from the anachronistic subject-matter. Albert Giraud's poems, translated by Hartleben, regress behind Expressionism to the level of commercial art, figured ornament and stylizing. The form and content which confront the subject remain its unconscious projection. It is not the subject-matter alone that brings Schoenberg's masterwork into paradoxical proximity to *kitsch*, thus jeopardizing everything exquisite in the piece; rather, through its propensity for isolated flowing and flashy *pointes*, the music itself sacrifices something of what Schoenberg had accomplished since *Erwartung*. All virtuoso spirituality notwithstanding and despite the fact that some of Schoenberg's most complex compositions are included in *Pierrot*, the musical project – the production of surface connections – retreats inconspicuously from his most advanced position. Yet this can in no way be attributed to a decline in compositional power. Schoenberg was never more sovereign in his use of technique than in the Arabesques, which playfully overcome all musical gravity. But he collides with the very historical necessity which he, more than any other composer of the epoch, embodies. He became entangled in the aporia of the false transition. Nothing spiritual has ever escaped this fate since Hegel, perhaps because non-contradiction can no longer be attained in the self-satisfied realm of the mind, if indeed it ever could. The aesthetic subject, like the philosophical subject, having developed fully and in control of itself, cannot stop at that self and its 'expression'; it must aim at objective authority, as Schoenberg's bestowing gesture intended from the very first. Yet this authority cannot be derived from mere subjectivity, even if the latter has drawn its sustenance from the entire dynamics of society, unless it is already present in society, from which the aesthetic subject must detach itself today precisely because that substantial content is lacking in society. In Schoenberg, the destiny of Nietzsche's 'New Table' repeated itself, as well as that of George, who invented a new god in order to ensure the possibility of cultic poetry; it was no accident that Schoenberg felt himself

drawn to both men. After *Pierrot* and the *Orchestral Songs*, he began composing an Oratorio. The musical fragments that were published display again
Schoenberg's ability to achieve the most extreme effects unfailingly, such as
the hammer-stroke in the *Glückliche Hand*. But the text reveals the desperate
nature of the enterprise. The literary inadequacy discloses the impossibility
of the object itself, the incongruity of a religious choral work in the midst
of late capitalist society, of the aesthetic figure of totality. The whole, as a positive entity, cannot be antithetically extracted from an estranged and splin-
tered reality by means of the will and power of the individual; if it is not to
degenerate into deception and ideology, it must assume the form of negation. The *chef d'oeuvre* remained unfinished and Schoenberg's admission of
failure, his recognition that it was 'a fragment, like everything else', says
perhaps more for him than any success. There is no question that he could
have forcibly completed what he had in mind, but he must have sensed something false in the project itself; the idea of the masterpiece has today been
twisted into the genre of masterpiece. The break between the substantiality
of the ego and the over-all structure of social existence, which denies the
ego not merely external sanction but its necessary preconditions as well, has
become too profound to permit works of art a synthesis. The subject knows
itself to be objective, removed from the contingency of mere existence, yet
this knowledge, which is true, is at the same time also untrue. The objectivity that inheres in the subject is barred from reconciliation with a state of
things which negates that objective substance precisely by aiming at full reconciliation with it, and yet which that objectivity must nevertheless become
if it is to be saved from the impotence of mere 'being-for-itself'. The greater
the artist, the stronger the temptation of the chimerical. For, like knowledge,
art cannot wait, but as soon as it succumbs to impatience it is trapped. In
this respect Schoenberg resembles not merely Nietzsche and George, but also
Wagner. The sectarian stigma that adhered to him and his circle is a symptom
of the false transition. His authoritarian nature is so constructed that, having
followed musical logic in making himself the principle of all music, he then
had to enthrone that principle above himself and obey it. The idea of freedom
is blocked in his music by the desperate need to submit to a heteronomous
authority, a need that arises because the effort to transcend mere individuality and reach objectivity is futile. The inner impossibility of music objectifying itself is manifested in the compulsive traits of its aesthetic complexion. It
cannot truly go outside of itself and hence must elevate its own arbitrary
will, which failed to attain objectivity, to a position of authority over itself.
The iconoclast becomes the fetishist. Cut off from its realization, the principle of music which is both rationally transparent and inclusive of the subject
becomes an abstraction, a rigid, unquestioned precept.

Schoenberg's pause in creation, of Biblical length, cannot be adequately explained in terms of his private destiny in the war and inflation. His forces regrouped as though after a mortal defeat. He busied himself with extraordinary intensity in those years with the 'Society for Private Musical Performances', which he had founded. His significance for musical interpretation can scarcely be overestimated. Schoenberg, who as composer had turned the subcutaneous outwards, discovered and taught a mode of presentation that rendered the subcutaneous structure visible, making the performance the integral realization of the musical construction. The ideal of interpretation converges with that of composition. The dream of the musical subject–object concretized itself technologically after the composer had abandoned the conclusion of *Jacob's Ladder*. He no longer looks to superpersonal ideas and forms to lead the way to aesthetic authority, but instead recognizes that this can be achieved only through the immanent movement of the subject-matter in the form of logically coherent composition. He thus showed himself to be incorruptibly superior to the blandishments of all the usurpatory and restorative tendencies that emerged in post-Expressionist music, even at points where he brushed the neo-Classical music he despised. But the stubborn loyalty of the later Schoenberg to the method, as a guarantee of comprehensive totality, merely deferred the aporia. Something almost imperceptible happened to his music under the primacy of the highly ingenious twelve-tone technique. Of course, the experiences and rules that precipitated necessarily and convincingly out of the compositional process were comprehended, codified and systematized. But this act does not leave the truth-content of those experiences untouched. They are no longer open and accessible to dialectical correction. Schoenberg is threatened by the nemesis of what Kandinsky, in an article written in 1912 and dedicated to him, describes as follows: 'The artist thinks that, having "finally found his form", he can now continue to create works of art in peace. Unfortunately, even he himself does not usually notice that from this moment (of "peace") on, he very rapidly begins to lose this finally found form.' This is so because each work of art is a force-field, and just as the act of thought cannot be separated from the truth-content of the logical judgement, works of art are true only in so far as they transcend their material preconditions. The element of delusion shared by both technical-aesthetic and cognitive systems does, it is true, assure them of their suggestive power. They become models. But in denying themselves self-reflection and making themselves static, they become moribund and cripple the very impulse that produced the system in the first place. There is no middle way that avoids the alternative. To ignore the insights that have coalesced into the system is to cling impotently to what has been superseded. Yet the system itself becomes a fixed idea and universal recipe. It is not the method itself that is false – no one can compose any longer who has not sensed with his own ears the gravitational pull towards twelve-tone technique – but rather its hypostasization, the rejection of all that is otherwise, of anything not already analytically assimilated. Music must not identify its methods, a part of subjective reason, with the subject-matter, which is objective. The pressures to do just this, however, increase as the aesthetic subject is less and less able to orient itself on something which is both distinct from it and yet in harmony with it – the magic formula replaces the comprehensive work which prohibits itself. To be true to Schoenberg is to warn against all twelve-tone schools. Devoid of experimentation as well as prudence, these schools no longer involve any risk, and hence have entered the service of a second conformity. The means have become ends. Schoenberg himself benefited greatly through his bond to the tradition of musical language; by means of the twelve-tone procedure he was able to organize music which was both highly complex and in need of such supports. With the composers that followed, the method gradually loses its function and is abused as a mere substitute for tonality; it does nothing more than to glue together musical phenomena which are so simple that such great pains are hardly worthwhile. For this turn of events, however, Schoenberg again is not wholly innocent. At times he wrote twelve-tone gigues and rondos, forms in which the twelve-tone technique becomes superfluous, while remaining fundamentally incompatible with musical types that so unmistakably presuppose tonal modulation. In the beginning he glaringly exposed the inconsistency of all too consistent music which depended on just this kind of borrowing, only to spend years thereafter striving to find a corrective.

To this day the potentiality of the twelve-tone technique has remained open. It does in fact permit the synthesis of a procedure which is completely free and yet completely strict. Inasmuch as thematic work wholly dominates the material, the composition itself can become truly athematic, 'prose', without succumbing to contingency in the process. But the reification of the method becomes flagrant when Schoenberg claims that the twelve-tone series, which solely predispose the material, have the power of creating large forms. What tonality was once able to achieve by virtue of modulatory proportions cannot be repeated by a technique, the very sense of which lies in its not appearing outwardly. When twelve-tone rows and relations become as evident in larger forms as key relations were in traditional music, the form rattles mechanically. The twelve-tone rows do not describe a musical space within which the work unfolds and which predetermines intuition. They are rather the smallest units which enable the construction of an integral whole comprising the most variegated relations. If they become manifest, the whole

disintegrates into its atoms. It was self-evident therefore for Schoenberg's
variative imagination to have concealed the rows behind the real musical progression. Thus hidden, however, they could not exercise the architectonic
influence for which he hoped. The contradiction between latent organization and manifest music reproduces itself at a higher stage. Schoenberg
invoked traditional formal means in order to exorcise it. Because he saddled
the twelve-tone technique with the burden of objectivity as a kind of universal, conceptual order – a burden it could not bear – he was compelled to
introduce external categories without regard for the material, so as to produce
that order. Faith in organizational musical categories was something he never
lost. Many of the large twelve-tone pieces, especially those composed in
America, are convincingly successful. The best, however, rely neither on the
twelve-tone rows nor on the traditional types. They are characterized by the
free use of authentic compositional techniques, as for instance, stacking thematic surfaces, which are based on distinct but disparate models, one on top
of the other. The logic of construction is intensified anew; the main theme
from the first movement of the Violin Concerto, for instance, is more
pregnant in its construction than anything prior to the introduction of the
twelve-tone technique. Schoenberg's compositional faculties were heightened
through such resistances. For the disciples, however, the technique came to
be regarded as 'natural', as the musical *ordo*, and in this sense, it became the
bad heir of tonality, which itself was not natural any more but rather the
product of rationalization; Schoenberg's followers thus succeeded only in
displaying their own weakness, their impotent longing for security. This can
be drastically demonstrated in the relation of twelve-tone technique to the
octave. The technique tacitly accepts the identity of the octave, without which
one of the most important twelve-tone principles, the interchangeability of
each tone in any octave range, becomes inconceivable. Yet at the same time
the octave retains something 'tonal' about it, and disturbs the equilibrium of
the twelve half-tones; whenever octaves are doubled there is the association
of the triad. The contradiction manifested itself in Schoenberg's fluctuating
praxis. Earlier, beginning already to a large extent in the works of free atonality, the octave was avoided. Then, however, Schoenberg wrote octaves, probably to clarify the bass sounds and main thematic parts; the first time came
in a piece which played with tonality, the *Ode to Napoleon* – here, just as in
the Piano Concerto, it is impossible not to hear a certain forced, impure
quality. The pseudo–nature betrays itself entirely in the early days of the technique in a tendency to the apocryphal, the shabby and the absurd. At times,
music constructed according to formulas, essentially meaningless, threatens to
undo all its sublimation and revert to raw material. Like the dogma of
astrologers, which links the movement of the stars to the progress of human

destinies while both remain unaffected by the cognitive act and are thus fortuitous, the sequence of twelve-tone events, determined down to its final
note, contains vestiges of contingency for lived experience. As though to
mock the potential synthesis of freedom and necessity, the latter, having been
made absolute, reveals itself to be contingent.

The great composer triumphed once again over the inventor, as Schoenberg in later life devoted all his energies to the task of eliminating the apocryphal elements in twelve-tone technique. The first serial compositions,
which were not strictly twelve-tone, were still free of such elements. In the
first four pieces of op. 23, the eruptive forces of the Expressionist phase echo
tremulously. There are hardly any rigid sections. The second piece, for
instance, a peripatie which in Schoenberg's hands became heir to the scherzo,
is only a totally composed diminuendo of supreme originality; the outburst
dies away rapidly, leaving a nocturnally tranquil, comforting concluding
postlude. The spirited fourth piece comes closer to the idea of an athematic
twelve-tone composition than almost any other work. The Piano Suite op.
25 and the Woodwind Quintet op. 26 are thoroughly twelve-tone. They bring
out the element of constraint with particular emphasis, a kind of Bauhaus-
music, metallic constructivism which derives its force from precisely the
absence of primary expression; even where expressive characteristics appear,
they are 'totally constructed'. The Quintet, probably the most difficult piece
to listen to of any that Schoenberg wrote, brusquely drives sublimation, in
one dimension, to an extreme – it declares war on colour. The basic impulse
against everything infantile, against musical stupidity, takes hold of the
medium which, more than any other, seems culinary, mere sensuous excita-
tion this side of intellectual activity. Of all of Schoenberg's accomplishments
in integrating musical means, not the least was that he conclusively separated
colour from the decorative sphere and elevated it to a compositional element
in its own right. It changes into a means for the elucidation of musical inter-
relations. By being thus included in the compositional process, however, it is
also condemned. In a passage from *Style and Idea* Schoenberg explicitly repu-
diated it. The more nakedly construction represents itself, the less it requires
colouristic help. The principle thus turns against Schoenberg's own achievements, comparable perhaps to the late Beethoven, in whom all sensuous
immediacy reduces itself to mere foreground, to allegory. It is easy enough
to imagine this late form of Schoenberg's asceticism, the negation of all
façades, extending to all musical dimensions. Mature music becomes suspicious of real sound as such. Similarly, with the realization of the 'subcutaneous', the end of musical interpretation becomes conceivable. The silent,
imaginative reading of music could render actual playing as superfluous as,
for instance, speaking is made by the reading of written material; such a prac-

tice could at the same time save music from the abuse inflicted upon the compositional content by virtually every performance today. The inclination to silence, which shapes the aura of every tone in Webern's lyrics, is related to the tendency stemming from Schoenberg. Its ultimate result, however, can only be that artistic maturity and intellectualization abolish not only sensuous appearance, but with it, art itself. In Schoenberg's late work, artistic intellectualization moves emphatically towards the dissolution of art, and so converges abysmally with anti-artistic, barbaric tendencies. For this reason, the efforts of Boulez and the younger twelve-tone composers in all countries to achieve total abstraction are by no means 'youthful blundering', but rather the continuation and development of one of Schoenberg's intentions. He never, however, made himself completely the slave of his own intention or of objective tendencies. Paradoxically enough, the composer who forcibly organized and co-ordinated his material, with ever-increasing severity as he aged, in many respects broke through the systematic constraints of the logic he had unleashed. His composing never simulated the primitive unity of composition and technical procedure. The experience that no musical subject–object can constitute itself here and today was not wasted on him. On the one hand, it saved his subjective freedom of movement; on the other, it kept the demon of the composing machine distant from the objective form. He regained that freedom as soon as he could function in the twelve-tone technique as in a familiar 'language', in the school of the untroubled, gay Chamber Suite op. 29 and of the almost didactic Orchestral Variations, from which Leibowitz distilled a compendium of the new technique. His close contact with the text and with the *pointes*, however modest, of the comic opera, *From Today to Tomorrow*, returned to him all the flexibility of the musical idiom. With the latter fully in mind, he tosses off a masterpiece for the second time, again postponing the conclusion with that enigmatic faith in an endless life behind which his despair at the 'it-shall-not-be' is concealed. The fact that his powers actually rose to a highpoint once again in the early thirties was brought out by the unforgettable Darmstadt première of the *Dance of the Golden Calf* in the summer of 1951, only a few days before Schoenberg's death. The performance, under Scherchen, was met with wild enthusiasm and marked the first time that a twelve-tone piece had received the approval which its creator both scorned and needed more than anyone else. The expressive intensity, disposition of colour and constructive power sweep away all obstacles. To judge from the text of the fragment, as a finished opera, *Moses and Aaron* would have been lost; unfinished, it ranks among the great fragments of music.

Schoenberg, who resisted all conventions within the sphere of music, accepted the role assigned to him by the social division of labour, which restricted him to the sphere of music. His impulse to go beyond it as painter and poet was frustrated; the division of labour is not to be revoked by the claims of universal genius. He thus took his place among the 'great composers', as though this notion was eternal. The slightest criticism of any of the masters since Bach he found intolerable. Not only did he reject qualitative differences within the work of each, but also, whenever possible, stylistic distinctions between works written in different genres, even those which are beyond question, such as that between Beethoven's symphonic and his chamber music. That the category of the great composer was susceptible to historical variation did not occur to him any more than the doubt that his own work would be established as a classic when the time came. Against his will, that which crystallized in his work embodied immanent musical opposition to such socially naïve conceptions. The impatience with sensuous appearance in his late style corresponds to the emasculation of art faced with the possibility of its promises being fulfilled in reality, but also to the horror which, in order to suppress that possibility, explodes every criterion of that which might become an image. In the midst of the blindness of specialization, his music suddenly saw the light that shines beyond the aesthetic realm. His incorruptible integrity once attained this awareness when, during the first months of the Hitler dictatorship, he unabashedly said that survival was more important than art. If his late work has been spared the fate of all art since the Second World War with the exception of Picasso's, it is because of this relativizing of the artistic, to which Schoenberg's anticultural element sublimated itself. Perhaps this is only fully revealed in his didactic traits. When Valéry remarked that the work of great artists has something of the quality of finger exercises, of studies for works that were never created, he could have used Schoenberg as his model. The utopia of art transcends individual works. Moreover, it is this medium alone which produces the characteristic consensus among musicians which holds that the distinction between production and reproduction is indifferent. Musicians sense that they labour on music and not on works, even if such labour progresses only through works. The late Schoenberg composed not works, but paradigms of a possible music. The idea of music itself grows all the more transparent as the works insist less and less on their appearance. They begin to acquire the character of the fragment, the shadow of which followed Schoenberg's art throughout his life. His last pieces give a fragmentary impression, not merely in their brevity but in their shrivelled diction. The dignity of the great works devolves on splinters. Oratorio and Biblical opera are outweighed by the tale of the *Survivor from Warsaw*, which lasts only a few minutes; in this piece, Schoenberg, acting on his own, suspends the aesthetic sphere through the recollection of experiences which are inaccessible to art. Anxiety, Schoenberg's expressive core, identifies itself with the terror of men in the agonies of death, under total domination. The sounds of *Erwartung*, the shocks of the *Music for the Film*, of 'impending danger, anxiety, catastrophe', finally meet what they had always prophesied. That which the feebleness and impotence of the individual soul seemed to express testifies to what has been inflicted on mankind in those who represent the whole as its victims. Horror has never rung as true in music, and by articulating it music regains its redeeming power through negation. The Jewish song with which the *Survivor from Warsaw* concludes is music as the protest of mankind against myth.

Note

1   The gesture traces the direction of Schoenberg's development, before the listener's ears – the revelation of the subcutaneous, not unlike contemporary Cubism, which transposed similar latent structures into the immediate phenomenon. The analogy is particularly relevant to the elimination of traditional perspective in painting and of tonal – 'spatial' – harmony in music. Both result from the anti-ornamental impulse. Artistic perspective, not without reason called 'trompe-l'oeil', contains an element of deception which is also present, in a manner that is difficult to define, of course, in tonal harmony, which creates the illusion of spatial depth. It is precisely this illusion that the movement of the piano pieces op. 11 destroys. The illusionary moment in harmony became intolerable and the reaction it produced contributed decisively to externalizing the inner dimension. The illusionary moment, however, was profoundly linked to the very *stile rappresentativo* from which Schoenberg distanced himself. In so far as art imitates, it has always involved illusion. But like painting, music does not simply abolish space; rather it replaces the illusion, the pretence of it, with an, as it were, expanded, peculiarly musical space.

17

Alienated Masterpiece: The *Missa Solemnis*

Adorno has been accused of constructing a Teutonocentric history of music. Although that charge has *prima facie* plausibility, Adorno is not, by any means, driven by chauvinism. After all, many of the writers whose work he sees as pre-eminent critical moments in modern literature were neither German nor Austrian (i.e. Proust, Joyce, Beckett). Adorno evaluates music in accordance with its embodiment of dialectical progress. That is, the transitions from Beethoven to Schoenberg (with Brahms, Wagner, and Mahler the major figures in between) have all come about through the efforts of each composer to respond authentically to the material given by the tradition. However, music, as we know from Adorno's sociology of art, is never just music: it is an intellectual phenomenon of its time, is part of the social totality in which it is produced, and represents that totality, however obliquely. Knowledge of the totality is latent and retrievable by the appropriate interpretation. What might appear as purely musicological problems – compositional dilemmas, stylistic and formal dead ends – can also be understood as issues produced by the totality. Thus if society should experience an alteration in its self-conception – e.g. the transition from a representation of itself as a harmonious totality to an individualist collective – this will be represented, in some way, in the task of aesthetic production. Many of us might indeed perceive some vague connection between art and society in this way: that forms of art are historically constituted and cannot be repeated today. Adorno shares this insight and attempts to demonstrate the connection.

We can see one of his most significant efforts in his reading of Beethoven's extraordinary *Missa Solemnis* or Mass in D, opus 123. Adorno's fascination with Beethoven's music was well-informed as we can see from the recently published *Beethoven: The Philosophy of Music*. Adorno does not want to deny the conventional view that the *Missa* is a masterpiece. However it is essential in gaining a critical understanding of what constitutes the work that we appreciate the strangeness of the work, that we 'alienate' it from the unapproachability given by its status as a masterpiece. Most commentators note a number of musicological difficulties with the *Missa*: it is liturgically compromised as it is too long; at crucial points Beethoven plays down the religious meanings of the text in favour of a humanistic philosophy (as such the *Credo* is particularly questionable as a liturgical setting); Beethoven struggles with the unfamiliar genre of the mass and turns to archaic forms, with the result that his normal coherence and carefully developed thematic unity is lost. For Adorno, these problems are not simply the inevitable outcome of Beethoven somehow failing artistically to meet his familiar patterns of musical coherence (the self-developing motifs – dialectic – in contrast to the discreet sections of the *Missa*). What Adorno particularly wants to argue, more philosophically, is that the oddness of the work is social in origin. Beethoven may once have been able to compose from within a conception of universal humanity (as Adorno sees Beethoven's early and middle works) but the late works – the *Missa* outstandingly – lie in a different context and lose the synthesis of the earlier conception. Beethoven's search for musical truth inevitably responds to the culture in which he produces. The problems with the *Missa*, by comparison with the great works of the earlier periods, is that it is not a work of bourgeois optimism, the belief in the unity of subjectivity and objectivity (the individual in society). Rather it expresses the lack of confidence in the possibility of that unity. The difficulties of the *Missa Solemnis* are not therefore those of abstracted artistic problems. Rather, the more artistic the composer is, that is, the more he struggles with the material which is social in origin, the more it represents the problems of the totality.

'Alienated Masterpiece: The *Missa Solemnis*' [1959], *Telos*, no. 28
(Summer, 1976), pp. 113–24.
Translated by Duncan Smith.

Neutralization of culture – the words have the ring of a philosophical concept. They posit as a more or less general reflection that intellectual constructs have forfeited their intrinsic meanings because they have lost any possible relation to social praxis and have become that which aesthetics retrospectively claims they are – objects of pure observation, of mere contemplation. As such they ultimately lose even their own aesthetic import; their aesthetic truth content disappears along with their tension *vis-à-vis* reality. They become cultural goods, exhibited in a secular pantheon in which contradictions, works which would tend to destroy each other, find a deceptively peaceful realm of co-existence, e.g., Kant and Nietzsche, Bismarck and Marx, Clemens Brentano and Büchner. This wax museum of great men finally admits its own disconsolateness in the innumerable ignored pictures of each museum and in the editions of the classics in miserly locked up bookcases. But no matter how widespread the consciousness of all this has meantime become, it is still as difficult as ever to grasp this phenomenon in its entirety, at least if one ignores the fashion of biographical writing which reserves a niche for this queen and that microbe hunter. For there is no superfluous work of Rubens in which at least the cognoscenti would not admire the incarnate value and no house poet of the Cotta Firm in whose work there are no non-contemporarily successful verses awaiting resurrection. Every now and then, however, it is possible to name a work in which the neutralization of culture has expressed itself most strikingly; a work, in fact, which in addition is also famous, which occupies an uncontested place in the repertoire even while it remains enigmatically incomprehensible; and one which, whatever else it may conceal, offers no justification for the admiration accorded it. No less a work than Beethoven's *Missa Solemnis* belongs in this category. To speak seriously of this work can mean nothing less than, in Brecht's terms, to alienate it; to break through the aura of irrelevant worship which protectively surrounds it and thereby perhaps to contribute something to an authentic aesthetic experience of it beyond the paralysing respect of the academic sphere. This attempt necessarily requires criticism as its medium. Qualities which have been assigned without any thought by traditional consciousness to the *Missa Solemnis* must be tested in order to prepare for a recognition of its content, a recognition which to this day is still missing. This effort is not one of debunking, of tearing down recognized greatness for the sake of tearing something down. The disillusioning gesture which pulls down from the heights the very thing it attacks is by that very act subservient to the substance of that which it pulls down. Instead, criticism with regard to a work of such demand and with regard to the total *oeuvre* of Beethoven, can only be a means of penetrating the work. It is the fulfillment of a duty *vis-à-vis* the work and not a means of gaining malicious satisfaction from knowing that once again there is one less great work in the world. It is necessary to point this out, because neutralized culture makes certain that the names of the authors are taboo while the constructs themselves are no longer perceived in their original contents. Rather they are merely consumed as socially acceptable works. Rage is immediately provoked whenever reflection about the work threatens to touch the authority of the author.

This situation must be anticipated whenever one prepares to say something heretical about a composer of the highest authority, one whose power is comparable only to the philosophy of Hegel and is still undiminished at a time when the historical preconditions of his work are irrevocably lost. But ·Beethoven's power of humanity and of demythologization demands by its very existence the destruction of mythical taboos. There is, of course, among musicians an underground tradition of critical reserve about the *Missa*. They have also long known that Handel is no Bach and that the actual compositional qualities of Gluck are questionable. Only fear of established public opinion made them keep their own opinions to themselves. So too they have known that there is something peculiar about the *Missa Solemnis*. Little truly penetrating has been written about it. Most of what has been written makes general pronouncements of awe about an immortal *chef d'oeuvre*, and it is easy to note the embarrassment of these writers which prevents them from stating wherein this supposed greatness actually lies. The neutralization of the *Missa* to cultural produce is reflected in such writings, but it is not overcome. Hermann Kretzschmar, who comes from a generation of music historians which had not yet cast off the experiences of the 19th century, expressed the most significant admiration for this work. According to his writing the earliest performances of the work, before its official acceptance into Valhalla, made no lasting impression. He sees the chief difficulty in the *Gloria* and *Credo* and supports his view with reference to the large number of short musical images which require the listener to organize them into a unity. Kretzschmar has at least named one of the alienating symptoms which the *Missa* exhibits. On the other hand, he has overlooked the manner in which this symptom is connected to the essence of the composition and has, therefore, expressed the erroneous opinion that the resultant musical difficulties could be overcome by the use of an enclosure of these short sections by powerful major themes in both the long movements. But this is as little the case as asserting, for example, that the listener comprehends the *Missa* as soon as he has present in mind the preceding parts in concentrated form in accordance with the principle of comprehending the great symphonic movements of Beethoven. The listener, then, supposedly follows in this manner the creation of unity from diversity. This unity itself is of a completely different type from the productive power of fantasy in the *Eroica* and in the *Ninth Symphony*. It is not a crime to doubt that his unity is so obviously comprehendable.

Indeed, the historical fate of this work is an alienating factor. It could only be performed twice during Beethoven's lifetime; once, but in incomplete form, in Vienna in 1824, together with the *Ninth Symphony*, and a second time that same year in Petersburg in complete form. Up to the beginning of the 1860s, it was performed only occasionally. It was more than 30 years after the composer's death that it achieved its current standing. The difficulties of interpretation — above all in the treatment of the vocal parts, and not, in most sections, any particular musical complexities — are not sufficient reason for this late discovery. Contrary to legend, the last quartets, which are in many ways far more expounded and far more demanding, found from the outset a respectable reception. But Beethoven had lent his own authority directly on behalf of the *Missa* in a manner decidedly different from his usual custom. He designated it *"l'oeuvre le plus accompli,"* his most successful work, when he offered it for subscription, and he wrote over the *Kyrie* the words "from the heart — may it go to hearts," a confession the like of which one may search for in vain in all the other printed editions of Beethoven's works. It is not possible to treat his own attitude to his work either lightly or to accept it blindly. The tone of that remark is conjuring, as if Beethoven had sensed something of the incomprehensible, reserved, and enigmatic quality of the *Missa* and had tried through the force of his will (as that force of will had ever stamped the content of his music) to force the work externally upon those whom it did not of its own power compel. This would hardly be conceivable if the work did not itself contain a secret quality which Beethoven believed justified him in influencing the history of this work. But when it had eventually established itself it was much aided by what had become in the meantime the unassailable prestige of the composer. His major sacred work was vouchsafed as a sister work the same admiration accorded to the *Ninth Symphony* without anyone daring to ask questions which might merely reveal the lack of depth of the questioner, as in the fairy tale of the emperor's new clothes.

The *Missa* would never have attained to an unquestioned place in the repetoire if it had caused a drastic shock, like *Tristan*, by its difficulty. But that is not the case. If one ignores the occasionally unusual demands made on the singing voice, a demand the work shares with the *Ninth Symphony*, the work may be seen to contain little that exceeds the circumference of traditional musical language. Very large parts are homophonous and even the fugues and fugati fit without difficulty into the thorough-bass pattern. The progressions of the harmonic intervals and with them the surface context, are seldom if ever problematic. The *Missa Solemnis* was composed far less against prevailing compositional traditions than are the quartets and variations, the five late sonatas and the Bagatelle cycli. The *Missa* is distinguished more by certain archaicizing moments of harmony — church modes — rather than by the advanced compositional daring of the great quartet fugue (opus 133). Not only did Beethoven always keep a stricter separation among the compositional genres than one suspects, but he also incorporated in them temporally different stages of his *oeuvre*. If the symphonies are in many respects simpler than the major works of the chamber music because of or despite the richer resources of the orchestra, the *Ninth Symphony* is clearly different and returns retrospectively to the classical symphonies of Beethoven without the sharp edges of the last quartets. In his late period the composer did not, as one might think, blindly follow the dictates of his inner ear, nor did he forcibly estrange himself from the sensual aspect of his work. Instead, he disposed sovereignly over all the possibilities which had grown up in the history of his composing. Desensualization was but one of these possibilities. The *Missa* shares with the last quartets an occasional abruptness, i.e., the lack of transitions. Otherwise there are few similarities. Altogether it reveals a sensuous aspect quite opposed to the intellectualized late style, an inclination to splendidness and tonal monumentality which usually is lacking in that late style. This aspect is incorporated technically in the process which in the *Ninth Symphony* is restricted to brief moments of ecstasy, doubling the parts through brasses, above all horns, which carry the melody. The frequently powerful octaves are related to this aspect as well, coupled with harmonic bass effects of the type contained in the well known "Die Himmel rühmen des Ewigen Ehre" and decisively in the passage "Ihr stürzt nieder" in the *Ninth Symphony*, later important in Bruckner. Clearly it is to no small extent these sensuous high points, an inclination to the tonally overwhelming, which gave the *Missa* its authority and helped its audiences over their own lack of understanding.

The real difficulty is greater than any of these. It is one of content, of the meaning of the music. It can perhaps be best formulated by asking whether someone ignorant of the work would recognize the *Missa*, apart from certain sections, as a work of Beethoven. If one played it to those who had never heard any part of it and had them guess who the composer was, one could expect some surprises. As little as the so-called imprint (*Handschrift*) of a composer forms a central criterion, its absence nevertheless reveals all the more that something isn't quite right. If one searches among Beethoven's other works of church music, one encounters this absence of the Beethoven imprint again. It is significant how difficult it is even to dredge up his *Christ on the Mount of Olives* or the by no means early *C Major Mass*, opus 86. The latter could, by contrast to the *Missa*, scarcely be attributed to Beethoven even in separate sections or phrases. Its indescribably calm "Kyrie" would seem at most to indicate a weak Mendelssohn. But throughout this work there are sections which reappear in the much more demandingly formed and more splendidly planned *Missa*. These include the dissolution into often short, hardly symphonically integrated parts, a lack of decisive thematic inspirations which otherwise characterize each work of Beethoven, and a lack of discharging dynamic developments. The *C Major Mass* reads as if Beethoven had decided only with difficulty to feel his way into what was

for him a strange genre. It is as if his humanism rebelled against the heteronomy of the traditional liturgical text and as if his composition of this
text surrendered to a routine which cost it all its genius. In order to get to
the enigma of the *Missa* at all it will be necessary to call to mind this moment
of his early church music. In the *Missa*, of course, it becomes a problem
against which he struggles, wearing out his strength, but it helps in identifying something of the conjuring nature of the work. The problem cannot be
separated from the paradox of Beethoven composing a mass at all. If one
could understand fully why he did it, one would certainly be able to understand the *Missa*.

It is customary to assert that the *Missa* far exceeds the traditional form of
the mass and to accord it the entire wealth of the secular compositions. Even
in the music volume of the Fischer Lexicon recently edited by Rudolf
Stephan, which otherwise does away with many conventional platitudes, the
piece is credited with being an "extraordinarily artistic thematic work." In so
far as one can talk about such work in the *Missa* at all, it utilizes a method
of kaleidoscopic mixing and supplementary combinations exceptional in
Beethoven. The motifs do not change with the dynamic pull of the composition – it has no such pull – but rather constantly reappear in changing light
though they are always identical. The idea of exploded form may apply to
the extenal dimensions at best, and Beethoven doubtless considered this idea
when he contemplated concert performance. But the *Missa* does not at all
break out of the pre-planned objectivity of the model through any subjective dynamic, nor does it create the totality in symphonic spirit out of itself.
On the contrary, the consequent denial of all this removes the *Missa* from
any direct connection with Beethoven's other works, with the exception of
his previously mentioned earlier church music. The internal construction of
this music, its fever, is radically different from everything which distinguishes
Beethoven's style. It is itself archaic. The form is not achieved through developing variations from basic motifs, but arises largely from sections imitative
in themselves, similar to the method of the Dutch composers around the
middle of the 15th century, and it is uncertain how well Beethoven knew
their work. The formal organization of the whole work is not that of a
process developing through its own impetus – it is not dialectical – but seeks
accomplishment by a balance of the individual sections, of the movements,
ultimately through contrapuntal enclosure. All the estranging characteristics
can be seen in this light. The fact that Beethoven did not use his own type
of themes in the *Missa* – who after all can sing a passage from it the way
one can sing a passage from any one of the symphonies or from *Fidelio* –
can be explained by the exclusion of the organizational principle. It is only
wherever a presented theme is developed and has, therefore, to be recogniz-

able in its subsequent development, that it needs plastic form. Such an idea was foreign to the *Missa* as well as to medieval music. One need only compare the Bach "Kyrie" with that of Beethoven. In Bach's fugue there is an incomparably memorable melody which suggests the image of humanity as a procession dragging itself along while bowed down under the heaviest of burdens. In Beethoven's work there are complexes almost without melodic profile which delineate the harmony and avoid expression with a gesture of monumentality. This comparison leads to a real paradox. According to the current if questionable view, Bach, in recapitulating the objective-closed musical world of the Middle Ages, had brought the fugue to its pure and authentic form even if he was not the creator of this musical form. The fugue was as much his product as he was the product of its spirit. He stood in a direct relationship to the fugue. For that reason many of his fugue themes, with the possible exception of his speculative late works, have a kind of freshness and spontaneity about them comparable only to the cantabile-like inspirations of the subjective composers. At the historic moment of Beethoven's creativity, however, that form of musical organization, the reflection of which Bach still regarded as an *a priori* of his compositions, was no longer valid. With it disappeared a harmony of the musical subject and the musical forms which had permitted something akin to naivete in Schiller's sense of the word. The objectivity of the musical forms with which Beethoven worked in the *Missa* is mediated and problematic – an object of reflection. The first part of the "Kyrie" includes Beethoven's own standpoint of subjective-harmonious being. But since this standpoint is also immediately pushed into the horizon of sacred objectivity, it takes on a mediated character as well, separated from the composed spontaneity – it is stylized. For that reason the smooth harmonious opening section of the *Missa* is more remote and less eloquent than the contrapuntal learnedness of Bach. That is particularly true of the actual fugues and fugati themes of the *Missa*. They have a peculiar character of quotation as if they had been built according to models. One could speak of compositional topics analogous to the wide spread literary custom in antiquity, or of the treatment of music according to latent patterns through which the objective demand is strengthened. That is very likely responsible for the peculiar incomprehensibility, for the withdrawness from any primary completion, which is characteristic of these fugue themes and is then also encountered in their further development in the work. The first fugal section of the *Missa*, the "Christe eleison" in B minor, is an example of this and at the same time demonstrates the work's archaicizing tone.

In point of fact, the work stands removed both from all subjective dynamics as well as from expression. The "Credo" hurries over the "Crucifixus" –

in Bach this is one of the expressive high points – marking it, however, with a very striking rhythm. Only at the "Et sepultus est," at the end of the Passion itself, does the section reach an expressive concentration in thoughts about the frailty of the human being, however, and not about the Passion of Christ. But that pathos cannot be attributed to the contrast of the following "Et resurrexit" which, at an analogous point in Bach, reaches toward the extreme of that emotion. Only one section, one which has also become the most famous of the work, is an exception to this, and that is the "Benedictus," the chief melody of which suspends stylization. The prelude to this section is a piece of intensely deep harmonious proportions having an equivalent only in the *Twentieth Diabelli Variation*. But the "Benedictus" melody itself, rightly praised as inspired, resembles the variation theme of the E-flat major quartet, opus 127. The entire "Benedictus" reminds one of that custom attributed to certain artists in the late Middle Ages – those who are said to have included their own portraits somewhere on their tabernacles for the host so that they would not be forgotten. But even the "Benedictus" remains true to the color of the entire work. It is divided into sections by intonations, like the other sections, and the polyphony always paraphrases the chords figuratively. That in turn is the result of the planned thematic looseness of the compositional process. It permits the themes to be treated imitatively yet to be conceived harmoniously in keeping with the basic homophonous consciousness of Beethoven and his era. The process of archaicizing was to respect the limits of Beethoven's musical experience. The great exception is the "Et vitam venturi" of the "Credo" in which Paul Becker correctly saw the nucleus of the entire work. It is a polyphonically fully developed fugue, in certain details, particularly in harmonic twists, it is related to the finale of the *Hammerklavier Sonata*, leading into a grand development. Therefore, it is also quite explicit melodically and heightened to an extreme by its intensity and power. This piece – perhaps the only one which is entitled to the epithet "explosive" – is the most difficult one in terms of complexity and performance, but together with the "Benedictus" is the simplest by virtue of the directness of the effect.

It is no accident that the transcendental moment of the *Missa Solemnis* does not refer to the mystical content of transubstantiation but to the hope of eternal life for humanity. The enigma of the *Missa Solemnis* is the tie between an archaic methodology mercilessly sacrificing all Beethoven's conquests and human tone which appears to mock precisely this archaic tone. That enigma – the combination of the idea of the human with a mysterious articulation-shyness – can perhaps be deciphered by assuming that there is in the *Missa* a tangible taboo which determines its reception – a taboo about the negativity of existence, derived from Beethoven's despairing will to survive. The *Missa* is expressive wherever it addresses or literally conjures up salvation. It usually cuts off that expression wherever evil and death dominate in the text of the mass, and precisely through this suppression the *Missa* demonstrates the gradually dawning superior power of the negative; despair and yet anxiety of having that despair become manifest. The "Dona nobis pacem" assumes in a certain sense the burden of the "Crucifixus." The expressive potential is accordingly held back. The dissonant parts are only rarely the bearers of this expression (e.g., in the "Sanctus" before the Allegro opening of the "Pleni sunt coeli"). The expression clings much more often to the archaic portions, to the church modal gradations, to the awe about the past, as if the suffering were to be thrown back into the transitory realm. Not the modern but the ancient is expressive in the *Missa*. The human idea asserts itself in this work, as it did in the works of the later Goethe, only by virtue of convulsive, mythic denial of the mythical abyss. It calls upon positive religion for help whenever the lonely subject no longer trusted that it could of itself, as pure human essence, dispel the forward surging chaos of conquered and protesting nature. The recourse to mention Beethoven's subjective piety as an explanation of the fact that the composer, emancipated to the extreme and self reliant, tended toward traditional form, is as unsatisfying as the opposite extreme found in the academic sphere. There the explanation for this which is offered claims that his religiosity in this work, which subjects itself with zealous discipline to the liturgical purpose, extends beyond dogma to a kind of universal religiosity. The claim, therefore, is made that his is a mass for Unitarians. But confessions or announcements of subjective piety in relation to Christology have been repressed by the work. In the section where the liturgy dictates unavoidably the "I believe," Beethoven, according to Steuermann's astonishing observation, betrayed the opposite of such certainty by having the fugue theme repeat the word Credo as if the isolated man had to assure himself and others of his actual belief by this frequent repetition. The religiosity of the *Missa*, if one can speak unconditionally of such a thing, is neither that of one secure in belief nor that of a world religion of such an idealistic nature that it would require no effort of its adherent to believe in it. Expressed in more modern terms, it is a matter for Beethoven of whether ontology, the objective intellectual organization of existence, is still possible. It is a question of the musical salvation of such ontology in the realm of subjectivism and the return to the liturgy is intended to effect this salvation in a manner paralleled only in Kant's evocation of the ideas of God, Freedom, and Immortality. In its aesthetic form the work asks what and how one may sing of the absolute without deceit, and because of this, there occurs that compression which alienates it and causes it to approach incomprehensibility. This is so perhaps because the question which it asks itself refuses even musically the valid answer. The subject then remains exiled in its finiteness. The objective cosmos can no longer be imagined as an obligatory construct. Thus the *Missa* balances on the point of ineffectivity which approaches nothingness.

Its humanistic aspect is defined by the plenitude of chords in the "Kyrie" and extends to the construction of the concluding section, the "Agnus Dei," which prefigures the "Dona nobis pacem," the plea for inner and outer peace. Beethoven superscribed the section with the equivalent German words, and the piece once more breaks out expressively after the threat of war allegorically presented by drums and trumpets. Already at the "Et homo factus est," the music begins to warm as if breathed upon. But these are the exceptions. Most of the time, despite stylization, the work procedes in tone and style back toward something unexpressed, undefined. This aspect, resulting from the mutually contradictory forces in the work, is perhaps the one which interferes most with its comprehension. Having been conceived in a flat and undynamic manner, the *Missa* is not arranged according to pre-classical "terraces." In fact, it often erases even the slightest contours. Short inserts frequently do not converge into the whole nor do they stand on their own; rather they rely upon their proportions to other parts. The style is contrary to the spirit of the sonata and yet not as much traditionally ecclesiastical as secular in a rudimentary ecclesiastical language dredged up from memory. The relationship to this language is as chaotic as it is to Beethoven's own style. It is distantly analogous to the position of the *Eighth Symphony* with regard to Haydn and Mozart. Except in the Et-vitam-venturi fugue, even the fugue sections are not genuinely polyphonic but are also in no measure homophonously melodious in the manner of the 19th century. While the category of totality, which in Beethoven's works is always the major one, results in other works from the internal development of the individual parts, it is retained in the *Missa* only at the price of a kind of leveling. The omnipresent stylization principle no longer tolerates anything which is truly unique and whittles the character of the work down to the level of the scholastic. These motifs and themes resist being named. The lack of dialectical contrasts which are replaced by the mere opposition of closed phrases weakens at times the totality. That is particularly obvious in conclusions of movements. Because no direction is traversed, because no individual resistance has been overcome, the trace of the accidental is carried over to the entire work itself, and the phrases, which no longer terminate in a specific goal prescribed by the thrust of the particular, frequently end exhausted; they cease without achieving the security of a conclusion. Despite an external manifestation of powerfulness, all this nevertheless causes a feeling of indirectness to prevail, a feeling which is at an equal distance both from a liturgical connection and from compositional fantasy. It rather brings about that enigmatic quality which at times, as in the brief allegro and presto sections of the "Agnus," borders on the absurd.

After all that has been written above, it might appear that the *Missa*, characterized in all its uniqueness, could now be understood. But the dark quality of the work, perceived as such, does not brighten without further analysis. To understand that one does not understand is the first step toward understanding but is not understanding itself. The above mentioned characteristics of the work can be confirmed by listening to it, and the attention which is concentrated on those characteristics may prevent a disoriented listening, but by themselves they do not allow the ear spontaneously to perceive a musical purpose or meaning in the *Missa*. If it exists at all, such a meaning lies precisely in the resistance to such spontaneity. This much at least is certain: the alienating aspects of the work do not disappear in the presence of the comfortable formula which asserts that the autonomous fantasy of the composer chose a heteronomous form removed from his will and fantasy, and that the specific development of his music had thereby been hindered. For it would seem apparent that Beethoven did not try in the *Missa* to legitimize himself in a genre not familiar to him as well as in his "actual" works. This kind of legitimation has been attempted before in the history of music. But in Beethoven's case, there was an attempt not to overburden that unfamiliar genre. Instead, each measure of the work as well as the length of the process of composition – unusual for Beethoven – shows the most insistent effort on the composer's part. But the effort is not, as in his other works, directed at the accomplishment of the subjective intention, but rather at its exclusion. The *Missa Solemnis* is a work of such exclusion, of permanent renunciation. It is already to be counted among those efforts of the later bourgeois spirit which no longer hope to conceive and form in any concrete manner the universally human, but which strive instead to accomplish this end through abstraction, through the process of exclusion of the accidental by means of maintaining a firm grasp on a universal which had gone astray in the reconciliation with the particular. The metaphysical truth in this work becomes a residue, as in Kantian philosophy the contentless simplicity of the pure "I think." This residual nature of truth, the rejection of the permeation of the particular, condemns the *Missa Solemnis* not merely to being enigmatic, but stamps it in a highest sense with the mark of impotence. It is the impotence not merely of the mightiest composer but of an historical position of the intellect which, of whatever it dares write here, can speak no longer or not yet.

But what compelled Beethoven, that immeasurably deep human being in whom the power of subjective creation rose to the hubris of the human being as the creator to the opposite of all this, to self-limitation? It was certainly not the psychology of this man who could traverse at one and the same time the composition of the *Missa* and the composition of works entirely its opposite. It was rather a pressure in the thing itself, which Beethoven, resisting to be sure to the last, obeyed and obeyed with all his energy. Here we find something common to both the *Missa* and to the last quartets in their intellectual structuring. They share a common avoidance. The musical experience of the late Beethoven must have become mistrustful of the unity of subjectivity and objectivity, the roundness of symphonic successes, the totality emerging from the movement of all the parts; in short, of everything that gave authenticity up to now to the works of his middle period. He exposed the classical as classicizing. He rejected the affirmative, that which uncritically endorsed Being in the idea of the classically symphonic. He rejected that trait which Georgiades in his article on the finale of the *Jupiter Symphony* called ceremonial. He must have felt the untruth in the highest demand of classical music, that untruth which asserts that the essence of the contradictory motion of all the parts which disappears in that essence is itself the positive, the affirmative. At this moment he transcended the bourgeois spirit whose highest musical manifestation was his own work. Something in his own genius, the deepest part of it, refused to reconcile in a single image what is not reconciled. Musically this may have become concretized in a vague sensitivity toward a filigree structure and developmental principle. It is related to the hostility which developed poetic sensibility had early seized upon in Germany toward dramatic complexity and intrigue. It is a sublimely plebeian hostility, inimical to all that is aristocratic and it was Beethoven who for the first time imbued German music with this feeling. Intrigue in the theater had always had something foolish about it. Its activity seemed to emanate from above, from the author and his idea, and was never motivated from below, from out of the characters themselves. The activity of the thematic work may have sounded to Beethoven's inner ear like the machinations of the courtiers in Schiller's plays, of costumed wives and broken jewel cases, and stolen letters. There is something realistic, in a true meaning of that word, in Beethoven which is not satisfied with conflicts so obviously contrived, with manipulated antitheses which all classicism creates and which are supposed to transcend all details but which instead are thrust upon those details as if by decree. Marks of this arbitrariness can be found in the decisive phrases of the developments in even the *Ninth Symphony*. The late Beethoven's demand for truth rejects the illusory appearance of the unity of subjective and objective, a concept practically at one with the classicist idea. A polarization results. Unity transcends into the fragmentary. In the last quartets this takes place by means of the rough, unmediated juxtaposition of callow aphoristic motifs and polyphonic complexes. The gap between both becomes obvious and makes the impossibility of aesthetic harmony into the aesthetic content of the work; makes failure in a highest sense a measure of success. In its way even the *Missa* sacrifices the idea of synthesis. But in so far as it refuses the subject, the listener, entry or access to the music and the subject or listener is no longer secure in the objectivity of the form and cannot produce this form unbroken out of himself, it is prepared now to pay for its human universality by having the individual soul be silent, perhaps already submissive. *That*, and not the concession to ecclesiastical tradition or the will to please Archduke Rudolf, his pupil, may lead to an explanation of the *Missa Solemnis*. The autonomous subject, that subject which otherwise cannot know itself capable of objectivity, secedes from freedom to heteronomy. Pseudo-morphosis to an alienated form, at one with the expression of alienation itself, is supposed to accomplish what otherwise would be incapable of accomplishment. The composer experiments with strict style because formal bourgeois freedom is not sufficient as a stylization principle. The composition unremittingly controls whatever is to be filled out by the subject under such externally dictated stylization principles. Not only is each motion which opposes this principle subjected to rigorous criticism, but each more concrete version of the objectivity itself, which degrades it to romantic fiction, is also so criticized, and either as a skeleton, real, tangible, or concrete it nonetheless disappears into that fiction. This dual criticism, a kind of permanent selection process, imposes upon the *Missa* its remote outline character. It brings the work despite its full resonance into such a rigorous contradiction to sensuous appearance as in the ascetic last quartets. The aesthetically fragile in the *Missa Solemnis*, the denial of conspicuous organization in favor of an almost cuttingly strict question as to what is at all still possible, corresponds in its deceptively closed surface to the open fractures which the last quartets demonstrate. The tendency to an archaicization which here is still tempered, is shared by the *Missa* with the late style of almost all great composers from Bach to Schoenberg. They have all, as exponents of the bourgeois spirit, reached the limits of that spirit without, however, in the bourgeois world ever being able to climb beyond it on their own. All of them had to dredge up the past in the anguish of the present as sacrifices to the future. Whether this sacrifice was fruitful in Beethoven's case, whether the essence of that which was left out is really the cipher of a realized cosmos, or whether as in the later attempts to reconstruct objectivity, the *Missa* already failed, all this can be judged only if historical-philosophical reflection on the structure of the work were to penetrate even into the innermost compositional calls. The fact that today, after the developmental principle has been driven to its historical conclusion and has lost its meaningfulness, composing sees itself obliged to segmentation of parts, to articulations restricted by fields without any thought given to the methodology of the *Missa*'s composition, encourages us to take Beethoven's plea in the greatest of his works for more than merely a plea.

18

Trying to Understand
Endgame

That Adorno wanted to dedicate *Aesthetic Theory* to Samuel Beckett tells us something of his estimation of Beckett's work. Adorno is not, of course, alone in placing Beckett highly among post-war writers. His reasons for so doing, however, are unique and often persuasive. He argues that Beckett's work – *Endgame* in particular – responds to (a loose) antinomy which challenges the very possibility of aesthetic production. This is the antinomy that autonomous subjectivity is recognized as a semblance produced within a totality which somehow both generates and is the result of this semblance. Art, however, unlike philosophy, cannot discursively name this semblance. ('The name of disaster can only be spoken silently.') This antinomy cannot be set aside: it is the condition within which alone authentic art can operate. Modernist art makes this antinomy its own process. Since art cannot explicitly express the truth about autonomous subjectivity it turns to form, altering traditional form to release possibilities which are otherwise unavailable to reified experience. Traditional drama, for instance, operates with forms that would preclude such an achievement. Instead we would have a plot, a sequence of events, all of which lead to a conclusion. There is nothing traditional about *Endgame*, yet it remains as art. The effort of the play, in its thoroughly modernist adherence to the antinomy of art, is to present itself in a way which effectively uncovers the conditions of social totality. It is no longer permissible to write poetry after Auschwitz ('Cultural Criticism and Society'), but *Endgame* indicates the degenerative conditions which allowed the Holocaust to happen.

In 'Trying to Understand *Endgame*' Adorno gives his most extended account of the significance of the formal transformation found in modernist art. *Endgame*, Adorno proposes, is a play about meaninglessness. However, it cannot name meaninglessness, as such. Nor, importantly, does the play itself fall into meaninglessness in the sense that it says nothing at all. We understand *Endgame*, he claims, when we recognize its incomprehensibility without making that incomprehensibility equivalent to meaninglessness. But what, we might ask, is socially revealing about incomprehensibility? Adorno connects the process of understanding *Endgame* – that it is unintelligible though formally coherent – with the idea that bourgeois society resists intelligibility. The real life processes of society are veiled by a version of reason that precludes access to objects which do not conform to its rules of intelligibility.

In offering this radical reading of *Endgame* Adorno takes issue with Sartre and, to a lesser extent, Lukács. Lukács dismissed Beckett's work as 'decadent', a term in Marxist aesthetics denoting art which eternalizes a debased version of humanity, thereby occluding a vision which would have revolutionary potential. Adorno simply confronts Lukács with the social truths contained monadologically within Beckett's drama. Sartre's positive estimation of Beckett is also rejected. Sartre sees Beckett as the author of the absurd, one whose plays and novels show that there is no metaphysical meaning and that the subject must construct meaning anew. However, the very idea of autonomy is shattered by *Endgame*, which Adorno describes as the history of the end of subjectivity. As such *Endgame* is anything but a literary companion to existentialism.

Adorno may not always perfectly fulfil the criteria of his own interpretation, that is, to uncover decisively the social totality within the autonomous work. What remains, however, and compensates the reader, is a brilliantly incisive, detailed and illuminating essay which changes forever how we should think of *Endgame*.

'Trying to Understand *Endgame*' [1961], *New German Critique*, no. 26
(Spring–Summer, 1982), pp. 119–50.
Translated by Michael J. Jones.

to S.B. in memory of Paris, Fall 1958

Beckett's *oeuvre* has several elements in common with Parisian existentialism. Reminiscences of the category of "absurdity," of "situation," of "decision" or their opposite permeate it as medieval ruins permeate Kafka's monstrous house on the edge of the city: occasionally, windows fly open and reveal to view the black starless heaven of something like anthropology. But form – conceived by Sartre rather traditionally as that of didactic plays, not at all as something audacious but rather oriented toward an effect – absorbs what is expressed and changes it. Impulses are raised to the level of the most advanced artistic means, those of Joyce and Kafka. Absurdity in Beckett is no longer a state of human existence thinned out to a mere idea and then expressed in images. Poetic procedure surrenders to it without intention. Absurdity is divested of that generality of doctrine which existentialism, that creed of the permanence of individual existence, nonetheless combines with Western pathos of the universal and the immutable. Existential conformity – that one should be what one is – is thereby rejected along with the ease of its representation. What Beckett offers in the way of philosophy he himself also reduces to culture-trash, no different from the innumerable allusions and residues of education which he employs in the wake of the Anglo-Saxon tradition, particularly of Joyce and Eliot. Culture parades before him as the entrails of *Jugendstil* ornaments did before that progress which preceded him, modernism as the obsolescence of the modern. The regressive language demolishes it. Such objectivity in Beckett obliterates the meaning that was culture, along with its rudiments. Culture thus begins to fluoresce. He thereby completes a tendency of the recent novel. What was decried as abstract according to the cultural criterion of aesthetic immanence – reflection – is lumped together with pure representation, corroding the Flaubertian principle of the purely self-enclosed matter at hand. The less events can be presumed meaningful in themselves, the more the idea of aesthetic *Gestalt* as a unity of appearance and intention becomes illusory. Beckett relinquishes the illusion by coupling both disparate aspects. Thought becomes as much a means of producing a meaning for the work which cannot be immediately rendered tangible, as it is an expression of meaning's absence. When applied to drama, the word "meaning" is multivalent. It denotes: metaphysical content, which objectively presents itself in the complexion of the artifact; likewise the intention of the whole as a structure of meaning which it signifies in itself; and finally the sense of the words and sentences which the characters speak, and that of their progression – the sense of the dialogue. But these equivocations point toward a common basis. From it, in Beckett's *Endgame*, emerges a continuum. It is historio-philosophically supported by a change in the dramatic *a priori:* positive metaphysical meaning is no longer possible in such a substantive way (if indeed it ever was), such that dramatic form could have its law in such meaning and its epiphany. Yet that afflicts the form even in its linguistic construction. Drama cannot simply seize on to negative meaning, or its absence, as content, without thereby affecting everything peculiar to it – virtually to the point of reversal to its opposite. What is essential for drama was constituted by that meaning. If drama were to strive to survive meaning aesthetically, it would be reduced to inadequate content or to a clattering machinery demonstrating world views, as often happens in existentialist plays. The explosion of metaphysical meaning, which alone guaranteed the unity of an aesthetic structure of meaning, makes it crumble away with a necessity and stringency which equals that of the transmitted canon of dramaturgical form. Harmonious aesthetic meaning, and certainly its subjectification in a binding tangible intention, substituted for that transcendent meaningfulness, the denial of which itself constituted the content. Through its own organized meaninglessness, the plot must approach that which transpired in the truth content of dramaturgy generally. Such construction of the senseless also even includes linguistic molecules: if they and their connections were rationally meaningful, then within the drama they would synthesize irrevocably into that very meaning structure of the whole which is denied by the whole. The interpretation of *Endgame* therefore cannot chase the chimera of expressing its meaning with the help of philosophical mediation. Understanding it can mean nothing other than understanding its incomprehensibility, or concretely reconstructing its meaning structure — that it has none. Isolated, thought no longer pretends, as the Idea once did, to be itself the structure's meaning — a transcendence which would be engendered and guaranteed by the work's own immanence. Instead, thought transforms itself into a kind of material of a second degree, just as the philosophemes expounded in Thomas Mann's *The Magic Mountain* and *Doctor Faustus*, as novel materials, find their destiny in replacing that sensate immediacy which is diminished in the self-reflective work of art. If such materiality of thought was heretofore largely involuntary, pointing to the dilemma of works which perforce confused themselves with the Idea they could not achieve, then Beckett confronts this challenge and uses thoughts *sans phrase* as phrases, as those material components of the *monologue intérieur* which mind itself has become, the reified residue of education. Whereas pre-Beckett existentialism cannibalized philosophy for poetic purposes as if it were Schiller incarnate, Beckett, as educated as anyone, presents the bill: philosophy, or spirit itself, proclaims its bankruptcy as the dreamlike dross of the experiential world, and the poetic process shows itself as worn out. Disgust (*dégoût*), a productive force in the arts since Baudelaire, is insatiable in Beckett's historically mediated impulses. Everything now impossible becomes canonical, freeing a motif from the prehistory of existentialism — Husserl's universal annihilation of the world — from the shadowy realm of methodology. Totalitarians like Lukács, who rage against the — truly terrifying — simplifier as "decadent," are not ill advised by the interests of their bosses. They hate in Beckett what they have betrayed. Only the nausea of satiation — the tedium of spirit with itself — wants something completely different: prescribed "health" nevertheless makes do with the nourishment offered, with simple fare. Beckett's *dégoût* cannot be forced to fall in line. He responds to the cheery call to play along with parody, parody of the philosophy spit out by his dialogues as well as parody of forms. Existentialism itself is parodied; nothing remains of its "invariants" other than minimal existence. The drama's opposition to ontology – as the sketch of a first or immutable principle – is unmistakable in an exchange of dialogue which unintentionally garbles Goethe's phrase about "old truths," which has degenerated to an arch-bourgeois sentiment:

HAMM: Do you remember your father.
CLOV: (wearily) Same answer. (Pause.) You've asked me these questions millions of times.
HAMM: I love the old questions. (With fervor.) Ah the old questions, the old answers, there's nothing like them.[1]

Thoughts are dragged along and distorted like the day's left-overs, *homo homini sapienti sat*. Hence the precariousness of what Beckett refuses to deal with, interpretation. He shrugs his shoulders about the possibility of philosophy today, or theory in general. The irrationality of bourgeois society on the wane resists being understood: those were the good old days when a critique of political economy could be written which took this society by its own *ratio*. For in the meantime it has thrown this *ratio* on the junk-heap and virtually replaced it with direct control. The interpretive word, therefore, cannot recuperate Beckett, while his dramaturgy – precisely by virtue of its limitation to exploded facticity – twitches beyond it, pointing toward interpretation in its essence as riddle. One could almost designate as the criterion of relevant philosophy today whether it is up to that task.

French existentialism had tackled history. In Beckett, history devours existentialism. In *Endgame*, a historical moment is revealed, the experience which was cited in the title of the culture industry's rubbish book *Corpsed*. After the Second War, everything is destroyed, even resurrected culture, without knowing it; humanity vegetates along, crawling, after events which even the survivors cannot really survive, on a pile of ruins which even renders futile self-reflection of one's own battered state. From the marketplace, as the play's pragmatic precondition, that fact is ripped away:

CLOV: (He gets up on ladder, turns the telescope on the without.) Let's see. (He looks, moving the telescope.) Zero . . . (he looks) . . . zero . . . (he looks) . . . and zero.
HAMM: Nothing stirs. All is –
CLOV: Zer –
HAMM: (violently) Wait till you're spoken to. (Normal voice.) All is . . . all is . . . all is what? (Violently.) All is what?

CLOV: What all is? In a word. Is that what you want to know? Just a moment. (He
   turns the telescope on the without, looks, lowers the telescope, turns toward
   Hamm.) Corpsed. (Pause.) Well? Content?[2]

That all human beings are dead is covertly smuggled in. An earlier passage
explains why the catastrophe may not be mentioned. Vaguely, Hamm himself
is to blame for that:

HAMM: That old doctor, he's dead naturally?
CLOV: He wasn't old.
HAMM: But he's dead?
CLOV: Naturally. (Pause.) *You* ask *me* that?[3]

The condition presented in the play is nothing other than that in which
"there's no more nature."[4] Indistinguishable is the phase of completed
reification of the world, which leaves no remainder of what was not made
by humans; it is permanent catastrophe, along with a catastrophic event caused
by humans themselves, in which nature has been extinguished and nothing
grows any longer.

HAMM: Did your seeds come up?
CLOV: No.
HAMM: Did you scratch round them to see if they had sprouted?
CLOV: They haven't sprouted.
HAMM: Perhaps it's still too early.
CLOV: If they were going to sprout they would have sprouted. (Violently.) They'll
   never sprout![5]

The *dramatis personae* resemble those who dream their own death, in a
"shelter" where "it's time it ended."[6] The end of the world is discounted, as
if it were a matter of course. Every supposed drama of the atomic age would
mock itself, if only because its fable would hopelessly falsify the horror of
historical anonymity by shoving it into the characters and actions of humans,
and possibly by gaping at the "prominents" who decide whether the button
will be pushed. The violence of the unspeakable is mimicked by the timid-
ity to mention it. Beckett keeps it nebulous. One can only speak euphemisti-
cally about what is incommensurate with all experience, just as one speaks
in Germany of the murder of the Jews. It has become a total *a priori*, so that
bombed-out consciousness no longer has any position from which it could
reflect on that fact. The desperate state of things supplies – with gruesome
irony – a means of stylization that protects that pragmatic precondition from
any contamination by childish science fiction. If Clov really were exaggerat-

ing, as his nagging, "common-sensical" companion reproaches him, that would not change much. If catastrophe amounted to a partial end of the world, that would be a bad joke: then nature, from which the imprisoned figures are cut off, would be as good as nonexistent; what remains of it would only prolong the torment.

This historical *nota bene* however, this parody of the Kierkegaardian one of the convergence of time and eternity, imposes at the same time a taboo on history. What would be called the *condition humaine* in existentialist jargon is the image of the last human, which is devouring the earlier ones – humanity. Existential ontology asserts the universally valid in a process of abstraction which is not conscious of itself. While it still – according to the old phenomenological doctrine of the intuition of essence – behaves as if it were aware, even in the particular, of its binding determinations, thereby unifying apriority and concreteness, it nonetheless distills out what appears to transcend temporality. It does so by blotting out particularity – what is individualized in space and time, what makes existence existence rather than its mere concept. Ontology appeals to those who are weary of philosophical formalism but who yet cling to what is only accessible formally. To such unacknowledged abstraction, Beckett affixes the caustic antitheses by means of acknowledged subtraction. He does not leave out the temporality of existence – all existence, after all, is temporal – but rather removes from existence what time, the historical tendency, attempts to quash in reality. He lengthens the escape route of the subject's liquidation to the point where it constricts into a "this-here," whose abstractness – the loss of all qualities – extends ontological abstraction literally *ad absurdum*, to that Absurd which mere existence becomes as soon as it is consumed in naked self-identity. Childish foolishness emerges as the content of philosophy, which degenerates to tautology – to a conceptual duplication of that existence it had intended to comprehend. While recent ontology subsists on the unfulfilled promise of concretion of its abstractions, concreteness in Beckett – that shell-like, self-enclosed existence which is no longer capable of universality but rather exhausts itself in pure self-positing – is obviously the same as an abstractness which is no longer capable of experience. Ontology arrives home as the pathogenesis of false life. It is depicted as the state of negative eternity. If the messianic Myshkin once forgot his watch because earthly time is invalid for him, then time is lost to his antipodes because it could still imply hope. The yawn accompanying the bored remark that the weather is "as usual"[7] gapes like a hellish abyss:

HAMM: But that's always the way at the end of the day, isn't it, Clov?
CLOV: Always.

HAMM: It's the end of the day like any other day, isn't it, Clov?
CLOV: Looks like it.[8]

Like time, the temporal itself is damaged; saying that it no longer exists would already be too comforting. It is and it is not, like the world for the solipsist who doubts its existence, while he must concede it with every sentence. Thus a passage of dialogue hovers:

HAMM: And the horizon? Nothing on the horizon?
CLOV: (lowering the telescope, turning towards Hamm, exasperated): What in God's name would there be on the horizon? (Pause.)
HAMM: The waves, how are the waves?
CLOV: The Waves? (He turns the telescope on the waves.) Lead.
HAMM: And the sun?
CLOV: (looking) Zero.
HAMM: But it should be sinking. Look again.
CLOV: (looking) Damn the sun.
HAMM: Is it night already then?
CLOV: (looking) No.
HAMM: Then what is it?
CLOV: (looking) Gray. (Lowering the telescope, turning towards Hamm, louder.) Gray! (Pause. Still louder.) GRRAY![9]

History is excluded, because it itself has dehydrated the power of consciousness to think history, the power of remembrance. Drama falls silent and becomes gesture, frozen amid the dialogues. Only the result of history appears – as decline. What preens itself in the existentialists as the once-and-for-all of being has withered to the sharp point of history which breaks off. Lukács' objection, that in Beckett humans are reduced to animality,[10] resists with official optimism the fact that residual philosophies, which would like to bank the true and immutable after removing temporal contingency, have become the residue of life, the end product of injury. Admittedly, as nonsensical as it is to attribute to Beckett – as Lukács does – an abstract, subjectivist ontology and then to place it on the excavated index of degenerate art because of its worldlessness and infantility, it would be equally ridiculous to have him testify as a key political witness. For urging the struggle against atomic death, a work that notes that death's potential even in ancient struggles is hardly appropriate. The simplifier of terror refuses – unlike Brecht – any simplification. But he is not so dissimilar from Brecht, insofar as his differentiation becomes sensitivity to subjective differences, which have regressed do the "conspicuous consumption" of those who can afford individuation.

Therein lies social truth. Differentiation cannot absolutely or automatically be recorded as positive. The simplification of the social process now beginning relegates it to "incidental expenses" (*faux frais*), somewhat as the formalities of social forms, from which emerged the capability for differentiation, are disappearing. Differentiation, once the condition of humanity, glides into ideology. But the non-sentimental consciousness of that fact does not regress itself. In the act of omission, that which is omitted survives through its exclusion, as consonance survives in atonal harmony. The idiocy of *Endgame* is recorded and developed with the greatest differentiation. The unprotesting depiction of omnipresent regression protests against a disposition of the world which obeys the law of regression so obligingly, that a counter-notion can no longer be conceived to be held against it. That it is only thus and not otherwise is carefully shown; a finely-tuned alarm system reports what belongs to the topology of the play and what does not. Delicately, Beckett suppresses the delicate elements no less than the brutal ones. The vanity of the individual who indicts society, while his rights themselves merge in the accumulation of the injustice of all individuals – disaster itself – is manifest in embarrassing declamations like the "Germany" poem of Karl Wolfskehl. The "too-late," the missed moment condemns such bombastic rhetoric to phraseology. Nothing of that sort in Beckett. Even the view that he negatively presents the negativity of the age would fit into a certain kind of conception, according to which people in the eastern satellite countries – where the revolution is carried out by bureaucratic decree – need only devote themselves happily to reflecting a happy-go-lucky age. Playing with elements of reality – devoid of any mirror-like reflection –, refusing to take a "position," and finding joy in such freedom as is prescribed: all of this reveals more than would be possible if a "revealer" were partisan. The name of disaster can only be spoken silently. Only in the terror of recent events is the terror of the whole ignited, but only there, not in gazing upon "origins." Humankind, whose general species-name fits badly into Beckett's linguistic landscape, is only that which humanity has become. As in utopia, the last days pass judgment on the species. But this lamentation – within mind itself – must reflect that lamenting has become impossible. No amount of weeping melts the armor; only that face remains on which the tears have dried up. That is the basis of a kind of artistic behavior denounced as inhuman by those whose humanity has already become an advertisement for inhumanity, even if they have as yet no notion of that fact. Among the motives for Beckett's regression to animal-like man, that is probably the deepest. By hiding its countenance, his poetic work participates in the absurd.

The catastrophies that inspire *Endgame* have exploded the individual whose substantiality and absoluteness was the common element between

Kierkegaard, Jaspers, and the Sartrian version of existentialism. Even to the
concentration camp victims, existentialism had attributed the freedom either
inwardly to accept or reject the inflicted martyrdom. *Endgame* destroys such
illusions. The individual as a historical category, as the result of the captalist
process of alienation and as a defiant protest against it, has itself become
openly transitory. The individualist position belonged, as polar opposite, to
the ontological tendency of every existentialism, even that of *Being and Time.*
Beckett's dramaturgy abandons it like an obsolete bunker. In its narrowness
and contingency, individual experience could nowhere locate the authority
to interpret itself as a cipher of being, unless it pronounced itself the fundamental characteristic of being. Precisely that, however, is untrue. The immediacy of individuation was deceptive: what particular human experience
clings to is mediated, determined. *Endgame* insinuates that the individual's
claim of autonomy and of being has become incredible. But while the prison
of individuation is revealed as a prison and simultaneously as mere semblance
– the stage scenery is the image of such self-reflection –, art is unable to
release the spell of fragmented subjectivity; it can only depict solipsism.
Beckett thereby bumps up against art's contemporary antinomy. The position
of the absolute subject, once it has been cracked open as the appearance of
an over-arching whole through which it first matures, cannot be maintained:
Expressionism becomes obsolete. Yet the transition to the binding universality of objective reality, that universality which could relativize the semblance
of individuation, is denied art. For art is different from the discursive cogni-
ton of the real, not gradually but categorically distinct from it; in art, only
what is transported into the realm of subjectivity, commensurable to it, is
valid. It can conceive reconciliation – its idea – only as reconciliation of that
which is alienated. If art simulated the state of reconciliation by surrender-
ing to the mere world of things, then it would negate itself. What is offered
in the way of socialist realism is not – as some claim – beyond subjectivism
but rather lags behind it and is at the same time its pre-artistic complement;
the expressionist "Oh Man" and ideologically spiced social reportage fit
together seamlessly. In art, unreconciled reality tolerates no reconciliation with
the object; realism, which does not reach the level of subjective experience,
to say nothing of reaching further, merely mimics reconciliation. The dignity
of art today is not measured by asking whether it slips out of this antinomy
by luck or cleverness, but whether art confronts and develops it. In that
regard, *Endgame* is exemplary. It yields both to the impossibility of dealing
with materials and of representation according to nineteenth-century practice, as well as to the insight that subjective modes of reaction, which mediate
the laws of form rather than reflecting reality, are themselves no absolute
first principle but rather a last principle, objectively posited. All content of

subjectivity, which necessarily hypostatizes itself, is trace and shadow of the world, from which it withdraws in order not to serve that semblance and conformity the world demands. Beckett responds to that condition not with any immutable "provisions" (*Vorrat*), but rather with what is still permitted, precariously and uncertainly, by the antagonistic tendencies. His dramaturgy resembles the fun that the old Germany offered – knocking about between the border markers of Baden and Bavaria, as if they fenced in a realm of freedom. *Endgame* takes place in a zone of indifference between inner and outer, neutral between – on the one hand – the "materials" without which subjectivity could not manifest itself or even exist, and – on the other – an animating impulse which blurs the materials, as if that impulse had breathed on the glass through which they are viewed. These materials are so meager that aesthetic formalism is ironically rescued – against its adversaries hither and thither, the stuff-pushers of dialectical materialism and the administrators of authentic messages. The concreteness of the lemurs, whose horizon was lost in a double sense, is transformed directly into the most extreme abstraction; the level of material itself determines a procedure in which the materials, by being lightly touched as transitory, approximate geometrical forms; the most narrow becomes the general. The localization of *Endgame* in that zone teases the spectator with the suggestion of a symbolism which it – like Kafka – refuses. Because no state of affairs is merely what it is, each appears as the sign of interiority, but that inward element supposedly signified no longer exists, and the signs mean just that. That iron ration of reality and people, with whom the drama reckons and keeps house, is one with that which remains of subject, mind (*Geist*), and soul in the face of permanent catastrophe: of the mind, which originated in mimesis, only ridiculous imitation; of the soul – staging itself – inhumane sentimentality; of the subject its most abstract determination, actually existing and thereby already blaspheming. Beckett's figures behave primitively and behavioristically, corresponding to conditions after the catastrophe, which has mutilated them to such an extent that they cannot react differently – flies that twitch after the swatter has half smashed them. The aesthetic *principium stilisationis* does the same to humans. Thrown back completely upon themselves, subjects – anti-cosmism become flesh – consist in nothing other than the wretched realities of their world, shrivelled down to raw necessities; they are empty *personae*, through which the world truly can only resound. Their "phonyness" is the result of mind's disenchantment – as mythology. In order to undercut history and perhaps thereby to hibernate, *Endgame* occupies the nadir of what philosophy's construction of the subject-object confiscated at its zenith: pure identity becomes the identity of annihilation, identity of subject and object in the state of complete alienation. While meanings in Kafka were beheaded or confused, Beckett calls a halt to the bad infinity of intentions: their sense is senselessness. Objectively and without any polemical intent, that is his answer to existential philosophy, which under the name of "thrownness" and later of "absurdity" transforms senselessness itself into sense, exploiting the equivocations inherent in the concept of sense. To this Beckett juxtaposes no world view, rather he takes it at its word. What becomes of the absurd, after the characters of the meaning of existence have been torn down, is no longer a universal – the absurd would then be yet again an idea – but only pathetic details which ridicule conceptuality, a stratum of utensils as in an emergency refuge: ice boxes, lameness, blindness, and unappetizing bodily functions. Everything awaits evacuation. This stratum is not symbolic but rather the post-psychological state, as in old people and torture victims.

Removed from their inwardness, Heidegger's states of being (Befindlichkeiten) and Jaspers' "situations" have become materialistic. With them, the hypostatis of individual and that of situation were in harmony. The "situation" was temporal existence itself, and the totality of living individuals was the primary certainty. It presupposed personal identity. Here, Beckett proves to be a pupil of Proust and a friend of Joyce, in that he gives back to the concept of "situation" what it actually says and what philosophy made vanish by exploiting it: dissociation of the unity of consciousness into disparate elements – non-identity. As soon as the subject is no longer doubtlessly self-identical, no longer a closed structure of meaning, the line of demarcation with the exterior becomes blurred, and the situations of inwardness become at the same time physical ones. The tribunal over individuality – conserved by existentialism as its idealist core – condemns idealism. Non-identity is both: the historical disintegration of the subject's unity and the emergence of what is not itself subject. That changes the possible meaning of "situation." It is defined by Jaspers as "a reality for an existing subject who has a stake in it."[11] He subsumes the concept of situation under a subject conceived as firm and identical, just as he insinuates that meaning accrues to the situation because of its relationship to this subject. Immediately thereafter, he also calls it "not just a reality governed by natural laws. It is a sense-related reality," a reality moreover which, strangely enough, is said by Jaspers to be "neither psychological nor physical, but both in one."[12] When situation becomes – in Beckett's view – actually both, it loses its existential-ontological constituents: personal identity and meaning. That becomes striking in the concept of "boundary situation" (Grenzsituation). It also stems from Jaspers: "Situations like the following: that I am always in situations; that I cannot live without struggling and suffering; that I cannot avoid guilt; that I must die – these are what I call boundary situations. They never change, except

in appearance; [with regard to our existence, they are final]."[13] The construction of *Endgame* takes that up with a sardonic "Pardon me?" Such wise
sayings as that "I cannot live without suffering, that I cannot avoid guilt, that
I must die" lose their triviality the moment they are retrieved back from their
apriority and portrayed concretely. Then they break to pieces – all those
noble, affirmative elements with which philosophy adorns that existence that
Hegel already called "foul" (*faul*). It does so by subsuming the non-conceptual under a concept, which magically disperses that difference pompously
characterized as "ontological." Beckett turns existential philosophy from its
head back on its feet. His play reacts to the comical and ideological mischief
of sentences like: "Courage in the boundary situation is an attitude that lets
me view death as an indefinite opportunity to be myself,"[14] whether Beckett
is familiar with them or not. The misery of participants in the *Endgame* is
the misery of philosophy.

These Beckettian situations which constitute his drama are the negative
of meaningful reality. Their models are those of empirical reality. As soon as
they are isolated and divested of their purposeful and psychological context
through the loss of personal unity, they assume a specific and compelling
expression – that of horror. They are manifest already in the practice of
Expressionism. The dread disseminated by Leonhard Frank's elementary
school teacher Mager, the cause of his murder, becomes evident in the
description of Mager's fussy manner of peeling an apple in class. Although it
seems so innocent, such circumspection is the figure of sadism: this image of
one who takes his time resembles that of the one who delays giving a ghastly
punishment. Beckett's treatment of these situations, that panicky and yet
artificial derivation of simplistic slapstick comedy of yesteryear, articulates
a content noted already in Proust. In his posthumous work *Immediacy and
Sense-Interpretation*, Heinrich Rickert considers the possibility of an objective
physiognomy of mind, rather than of a merely projected "soul" of a landscape or a work of art.[15] He cites a passage from Ernst Robert Curtius, who
considers it "only partially correct to view Proust only or primarily as a great
psychologist. A Stendhal is appropriately characterized in this manner. He is
indeed part of the Cartesian tradition of the French mind. But Proust does
not recognize the division between thinking and the extended substance. He
does not sever the world into psychological and physical parts. To regard his
work from the perspective of the 'psychological novel' is to misunderstand
its significance. In Proust's books, the world of sensate objects occupies the
same space as that of mind." Or: "If Proust is a psychologist, he is one in a
completely new sense – by immersing all reality, including sense perception,
in a mental fluid." To show "that the usual concept of the psychic is not
appropriate here," Rickert again quotes Curtius: "But here the concept of the

psychological has lost its opposite – and is thereby no longer a useful characterization."[16] The physiognomy of objective expression however retains an enigma. The situations say something, but what? In this regard, art itself, as the embodiment of situations, converges with that physiognomy. It combines the most extreme determinacy with its radical opposite. In Beckett, this contradiction is inverted outward. What is otherwise entrenched behind a communicative facade is here condemned merely to appear. Proust, in a subterranean mystical tradition, still clings affirmatively to that physiognomy, as if involuntary memory disclosed a secret language of things; in Beckett, it becomes the physiognomy of what is no longer human. His situations are counterparts to the immutable elements conjured by Proust's situations; they are wrested from the flood of schizophrenia, which fearful "health" resists with murderous cries. In this realm Beckett's drama remains master of itself, transforming even schizophrenia into reflection:

HAMM: I once knew a madman who thought the end of the world had come. He was a painter – and engraver. I had a great fondness for him. I used to go and see him, in the asylum. I'd take him by the hand and drag him to the window. Look! There! All that rising corn! And there! Look! The sails of the herring fleet! All that loveliness! (Pause.) He'd snatch away his hand and go back into his corner. Appalled. All he had seen was ashes. (Pause.) He alone had been spared. (Pause.) Forgotten. (Pause.) It appears the case is . . . was not so . . . so unusual.[17]

The madman's perception would approximate that of Clov peering on command through the window. *Endgame* draws back from the nadir through no other means than by calling to itself like a sleepwalker: negation of negativity. There sticks in Beckett's memory something like an apoplectic middle-aged man taking his midday nap, with a cloth over his eyes to keep out the light or the flies; it makes him unrecognizable. This image – average and optically barely unusual – becomes a sign only for that gaze which perceives the face's loss of identity, sees the possibility that being concealed is the face of a dead man, and becomes aware of the repulsive nature of that physical concern which reduces the man to his body and places him already among corpses.[18] Beckett stares at such aspects until that family routine – from which they stem – pales into irrelevance. The tableau begins with Hamm covered by an old sheet; at the end, he places near his face the handkerchief, his last possession:

HAMM: Old Stancher! (Pause.) You . . . remain.[19]

Such situations, emancipated from their context and from personal character, are reconstructed in a second autonomous context, just as music joins

together the intentions and states of expression immersed in it until
its sequence becomes a structure in its own right. A key point in the drama
– "If I can hold my peace, and sit quiet, it will be all over with sound,
and motion, all over and done with"[20] – betrays the principle, perhaps as a
reminiscence of how Shakespeare employed his principle in the actors' scene
of *Hamlet*.

HAMM: Then babble, babble, words, like the solitary child who turns himself into
    children, two, three, so as to be together, and whisper together, in the dark. (Pause.)
    Moment upon moment, pattering down, like the millet grains of . . . (he hesitates)
    that old Greek, and all life long you wait for that to mount up to a life.[21]

In the tremors of "not being in a hurry," such situations allude to the indifference and superfluity of what the subject can still manage to do. While
Hamm considers riveting shut the lids of those trash cans where his parents
reside, he retracts that decision with the same words as when he must urinate
with the tortuous aid of the catheter: "Time enough."[22] The imperceptible
aversion to medicine bottles, dating back to the moment one perceived one's
parents as physically vulnerable, mortal, deteriorating, reappears in the
question:

HAMM: Is it not time for my pain-killer?[28]

Speaking to each other has completely become Strindbergian grumbling:

HAMM: You feel normal?
CLOV: (irritably) I tell you I don't complain.[24]

And another time:

HAMM: I feel a little too far to the left. (Clov moves chair slightly.) Now I feel a
    little too far to the right. (Clov moves chair slightly.) Now I feel a little too far
    forward. (Clov moves chair slightly.) Now I feel a little too far back. (Clov moves
    chair slightly.) Don't stay there, (i.e. behind the chair) you give me the shivers.
    (Clov returns to his place beside the chair.)
CLOV: If I could kill him I'd die happy.[25]

The waning of a marriage is the situation where one scratches the other:

NELL: I am going to leave you.
NAGG: Could you give me a scratch before you go?
NELL: No. (Pause.) Where?

NAGG: In the back.
NELL: No. (Pause.) Rub yourself against the rim.
NAGG: It's lower down. In the hollow.
NELL: What hollow?
NAGG: The hollow! (Pause.) Could you not? (Pause.) Yesterday you scratched me
    there.
NELL: (elegiac) Ah yesterday!
NAGG: Could you not? (Pause.) Would you like me to scratch you? (Pause.) Are
    you crying again?
NELL: I was trying.[26]

After the dismissed father – preceptor of his parents – has told the Jewish
joke, metaphysically famous, about the trousers and the world, he himself
bursts into laughter. The shame which grips the listener when someone
laughs at his own words becomes existential; life is merely the epitome of
everything about which one must be ashamed. Subjectivity is frightening
when it simply amounts to domination, as in the situation where one whistles and the other comes running.[27] But what shame struggles against has its
social function: in those moments when the bourgeois (*Bürger*) acts like a real
bourgeois, he besmirches the concept of humanity on which his claim rests.
Beckett's archaic images (*Urbilder*) are also historical, in that he shows as
humanly typical only those deformations inflicted on humans by the form
of their society. No space remains for anything else. The rudeness and ticks
of normal character, which *Endgame* inconceivably intensifies, is that universality of the whole that already preforms all classes and individuals; it merely
reproduces itself through bad particularity, the antagonistic interests of single
individuals. Because there was no other life than the false one, the catalogue
of its defects becomes the mirror image of ontology.

This shattering into unconnected, non-identical elements is nevertheless
tied to identity in a theater play, which does not abandon the traditional cast
of characters. Only against identity, by dismantling its concept, is dissociation
at all possible; otherwise, it would be pure, unpolemical, innocent pluralism.
For the time being, the historical crisis of the individual runs up against the
single biological being, its arena. The succession of situations in Beckett,
gliding along without resistance from individuals, thus ends with those obsti-
nate bodies to which they have regressed. Measured by a unit, such as the
body, the schizoid situations are comical like optical illusions. That explains
the *prima vista* clowning evident in the behavior and constellations of
Beckett's figures.[28] Psychoanalysis explains clownish humor as a regression
back to a primordial ontogenetic level, and Beckett's regressive play descends
to that level. But the laughter it inspires ought to suffocate the laughter. That
is what happened to humor, after it became – as an aesthetic medium – obso-

lete, repulsive, devoid of any canon of what can be laughed at; without any place for reconciliation, where one could laugh; without anything between heaven and earth harmless enough to be laughed at. An intentionally idiotic *double entendre* about the weather runs:

CLOV: Things are livening up. (He gets up on ladder, raises the telescope, lets it fall.) It did it on purpose. (He gets down, picks up the telescope, turns it on auditorium.) I see . . . a multitude . . . in transports . . . of joy. (Pause.) That's what I call a magnifier. (He lowers the telescope, turns toward Hamm.) Well? Don't we laugh?[29]

Humor itself has become foolish, ridiculous – who could still laugh at basic comic texts like *Don Quixote* or *Gargantua* – and Beckett carries out the verdict on humor. The jokes of the damaged people are themselves damaged. They no longer reach anybody; the state of decline, admittedly a part of all jokes, the *Kalauer* (pun), now covers them like a rash. When Clov, looking through the telescope, is asked about the weather and frightens Hamm with the word "gray," he corrects himself with the formulation "a light black." That smears the punchline from Molière's *Miser*, who describes the allegedly stolen casket as gray-red. The marrow has been sucked out of the joke as well as out of the colors. At one point, the two anti-heroes, a blind man and a lame man – the stronger is already both while the weaker will become so – come up with a "trick," an escape, "some kind of plan" à la *Three Penny Opera*; but they do not know whether it will only lengthen their lives and torment, or whether both are to end with absolute obliteration:

CLOV: Ah good. (He starts pacing to and fro, his eyes fixed on the ground, his hands behind his back. He halts.) The pains in my legs! It's unbelievable! Soon I won't be able to think any more.
HAMM: You won't be able to leave me. (Clov resumes his pacing.) What are you doing?
CLOV: Having an idea. (He paces.) Ah. (He halts.)
HAMM: What a brain! (Pause.) Well?
CLOV: Wait! (He meditates. Not very convinced.) Yes . . . (Pause. More convinced.) Yes! (He raises his head.) I have it! I set the alarm![30]

That is probably associated with the originally Jewish joke from the Busch circus, when stupid August, who has caught his wife with his friend on the sofa, cannot decide whether to throw out his wife or the friend, because they are both so dear to him, and comes up with the idea of selling the sofa. But even the remaining trace of silly, sophistic rationality is wiped away. The only comical thing remaining is that along with the sense of the punchline,

comedy itself has evaporated. That is how someone suddenly jerks upright
after climbing to the top step, climbing further, and stepping into the void.
The most extreme crudity completes the verdict on laughter, which has long
since participated in its own guilt. Hamm lets his stumps of parents completely starve, those parents who have become babies in their trashcans – the
son's triumph as a father. There is this chatter:

NAGG: Me pap!
HAMM: Accursed progenitor!
NAGG: Me pap!
HAMM: The old folks at home! No decency left! Guzzle, guzzle, that's all they think
   of. (He whistles. Enter Clov. He halts beside the chair.) Well! I thought you were
   leaving me.
CLOV: Oh not just yet, not just yet.
NAGG: Me pap!
HAMM: Give him his pap.
CLOV: There's no more pap.
HAMM: (to Nagg) Do you hear that? There's no more pap. You'll never get any
   more pap.[31]

To the irreparable harm already done, the anti-hero adds his scorn – the
indignation at the old people who have no manners, just as the latter
customarily decry dissolute youth. What remains humane in this scene – that
the two old people share the zwieback with each other – becomes repulsive
through its contrast with transcendental bestiality; the residue of love becomes
the intimacy of smacking. As far as they are still human, they "humanize":

NELL: What is it, my pet? (Pause.) Time for love?
NAGG: Were you asleep?
NELL: Oh no!
NAGG: Kiss me.
NELL: We can't.
NAGG: Try. (Their heads strain towards each other, fail to meet, fall apart again.)[32]

Dramatic categories as a whole are treated just like humor. All are parodied. But not ridiculed. Emphatically, parody entails the use of forms in the
epoch of their impossibility. It demonstrates this impossibility and thereby
changes the forms. The three Aristotelian unities are retained, but drama itself
perishes. Along with subjectivity, whose final epilogue (*Nachspiel*) is *Endgame*,
the hero is also withdrawn; the drama's freedom is only the impotent, pathetic
reflex of futile resolutions.[33] In that regard too, Beckett's drama is heir to
Kafka's novels, to whom he stands in a similar relation as the serial com-

posers to Schoenberg: he reflects the precursor in himself, altering the latter through the totality of his principle. Beckett's critique of the earlier writer, which irrefutably stresses the divergence between what happens and the objectively pure, epic language, conceals the same difficulty as that confronted by contemporary integral composition with the antagonistic procedure of Schoenberg. What is the *raison d'être* of forms when the tension between them and what is not homogeneous to them disappears, and when one nevertheless cannot halt the progress of mastery over aesthetic material? *Endgame* pulls out of the fray, by making that question its own, by making it thematic. That which prohibits the dramatization of Kafka's novels becomes subject matter. Dramatic components reappear after their demise. Exposition, complication, plot, peripeteia, and catastrophe return as decomposed elements in a post-mortem examination of dramaturgy: the news that there are no more painkillers depicts catastrophe.[34] Those components have been toppled along with that meaning once discharged by drama; *Endgame* studies (as if in a test-tube) the drama of the age, the age that no longer tolerates what constitutes drama. For example, tragedy, at the height of its plot and with antithesis as its quintessence, manifested the utmost tightening of the dramatic thread, stychomythia – dialogues in which the trimeter spoken by one person follows that of the other. Drama had renounced this technique, because its stylization and resulting pretentiousness seemed alien to secular society. Beckett employs it as if the detonation had revealed what was buried in drama. *Endgame* contains rapid, monosyllabic dialogues, like the earlier question-and-answer games between the blinded king and fate's messenger. But where the bind tightened then, the speakers now grow slack. Short of breath until they almost fall silent, they no longer manage the synthesis of linguistic phrases; they stammer in protocol sentences that might stem from positivists or Expressionists. The boundary value (*Grenzwert*) of Beckett's drama is that silence already defined as "the rest" in Shakespeare's inauguration of modern tragedy. The fact that an "act without words" follows *Endgame* as a kind of epilogue is its own *terminus ad quem*. The words resound like merely makeshift ones because silence is not yet entirely successful, like voices accompanying and disturbing it.

What becomes of form in *Endgame* can be virtually reconstructed from literary history. In Ibsen's *The Wild Duck*, the degenerate photographer Hjalmar Ekdal – himself a potential anti-hero – forgets to bring to the teenager Hedwig the promised menu from the sumptuous dinner at old Werle's house, to which he had been invited without his family. Psychologically, that is motivated by his slovenly egotistical character, but it is symbolically significant also for Hjalmar, for the course of the plot, and for the play's meaning: the girl's futile sacrifice. That anticipates the later Freudian theory

of "parapraxis,"[35] Which explicates such slip-ups by means of their relation
to past experiences and wishes of an individual, to the individual's identity.
Freud's hypotheses, "all our experiences have a sense,"[36] transforms the traditional dramatic idea into psychogical realism, from which Ibsen's tragi-
comedy of the *Wild Duck* incomparably extracts the spark of form one more
time. When such symbolism liberates itself from its psychological determination, it congeals into a being-in-itself, and the symbol becomes symbolic as
in Ibsen's late works like *John Gabriel Borkmann*, where the accountant Foldal
is overcome by so-called "youth." The contradiction between such a consistent symbolism and conservative realism constitutes the inadequacy of the
late plays. But it thereby also constitutes the leavening ferment of the Expressionist Strindberg. His symbols, torn away from empirical human beings, are
woven into a tapestry in which everything and nothing is symbolic, because
everything can signify everything. Drama need only become aware of the
ineluctably ridiculous nature of such pan-symbolism, which destroys itself; it
need only take that up and utilize it, and Beckettian absurdity is already
achieved as a result of the immanent dialectic of form. Not meaning anything becomes the only meaning. The mortal fear of the dramatic figures, if
not of the parodied drama itself, is the distortedly comical fear that they could
mean something or other:

HAMM: We're not beginning to . . . to . . . mean something?
CLOV: Mean something! You and I, mean something! (Brief laugh.) Ah that's a
   good one![37]

With this possibility, long since crushed by the overwhelming power of
an apparatus in which individuals are interchangeable and superfluous, the
meaning of language also disappears. Hamm, irritated by the impulse of life
which has regressed to clumsiness in his parents' trashcan conversations, and
nervous because "it doesn't end," asks: "Will you never finish? Will this never
finish?"[38] The play takes place on that level. It is constructed on the ground
of a proscription of language, and it articulates that in its own structure.
However, it does not thereby avoid the aporia of Expressionist drama: that
language, even where it tends to be shortened to mere sound, yet cannot
shake off its semantic element. It cannot become purely mimetic[39] or gestural, just as forms of modern painting, liberated from referentiality (*Gegen-
ständlichkeit*), cannot cast off all similarity to objects. Mimetic values,
definitively unloosed from significative ones, then approach arbitrariness, contingency, and finally a mere secondary convention. The way *Endgame* comes
to terms with that differentiates it from *Finnegans Wake*. Rather than striving to liquidate the discursive element of language through pure sound,

Beckett turns that element into an instrument of its own absurdity and he does that according to the ritual of clowns, whose babbling becomes nonsensical by presenting itself as sense. The objective disintegration of language – that simultaneously stereotyped and faulty chatter of self-alienation, where word and sentence melt together in human mouths – penetrates the aesthetic arcanum. The second language of those falling silent, a conglomeration of insolent phrases, pseudo-logical connections, and galvanized words appearing as commodity signs – as the desolate echo of the advertising world – is "refunctioned" (*umfunktioniert*) into the language of a poetic work that negates language.[40] Beckett thus approximates the drama of Eugène Ionesco. Whereas a later work by him is organized around the image of the tape recorder, the language of *Endgame* resembles another language familiar from the loathsome party game, where someone records the nonsense spoken at a party and then plays it back for the guests' humiliation. The shock, overcome on such an occasion only by stupid tittering, is here carefully composed. Just as alert experience seems to notice everywhere situations from Kafka's novels after reading him intensely, so does Beckett's language bring about a healing illness of those already ill: whoever listens to himself worries that he also talks like that. For some time now, the accidental events on the street seem to the movie-goer just leaving the theater like the planned contingency of a film. Between the mechanically assembled phrases taken from the language of daily life, the chasm yawns. Where one of the pair asks with the routine gesture of the hardened man, certain of the uncontestable boredom of existence, "What in God's name could there be on the horizon?"[41] then this shoulder-shrugging in language becomes apocalyptic, particularly because it is so familiar. From the bland yet aggressive impulse of human "common sense," "What do you think there is?" is extracted the confession of its own nihilism. Somewhat later, Hamm the master commands the *soi-disant* servant Clov, in a circus-task, to undertake the vain attempt to shove the chair back and forth, to fetch the "gaff." There follows a brief dialogue:

CLOV: Do this, do that, and I do it. I never refuse. Why?
HAMM: You're not able to.
CLOV: Soon I won't do it any more.
HAMM: You won't be able to any more. (Exit Clov.) Ah the creatures, everything has to be explained to them.[42]

That "everything has to be explained to the creatures" is drummed daily by millions of superiors into millions of subordinates. However, by means of the nonsense thus supposedly established in the passage – Hamm's explanation contradicts his own command – the cliché's inanity, usually hidden by custom, is garishly illuminated, and furthermore, the fraud of speaking with each other is expressed. When conversing, people remain hopelessly distant from each other no more reaching each other than the two old cripples in the trash bins do. Communication, the universal law of clichés, proclaims that there is no more communication. The absurdity of all speaking is not unrelated to realism but rather develops from it. For communicative language postulates – already in its syntactic form, through logic, the nature of conclusions, and stable concepts – the principle of sufficient reason. Yet this requirement is hardly met any more: when people speak with each other, they are motivated partly by their psychology or pre-logical unconscious, and partly by their pursuit of purposes. Since they aim at self-preservation, these purposes deviate from that objectivity deceptively manifest in their logical form. At any rate, one can prove that point to people today with the help of tape recorders. In Freud's as in Pareto's understanding, the *ratio* of verbal communication is always also a rationalization. *Ratio* itself emerged from the interest in self-preservation, and it is therefore undermined by the obligatory rationalizations of its own irrationality. The contradiction between the rational facade and the immutably irrational is itself already the absurd. Beckett must only mark the contradiction and employ it as a selective principle, and realism, casting off the illusion of rational stringency, comes into its own.

Even the syntactic form of question and answer is undermined. It presupposes an openness of what is to be spoken, an openness which no longer exists, as Huxley already noted. In the question one hears already the anticipated answer, and that condemns the game of question and answer to empty deception, to the unworkable effort to conceal the unfreedom of informative language in the linguistic gesture of freedom. Beckett tears away this veil, and the philosophical veil as well. Everything radically called into question when confronted by nothingness resists – by virtue of a pathos borrowed from theology – these terrifying consequences, while insisting on their possibility; in the form of question and answer, the answer is infiltrated with the meaning denied by the whole game. It is not for nothing that in fascism and pre-fascism such destructionists were able heartily to scorn destructive intellect. But Beckett deciphers the lie of the question mark: the question has become rhetorical. While the existential-philosophical hell resembles a tunnel, where in the middle one can already discern light shining at the end, Beckett's dialogues rip up the railroad tracks of conservation; the train no longer arrives at the bright end of the tunnel. Wedekind's old technique of misunderstanding becomes total. The course of the dialogues themselves approximates the contingency principle of literary production. It sounds as if the laws of its continuation were not the "reason" of speech and reply, and not even their psychological entwinement, but rather a test of listening, related to that of a music which frees itself from preformed types. The drama attends carefully to what kind of sentence might follow another. Given the accessible spontaneity of such questions, the absurdity of content is all the more strongly felt. That, too, finds its infantile model in those people who, when visiting the zoo, wait attentively for the next move of the hippopotamus or the chimpanzee.

In the state of its disintegration, language is polarized. On the one hand, it becomes Basic English, or French, or German – single words, archaically ejected commands in the jargon of universal disregard, the intimacy of irreconcilable adversaries; on the other hand, it becomes the aggregate of its empty forms, of a grammar that has renounced all reference to its content and therefore also to its synthetic function. The interjections are accompanied by exercise sentences, God knows why. Beckett trumpets this from the rooftops, too: one of the rules of the *Endgame* is that the unsocial partners – and with them the audience – are always eyeing each other's cards. Hamm considers himself an artist. He has chosen as his life maxim Nero's *qualis artifex pereo*. But the stories he undertakes run aground on syntax:

HAMM: Where was I? (Pause. Gloomily.) It's finished, we're finished. (Pause.) Nearly finished.[43]

Logic reels between the linguistic paradigms. Hamm and Clov converse in their authoritative, mutually cutting fashion:

HAMM: Open the window.
CLOV: What for?
HAMM: I want to hear the sea.
CLOV: You wouldn't hear it.
HAMM: Even if you opened the window?
CLOV: No.
HAMM: Then it's not worthwhile opening it?
CLOV: No.
HAMM: (violently) Then open it! (Clov gets up on the ladder, opens the window. Pause.) Have you opened it?
CLOV: Yes.[44]

One could almost see in Hamm's last "then" the key to the play. Because it is not worthwhile to open the window, since Hamm cannot hear the sea – perhaps it is dried out, perhaps it no longer moves –, he insists that Clov open it. The nonsense of an act becomes a reason to accomplish it – a late legitimation of Fichte's free activity for its own sake. That is how contemporary actions look, and they arouse the suspicion that things were never very different. The logical figure of the absurd, which makes the claim of stringency for stringency's contradictory opposite, denies every context of meaning apparently guaranteed by logic, in order to prove logic's own absurdity: that logic, by means of subject, predicate, and copula, treats non-identity as if it were identical, as if it were consumed in its forms. The absurd does not take the place of the rational as one world view of another; in the absurd, the rational world view comes into its own.

The pre-established harmony of despair reigns between the forms and the residual content of the play. The ensemble – smelted together – counts only four heads. Two of them are excessively red, as if their vitality were a skin disease; the two old ones, however, are excessively white, like sprouting potatoes in a cellar. None of them still has a properly functioning body; the old people consist only of rumps, having apparently lost their legs not in the catastrophe but in a private tandem accident in the Ardennes, "on the road to Sedan,"[45] an area where one army regularly annihilates another. One should not suppose that all that much has changed. Even the memory of their own particular (*bestimmt*) misfortune becomes enviable in relation to the indeterminacy (*Unbestimmtheit*) of universal misfortune – they laugh at it. In contrast to Expressionism's fathers and sons, they all have their own names, but all four names have one syllable, "four-letter words" like obscenities. Practical, familiar abbreviations, popular in Anglo-Saxon countries, are exposed as mere stumps of names. Only the name of the old mother, Nell, is somewhat common even if obsolete; Dickens uses it for the touching child in *Old Curiosity Shop*. The three other names are invented as if for bill-boards. The old man is named Nagg, with the association of "nagging" and perhaps also a German association: an intimate pair is intimate through "gnawing" (*Nagen*). They talk about whether the sawdust in their cans has been changed; yet it is not sawdust but sand. Nagg stipulates that it used to be sawdust, and Nell answers boredly: "Once!"[46] – a woman who spitefully exposes her husband's frozen, repetitive declarations. As sordid as the fight about sawdust or sand is, the difference is decisive for the residual plot, the transition from a minimum to nothing. Beckett can claim for himself what Benjamin praised in Baudelaire, the ability to "express something extreme with extreme discretion;"[47] the routine consolation that things could be worse becomes a condemnation. In the realm between life and death, where even pain is no longer possible, the difference between sawdust and sand means everything. Sawdust, wretched by-product of the world of things, is now in great demand; its removal becomes an intensification of the life-long death penalty. The fact that both lodge in trash bins – a comparable motif appears, moreover, in Tennessee Williams' *Camino Real*, surely without one play having been influenced by the other – takes the conversational phrase literally, as in Kafka. "Today old people are thrown in the trashcan" and it happens. *Endgame* is the true gerontology. According to the measure of socially useful labor, which they can no longer perform, old people are superfluous and must be discarded. That is extracted from the scientific ruckus of a welfare system that accentuates what it negates. *Endgame* trains the viewer for a condition where everyone involved expects – upon lifting the lid from the nearest dumpster – to find his own parents. The natural cohension of life has become organic refuse. The national socialists irreparably overturned the taboo of old age. Beckett's trashcans are the emblem of a culture restored after Auschwitz. Yet the sub-plot goes further than too far, to the old people's demise. They are denied children's fare, their pap, which is replaced by a biscuit they – tooth-less – can no longer chew; and they suffocate, because the last man is too sensitive to grant life to the next-to-last ones. That is entwined with the main plot, because the old pair's miserable end drives it forward to that exit of life whose possibility constitutes the tension in the play. Hamlet is revised: croak or croak, that is the question.

The name of Shakespeare's hero is grimly foreshortened by Beckett – the last, liquidated dramatic subject echoing the first. It is also associated with one of Noah's sons and thereby with the flood: the progenitor of blacks, who replaces the white "master race" in a Freudian negation. Finally, there is the English "ham actor." Beckett's Hamm, the key to power and helpless at the same time, plays at what he no longer is, as if he had read the most recent sociological literature defining *zoon politikon* as a role. Whoever cleverly presented himself became a "personality" just like helpless Hamm. "Personality" may have been a role originally – nature pretending to transcend nature. Fluctuation in the play's situations causes one of Hamm's roles: occasionally, a stage direction drastically suggests that he speak with the "voice of a rational being;" in a lengthy narrative, he is to strike a "narrative tone." The memory of what is irretrievably past becomes a swindle. Disintegration retrospectively condemns as fictional that continuity of life which alone made life possible. Differences in tone – between people who narrate and those who speak directly – pass judgment on the principle of identity. Both alternate in Hamm's long speech, a kind of inserted aria without music. At the transition points he pauses – the artistic pauses of the veteran actor of heroic roles. For the norm of existential philosophy – people should be themselves because they can no longer become anything else –, *Endgame* posits the antithesis, that precisely this self is not a self but rather the aping imitation of something non-existent. Hamm's mendacity exposes the lie concealed in saying "I" and thereby exhibiting substantiality, whose opposite is the content disclosed by the "I." Immutability, the epitome of transience, is its ideology.

What used to be the truth content of the subject – thinking – is only still preserved in its gestural shell. Both main figures act as if they were reflecting on something, but without thinking.

HAMM: The whole thing is comical, I grant you that. What about having a good guffaw the two of us together?
CLOV: (after reflection) I couldn't guffaw today.
HAMM: (after reflection) Nor I.[48]

According to his name, Hamm's counterpart is what he is, a truncated clown, whose last letter has been severed. An archaic expression for the devil sounds similar – cloven foot; it also resembles the current word "glove." He is the devil of his master, whom he has threatened with the worst, leaving him; yet at the same time he is also the glove with which the master touches the world of things, which he can no longer directly grasp. Not only the figure of Clov is constructed through such associations, but also his connection with the others. In the old piano edition of Stravinsky's "Ragtime for Eleven Instruments," one of the most significant works of his Surrealist phase, there was a Picasso drawing which – probably inspired by the title "rag" – showed two ragged figures, the ancestors of those vagabonds Vladimir and Estragon, who are waiting for Godot. This virtuoso sketch is a single entangled line. The double-sketch of *Endgame* is of this spirit, as well as the damaged repetitions irresistably produced by Beckett's entire work. In them, history is cancelled out. This compulsory repetition is taken from the regressive behavior of someone locked up, who tries it again and again. Beckett converges with the newest musical tendencies by combining, as a Westerner, aspects of Stravinsky's radical past – the oppressive stasis of disintegrating continuity – with the most advanced expressive and constructive means from the Schoenberg school. Even the outlines of Hamm and Clov are one line; they are denied the individuation of a tidily independent monad. They cannot live without each other. Hamm's power over Clov seems to be that only he knows how to open the cupboard, somewhat like the situation where only the principal knows the combination of the safe. He would reveal the secret to Clov, if Clov would swear to "finish" him – or "us." In a reply thoroughly characteristic of the play's tapestry, Clov answers: "I couldn't finish you;" as if the play were mocking the man who feigns reason, Hamm says: "Then you won't finish me."[49] He is dependent on Clov, because Clov alone can accomplish what keeps both alive. But that is of questionable value, because both – like the captain of the ghostly ship – must fear not being able to die. The tiny bit that is also everything – that would be the possibility that something could perhaps change. This movement, or its absence, is the plot. Admittedly, it does not become much more explicit than the repeated motif "Something is taking its course,"[50] as abstract as the pure form of time. The Hegelian dialectic of master and slave, mentioned by Günther Anders with reference to *Godot*, is derided rather than portrayed according to the tenets of traditional aesthetics. The slave can no longer grasp the reins and abolish domination. Crippled as he is, he would hardly be capable of this, and according to the play's historico-philosophical sundial, it is too late for spontaneous action anyway. Clov has no other choice than to emigrate out into the world that no longer exists for the play's recluses, with a good chance of dying. He cannot even depend on freedom unto death. He does manage to make the decision to go, even comes in for the farewell: "Panama hat, tweed coat, raincoat over his arm, umbrella, bag"[51] – a strong, almost musical conclusion. But one does not see his exit, rather he remains "impassive and motionless, his eyes fixed on Hamm, till the end."[52] That is an allegory whose intention has evaporated. Aside from some differences, which may be decisive or completely irrelevant, this is identical with the beginning. No spectator and no philosopher can say if the play will not begin anew. The dialectic swings to a standstill.

As a whole, the play's plot is musically composed with two themes, like the double fugue of earlier times. The first theme is that it should end, a Schopenhauerian negation of the will to live become insignificant. Hamm strikes it up; the persons, no longer persons, become instruments of their situation, as if they were playing chamber music. "Of all of Beckett's bizarre instruments, Hamm, who in *Endgame* sits blindly and immovably in his wheelchair, resounds with the most tones, the most surprising sound."[53] Hamm's non-identity with himself motivates the course of the play. While he desires the end of the torment of a miserably infinite existence, he is concerned about his life, like a gentleman in his ominous "prime" years. The peripheral paraphernalia of health are utmost in his mind. Yet he does not fear death, rather that death could miscarry; Kafka's motif of the hunter Grachus still resonates.[54] Just as important to him as his own bodily necessities is the certainty that Clov, ordered to gaze out, does not espy any sail or trail of smoke, that no rat or insect is stirring, with whom the calamity could begin anew; that he also does not see the perhaps surviving child, who could signify hope and for whom he lies in wait like Herod the butcher for the *agnus dei*. Insecticide, which all along pointed toward the genocidal camps, becomes the final product of the domination of nature, which destroys itself. Only this content of life remains: that nothing be living. All existence is levelled to a life that is itself death, abstract domination. The second theme is attributed to Clov the servant. After an admittedly obscure history he sought refuge with Hamm; but he also resembles the son of the raging yet impotent patriarch. To give up obedience to the powerless is most difficult; the insignificant and obsolete struggles irresistably against its abolition. Both plots are counterpointed, since Hamm's will to die is identical with his life principle, while Clov's will to live may well bring about the death of both; Hamm says: "Outside of here it's death."[55] The antithesis of the heroes is also not fixed, rather their impulses converge; it is Clov who first speaks of the end. The scheme of the play's progression is the end game in chess, a typical, rather standard situation, separated from the middle game and its combinations by a caesura; these are also missing in the play, where intrigue and "plot" are silently suspended. Only artistic mistakes or accidents, such as something growing somewhere, could cause unforeseen events, but not resourceful spirit. The field is almost empty, and what happened before can only be poorly construed from the positions of the few remaining figures. Hamm is the king, about whom everything turns and who can do nothing himself. The incongruity between chess as pastime and the excessive effort involved becomes on the stage an incongruity between athletic pretense and the lightweight actions that are performed. Whether the game ends with stalemate or with perpetual check, or whether Clov wins, remains unclear, as if clarity in that would already be too much meaning. Moreover, it is probably not so important, because everything would come to an end in stalemate as in checkmate. Otherwise, only the fleeting image of the child[56] breaks out of the circle, the most feeble reminder of Fortinbras or the child king. It could even be Clov's own abandoned child. But the oblique light falling from thence into the room is as weak as the helplessly helping arms extending from the windows at the conclusion of Kafka's *Trial*.

The history of the subject's end becomes thematic in an intermezzo, which can afford its symbolism, because it depicts the subject's own decrepitude and therefore that of its meaning. The hubris of idealism, the enthroning of man as creator in the center of creation, has entrenched itself in that "bare interior" like a tyrant in his last days. There man repeats with a reduced, tiny imagination what man was once supposed to be; man repeats what was taken from him by social strictures as well as by today's cosmology, which he cannot escape. Clov is his male nurse. Hamm has himself shoved about by Clov into the middle of that *intérieur* which the world has become but which is also the interior of his own subjectivity:

HAMM: Take me for a little turn. (Clov goes behind the chair and pushes it forward.) Not too fast! (Clov pushes chair.) Right round the world! (Clov pushes chair.) Hug the walls, then back to the center again. (Clov pushes chair.) I was right in the center, wasn't I?[57]

The loss of the center, parodied here because that center itself was a lie, becomes the paltry object of carping and powerless pedantry:

CLOV: We haven't done the round.
HAMM: Back to my place. (Clov pushes chair back to center.) Is that my place?
CLOV: I'll measure it.
HAMM: More or less! More or less!
CLOV: (moving chair slightly) There!
HAMM: I'm more or less in the center?
CLOV: I'd say so.
HAMM: You'd say so! Put me right in the center!
CLOV: I'll go and get the tape.
HAMM: Roughly! Roughly! (Clov moves chair slightly.) Bang in the center![58]

What is paid back in this ludicrous ritual is nothing originally perpetrated by the subject. Subjectivity itself is guilty; that one even is. Original sin is heretically fused with creation. Being, trumpeted by existential philosophy as the meaning of being, becomes its antithesis. Panic fear of the reflex movements of living entities does not only drive untiringly toward the domination of nature: it also attaches itself to life as the ground of that calamity which life has become:

HAMM: All those I might have helped. (Pause.) Helped! (Pause.) Saved. (Pause.) Saved! (Pause.) The place was crawling with them! (Pause. Violently.) Use your head, can't you, use your head, you're on earth, there's no cure for that![59]

From that he draws the conclusion: "The end is in the beginning and yet you go on."[60] The autonomous moral law reverts antinomically from pure domination over nature into the duty to exterminate, which always lurked in the background:

HAMM: More complications! (Clov gets down.) Not an underplot, I trust. (Clov moves ladder nearer window gets up on it, turns telescope on the without.)
CLOV: (dismayed) Looks like a small boy!
HAMM: (sarcastic) A small . . . boy!
CLOV: I'll go and see. (He gets down, drops the telescope, goes towards door, turns.)
HAMM: No! (Clov halts.)
CLOV: No? A potential procreator?[61]

Such a total conception of duty stems from idealism, which is judged by a question the handicapped rebel Clov poses to his handicapped master:

CLOV: Any particular sector you fancy? Or merely the whole thing?[62]

That sounds like a reminder of Benjamin's insight that an intuited cell of reality counterbalances the remainder of the whole world. Totality, a pure postulate of the subject, is nothing. No sentence sounds more absurd than this most reasonable of sentences, which bargains "the whole thing" down to "merely," to the phantom of an anthropocentrically dominated world. As reasonable as this most absurd observation is, it is nevertheless impossible to dispute the absurd aspects of Beckett's play just because they are confiscated by hurried apologetics and a desire for easy disposal. *Ratio*, having been fully instrumentalized, and therefore devoid of self-reflection and of reflection on what it has excluded, must seek that meaning that it has itself extinguished. But in the condition that necessarily gave rise to this question, no answer is possible other than nothingness, which the form of the answer already is. The historical inevitability of this absurdity allows it to seem ontological; that is the veil of delusion produced by history itself. Beckett's drama rips through this veil. The immanent contradition of the absurd, reason terminating in senselessness, emphatically reveals the possibility of a truth which can no longer even be thought; it undermines the absolute claim exercised by what merely is. Negative ontology is the negation of ontology: history alone has brought to maturity what was appropriated by the mythic power of timelessness. The historical fiber of situation and language in Beckett does not concretize – *more philosophico* – something unhistorical: precisely this procedure, typical of existential dramatists, is both foreign to art and philosophically obsolete. Beckett's once-and-for-all is rather infinite catastrophe; only "that the earth is extinguished, although I never saw it lit"[63] justifies Clov's answer to Hamm's question: "Do you not think this has gone on long enough?" "Yes."[64] Pre-history goes on, and the phantasm of infinity is only its curse. After Clov, commanded to look outside,[65] reports to the totally lame man what he sees of earth, Hamm entrusts to him his secret:

CLOV: (absorbed) Mmm.
HAMM: Do you know what it is?
CLOV: (as before) Mmm.
HAMM: I was never there.[66]

Earth was never yet tread upon; the subject is not yet a subject.

Determinate negation becomes dramaturgical through consistent reversal. Both social partners qualify their insight that there is no more nature with the bourgeois "You exaggerate."[67] Prudence and circumspection are the tried-

and–true means of sabotaging contemplation. They cause only melancholy reflection:

CLOV: (sadly) No one that ever lived ever thought so crooked as we.[68]

Where they draw nearest to the truth, they experience their consciousness – doubly comical – as false consciousness; thus a condition is mirrored that reflection no longer reaches. The entire play is woven with the technique of reversal. It transfigures the empirical world into that world desultorily named already by the late Strindberg and in Expressionism. "The whole house stinks of corpses . . . The whole universe."[69] Hamm, who then says "to hell with the universe," is just as much the descendant of Fichte, who disdains the world as nothing more than raw material and mere product, as he is the one without hope except for the cosmic night, which he implores with poetic quotes. Absolute, the world becomes a hell; there is nothing else. Beckett graphically stresses Hamm's sentence: "Beyond is the . . . OTHER hell."[70] With a Brechtian commentary, he lets the distorted metaphysics of "the here and now" shine through:

CLOV: Do you believe in the life to come?
HAMM: Mine was always like that. (Exit Clov.) Got him that time![71]

In his conception, Benjamin's notion of the "dialectic at a standstill" comes into its own:

HAMM: It will be the end and there I'll be, wondering what can have brought it on and wondering what can have (he hesitates) . . . why it was so long coming. (Pause.) There I'll be, in the old shelter, alone against the silence and . . . (he hesitates) . . . the stillness. If I can hold my peace, and sit quiet, it will be all over with sound and motion, all over and done with.[72]

That "stillness" is the order which Clov supposedly loves and which he defines as the purpose of his functions:

CLOV: A world where all would be silent and still and each thing in its last place, under the last dust.[73]

To be sure, the Old Testament saying "You shall become dust (*Staub*) again" is translated here into "dirt" (*Dreck*). In the play, the substance of life, a life that is death, is the excretions. But the imageless image of death is one of indifference. In it, the distinction disappears: the distinction between absolute domination, the hell in which time is banished into space, in which nothing will change any more – and the messianic condition where everything would be in its proper place. The ultimate absurdity is that the repose of nothingness and that of reconciliation cannot be distinguished from each other. Hope creeps out of a world in which it is no more conserved than pap and pralines, and back where it came from, back into death. From it, the play derives its only consolation, a stoic one:

CLOV: There are so many terrible things now.
HAMM: No, no, there are not so many now.[74]

Consciousness begins to look its own demise in the eye, as if it wanted to survive the demise, as these two want to survive the destruction of their world. Proust, about whom the young Beckett wrote an essay, is said to have attempted to keep protocol on his own struggle with death, in notes which were to be integrated into the description of Bergotte's death. *Endgame* carries out this intention like a mandate from a testament.

Notes

1   Samuel Beckett, *Endgame: A Play in One Act* (New York: Grove Press, 1958), p. 38.
2   Ibid., pp. 29–30.
3   Ibid., pp. 24–5.
4   Ibid., p. 11.
5   Ibid., p. 13.
6   Ibid., p. 3.
7   Ibid., p. 27.
8   Ibid., p. 13.
9   Ibid., p. 31.
10 Cf. Theodor W. Adorno, "Reconciliation under Duress," in Ernst Bloch et al., *Aesthetics and Politics*, afterword Frederic Jameson (London: New Left Books, 1977), p. 161; and Georg Lukács, *The Meaning of Contemporary Realism*, trans. John and Necke Mander (London: Merlin Press, 1963), p. 31.
11 Karl Jaspers, *Philosophy*, trans. E. B. Ashton (Chicago and London: University of Chicago Press, 1970), II, p. 177.
12 *Philosophy*, II, p. 177.
13 *Philosophy*, II, p. 178; bracketed material omitted in English translation.
14 *Philosophy*, II, p. 197.
15 Heinrich Rickert, *Unmittelbarkeit und Sinndeutung* (Tübingen: Mohr, 1939), pp. 133ff.

16 Ernst Robert Curtius, *Französischer Geist im neuen Europa* (1925), rpt. in his *Französischer Geist im zwanzigsten Jahrhundert* (Bern: Francke, 1952), pp. 312–313; quoted in Rickert, *Unmittelbarkeit*, pp. 133ff, footnote.

17 *Endgame*, p. 44.

18 Max Horkheimer and Theodor W. Adorno, *Dialectic of Englightenment*, trans. John Cumming (New York: Seabury Press, 1972/London: Verso, 1979), p. 234.

19 *Endgame*, p. 84.

20 Ibid., p. 69.

21 Ibid., p. 70.

22 Ibid., p. 24.

23 Ibid., p. 7.

24 Ibid., p. 4.

25 Ibid., p. 27.

26 Ibid., pp. 19–20.

27 Ibid., p. 45.

28 Cf. Günther Anders, *Die Antiquiertheit des Menschen* (Munich: Beck, 1956), p. 217.

29 *Endgame*, p. 29.

30 Ibid., pp. 46–7.

31 Ibid., p. 9.

32 Ibid., p. 14.

33 Theodor W. Adorno, "Notes on Kafka," in *Prisms*, trans. Samuel and Shierry Weber (1967; rpt. Cambridge: MIT Press, 1981), pp. 262–3n.

34 *Endgame*, p. 14.

35 'Parapraxes' is the usual translation of Freud's *Fehlleistungen*, although Adorno writes *Fehlhandlung*: faulty acts, slip-ups.

36 Sigmund Freud, *The Standard Edition of the Complete Psychological Works*, trans. and ed. James Strachey (London: Hogarth Press, 1963), XV, p. 40. [The context is discussing "parapraxes," and Freud asserts that "we formed an impression that in particular cases they seemed to be betraying a sense of their own."]

37 *Endgame*, pp. 32–3.

38 Ibid., p. 23.

39 Theodor W. Adorno, "Presuppositions", in *Notes to Literature* Vol. 2, trans. Shierry Weber Nicholsen (New York: Columbia U.P., 1992), pp. 95–108. Horkheimer and Adorno, *Dialectic of Enlightenment*, pp. 24ff.

40 Cf. Theodor W. Adorno, *Dissonanzen: Musik in der verwalteten Welt*, 2nd edn (Göttingen: Vandenhoeck and Ruprecht, 1958), pp. 34 and 44.

41 *Endgame*, p. 31.

42 Ibid., p. 43.

43 Ibid., p. 50.

44 Ibid., pp. 64–5.

45 Ibid., p. 16.

46 Ibid., p. 17.

47 Walter Benjamin, "On Some Motifs in Baudelaire," in his *Illuminations*, trans. Harry Zohn (New York: Schocken Books, 1969), pp. 183–4.

48 *Endgame*, p. 60.
49 Ibid., p. 36.
50 Ibid., p. 13; cf. p. 32.
51 Ibid., p. 82.
52 Ibid., p. 82.
53 Marie Luise von Kaschnitz, "Lecture on Lucky," Frankfurt University.
54 Adorno, "Notes on Kafka," *Prisms*, p. 260.
55 *Endgame*, p. 9.
56 Ibid., p. 78.
57 Ibid., p. 25.
58 Ibid., pp. 26–7.
59 Ibid., p. 68.
60 Ibid., p. 69.
61 Ibid., p. 78. [Adorno cites the divergent German edition, which here includes Clov's belief that he sees someone and Hamm's command to him to do his duty and extirpate that person.]
62 Ibid., p. 73.
63 Ibid., p. 81.
64 Ibid., p. 45. [In the German edition, Clov says "from time immemorial."]
65 Ibid., p. 72.
66 Ibid., p. 74.
67 Ibid., p. 11.
68 Ibid., p. 11.
69 Ibid., p. 46.
70 Ibid., p. 26. [Not capitalized in the English edition.]
71 Ibid., p. 49.
72 Ibid., p. 69.
73 Ibid., p. 57.
74 Ibid., p.44.

Select Bibliography

This bibliography lists all of Adorno's philosophical works both in the original (1.1) and in available translations (books 1.2, articles 1.3). The list of books on Adorno is selective and limited to English language publications. For the list of articles in translation (1.3) I am indebted to the bibliography compiled by Tom Huhn and Lambert Zuidervaart in *The Semblance of Subjectivity* (see below). For further references to Adorno bibliographies, readers should consult Huhn and Zuidervaart and also Zuidervaart's *Adorno's Aesthetic Theory* (see below). (In the following square brackets indicate a work's original year of publication or final year of writing if unpublished.)

1.1 Adorno: Collected Works

Theodor W. Adorno, *Gesammelte Schriften* (Frankfurt am Main: Suhrkamp), editor in chief, Rolf Tiedemann.
Vol. 1 (1973) *Philosophische Frühschriften*:
 Die Transzendenz des Dinglichen und Noematischen in Husserls Phänomenologie [1924]
 Der Begriff des Unbewußten in der transzendentalen Seelenlehre [1927]
 Vorträge und Thesen [early 1930s]
Vol. 2 (1979):
 Kierkegaard. Konstruktion des Ästhetischen [1933]
Vol. 3 (1980):
 (With Max Horkheimer) *Dialektik der Aufklärung. Philosophische Fragmente* [1944]
Vol. 4 (1979):
 Minima Moralia. Reflexionen aus dem beschädigten Leben [1951]
Vol. 5 (1971):
 Zur Metakritik der Erkenntnistheorie. Studien über Husserl und die phänomenologischen

Antinomien [1956]

Drei Studien zu Hegel [1963]

Vol. 6 (1972):

Negative Dialektik [1966]

Jargon der Eigentlichkeit. Zur deutschen Ideologie [1964]

Vol. 7 (1971):

Ästhetische Theorie [1970]

Vol. 8 (1972) *Soziologische Schriften I* (various pieces assembled by the editors)

Vol. 9.1 (1975) *Soziologische Schriften II*:

The Psychological Technique of Martin Luther Thomas' Radio Addresses [1943]

Studies in the Authoritarian Personality [1950]

Vol. 9.2 (1975) *Soziologische Schriften II*:

The Stars Down to Earth [1957]

Schuld und Abwehr [1955]

Vol. 10.1 (1977) *Kulturkritik und Gesellschaft I*:

Prismen. Kulturkritik und Gesellschaft [1955]

Ohne Leitbild. Parva Aesthetica [1967]

Vol. 10.2 (1977) *Kulturkritik und Gesellschaft II*:

Eingriffe. Neun kritische Modelle [1963]

Stichworte. Kritische Modelle 2 [1969]

Kritische Modelle 3 (various pieces)

Vol. 11 (1974) *Noten zur Literatur*:

Part I [1958]

Part II [1961]

Part III [1965]

Part IV (various pieces assembled by the editors)

Vol. 12 (1975):

Philosophie der neuen Musik [1949]

Vol. 13 (1971) *Die musikalische Monographien*:

Versuch über Wagner [1952]

Mahler. Eine musikalische Physiognomik [1960]

Berg. Der Meister des kleinsten Übergangs [1968]

Vol. 14 (1973):

Dissonanzen. Musik in der verwalten Welt [1956]

Einleitung in die Musiksoziologie [1962]

Vol. 15 (1976):

(With Hanns Eisler) *Komposition für den Film* [1944, in English, bearing only Eisler's name, and 1969]

Der getreue Korrepetitor. Lehrschriften zur musikalischen Praxis [1963]

Vol. 16 (1978) *Musikalische Schriften I–III*:

Klangfiguren. Musikalische Schriften I [1959]

Quasi una fantasia. Musikalische Schriften II [1963]

Musikalische Schriften III (unfinished collection)

Vol. 17 (1982) *Musikalische Schriften IV*:

Moments musicaux. Neu gedruckte Aufsätze 1928–1926 [1964]

Impromptus. Zweite Folge neu gedruckter musikalischer Aufsätze [1968]

Vol. 18 (1984) *Musikalische Schriften V* (various pieces assembled by the editors):
Musikalische Aphorismen
Theorie der neuen Musik. Neunzehn Beiträge über neue Musik
Komponisten und Kompositionen
Konzert-Einleitungen und Rundfunkvorträge mit Musikbeispielen
Musiksoziologisches

Vol. 19 (1984) *Musikalische Schriften VI* (various pieces assembled by the editors):
Frankfurter Opern- und Konzertkritiken
Andere Opern- und Konzertkritiken
Kompositionskritiken
Buchrezensionen
Zur Praxis des Musiklebens

Vol. 20.1 (1986) *Vermischte Schriften I* (various pieces assembled by the editors):
Theorien und Theoretiker
Gesellschaft, Unterricht, Politik

Vol. 20.2 (1986) *Vermischte Schriften II* (various pieces assembled by the editors):
Aesthetica
Miscellanea
Institüt für Sozialforschung und Deutsche Gesellschaft für Soziologie

Adorno's posthumous works – *Nachgelassene Schriften* (Frankfurt am Main: Suhrkamp Verlag) – are currently being edited by the Theodor W. Adorno Archiv (director: Rolf Tiedemann). As well as including unpublished manuscripts it contains transcriptions of recorded lectures series and interviews. Some volumes of the projected edition have already appeared:

Part I. *Fragment gebliebene Schriften*
Vol. 1. (1993). *Beethoven. Philosophie der Musik*
Vol. 2. *Theorie der musikalischen Reproduktion*
Vol. 3. *Currents of Music. Elements of a Radio Theory*
Part II. *Philosophische Notizen* (*c.* 5 volumes)
Part III. *Poetische Versuche* (1 volume)
Part IV. *Vorlesungen* (Square brackets indicate the year in which the lectures took place.)
Vol. 1. *Erkenntnistheorie* [1957/58]
Vol. 2. *Einführung in die Dialektik* [1958]
Vol. 3. *Ästhetik* [1958/59]
Vol. 4 (1995). *Kants "Kritik der reinen Vernunft"* [1959]
Vol. 5. *Einleitung in die Philosophie* [1959/60]
Vol. 6. *Philosophie und Soziologie* [1960]
Vol. 7. *Ontologie und Dialektik* [1960/61]
Vol. 8. *Ästhetik* [1961/62]

Vol. 9. *Philosophische Terminologie* [1962/63]

(A transcription of these lectures has already appeared under a separate edition (Suhrkamp Verlag, Vol. I, 1973, Vol. II, 1974).)

Vol. 10. (1996). *Probleme der Moralphilosophie* [1963]

Vol. 11. *Fragen der Dialektik* [1963/64]

Vol. 12. *Philosophische Elemente einer Theorie der Gesellschaft* [1964]

Vol. 13. *Zur Lehre von der Geschichte und der Freiheit* [1964/65]

Vol. 14. (1998). *Metaphysik, Begriff und Probleme* [1965]

Vol. 15. (1993). *Einleitung in die Soziologie* [1968]

Vol. 16. *Stichworte und Stenogramm-Fragmente zu nicht erhaltenen Vorlesungen*

Part V. *Improvisierte Vorträge* (*c.* 2 volumes)

Part VI. *Gespräche, Diskussionen, Interviews*

1.2   Adorno: Books and Edited Collections in English

Aesthetic Theory [1970], trans. C. Lenhardt (London: Routledge and Kegan Paul, 1984).

Aesthetic Theory [1970], trans. Robert Hullot-Kentor (Minneapolis: University of Minnesota Press, 1997).

Aesthetics and Politics, Adorno et al., ed. Ronald Taylor (London: NLB, 1977).

Against Epistemology: A Metacritique. Studies in Husserl and the Phenomenological Antinomies [1956], trans. Willis Domingo (Oxford: Basil Blackwell, 1982).

Alban Berg: Master of the Smallest Link [1968], trans. Julian Brand and Christopher Hailey (Cambridge: Cambridge University Press, 1991).

Aspects of Sociology [1956], The Frankfurt Institute of Social Research, trans. John Viertel (Boston: Beacon Press, 1972).

The Authoritarian Personality, in collaboration with Else Frenkel-Brunswick, Daniel Levinson, R. Nevitt Sanford (New York: Harper and Brothers, 1950). Abridged edition, *The Authoritarian Personality* (New York: W. W. Norton and Company, 1982).

Beethoven: The Philosophy of Music [various], trans. Edmund Jephcott (Stanford: Stanford University Press, 1997).

Composing for the Films, in collaboration with Hanns Eisler (New York: Oxford University Press, 1947). (This 1947 edition does not note Adorno's authorship.)

Critical Models: Interventions and Catchwords [1963 and 1969], trans. Henry W. Pickford (New York: Columbia University Press, 1998).

The Culture Industry: Selected Essays on Mass Culture, ed. J. M. Bernstein (London: Routledge, 1991).

Dialectic of Enlightenment [1947], trans. John Cumming (London: Verso, 1979).

The Essential Frankfurt School Reader, (Adorno et al) eds. Andrew Arato and Eike Gebhardt (Oxford: Basil Blackwell, 1978).

Hegel: Three Studies [1963], trans. Shierry Weber Nicholsen (Cambridge, Mass.: MIT Press, 1993).

In Search of Wagner [1952], trans. Rodney Livingstone (London: NLB, 1981).

Introduction to the Sociology of Music [1962], trans. E. B. Ashton (New York: Seabury Press, 1976).

The Jargon of Authenticity [1964], trans. Knut Tarnowski and Frederic Will (London: Routledge and Kegan Paul, 1973).

Kierkegaard: Construction of the Aesthetic [1933], trans. Robert Hullot-Kentor (Minneapolis: University of Minnesota Press, 1989).

Mahler: A Musical Physiognomy [1960], trans. Edmund Jephcott (Chicago: University of Chicago Press, 1992).

Minima Moralia: Reflections from Damaged Life [1951], trans. E. F. N. Jephcott (London: NLB, 1974).

Negative Dialectics [1966], trans. E. B. Ashton (London: Routledge and Kegan Paul, 1973).

Notes to Literature [1958 and 1961], vol. One, trans. Shierry Weber Nicholsen (New York: Columbia University Press, 1991).

Notes to Literature [1965 and various], vol. Two, trans. Shierry Weber Nicholsen (New York: Columbia University Press, 1992).

Philosophy of Modern Music [1949], trans. Anne G. Mitchell and Wesley Blomster (London: Sheed and Ward, 1973).

The Positivist Dispute in German Sociology, Adorno et al., trans. Glyn Adey and David Frisby (London: Heinemann, 1976).

Prisms [1955], trans. Samuel and Shierry Weber (Cambridge, Mass.: MIT Press, 1981).

Quasi una Fantasia: Essays on Modern Music [1963], trans. Rodney Livingstone (London: Verso, 1992).

The Stars Down to Earth and Other Essays on the Irrational in Culture, ed. Stephen Crook (London: Routledge, 1995).

1.3   Adorno: Articles in English

The following lists only those articles not found in some form either in 1.2 above or in the present collection.

'The Aging of the New Music' [1955], *Telos* 77 (1988), pp. 95–116.

'Analytical Study of the NBC Music Appreciation Hour' [between 1938 and 1941], *Musical Quarterly* 78 (1994), pp. 325–77.

'Bibliographical Musings' [1965], *Grand Street* 10 (1991), pp. 135–48.

'Bloch's Traces: The Philosophy of Kitsch' [1960], *New Left Review* 121 (1980), pp. 49–62.

'Bourgeois Opera' [1959], *Opera through Other Eyes*, ed. David J. Levin (Stanford: Stanford University Press), pp. 25–43.

'Contemporary German Sociology' [1959], *Transactions of the Fourth World Congress of Sociology*, vol. 1 (London: International Sociological Association, 1959), pp. 33–56.

'The Curves of the Needle' [1928], *October* 55 (1990), pp. 49–55.

'Education for Autonomy' (with Hellmut Becker) [1969/1970], *Telos* 56 (1983), pp. 103–10.

'The Form of the Phonograph Record' [1934], *October* 55 (1990), pp. 56–61.

'Functionalism Today' [1966], *Oppositions* 17 (1979), pp. 31–41.

'Goldmann and Adorno: To Describe, Understand and Explain' [1968], in Lucien Goldmann, trans. Bart Grahl, *Cultural Creation in Modern Society* (Oxford: Basil Blackwell, 1976), pp. 129–45.

'Husserl and the Problem of Idealism', *The Journal of Philosophy* 37 (1940), pp. 5–18.

'The Idea of Natural History' [1932], *Telos* 60 (1984), pp. 111–24.

'Is Marx Obsolete?' [1968], *Diogenes* 64 (1968), pp. 1–16.

'Jazz', *Encyclopaedia of the Arts*, eds Dagobert D. Runes and Harry G. Schrickel (New York: Philosophical Library, 1946), pp. 511–13.

'Late Style in Beethoven' [1937], *Raritan* 13 (1993), pp. 102–7.

'Looking Back on Surrealism' [1956], *The Idea of the Modern in Literature and the Arts*, ed. Irving Howe (New York, Horizon Press, 1967), pp. 220–4.

'Messages in a Bottle' [1951], *New Left Review* 200 (1993), pp. 5–14.

'Music and Technique' [1958], *Telos* 32 (1977), pp. 79–94.

'Music, Language, and Composition' [1956], *Musical Quarterly* 77 (1993), pp. 401–14.

'New Music and the Public: Some Problems of Interpretation' [1957], *Twentieth Century Music*, ed. Rollo H. Myers (London: Calder and Boyors, 1968), pp. 63–74.

'Of Barricades and Ivory Towers: An Interview with T. W. Adorno', *Encounter* 33 (1969), pp. 63–9.

'On Jazz' [1937], *Discourse* 12 (1989–90), pp. 36–69.

'On Kierkegaard's Doctrine of Love', *Studies in Philosophy and Social Science* 8 (1939–40), pp. 413–29.

'On Popular Music' (with George Simpson), *Studies in Philosophy and Social Science* 9 (1941), pp. 17–48.

'On Some Relationships between Music and Painting' [1965], *Musical Quarterly* 79 (1995), pp. 66–79.

'On the Historical Adequacy of Consciousness' (with Peter von Haselberg) [1965], *Telos* 56 (1983), pp. 97–103.

'On the Score of Parsifal' [1956], *Music and Letters* 76 (1995), pp. 384–97.

'On the Social Situation of Music' [1932], *Telos* 35 (1978), pp. 128–64.

'On Tradition' [1966], *Telos* 94 (1993), pp. 75–81.

'Opera and the Long-Playing Record' [1969], *October* 55 (1990), pp. 62–6.

'Punctuation Marks' [1956], *Antioch Review* 48 (1990), pp. 300–5.

'The Radio Symphony: An Experiment in Theory', *Radio Research 1941*, ed. Paul F. Lazarfeld and Frank N. Stanton (New York: Duell, Sloan and Pearce, 1941), pp. 110–39.

'Review of Jean Wahl, *Études Kierkegaardiennes*; Walter Lowrie, *Kierkegaard*; and *The Journals of Soren Kierkegaard*', *Studies in Philosophy and Social Science* 8 (1939), pp. 232–5.

'Review of Wilder Hobson, *American Jazz Music*; Winthrop Sargeant, *Jazz Hot and Hybrid*' (with Eunice Cooper), *Studies in Philosophy and Social Science* 9 (1941), pp. 167–78.

'Richard Strauss at Sixty' [1924], *Richard Strauss and His World*, ed. Bryan Gilliam (Princeton, NJ: Princeton University Press, 1992), pp. 406–15.

'A Social Critique of Radio Music', *Kenyon Review* 7 (1945), pp. 208–17.

'Society' [1966], *Salmagundi* 10–11 (1969–1970), pp. 144–53.

'Sociology and Psychology' [1955], *New Left Review* 46 (1967), pp. 79–97.

'Spengler Today', *Studies in Philosophy and Social Science* 9 (1941), pp. 305–25.

'"Static" and "Dynamic" as Sociological Categories' [1956], *Diogenes* 33 (1961), pp. 28–49.

'Theory of Pseudo-Culture' [1959], *Telos* 95 (1993), pp. 15–38.

'Theses on the Sociology of Art' [1967], *Working Papers in Cultural Studies 2* (Birmingham, 1972), pp. 121–8.

'Theses upon Art and Religion Today', *Kenyon Review* 7 (1945), pp. 677–82.

'Veblen's Attack on Culture: Remarks Occasioned by the Theory of the Leisure Class', *Studies in Philosophy and Social Science* 9 (1941), pp. 389–413.

'Wagner, Nietzsche and Hitler' (review), *Kenyon Review* 9 (1947), pp. 165–72.

'Wagner's Relevance for Today' [1964/1965], *Grand Street* 11 (1993), pp. 32–59.

'What Does Coming to Terms with the Past Mean?' [1960], *Bitburg in Moral and Political Perspective*, ed. G. Hartmann (Indianapolis: Indiana University Press, 1986), pp. 114–29.

2   Books in English on Adorno

Bernstein, J. M., *The Fate of Art: Aesthetic Alienation from Kant to Derrida and Adorno* (Cambridge: Polity Press, 1991).

——, (ed.) *The Frankfurt School: Critical Assessmentss* (London, Routledge, 1995), vols 3 and 4.

Bronner, Stephen Eric, *Of Critical Theory and Its Theorists* (Oxford: Blackwell, 1994).

Buck-Morss, Susan, *The Origin of Negative Dialectics: Theodor W. Adorno, Walter Benjamin, and the Frankfurt Institute* (Sussex: The Harvester Press, 1977).

Connerton, Paul, *The Tragedy of Enlightenment: An Essay on the Frankfurt School* (Cambridge: Cambridge University Press, 1980).

Cook, Deborah, *The Culture Industry Revisited: Theodor W. Adorno on Mass Culture* (Landham, Md.: Rowman and Littlefield, 1996).

Dennis, Christopher J., *Adorno's Philosophy of Modern Music* (New York: Edwin Mellen Press, 1997).

Harding, James Martin, *Adorno and 'A Writing of the Ruins': Essays on Modern Aesthetics and Anglo-American Literature and Culture* (Albany: SUNY Press, 1997).

Held, David, *Introduction to Critical Theory: Horkheimer to Habermas* (Berkeley: University of California Press, 1980).

Hohendahl, Peter Uwe, *Prismatic Thought: Theodor W. Adorno* (Lincoln: University of Nebraska Press, 1995).

Huhn, Tom and Zuidervaart, Lambert (eds), *The Semblance of Subjectivity: Essays in Adorno's Aesthetic Theory* (Cambridge, Mass.: MIT Press, 1987).

Jameson, Fredric, *Late Marxism: Adorno, or, The Persistence of the Dialectic* (London: Verso, 1990).

Jarvis, Simon, *Adorno: A Critical Introduction* (Cambridge: Polity Press, 1998).

Jay, Martin, *The Dialectical Imagination: A History of the Frankfurt School and the Institute of Social Research 1923–50* (Berkeley: University of California Press, 2nd edn, 1996).

——, *Marxism and Totality: The Adventures of a Concept from Lukács to Habermas* (Berkeley: University of California Press, 1984).

——, *Adorno* (London: Fontana, 1984).

Lunn, Eugene, *Marxism and Modernism: A Historical Study of Lukács, Brecht, Benjamin, and Adorno* (Berkeley: University of California Press, 1982).

Menke-Eggers, Christoph, trans. Neil Solomon, *The Sovereignty of Art: Aesthetic Negativity in Adorno and Derrida* (Cambridge, Mass.: MIT Press, 1998).

Nicholsen, Shierry Weber, *Exact Imagination, Late Work: On Adorno's Aesthetics* (Cambridge, Mass.: MIT Press, 1997).

Paddison, Max, *Adorno's Aesthetics of Music* (Cambridge: Cambridge University Press, 1993).

——, *Adorno, Modernism and Mass Culture: Essays on Critical Theory and Music* (London: Kahn and Averill, 1996).

Pensky, Max (ed.), *The Actuality of Adorno: Critical Essays on Adorno and the Postmodern* (Albany: SUNY Press, 1997).

Roberts, David, *Art and Enlightenment: Aesthetic Theory after Adorno* (Lincoln: University of Nebraska Press, 1991).

Rose, Gillian, *The Melancholy Science: An Introduction to the Thought of Theodor W. Adorno* (London: Macmillan, 1978).

Schultz, Karla L., *Mimesis on the Move: Theodor W. Adorno's Concept of Imitation* (New York: Peter Lang, 1990).

Tar, Zoltan, *The Frankfurt School: The Critical Theories of Max Horkheimer and Theodor W. Adorno* (New York: John Willey, 1977).

Wiggershaus, Rolf, trans. Michael Robertson, *The Frankfurt School: Its History, Theories and Political Significance* (Cambridge: Polity Press, 1994).

Witkin, Robert W., *Adorno on Music* (London: Routledge, 1998).

Wolin, Richard, *Walter Benjamin: An Aesthetic of Redemption* (New York: Columbia University Press, 1994).

Zuidervaart, Lambert, *Adorno's Aesthetic Theory: The Redemption of Illusion* (Cambridge, Mass.: MIT Press, 1991).

Name Index

Subject Index

Feb 21107